First World War
and Army of Occupation
War Diary
France, Belgium and Germany

61 DIVISION
Headquarters, Branches and Services
General Staff
1 September 1918 - 30 July 1919

WO95/3036/1

The Naval & Military Press Ltd
www.nmarchive.com
Published in association with The National Archives

Published by

The Naval & Military Press Ltd

Unit 10 Ridgewood Industrial Park,

Uckfield, East Sussex,

TN22 5QE England

Tel: +44 (0) 1825 749494

www.naval-military-press.com

www.nmarchive.com

This diary has been reprinted in facsimile from the original. Any imperfections are inevitably reproduced and the quality may fall short of modern type and cartographic standards.

© Crown Copyright
Images reproduced by permission of The National Archives, London, England, 2015.

Contents

Document type	Place/Title	Date From	Date To
Heading	WO95/3036/1		
Heading	61st Division General Staff 1918 Sep-Jly 1919		
Heading	War Diary 61st Divn Sept 1918 Vol XXIX		
War Diary	Croix Marraisse J.21.c. (Sht.36A)	01/09/1918	08/09/1918
War Diary	Rill Works L.33.b.3.7 (Sht.36A)	09/09/1918	30/09/1918
Miscellaneous	61st Division Locations of Units At 6 a.m. 1.9.18	31/08/1918	31/08/1918
Operation(al) Order(s)	61st Division Order No.199	01/09/1918	01/09/1918
Miscellaneous	A Form Messages And Signals.		
Miscellaneous	61st Division Locations of Units At 6 a.m. 2.9.18	01/09/1918	01/09/1918
Operation(al) Order(s)	61st Division Order No.209	02/09/1918	02/09/1918
Miscellaneous	A Form Messages And Signals.		
Miscellaneous	Appendix VI		
Miscellaneous	184 Bde. G. 602. 2nd		
Miscellaneous	182 Bde 59 Div G. 616 2nd.		
Miscellaneous	H.Q.61 Div. F.771.2nd		
Miscellaneous	61st Division Locations of Units At 6 a.m. 4.9.18	03/09/1918	03/09/1918
Miscellaneous	Appendix XI		
Miscellaneous	Appendix XII		
Miscellaneous	Major-General Duncan 61st Divn.		
Operation(al) Order(s)	61st Division Order No.201	04/09/1918	04/09/1918
Miscellaneous	61 Bn. M.O.C. by wire.		
Miscellaneous	61st Division Instructions No.1	04/09/1918	04/09/1918
Miscellaneous	Appendix XVI		
Operation(al) Order(s)	61st Division Order No.202	05/09/1918	05/09/1918
Miscellaneous	Appendix XVIII		
Miscellaneous	Appendix XVIIIa		
Miscellaneous	182 Inf. Bde.		
Miscellaneous	A Form Messages And Signals.		
Miscellaneous	61st Division Locations of Units At 6 a.m., 9.9.18	09/09/1918	09/09/1918
Miscellaneous	61st Division Instructions No.2 Intelligence	08/09/1918	08/09/1918
Miscellaneous	61st Division Locations of Units At 6 a.m.	10/09/1918	10/09/1918
Miscellaneous	Appendix XXIV		
Operation(al) Order(s)	61st Division Order No.203	10/09/1918	10/09/1918
Miscellaneous	61st Division Instructions No.3 Anti-Aircraft Defence.	10/09/1918	10/09/1918
Miscellaneous	Appendix "A" to 61st Division Defence Instructions No.3 Anti-Aircraft Defence.	10/09/1918	10/09/1918
Miscellaneous	Appendix XXVII		
Miscellaneous	Appendix XXVIII		
Miscellaneous	Appendix XXIX		
Miscellaneous	61st Division Locations of Units At 6 a.m. 13.9.18	12/09/1918	12/09/1918
Miscellaneous	61st Division Instructions No.4	13/09/1918	13/09/1918
Operation(al) Order(s)	61st Division Order No.204	13/09/1918	13/09/1918
Miscellaneous	61st Division Instructions No.5 Defence Against Gas.	14/09/1918	14/09/1918
Miscellaneous	Amendment No.1 To 61 Div. Instructions No.4	14/09/1918	14/09/1918
Miscellaneous	Appendix XXXV	14/09/1918	14/09/1918
Miscellaneous	Not To Be Taken Beyond Battalion H.Q. in The Line 61st Division Intelligence Summary No.1	14/09/1918	14/09/1918
Miscellaneous	(Appendix to 61 Div. Int. Summary No.1)	13/09/1918	13/09/1918
Miscellaneous	G.C. 40/5.	15/09/1918	15/09/1918

Type	Description	Date	Date
Miscellaneous	Not To Be Taken Beyond Battalion H.Q. in The Line 61st Division Intelligence Summary No.2.	15/09/1918	15/09/1918
Miscellaneous	61st Division Locations of Units At 6 a.m. 16.9.18	16/09/1918	16/09/1918
Miscellaneous	G.O.C., 5th Divn		
Miscellaneous	Appendix XL		
Miscellaneous	Appendix XLI		
Miscellaneous	Not To Be Taken Beyond Battalion H.Q. in The Line 61st Division Intelligence Summary No.3	16/09/1918	16/09/1918
Miscellaneous	A Form Messages And Signals.		
Miscellaneous	Appendix XLIV		
Miscellaneous	Not To Be Taken Beyond Battalion H.Q. in The Line 61st Division Intelligence Summary No.4	17/09/1918	17/09/1918
Operation(al) Order(s)	61st Division Order No.205	17/09/1918	17/09/1918
Miscellaneous	Amendment No.1 To 61st Div. Instructions No.3	18/09/1918	18/09/1918
Miscellaneous	Not To Be Taken Beyond Battalion H.Q. in The Line 61st Division Intelligence Summary No.5	18/09/1918	18/09/1918
Miscellaneous	Not To Be Taken Beyond Battalion H.Q. in The Line 61st Division Intelligence Summary No.6	19/09/1918	19/09/1918
Miscellaneous	61st Division Locations of Units At 6 a.m.	19/09/1918	19/09/1918
Miscellaneous	Not To Be Taken Beyond Battalion H.Q. in The Line 61st Division Intelligence Summary No.7	20/09/1918	20/09/1918
Miscellaneous	Appendix LIa		
Miscellaneous	61st Division Locations of Units At 6 a.m., 22.9.18	21/09/1918	21/09/1918
Miscellaneous	Not To Be Taken Beyond Battalion H.Q. in The Line 61st Division Intelligence Summary No.8	21/09/1918	21/09/1918
Miscellaneous	Not To Be Taken Beyond Battalion H.Q. in The Line 61st Division Intelligence Summary No.9	22/09/1918	22/09/1918
Miscellaneous	Commanding Northumberland Fusiliers		
Miscellaneous	Not To Be Taken Beyond Battalion H.Q. in The Line 61st Division Intelligence Summary No.10	23/09/1918	23/09/1918
Miscellaneous	Appendix LVII		
Miscellaneous	61st Division Locations of Units At 6.a.m., 25.9.18	24/09/1918	24/09/1918
Miscellaneous	Not To Be Taken Beyond Battalion H.Q. in The Line 61st Division Intelligence Summary No.11	24/09/1918	24/09/1918
Miscellaneous	Not To Be Taken Beyond Battalion H.Q. in The Line 61st Division Intelligence Summary No.12	25/09/1918	25/09/1918
Operation(al) Order(s)	61st Division Order No.206	25/09/1918	25/09/1918
Miscellaneous	61st Division Instructions No.6 Operations	25/09/1918	25/09/1918
Miscellaneous	Amendment No.1 To 61st Division Order No.206	26/09/1918	26/09/1918
Miscellaneous	Not To Be Taken Beyond Battalion H.Q. in The Line 61st Division Intelligence Summary No.13	26/09/1918	26/09/1918
Miscellaneous	Not To Be Taken Beyond Battalion H.Q. in The Line 61st Division Intelligence Summary No.14	27/09/1918	27/09/1918
Miscellaneous	Appendix LXVI		
Operation(al) Order(s)	61st Division Order No.207	27/09/1918	27/09/1918
Miscellaneous	Not To Be Taken Beyond Battalion H.Q. in The Line 61st Division Intelligence Summary No.15	28/09/1918	28/09/1918
Miscellaneous	General Routine Order No.5104	26/09/1918	26/09/1918
Miscellaneous	Appendix LXX	25/09/1918	25/09/1918
Operation(al) Order(s)	61st Division Order No.208	28/09/1918	28/09/1918
Miscellaneous	61st Division Locations of Units	28/09/1918	28/09/1918
Miscellaneous	Not To Be Taken Beyond Battalion H.Q. in The Line 61st Division Intelligence Summary No.16	29/09/1918	29/09/1918
Miscellaneous	Appendix LXXIV 61st Divn.		
Miscellaneous	Brigadier General Pagan 184th Infy Brigade		

Miscellaneous	Lieut. Colonel Christie Miller, Commanding 5th Gloucesters.		
Miscellaneous	Not To Be Taken Beyond Battalion H.Q. in The Line 61st Division Intelligence Summary No.17	30/09/1918	30/09/1918
Miscellaneous	61st Division Locations of Units At 6 a.m. 1.10.18	01/10/1918	01/10/1918
Map	Map		
Heading	Appendix LXXVII		
Miscellaneous	Total Captures During Septr. 1918 By 61st Division		
Heading	War Diary 61st Divn October 1918 Vol XXX		
War Diary	Rill Works L.33.b. Sht.36A	01/10/1918	04/10/1918
War Diary	La Lacque Camp I.32.b. Sht.36.A	04/10/1918	05/10/1918
War Diary	Doullens	06/10/1918	08/10/1918
War Diary	Lagnicourt C.24.c.4.5 (Sht.57C)	09/10/1918	10/10/1918
War Diary	Lagnicourt C.O.24.c.4.5 (Sht.57C)	10/10/1918	12/10/1918
War Diary	Noyelles. L.11. (Sht. 57C)	13/10/1918	18/10/1918
War Diary	Rieux U.20.c.9.9. (Sh.51A)	19/10/1918	22/10/1918
War Diary	St. Aubert U.24.b.6.1	23/10/1918	24/10/1918
War Diary	Montrecourt (V.14.a.0.8.)	24/10/1918	25/10/1918
War Diary	Vendegies (Q.14.a.1.7.)	25/10/1918	31/10/1918
Miscellaneous	61st Division Locations of Units At 6 a.m. 1.10.18	30/09/1918	30/09/1918
Operation(al) Order(s)	61st Division Order No.209	01/10/1918	01/10/1918
Miscellaneous	61st Division Order No.210	01/10/1918	01/10/1918
Miscellaneous	Reference D.O.211 Of 1.10.18	03/10/1918	03/10/1918
Operation(al) Order(s)	61st Division Order No.211	01/10/1918	01/10/1918
Miscellaneous	Movement Table To Accompany 61st Division Order No.211 Dated 1.10.18		
Miscellaneous	Appendix V	02/10/1918	02/10/1918
Map	Map		
Miscellaneous	61st Division Locations of Units At 09.00 3.10.18	02/10/1918	02/10/1918
Miscellaneous	Appendix VII	03/10/1918	03/10/1918
Miscellaneous	61st Division Locations of Units At 12.00, 4.10.18	03/10/1918	03/10/1918
Operation(al) Order(s)	61st Division Order No.212	04/10/1918	04/10/1918
Miscellaneous	61st Division Amendment To Locations.	04/10/1918	04/10/1918
Miscellaneous	61st Division Order No.213 Warning Order.	07/10/1918	07/10/1918
Miscellaneous	Amendment No.1 To 61st Division Order No.214	08/10/1918	08/10/1918
Operation(al) Order(s)	61st Division Order No.214	07/10/1918	07/10/1918
Miscellaneous	Movement Table To Accompany 61 Div. Order No. 214 Dated 7.10.18.	07/10/1918	07/10/1918
Miscellaneous	61st Division Locations of Units At 1800, 7.10.18	07/10/1918	07/10/1918
Miscellaneous	Locations of 61st Division at 0600, 9.10.18	08/10/1918	08/10/1918
Miscellaneous	61st Division Locations of Units At 0600, 10.10.18	09/10/1918	09/10/1918
Operation(al) Order(s)	61st Division Order No.215	10/10/1918	10/10/1918
Diagram etc	Diagram		
Miscellaneous	61st Division Order No.216 Warning Order	10/10/1918	10/10/1918
Operation(al) Order(s)	61st Division Order No.217	10/10/1918	10/10/1918
Operation(al) Order(s)	61st Division Order No.218	10/10/1918	10/10/1918
Miscellaneous	61st Division Locations of Units At 1200	12/10/1918	12/10/1918
Miscellaneous	61st Division Order No.219. Warning Order.	12/10/1918	12/10/1918
Miscellaneous	61 Division Locations of Units At 0600 14.10.18	13/10/1918	13/10/1918
Miscellaneous	61st Division Locations of Units At 0600, 15.10.18	15/10/1918	15/10/1918
Miscellaneous	61st Division Instructions No.7 Intelligence.	16/10/1918	16/10/1918
Miscellaneous	G.C. 31/3 Appx XXVI	16/10/1918	16/10/1918
Miscellaneous	Reference D.O. 222 Of 18.10.18	18/10/1918	18/10/1918
Operation(al) Order(s)	61st Division Order No. 221	17/10/1918	17/10/1918
Miscellaneous	Movement Table Issued With 61st Div. Order No.221 Dated 17.10.18	17/10/1918	17/10/1918

Type	Description	Date 1	Date 2
Operation(al) Order(s)	61st Division Order No.222	18/10/1918	18/10/1918
Miscellaneous	Movement Table Issued With 61st Div Order No.222, Dated 18.10.18	18/10/1918	18/10/1918
Miscellaneous	Locations of 61st Division at 0600 hours, October 20th, 1918	19/10/1918	19/10/1918
Operation(al) Order(s)	61st Division (Preliminary) Order No.223	21/10/1918	21/10/1918
Operation(al) Order(s)	61st Division Order No.224	22/10/1918	22/10/1918
Miscellaneous	Movement Table To Accompany 61st Division Order No.224 Dated 22.10.18	22/10/1918	22/10/1918
Operation(al) Order(s)	61st Division Order No.225	22/10/1918	22/10/1918
Map	Map		
Miscellaneous	App XXXII		
Miscellaneous	Reference 61st Division Order No.225 Dated 22nd October 1918.	23/10/1918	23/10/1918
Operation(al) Order(s)	61st Division Order No.226	23/10/1918	23/10/1918
Miscellaneous	A Form Messages And Signals.		
Miscellaneous	61st Division Locations of Advanced H.Q. At 0600, 25th October 1918.	24/10/1918	24/10/1918
Miscellaneous	61st Division Locations of Units At 1800 Hrs, 25.10.18.	25/10/1918	25/10/1918
Miscellaneous	A Form Messages And Signals.		
Miscellaneous	61st Division Locations of Units At 0600 Hrs. 26.10.18	25/10/1918	25/10/1918
Miscellaneous	A Form Messages And Signals.		
Miscellaneous	61st Division Locations of Units At 0600 Hrs., 27.10.18	27/10/1918	27/10/1918
Operation(al) Order(s)	61st Division Order No.227	27/10/1918	27/10/1918
Miscellaneous	61st Division Locations of Units At 0600 Hrs. 28.10.1918	28/10/1918	28/10/1918
Miscellaneous	61st Division Locations of Units At 0600 Hours, 30.10.18	29/10/1918	29/10/1918
Miscellaneous	C Form Messages And Signals.		
Operation(al) Order(s)	61st Division Order No.229	30/10/1918	30/10/1918
Miscellaneous	Appendix XLVII	30/10/1918	30/10/1918
Map	Map		
Heading	61st Division War Diary Vol XXXI November 1918.		
War Diary	Vendegies Q.14.d.1.7. (Sht.51A)	31/10/1918	03/11/1918
War Diary	St. Aubert U.24.b.6.1	04/11/1918	07/11/1918
War Diary	Vendegies (Q.14.d.1.7) Sht.51A.	08/11/1918	14/11/1918
War Diary	Rieux	14/11/1918	14/11/1918
War Diary	Cambrai	15/11/1918	25/11/1918
War Diary	Bernaville	26/11/1918	30/11/1918
Miscellaneous	Amendment No.1 To 61st Div Order No.228 Of 29.10.18	29/10/1918	29/10/1918
Miscellaneous	A Form Messages And Signals.		
Miscellaneous	G.C.40/5	29/10/1918	29/10/1918
Map	Map		
Operation(al) Order(s)	61st Division Order No.228	29/10/1918	29/10/1918
Miscellaneous	61st Division Locations of Units At 0600, 1.11.18	31/10/1918	31/10/1918
Miscellaneous	G.C.45/7	31/10/1918	31/10/1918
Miscellaneous	Notes on The Enemy's Counter-preparation In Reply To our Smoke Barrage on 29th October	30/10/1918	30/10/1918
Miscellaneous	C.R.A.	01/11/1918	01/11/1918
Miscellaneous	A Form Messages And Signals.		
Operation(al) Order(s)	61st Division Order No.230	31/10/1918	31/10/1918
Map	Map		
Operation(al) Order(s)	61st Division Order No.231	01/11/1918	01/11/1918
Miscellaneous	Movement Table Issued With 61st Div. Order No.231, Dated 1.11.18	01/11/1918	01/11/1918

Miscellaneous	Reference Movement Table Issued With D.O. 231 Dated 1.11.18.	01/11/1918	01/11/1918
Miscellaneous	Reference Movement Table Issued With D.O.231	01/11/1918	01/11/1918
Miscellaneous	Reference Movement Table Issued With D.O.231	02/11/1918	02/11/1918
Miscellaneous	61st Division Locations of Units At 0600, 2.11.18	01/11/1918	01/11/1918
Miscellaneous	61st Division Locations of Units At 0600, 3.11.18	02/11/1918	02/11/1918
Operation(al) Order(s)	61st Division Order No. 232	03/11/1918	03/11/1918
Miscellaneous	Movement Table Issued With 61 Division Order No.232 Dated 3.11.18	03/11/1918	03/11/1918
Miscellaneous	61st Division Locations of Units At 0600,4.11.18	03/11/1918	03/11/1918
Miscellaneous	61st Division Locations of Units At 0600,5.11.18	04/11/1918	04/11/1918
Miscellaneous	61st Division Locations of Units At 0600, 7.11.18	06/11/1918	06/11/1918
Operation(al) Order(s)	61st Division Order No.233		
Miscellaneous	Movement Table Issued With 61 Division Order No.233 Dated 7.11.18.	07/11/1918	07/11/1918
Miscellaneous	A Form Messages And Signals.		
Miscellaneous	61st Division Locations of Units At 0600, 9th Nov 1918	08/11/1918	08/11/1918
Miscellaneous	A Form Messages And Signals.		
Operation(al) Order(s)	61st Division Order No.234	13/11/1918	13/11/1918
Miscellaneous	Movement Table To Accompany 51 Div Order No.234 Dated 13.11.18	13/11/1918	13/11/1918
Operation(al) Order(s)	61st Division Order No.235	14/11/1918	14/11/1918
Miscellaneous	Movement Table Issued With 61st Div. Order No.235	14/11/1918	14/11/1918
Miscellaneous	61st Division Locations of Units At 600 Hrs., 16.11.18	16/11/1918	16/11/1918
Miscellaneous	61st Division Locations of Units At 0600 Hrs. 20.11.18	19/11/1918	19/11/1918
Miscellaneous	61st Division Order No.236 Warning Order.	21/11/1918	21/11/1918
Miscellaneous	March Table Issued With 61 Div. Order No.236 Dated 21.11.18.	21/11/1918	21/11/1918
Operation(al) Order(s)	61st Division Order No.237	22/11/1918	22/11/1918
Miscellaneous	March Table Issued With 61st Div. Order No.237, Dated 22.11.18	22/11/1918	22/11/1918
Miscellaneous	2nd Division.	02/11/1918	02/11/1918
Map	Map		
Miscellaneous	Amendment To 61 Div. Order No. 237, Dated 22.11.18	22/11/1918	22/11/1918
Miscellaneous	A Form Messages And Signals.		
Miscellaneous	61st Division Locations of Units At 0600, 28.11.18	27/11/1918	27/11/1918
Heading	61st Division War Diary Vol. XXXII December 1918.		
Miscellaneous	61st Division No.A.36.	14/12/1918	14/12/1918
War Diary	Bernaville	01/12/1918	07/12/1918
War Diary	St. Riquier	08/12/1918	29/12/1918
Miscellaneous	Amendment To Locations Dated 28.11.18	01/12/1918	01/12/1918
Miscellaneous	Reference 61 Div. Order No.238	06/12/1918	06/12/1918
Operation(al) Order(s)	61st Division Order No.238	06/12/1918	06/12/1918
Miscellaneous	Movement Table To Accompany 61st Div. Order No. 238, Dated 6.12.18	06/12/1918	06/12/1918
Map	Map		
Miscellaneous	61st Division Locations of Units At 0600 Hours	08/12/1918	08/12/1918
Miscellaneous	61st Division Amendment To Location List Dated 9.12.18	09/12/1918	09/12/1918
Miscellaneous	61st Division Locations of Units At 0600 Hours, 12.12.18	11/12/1918	11/12/1918
Miscellaneous	A Form Messages And Signals.		
Heading	War Diary 61st Division January 1919 Vol XXXIII		
War Diary	St. Riquier	01/01/1919	31/01/1919
Heading	War Diary 61st Div February 1919 Vol XXXIV		
War Diary	St. Riquier	01/02/1919	28/02/1919

Miscellaneous	Amendment No.1 To 61st Division Order No.239	12/02/1919	12/02/1919
Operation(al) Order(s)	61st Division Order No.239.	12/02/1919	12/02/1919
Miscellaneous	61st Division Locations of Units At 1200 Hours 15.2.19	14/02/1919	14/02/1919
Heading	War Diary 61st Division March 1919 Vol XXXV		
War Diary	St. Riquier	01/03/1919	31/03/1919
Miscellaneous	G.C.31/1/1	03/03/1919	03/03/1919
Miscellaneous	Reference G.C. 31/1 Of 14.3.19	13/03/1919	13/03/1919
Miscellaneous	G.C. 31/1	14/03/1919	14/03/1919
Miscellaneous	G.C.31/1	21/03/1919	21/03/1919
Operation(al) Order(s)	61st Division Order No.240	21/03/1919	21/03/1919
Miscellaneous	61st Division Locations of Units At 1200 Hours 31.3.1919	31/03/1919	31/03/1919
Heading	War Diary 61st Division April 1919 Vol XXXVI		
War Diary	Le Treport	04/04/1919	06/04/1919
Miscellaneous	Appendix I	04/04/1919	04/04/1919
Heading	War Diary 61st Division May 1919 Vol XXXVII		
War Diary	Le Treport.		
Heading	War Diary 61st Division June 1919 Vol XXXVIII		
War Diary	Le Treport	02/06/1919	27/06/1919
Heading	War Diary 61st Division July 1919 Vol XXXIX		
War Diary	Le Treport	01/07/1919	30/07/1919

WO 95/3036/1

61ST DIVISION

GENERAL STAFF
MAY 1918 - JLY 1919

1918 SEP

War Diary.
61st Dvn.
Sept 1918
Vol. XXIX

Army Form C. 2118.

WAR DIARY
-or-
INTELLIGENCE SUMMARY

VOLUME XXIX.

(Erase heading not required.)

Instructions regarding War Diaries and Intelligence Summaries are contained in F.S. Regs., Part II. and the Staff Manual respectively. Title pages will be prepared in manuscript.

Place	Date	Hour	Summary of Events and Information	Remarks and references to Appendices
CROIX MARRAISSE. J.21.c. (Sht.36A).	SEPTR. 1918. 1st		The opening of the month found the Division still holding the left sector of the XI Corps front. For locations of units, and positions held by the Advanced Guard Brigade (184th), also Main Line of Retention in case of counter-attack, see attached location list and map "A" respectively. A quiet day, and much cooler. The night was quiet on the Divisional front; excepting that our patrols reached L.11.b.5.3 and KENNETT CROSS, there was no change in the line. Enemy artillery was active all night, and their activity included a barrage on RUE MONTIGNY & REGAL LODGE. Hostile M.Gs. also were busy, particularly from L.11.d.8.9 and WELWYN & FAGGOT FARMS. The 40th and 59th Divisions on our flanks advanced their line during the early morning. 184 Inf. Bde. reported at 11 a.m. that the strong points in L.23.d. and at L.28.b.9.9 were in their hands, and that a patrol was investigating between LEAM & FAGGOT Farms, where the situation was not quite clear. The enemy destroyed LA GORGUE church tower during the night, and explosions - thought to be road mines - were heard just E. of ESTAIRES. A later report from the Advanced Guard Bde. gave our line as now running - N. to S. - G.1.d.2.3 - WELWYN FM. - PETIT BOIS Bridge - FAGGOT FM. - L.23.c.0.0 - L.28.b.2.6 to the Canal at L.28.d.2.0, and this was shortly afterwards supplemented by the information that patrols had met with considerable M.G. fire. Fires and explosions continued behind enemy's lines. At noon, 61st Div. Order No. 199 was issued to all concerned. The chief points of this order were (1) That the battalion of the 183 Inf.Bde. placed at the disposal of the G.O.C. Advanced Guard Bde ※ would be relieved by a battalion of 182 Inf.Bde; (2) That the 182 Inf.Bde. (less the afore-mentioned battalion) would move forward and occupy the general line CRINQUETTE LOTTE - PULLET FM. - COCHIN CORNER; (3) That, upon this move being complete, 183 Inf.Bde. would withdraw into Divisional reserve. These reliefs and moves to be carried out tonight; the Main Line of Retention to remain as at present, and the responsibility for holding it to rest on 182 Inf.Bde. Details regarding the movement of M.G. Coys. in the event of the M.L.R. being threatened were also contained in this Order. Hostile shelling was normal during the day, but E.A. were active, 6 low-flying machines being reported over NEUF BERQUIN. By order of the Divisional Commander, SAILLY SUR LYS church tower was engaged and destroyed by our artillery during the afternoon. Patrols of the Advanced Guard Bde. made excellent progress, and by 8.15 p.m. had pushed through the town of ESTAIRES and established a line from the fork roads at G.25.d.9.6 along the road running N.E. through G.26.a. Patrols further north advanced also, and at 10.30 p.m. our line was reported to run - N. to S. - as follows - G.3.c.0.0. - G.9.c.0.0. - G.14.central - TROU BAYARD -	Appx. I. Appx. II. ※ (See Appx. XXVIII, Vol XXVIII).

Army Form C. 2118.

WAR DIARY
INTELLIGENCE SUMMARY

(Erase heading not required.)

Instructions regarding War Diaries and Intelligence Summaries are contained in F.S. Regs., Part II. and the Staff Manual respectively. Title pages will be prepared in manuscript.

Place	Date Hour	Summary of Events and Information	Remarks and references to Appendices
CROIX MARRAISSE, J.21.c. (Sht.36A.)	SEPTR. 1918. 1st (ctd.)	G.26.a.9.9, and thence down to PONT LEVIS. Touch was maintained on the left, where 40th Div. had made ground, but the 59th Div. on our right had found the enemy resistance stiff, and were a considerable distance in rear of our advanced troops. The Outpost Line of Resistance for the night, as taken up by 184 Inf.Bde., was the general line LYS Bridge - L.29.a.0.9 - FAGGOT FM. - PETIT BOIS Bridge - road junction at L.18.a.1.4 - WELWYN FM. - POM COTTAGE. Reliefs and moves in accordance with Div. Order No. 199 were completed before midnight. G.592, sent out at 11.15 p.m., ordered the R.F.A.Bde. covering the M.L.R. to move forward tomorrow to positions of readiness about LES PURESBECQUES, under orders of C.R.A. At 11 p.m. a hostile aeroplane dropped 10 bombs within 200 yds. of Advanced Div.H.Q.: no casualties or damage were sustained. For locations of units after relief, see location list -	(See Appx. II). Appx.IIa. Appx.III.
	2nd	Dull, with showers at intervals. Hostile artillery shelled FME. DE BRETAGNE heavily during the night, but his attitude, both on our front and flanks was otherwise quiet. 61 Div. Order No. 200,issued at 7 a.m., ordered the relief of 184 Inf.Bde. in the Advanced Guard position tonight; on relief, 184 Bde. to take over the responsibility for defence of the M.L.R., and to be located as follows :- 2 Bns. CRINQUETTE LOTTE, PULLET FM., COCHIN CORNER area, and 1 Bn. about LES PURESBECQUES; this Brigade to be prepared to move forward to the CHAPELLE DUVELLE - RUE MONTIGNY area. G.306, sent out as an amendment to this Order, ordered 2 Bns. of 184 Inf.Bde. to go to the CHAPELLE DUVELLE - RUE MONTIGNY area, and the remaining Bn. to NEUF BERQUIN neighbourhood. G.598, sent to all concerned, at 10.25 a.m., gave objective for Advanced Guard Bde. today. Continued good progress by 184 Bde.'s patrols resulted in their reaching, by 10 a.m., a general line of the road running from PONT LEVIS to G.10.a.8.4, with an unconfirmed statement that a party had crossed the river LYS and entered SAILLY SUR LA LYS, which eventually proved to be not so. The southern Divl. boundary was changed to the following line :- G.25.d.6.3 to G.26.c.2.2 (road junction exclusive- thence straight to G.34.d.3.2, thence due East. G.602, sent to 184 Inf.Bde., ordered them to furnish a special liaison platoon on their left flank, to ensure touch being kept with 40th Divn., the latter having arranged a similar party to work in conjunction. A noon situation wire from 184 Inf.Bde. stated that all bridges across the LYS River on their front had been destroyed, and were under hostile M.G. fire, which was considerable, likewise enemy	Appx.IV. Appx.V. Appx.VI. Appx.VII.

Army Form C. 2118.

WAR DIARY
-or-
-INTELLIGENCE-SUMMARY.-

(Erase heading not required.)

Instructions regarding War Diaries and Intelligence Summaries are contained in F.S. Regs., Part II. and the Staff Manual respectively. Title pages will be prepared in manuscript.

Place	Date	Hour	Summary of Events and Information	Remarks and references to Appendices
CROIX MARAISSE, J.21.c. (Sht.36A)	SEPTR.1918. 2nd (ctd.)		sniping; some shelling, too, on left patrols. This activity continued during the afternoon, and seemed to indicate that we were nearing the German line of resistance, an opinion shared by the Divisions on our flanks. Although not able to force a crossing of the river, our patrols succeeded in pushing forward posts close to the W. bank along our whole front. No further progress was made before night. It was decided that our easiest chance of crossing the LYS would be by working round on our right flank after crossing the river by the MEUSE & LYS bridges. 184 Inf.Bde. were therefore ordered to detach 2 coys. of infantry, together with M.Gs., to carry out this operation, reinforcing these as they worked E. & N.E. along the river by bringing troops over by the crossings thus cleared; this to be carried out early tomorrow; the final objectives of the Advanced Guard Bde. to be the CROIX DU BAC (exclusive) - BAC ST. MAUR, and S.W. along the railway to G.34.d.2.2 (see G.616 - Appx. VIII). The attached wire was received from Major-General COLIN MACKENZIE, K.C.B., late G.O.C., 61st Division.	Appx.VIII. Appx.IX.
	3rd		Relief, in accordance with Div. Order No. 200, was reported complete at 2.45 a.m., and at that hour G.O.C. 182 Bde. assumed charge of the Advanced Guard Bde. positions. For locations after relief, see location list attached. Weather dull and cloudy, but fine. Intermittent hostile M.G. and artillery fire during the night, but the Right Bn. of the Advanced Guard Bde. was able to push forward still closer to the W. bank of the LYS River. At 9 a.m. 182 Inf.Bde. reported as follows :- Bridge at G.27.a.98.40 repaired, and 2 coys. had crossed river; they were then on line 300 yds. E. of river from approx. G.27.c.9.7 to G.22.c.1.4; 2 coys. also crossed MEUSE Bridge, and were working E. through G.26.d. & 27.c. Both crossings drew heavy hostile M.G. fire and sniping. Patrols had also forced crossing W. of SAILLY. This operation yielded a prisoner of the 100th Res. Grenadier Regt. (captured in G.27) and 1 M.G. A further report from 182 Inf.Bde. about 1 p.m. stated that although there was no material change on the right front, patrols who had crossed the river near SAILLY had joined up with patrols who had crossed to the south, and were advancing on SAILLY from about G.22.central. Near the BRICKFIELDS 500 yds. had been gained, and touch was maintained with the 40th Divn: patrols were then pushing forward along the whole front.	(See Appx. IV). Appx.X.

A5834 Wt.W4973 M687 750,000 8/16 D.D.&L.Ltd. Forms/C.2118/13.

Army Form C. 2118.

WAR DIARY
— or —
INTELLIGENCE SUMMARY

(Erase heading not required.)

Instructions regarding War Diaries and Intelligence Summaries are contained in F.S. Regs., Part II. and the Staff Manual respectively. Title pages will be prepared in manuscript.

Place	Date SEPTR. 1918.	Hour	Summary of Events and Information	Remarks and references to Appendices
CROIX MARRAISSE, J.21.c. (Sht.36A).	3rd (ctd)		At 5 p.m. the line held was as follows - N. to S: G.12.a.1.3 - G.12.c.3.2 - G.18.central - G.22.central - G.28.b.6.4 - G.28.d.8.0 - G.34.b.6.0 - G.34.d.5.0. Situation between G.18.cent. and G.22.cent. obscure. In touch still with left Div., but none with right Div. yet obtained. To enable this to be gained, a liaison post was arranged for, to be established at G.33.c.8.4 at daybreak tomorrow.	
			A later report from the Advanced Guard Bde. gave their line N. to S. as G.12.a.3.0 - G.18.a.5.6 - G.17.b.5.3 - G.23.d.5.0 - thence along railway to G.34.d.2.3; the O.L.R. for the night taken up being the W. bank of the LYS from G.26.c.0.6 to G.16.b.8.8, thence N. along the STIEBEKE to the N. Divl. boundary.	
			Enemy attitude throughout the day was normal, and no undue amount of M.G. opposition was experienced by our patrols.	
			G.627, sent out at 11 p.m., gave line of objectives for Advanced Guard Bde. tomorrow.	Appx.XI.
	4th		Dull, with rain at times. Some gas shelling in G.9.d., and considerable M.G. fire from houses along the road in G.35.a. and G.29.d. during the night.	
			Our patrols resumed operations at dawn, and reported at 8.30 a.m. that on their left they had gained the W. bank of the LYS in H.13.a, while further south they had crossed the BAC ST.MAUR - LAVENTIE Railway practically along their whole front, and parties were working East of this; the village of BAC ST. MAUR thought to be clear of the enemy. Our advance encountered some M.G. and rifle fire, but no hostile shelling.	
			Information from yesterday's prisoners points to the 187 Div. having been withdrawn altogether from the sector opposite us, and that apparently only the 23rd Res.Div. (Saxon) which was very weak, and possibly elements of 4th Div., were opposed to the XI Corps. (The 187 Div. was identified on the SCARPE - SOMME front on the 7th).	
			The Fifth Army Commander visited Div.H.Q. during the morning.	
			G.632, sent out at 11.10 a.m., gave Corps objectives for today, and instructed 182 Inf.Bde. to push on to this line and keep touch with the enemy.	Appx.XII.
			The advance of the early morning was continued, and patrols gained a general line running N. to S: H.7.d - FORT ROMPU - H.13.d - H.19.central - through the cross-roads at G.36.d.8.7 down to M.6.b.9.1, and touch with both flanks was established. Hostile M.Gs. were active against our troops on the left.	
			A badly wounded prisoner of the 11th Railway Construction Coy. was captured in G.29; he stated in his examination that his coy. was engaged in taking up and destroying lines back to	

Army Form C. 2118.

WAR DIARY
—or—
—INTELLIGENCE—SUMMARY—
(Erase heading not required)

Instructions regarding War Diaries and Intelligence Summaries are contained in F.S. Regs., Part II. and the Staff Manual respectively. Title pages will be prepared in manuscript.

Place	Date	Hour	Summary of Events and Information	Remarks and references to Appendices
CROIX MARRAISSE, J.21.c. (Sht.36A)	SEPTR. 1918.	4th (ctd)	FROMELLES. The remainder of the day passed quietly, and the Advanced Guard Bde. took up their O.L.R. along the line of the railway from LAVENTIE Station to H.13.c.5.7, thence to H.13.c.45.95, and to the other boundary at G.12.b.3.0. The attached wire of congratulation from the Corps Commander was forwarded to O.C. 182 Inf.Bde. During the day the following instructions and orders were issued :- At 6 p.m. 61 Div. Order No. 201, ordering both the Intermediate and Reserve Bdes. to move forward - the former (184) to FAGGOT FM. - TROU BAYARD - G.9. area, and the latter (183) to the CHAPELLE DUVELLE - RUE MONTIGNY area; moves to take place today and tomorrow.respectively. G.635, sent out at 7.45 p.m., order M.G.Bn. (less coys. in the line) to move from HAVERSKERQUE to LA GORGUE tomorrow. 61 Div. Instructions No. 1, relating to current operations, were issued. The gist of these was as follows :- The Advanced Guard Bde. policy of maintaining touch with and vigorously acting against the enemy rearguards, to be maintained, with the object of pushing on to successive lines given; an Outpost Line of Resistance to be selected from time to time, according to the extent of the advance upon which, should an enemy counter-attack develop, the Advanced Guard Bde. would give battle. In place of the Main Line of Retention, a Corps Battle Line was being selected 3,000 to 5,000 yards behind the objectives of the Advanced Guard Bde; this line to be held by the two remaining Brigades in depth of three echelons. The Instructions contained further details regarding dispositions, accommodation, defences, communications, artillery and machine guns, and were issued to all concerned. G.638, sent out at 11.50 p.m., gave line of objectives for tomorrow to the Advanced Guard Bde.	Appx.XIII. Appx.XIIIa Appx.XIV. Appx.XV. Appx.XVI.
		5th	Dull and showery. Early morning reports stated that the line was unchanged. Hostile artillery active all night with H.E. and gas. C.R.E. reported at 10.20 a.m. that 5 bridges were in position over the LYS, and 1 over the METEREN BECQUE. G.643, sent out at 11.30 a.m., gave the Corps Battle Line selected (see Instructions No. 1, dated 4th (Appx.XV); also a second line to be taken up upon the Advanced Guard Bde. reaching certain objectives. Another wounded prisoner of the 11th Rly. Cons. Coy. was captured in H.31 during the morning, and a further identification (188 I.R.) was obtained from a corpse found in H.25.d; this man was shot yesterday morning.	

Army Form C. 2118.

WAR DIARY
—or—
INTELLIGENCE SUMMARY

(Erase heading not required.)

Instructions regarding War Diaries and Intelligence Summaries are contained in F.S. Regs., Part II. and the Staff Manual respectively. Title pages will be prepared in manuscript.

Place	Date SEPTR. 1918.	Hour	Summary of Events and Information	Remarks and references to Appendices
CROIX MARRAISSE, J.21.c. (Sht.36A).	5th. (ctd)		The 40th Div. made good progress during the day, but the 59th Div. encountered strong opposition from TWO TREE FM. and did not succeed in making much ground. Advanced Guard Bde. reported, at 5 p.m., that their line ran approximately from M.6.b.9.9 to N.1.a.6.9, thence along trench through H.31.d, from H.31.d.9.9 north through H.25.b.&.d. to H.19.cent., and from there to H.13.b.6.6 and along road N.E. to FORT ROMPU. Enemy had been active shelling with H.31.a. with 4.2s and T.Ms., and shelling had been heavy at times over whole area E. of LYS. M.Gs. and T.Ms. resisted our advance strongly in H.13.d. and H.25.a.& c. SAILLY heavily shelled at times with 5.9s. E.A. showed exceptional boldness all day, flying at varying altitudes E. and W. of LYS. An observed shoot tiwh 5.9s on the pontoon bridge at G.16.c.7.6 resulted in its destruction. 40 enemy dead have been counted, all killed by our infantry since crossing the river. The O.L.R. taken up at dusk was the line of the railway from LAVENTIE Station to H.13.c.3.6, and then N. along road to G.12.b.3.0. 61 Div. Order No. 202, issued at 6 p.m., ordered various readjustments and moves in connection with the recently selected Corps Battle Line; tomorrow 183 Inf.Bde. to take over the Northern Bde. area and 184 Bde. the southern Bde. area of this line; details of locations, inter-Brigade boundary, and distribution of M.G.Coys., were also given; further, the 183 Bde. were ordered to relieve the 182 Bde. in the Advanced Guard positions, one battn. on the night 6th/7th, and the remainder of the Brigade on the night 7th/8th, after which the 182 Bde. would withdraw to the northern Brigade area of the C.B.L.	Appx.XVII.
	6th		Bright, with showers at intervals. The night was fairly quiet, but enemy artillery continued its activity against SAILLY; G.26 was also shelled. Patrols made good progress throughout the day, and finally gained the general line- N. to S: Copse in H.8.b. (incl.) - H.9.c.3.4 - H.9.c.5.2 - H.14.central - H.25.b.8.3 - H.31.d.5.8 - N.1.a.6.9. A good deal of opposition was experienced. A hostile party at the cross-roads at H.8.b.9.3 was engaged by Lewis guns and forced to retire; enemy M.G. fire was heavy from houses in H.13.d. and H.14.c. until these were dealt with by our artillery; our patrols following up quickly, captured 15 prisoners and 2 M.Gs. in this vicinity, killing in addition 30 of the enemy. M.G. fire was also severe from the Copse in H.8.b. before our troops took it. Scattered shelling by 5.9s and 4.2s was reported over the whole area of advance. The prisoners belonged to the 14 I.R; a report on their preliminary examination is attached.	Appx.XVIII.

Army Form C. 2118.

WAR DIARY
of
INTELLIGENCE-SUMMARY.
(Erase heading not required.)

Instructions regarding War Diaries and Intelligence Summaries are contained in F.S. Regs., Part II. and the Staff Manual respectively. Title pages will be prepared in manuscript.

Place	Date 1918.	Hour	Summary of Events and Information	Remarks and references to Appendices
CROIX MARRAISSE, J.21.c. (Sht.36A)	SEPTR. 6th	(ctd)	The O.L.R. taken up for the night was the road from G.34.d.3.0 to H.14.a.7.3, and thence to FORT ROMPU. Moves to the C.R.L. area, according to Div. Order No. 202, were carried out during the afternoon and evening. G.660, sent out at 9.30 p.m., announced that the Corps Battle Line had been moved forward to a general line from NOUVEAU MONDE along the W. bank of the LYS and the W. bank of the STILBEKE; no further movement of troops responsible for its defence was, however, necessary. The attached message of congratulation to the 182 Inf.Bde. and C.R.E. respectively was sent by the Divisional Commander during the evening.	(See Appx. XVII). Appx.XVIII*a* Appx.XIX.
	7th		Hostile artillery was active throughout the night, especially on our left, and M.Gs. kept up a continuous fire. 500 Yellow Cross Gas shells fell in H.8.c. during the early hours of darkness. CHAPELLE DUVELLE vicinity received attention from a H.V. gun at 3 a.m. Our line was slightly advanced during the day, and by evening had reached the line – N.to S: H.9.a.1.5 – H.9.c.5.5 – H.14.b.2.6 – H.14.c.6.9 – H.19.c.7.8 – H.25.b.7.5 – H.25.d.8.8 – H.25.d.7.0 – H.31.b.9.0 – H.31.d.9.7 – N.1.b.2.8. On the extreme left, patrols encountered heavy M.G. fire from the railway in H.9.d. and H.15.c; also from a strong point at H.9.b. On the right strong resistance was made from BARTLETTS FARM. One L.F.E.A. was in evidence during operations. 2 M.Gs. were captured in H.14.b. The O.L.R. taken up at dusk was along the line just given. The 59th Div. made further unsuccessful attempts to push forward, and the 40th Div., after making some ground, were counter-attacked and forced to withdraw slightly on their left.	
	8th		Relief of 182 Inf.Bde. by 183 Inf.Bde. in Advanced Guard Bde. area was completed at 1.40 a.m. (Div.Order No.202 - Appx. XVII). Fine during the day, but very heavy showers during the evening, which continued at intervals until midnight. Activity of hostile artillery and M.Gs. was rather decreased during the night. The day, too, was fairly quiet. We established posts at N.1.b.6.7, N.1.b.95.95, H.32.c.0.5, & H.32.c.0.3. JUNCTION POST, BARTLETTS FM., TWO TREE FM., and copse in N.2.b. were strong centres of resistance. Enemy guns were quiet, but T.Ms. were fairly troublesome. A fire was observed in FLEURBAIX during the evening.	

Army Form C. 2118.

WAR DIARY
or
INTELLIGENCE SUMMARY.

(Erase heading not required.)

Instructions regarding War Diaries and Intelligence Summaries are contained in F. S. Regs., Part II. and the Staff Manual respectively. Title pages will be prepared in manuscript.

Place	Date 1918	Hour	Summary of Events and Information	Remarks and references to Appendices
CROIX MARRAISSE. J.21.b. (Sht.36A)	SEPTR. 8th (ctd)		G.679, sent out at noon, announced move of Div.H.Q. (Advanced) tomorrow. For locations of units, see attached list. 61st Div. Instructions No. 2 were issued today - subject "Intelligence".	Apdx.XX. Appx.XXI. Appx.XXII.
RILL WORKS L.33.b.3.7 (Sht.36A)	9th		Very heavy showers, lasting some time, throughout the day; otherwise dull and cold. There was no change in the situation during the night. Enemy M.Gs. were active, but beyond that all was quiet. In accordance with G.679, Advanced Div.H.Q. closed at CROIX MARRAISE at 10 a.m., opening at RILL WORKS, L.33.b.3.7, at the same hour. At 10.30 a.m. 183 Bde. reported that attempt to take JUNCTION POST, BARTLETTS FARM, and Farm at H.20.c.5.5 was unsuccessful. Strong M.G., T.M., and rifle fire resistance all along front. Hostile artillery active on G.29.b, H.31.a.&c, and H.13.c. Several small explosions were observed in FLEURBAIX about 1 p.m. 4 E.A. patrolled the right front during the afternoon. Towards evening the Advanced Guard Bde. established posts on the left at H.3.c.7.1, H.9.a.8.3, and H.9.d.3.1, in face of severe M.G. fire. A fairly heavy M.G. barrage came down on H.25.c, H.31.a, xxx. H.15.c.& d. The situation on the flanks remained unchanged. Prisoner captured by the 40th Divn. yesterday stated that the enemy intended returning to his old front line E. of ARMENTIERES. An explosion, thought to be an enemy delayed-action mine, occurred this afternoon in a house at G.16.b.25.80, which was unoccupied at the time. In consequence of this, a wire (G.695) was sent to all units in the forward area, warning them about houses at present intact, and instructing that careful search be made for any suspicious excavations in walls, cellars, etc; to assist this, Tunnelling personnel was being attached to Brigades. Location list attached shows changes that took place on this date.	(See Appx. XX). Appx.XXIII.
	10th		Very strong wind, with heavy rain at intervals. Enemy shelled TROU BAYARD & ROUGE DE BOUT during the night, and dropped T.M. bombs in H.25. A further attempt to take JUNCTION POST was stopped at H.32.a.5.2 by heavy M.G., T.M., and rifle grenade fire. G.697, sent to 183 & 184 Inf.Bdes. during the morning, ordered the relief of the former by the	Appx.XXIV

A5834 Wt.W4973 M687 750,000 8/16 D.D.&L. Ltd. Forms/C.2118/13.

Army Form C. 2118.

WAR DIARY
—of—
—INTELLIGENCE-SUMMARY.—

(Erase heading not required.)

Instructions regarding War Diaries and Intelligence Summaries are contained in F.S. Regs., Part II. and the Staff Manual respectively. Title pages will be prepared in manuscript.

Place	Date	Hour	Summary of Events and Information	Remarks and references to Appendices
RILL WORKS L.33.b.3.7 (Sht. 36A)	SEPTR. 1918. 10th		(ctd) latter in the Advanced Guard Bde. positions; 1 Bn. to be relieved tonight, and the remainder of the Brigade tomorrow night; this wire was confirmed by 61 Div. Order No. 203, issued at noon to all concerned.	Appx. XXV.
			During the day there was continued opposition to our patrols from JUNCTION POST; the Advanced Guard Bde. Artillery engaged this heavily. Hostile shelling was slight, and E.A. did not appear at all. A hostile sniper in a tree at N.1.b.5.3 was tumbled off his perch by one of our snipers; 2 Germans were seen in the trench at H.26.d.8.7.	
			Posts were established during the afternoon at H.9.a.75.80 and H.3.c.65.30, and towards dusk at H.3.d.0.4, H.9.b.1.9, and H.9.b.2.8.	
			Our gunners obtained a direct hit on a house at H.20.d.7.6, and several Germans bolted from the place.	
			Corps "I" informed us that increased hostile wireless activity pointed to possibility of the withdrawal of elements of the 4th Divn. opposite us.	
			2 horses were killed at FELM FM. early this morning by an enemy mine, and at 6.30 p.m. an explosion occurred at the road junction at L.29.d.85.85 (ESTAIRES) without causing casualties or undue damage. An unexploded charge was removed from the inner flange of a railway line at G.36.b.75.80.	
			61 Divl. Instructions No. 3 were issued today; subject - "Anti-Aircraft Defence".	Appx. XXVI.
	11th		Continued strong wind and rain at times.	
			The usual hostile M.G. fire was reported during the night, and FORT ROMPU & BAC ST. MAUR were shelled with 5.9s.	
			Shortly after dawn the left Bn. of the Advanced Guard Bde. attempted to push forward along the BAC ST. MAUR - ERQUINGHEM Road. Our patrols were strongly resisted by the enemy, who opened very heavy M.G. fire from the south and east; also, in reply to a single red rocket, a strong 5.9" barrage came down along the road for some distance; no progress was made by our troops.	
			Touch was established with the 40th Divn. at noon, by one of their patrols working between GOSPEL VILLA and our post at H.3.a.5.1.	
			Fork roads and 2 houses in ESTAIRES went up during the morning, apparently by the explosion of enemy mines; no casualties resulted.	
			G.719, sent out at 3.45 p.m. to all concerned, stated that a minor operation would be carried out by the Advanced Guard Bde. at an early hour tomorrow morning, supported by 59th Div. Arty.	Appx. XXVII.
			The day was very quiet, and hostile artillery inactive.	

Army Form C. 2118.

WAR DIARY
— or —
INTELLIGENCE-SUMMARY:—
(Erase heading not required.)

Instructions regarding War Diaries and Intelligence Summaries are contained in F.S. Regs., Part II. and the Staff Manual respectively. Title pages will be prepared in manuscript.

Place	Date	Hour	Summary of Events and Information	Remarks and references to Appendices
RILL WORKS L.33.b.3.7 (Sht.36A)	SEPTR. 1918. 11th (ctd)		E.A. who attempted to cross our lines in the evening were driven back by A.A. fire. Towards dusk dusk patrols of the Advanced Guard were active on the left, but were much hampered by continuous M.G. & T.M. fire and sniping. A hostile T.M. at H.10.a.0.3 was silenced by our artillery, as were M.Gs. in H.15.a.& c. G.732, sent out at 9.35 p.m. to Advanced Guard Bde. and C.R.A., gave warning that wireless interception indicated a possible hostile raid, with artillery support, between ERQUINGHEM and FAUQUISSART tonight. The 59th Divn. were raided early this morning in the vicinity of PICANTIN POST; the Germans were driven off, and 2 wounded raiders captured; they stated they were ordered to hold their present line at all costs, and had heard nothing about a further retirement; they held no posts W. of RUE TILLELOY, and their trenches were in a bad state, no work having been done on them, or on the wire; object of raid was to ascertain what Divn. was opposite. Our H.T.Ms. fired a shoot on BARTLETT'S FM. at 6 p.m., and good results were observed.	Appx.XXVIII
	12th		Completion of relief according to 61 Div. Order No. 203 was accomplished at 2.10 a.m., and 184 Bde. became the Advanced Guard Bde. from that hour. A showery night developed into heavy rain, which continued most of the day. After a quiet night, 184 Inf.Bde. carried out an operation with two coys. with JUNCTION POST & BARTLETT'S FM. as objectives; troops encountered 4 hostile M.Gs. in a trench at H.32.a.0.7; these were bombed out of action and the crews killed; our patrol penetrated into JUNCTION POST, but were almost immediately counter-attacked from the S., and, their rifles having become useless owing to the mud, they were forced to withdraw. Further to the left our line was advanced on to a line H.26.a.25.90 to H.26.a.25.50; a post was established at H.32.a.5.5. The attacking troops sustained over 30 casualties, and throughout the operation were much handicapped by the very bad weather conditions. The enemy artillery reply to our barrage was extremely slight. An Alsatian deserter, belonging to the 1st M.G.Coy., 140 I.R., 4th Divn., gave himself up in H.19.b during the morning. Enemy artillery and M.Gs. kept up an intermittent fire all day. Our aeroplanes, who took advantage of fine spells in the afternoon and evening to go up, met with unusually heavy hostile M.G. fire. G.747, sent out at 9.45 p.m., gave O.L.R. for tonight and until further orders. Some doubt existed regarding the post established at H.32.a.5.5 during this morning's operations; an orderly of the coy. affected reported that he failed to find the garrison (1 officer	(See Appx. XXV). Appx.XXIX.

Army Form C. 2118.

WAR DIARY
-or-
--INTELLIGENCE SUMMARY--
(Erase heading not required.)

Instructions regarding War Diaries and Intelligence Summaries are contained in F.S. Regs., Part II. and the Staff Manual respectively. Title pages will be prepared in manuscript.

Place	Date	Hour	Summary of Events and Information	Remarks and references to Appendices
RILL WORKS, L.33.b.3.7. (Sht.36A)	SEPTR. 1918. 12th(ctd)		and a section) on returning from Coy.H.Q. to the post; owing to hostile fire it was considered impossible to investigate before dark as to the whereabouts of the missing garrison, who, it was afterwards ascertained, had been captured by the enemy, who must have returned to their positions after the bombardment had ceased. For locations of units, see attached list. The enemy was reported today to be firing 18-pdr. shrapnel.	Appx.XXX.
	13th		A wet and cold day, with few bright intervals. A very quiet night, with hostile shelling subnormal. Our patrols were active; posts at H.20.a.4.9 & 7.8 were found unoccupied, but the enemy was holding H.9.a.25.15, H.14.d.3.9 & 1.9. M.Gs. active from H.25.b.7.9, H.32.c.5.5, and H.9.c.3.0 (2 guns); work was in progress at H.14.c.9.7; a hostile patrol, 7 strong, was seen at H.9.b.3.9. The day was also quiet, with enemy artillery unusually inactive, until 5.30 p.m., when a heavy concentration from 150mm. and 105mm. guns, lasting 15 minutes, was put down on road between G.16.d.6.3 & G.17.c.4.8; some gas was mixed with the H.E. and could be smelt 1,000 yds. away. Hostile snipers were active in the evening against individual movement some distance in rear of our lines. 61 Div. Instructions No. 4 were issued; subject - "Operations". 61 Div. Order No. 204 was issued at 6 p.m., ordering relief of 184 Inf.Bde. by 182 Inf.Bde. in the Advanced Guard positions - one Bn. on night 14th/15th, and the remainder of the Brigade on the night 15th/16th.	Appx.XXXI. Appx.XXXII.
	14th		Showery, with sunny intervals. The night was very quiet, and hostile artillery was less active than usual, being confined to searching fire on the main roads. E.A. showed an increased activity when the weather permitted. Beyond this, the day and evening were uneventful. 61st Div. Instructions No. 5 were issued: subject - "Defence against Gas". Amendment No. 1 to Instructions No. 4 was also issued. IG.44/2 was sent out to all concerned; the effect of this was that, owing to operations being more or less stationary, a need had arisen for a permanent record of Intelligence for the purpose of handing over when reliefs in the Advanced Guard area took place; in accordance with this, Divl. Intelligence Summary No. 1 was issued.	Appx.XXXIII Appx.XXXIV Appx.XXXV. Appx.XXXVa.

WAR DIARY
— or —
INTELLIGENCE SUMMARY.

(Erase heading not required.)

Army Form C. 2118.

Instructions regarding War Diaries and Intelligence Summaries are contained in F.S. Regs., Part II. and the Staff Manual respectively. Title pages will be prepared in manuscript.

Place	Date	Hour	Summary of Events and Information	Remarks and references to Appendices
RILL WORKS, L.33.b.3.7. (Sht.36A)	SEPTR.1918			
	14th (ctd)		Acting on instructions contained in 61 Div. Instructions No. 4, nucleus garrisons were established in the evening by 182 Inf.Bde. in the left subsector of the C.B.L.	(See Appx. XXXI).
	15th		Fine and sunny, with a fresh wind.	
			Hostile harassing fire was considerable during the night, especially on roads immediately E. & W. of the LYS; otherwise enemy attitude was normal, and our patrols maintained entire command of NO MAN'S LAND.	
			Two escaped Portuguese prisoners came into our lines in H.21.c. shortly after midnight. There was no change in the situation during the day. E.A. continued an abnormal activity, and drove down one of our R.E.8s; it crashed in G.7.d; the pilot was slightly wounded. Retaliation was carried out on an E.O.B., which went down for the last time at 5 p.m.	
			In accordance with 61 Div. Instructions No. 4, 183 Bde. and M.G.Bn. took up positions in the C.B.L. during the day. On the extreme left of this line a liaison post was established with the 40th Div. at G.10.b.0.1.	(See Appx. XXXI).
			An appreciation of the situation was sent to XI Corps (G.C. 40/5).	
			Div. Intelligence Summary No. 2 is attached.	Appx. XXXVI.
			Relief of 184 Inf.Bde. by 182 Inf.Bde. in the Advanced Guard positions (reference Div.Order 204 - Appx. XXXII) - was completed by 11.20 p.m.	Appx. XXXVII.
			For locations after relief, see attached location list.	Appx. XXXVIII.
			A wire of congratulation was sent to G.O.C. 5th Divn. by General DUNCAN on their being mentioned for good work in recent operations.	Appx. XXXIX.
	16th		Very fine, and much warmer.	
			Hostile artillery was fairly active during the night. Throughout the hours of darkness our patrols kept constant touch with enemy posts, and found the garrisons alert, and keeping his machine guns well employed. Shortly after dawn we established a post at H.9.a.9.5.	
			Another Portuguese escaped prisoner wandered into our lines in H.31 early this morning.	
			The enemy kept up scattered shelling all day, and his aircraft were again very active at verying altitudes.	
			Explosions, due to enemy delayed-action mines, continued in various localities, cellars and roads being frequently reported as having gone up; also some of the small cubby-shelters with which the area is thickly supplied have been mined. A pill-box also exploded today, and caused casualties to artillery personnel.	

WAR DIARY
-or-
-INTELLIGENCE-SUMMARY--
(Erase heading not required.)

Army Form C. 2118

Instructions regarding War Diaries and Intelligence Summaries are contained in F.S. Regs., Part II. and the Staff Manual respectively. Title Pages will be prepared in manuscript.

Place	Date	Hour	Summary of Events and Information	Remarks and references to Appendices
RILL WORKS L.33.b.3.7 (Sht.36A)	SEPTR. 1918 16th (ctd)		T.647 contained a warning from R.E. H.Q. respecting charges inserted in drains running from houses.	Appx.XL.
			G.793, sent to all concerned, laid down the Outpost line of resistance to be maintained during the present stationary period.	Appx.XLI.
			Div. Intelligence Summary No. 3 is attached.	Appx.XLII.
			Orders having been received from Corps to the effect that one battalion was to be sent to LINGHEM tomorrow (17th) to work on the new Corps School, under orders of XI Corps "Q", G.792 ordered 184 Inf.Bde. to supply a battalion in compliance with this order.	Appx.XLIII.
			In reply to our wire of congratulation, the attached was received from 5th Divn.	Appx.XLIV.
	17th		Very fine.	
		4 to 6 a.m.	The enemy's attitude was quiet during the night, but his artillery was very active from 4 to 6 a.m. Our patrols found his posts strongly held, and the garrisons alert. BAC ST.MAUR, SAILLY, and G.17 were shelled intermittently throughout the day. E.A. activity was much decreased. Abnormal wireless traffic was reported by Corps on the front of the 23rd Res.Div., and this was thought to possibly mean an enemy relief; in view of this, the Divisional Commander ordered extra artillery, machine gun, and trench mortar fire to be applied during the evening and night; particularly vigilant patrolling also to be carried out, with the object of taking the opportunity to kill enemy and round up posts.	
			Four houses went up today, and another cubby-shelter - no casualties caused.	
			Divl. Intelligence Summary No. 4 is attached.	Appx.XLV.
		6 p.m.	61 Div. Order No. 205, issued at 6 p.m., gave instructions that 183 Inf.Bde. would relieve 182 Inf.Bde. as Advanced Guard Bde: 1 Bn. on night 20th/21st, and remainder of Brigade on night 21st/22nd.	Appx.XLVI.

Army Form C. 2118

WAR DIARY
INTELLIGENCE-SUMMARY
(Erase heading not required.)

Instructions regarding War Diaries and Intelligence Summaries are contained in F.S. Regs., Part II. and the Staff Manual respectively. Title Pages will be prepared in manuscript.

Place	Date	Hour	Summary of Events and Information	Remarks and references to Appendices
RILL WORKS L.33.b.3.7 (Sht.36A)	SEPTR.1918 18th		A very fine day, and much warmer. A quiet night and morning, and hostile artillery inactive Our gunners and machine gunners were exceptionally busy during the hours of darkness, and the enemy's forward zone had little rest. A fighting patrol, working along the S. bank of the LYS, drew the attention of hostile M.Gs. in ERQUINGHEM, and were forced to retire. An enemy party of 30 on our southern boundary were dispersed by our small-arms fire, and were thought to have sustained loss. E.A. were completely absent during the day, whereas our machines were very active. German A.A. guns and field guns were thought to be firing from further back than yesterday. Amendment No. 1 to 61st Divl. Instructions No. 5 was issued. Div. Intelligence Summary No. 5 is attached.	Appx.XLVII. Appx.XLVIII.
	19th		Fine weather continued. Enemy artillery fairly active during the night. Our patrols were on the German wire throughout the hours of darkness, and found his attitude still very alert, and his machine guns well employed. The day was exceptionally quiet, with nothing of note to report, artillery activity being normal and E.A. inactive. Div. Intelligence Summary No. 6, and a location list, are attached.	Appx.XLIX) Appx.L.)
	20th		Cloudy and cool, but fine. A quiet night. Our patrols made several attempts to cut the enemy's wire, but owing to the bright moonlight the task was a very difficult one, and the enemy resisted their efforts strongly with M.G. fire. The day was again peaceful. The 59th Div. advanced the left of their line slightly. The MILL at G.22.b., and the SAILLY cross-roads, both went up during the afternoon, the roads being completely blocked by the latter explosion. A pigeon shot in our lines today carried a message from the 140 I.R. dated 16th Septr. Div. Intelligence Summary No. 7 is attached.	Appx.LI.

Army Form C. 2118

WAR DIARY
-or-
--INTELLIGENCE-SUMMARY--
(Erase heading not required.)

Instructions regarding War Diaries and Intelligence Summaries are contained in F. S. Regs., Part II. and the Staff Manual respectively. Title Pages will be prepared in manuscript.

Place	Date	Hour	Summary of Events and Information	Remarks and references to Appendices
RILL WORKS L.33.b.3.7. (Sht.36A).	SEPTR. 1918 21st		Dull and cloudy, with heavy rain at times. Very determined patrolling was carried out by the Advanced Guard Bde. during the night. Although much hampered by moonlight and the extreme alertness of the enemy, the hostile wire was thoroughly reconnoitred in face of heavy M.G. fire, and touch maintained with the enemy. One patrol of the 2/8 WORCESTERS, under the command of Lieut. THOMAS, remained in close vicinity of BARTLETTE FM. and encountered two strong hostile parties, which were engaged with effect by our patrol, which withdrew after gaining much information. The Divisional Commander sent the attached wire of congratulation to the 182 Inf.Bde., to be conveyed to Lieut. THOMAS. Hostile artillery rather less active, but E.A. activity somewhat increased; otherwise the day passed quietly. Relief of 182 Bde. by 183 Bde. in the Advanced Guard area was completed about midnight (in accordance with Div. Order 205 (see Appx. XLVI). For locations after relief, see location list. Div. Intelligence Summary No. 8 is attached.	Appx. LIa Appx. LII. Appx. LIII.
	22nd		Fine, but squally, with some showers. No hostile parties were seen by our patrols, who were active throughout the night. Ample evidence was, however, forthcoming that the enemy continued to hold his posts in strength, and his M.Gs. continued to engage our line and NO MAN'S LAND heavily; hostile artillery fire was again normal. Fires in the direction of ARMENTIERES were observed. The day was quiet; E.A. showed considerable activity despite high wind, meeting heavy opposition from our A.A. batteries. Div. Intelligence Summary No. 9 is attached; also a wire sent to the 9th (North. Hussars) Bn. The North. Fus., expressing the sympathy of the Divisional Commander on the death of Lieut.- Colonel EBSWORTH, M.C., commanding that unit, who was killed by a sniper last evening.	Appx. LIV. Appx. LV.

Army Form C. 2118.

WAR DIARY
-- or --
INTELLIGENCE SUMMARY.

(Erase heading not required.)

Instructions regarding War Diaries and Intelligence Summaries are contained in F. S. Regs., Part II. and the Staff Manual respectively. Title pages will be prepared in manuscript.

Place	Date	Hour	Summary of Events and Information	Remarks and references to Appendices
HILL WORKS, (L.33.b.3.7) Sht.36A.	SEPTR.1918. 23rd		Fine until afternoon, when it became showery. Our patrols maintained great activity, and consistently harassed the enemy's posts, revolver shots being fired into one in reply to bombs thrown at our patrol. Hostile activity was considerably slighter than usual during the night. The day passed very quietly, there being no incident of interest to report. Div. Intelligence Summary No. 10 is attached.	Appx.LVI.
	24th		Very bright and sunny. Liaison with hostile posts was maintained throughout the hours of darkness, and our artillery carried out special concentration shoots. M. & L.T.Ms. fired a wire-cutting programme. The day was again very quiet, except for enemy aircraft, who for once showed an inclination to see our side of the lines. Following a message from Corps "I" to the effect that German wireless stations had moved further back, orders were issued to all concerned to keep a vigilant observation for any signs of enemy withdrawal. (G.870). 2/4 Oxford & Bucks, who had been detached for work at LINGHEM, under Corps orders, rejoined 184 Inf.Bde. A Location list, and Div. Intelligence Summary No. 11, are attached. At 11.45 p.m. 460 gas projectors and 40 smoke projectors were discharged by "M" Special Coy. R.E. on JUNCTION POST & BARTLETTE'S FARM. These two strongholds of the enemy have received a great deal of attention lately. Hostile retaliation to this operation was nil.	Appx.LVII. Appx.LVIII. & LIX.
	25th		Fine, with a few showers. Hostile parties were occasionally active during the night. One of our patrols was bombed by an enemy patrol lying among their own wire. Two wiring parties were dispersed by our L.G. and rifle grenade fire. Our patrols carried out a thorough reconnaissance of enemy wire. The Divn. on our left, advanced their line slightly, and met with a good deal of M.G. opposition. Nothing unusual happened during the day, and E.A. were inactive. Div. Intelligence Summary No. 12 is attached. 61st Div. Order No. 206, issued at 6 p.m., ordered the relief of the 183 Inf.Bde. by the 184 Inf.Bde. in the Advanced Guard positions on the nights 26th/27th and 27th/28th.	Appx.LX. Appx.LXI.

Army Form C. 2118.

WAR DIARY
— or —
— INTELLIGENCE-SUMMARY. —

(Erase heading not required.)

Instructions regarding War Diaries and Intelligence Summaries are contained in F. S. Regs., Part II. and the Staff Manual respectively. Title pages will be prepared in manuscript.

Place	Date	Hour	Summary of Events and Information	Remarks and references to Appendices
RILL WORKS L.33.b.3.7. (Sht.36A).	SEPTR.1918. 25th	(cotd.)	61 Div. Instructions No. 6 were issued - subject "Operations". The gist of these Instructions was that, owing to indications of a possible further withdrawal on the part of the enemy, the Advanced Guard Bde. would be prepared, at 48 hours' notice, to carry out a reconnaissance in force, in the form of an operation, with the object of closely following up the hostile retreat. Two lines of objectives were also given, and special orders on dispositions, positions of headquarters, accommodation in evacuated area, Brigade forward observation stations, & communications.	Appx. LXII. LXIII.
	26th		Very bright and fine, with a cold wind. Amendment No. 1 to Div. Order 206 was sent out, postponing all dates. Patrols were very active during the hours of darkness, and found the enemy very alert and somewhat nervous. Our artillery and T.Ms. continued wire-cutting, and good results were observed. Enemy shelling was rather below normal. A heavy gas concentration was put down on LAVENTIE during the night. Hostile attitude throughout the day was quiet, though high-flying E.A. activity was above normal. Several indecisive air combats were reported. Div. Intelligence Summary No. 13 is attached.	Appx. LXIII.
			At 10.10 p.m. fighting patrols of the 1st R. Lancs Regt. attacked and captured BARTLETT'S FARM & JUNCTION POST under cover of a smoke and harmless gas projection, and with artillery, T.M., and M.G. support. A number of the enemy were killed, and 9 prisoners (1 wounded) and 1 M.G. taken. Our casualties were light. Prisoners belonged to the 49 I.R. and 100 R.G.R. Hostile artillery retaliation was intense on H.25; otherwise was not marked; M.G. fire also was heavy. During this attack 2 escaped Portuguese prisoners of war wandered into our lines.	Appx. LXIV.
	27th		Very heavy rain during the night, becoming fine after dawn. At 6 a.m. a strong hostile counter-attack developed against JUNCTION POST & BARTLETTE'S FM., and our troops were forced to withdraw, sustaining losses. 9th (North'd Hussar Bn.) North'd Fus. established posts, by means of daylight patrols, at H.19.b.60.25, H.19.d.35.35, & H.19.d.77.75. The day was exceptionally quiet, hostile artillery and aircraft activity being very slight. The results of the examination of prisoners captured during yesterday's attack are contained	

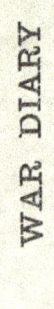

Army Form C. 2118.

WAR DIARY
—or—
INTELLIGENCE SUMMARY.
(Erase heading not required.)

Instructions regarding War Diaries and Intelligence Summaries are contained in F.S. Regs., Part II and the Staff Manual respectively. Title pages will be prepared in manuscript.

Place	Date SEPTR. 1918	Hour	Summary of Events and Information	Remarks and references to Appendices
RILL WORKS L.33.b.3.7. (Sht.36A)	27th (ctd)		in Div. Intelligence Summary No. 14. The attached congratulatory messages were received and sent out with reference to last night's operation.	Appx.LXV.
			At 9.15 p.m. 61 Div. Order No. 207 was issued to all concerned. This Order was to the effect that all moves laid down in Div.Order 206 (see Appx.LXI) were cancelled. In accordance with 61 Div. Instructions No. 6, preparations to renew the advance were to be immediately made, and the Divl. front reorganized into a two-Brigade front disposed on depth on a frontage of two battalions, the third Brigade being in Div. reserve. Accordingly, on the night 28th/29th, 184 Inf.Bde. to relieve all troops of 183 Inf.Bde. S. of H.19.central and become the Right Brigade; similarly, 182 Inf.Bde. to relieve all troops of 183 Inf.Bde. N. of the same point and become the Left Brigade; 183 Inf.Bde. to withdraw into Divl. reserve.	Appx.LXVI. Appx. LXVII.
	28th		Very wet during the early part of the day, afterwards becoming bright and sunny, with a suspicion of frost in the air. The night passed quietly, and enemy attitude was normal. Two Germans, approaching our posts in H.14, were fired on, and one badly wounded was brought into our lines; he was subsequently found to be a prisoner of war trying to escape into the enemy territory; turnips were found in his pocket, and had apparently been his only means of subsistence. The other man could not be discovered, though a thorough search was at once made. Nothing of an unusual nature happened during the day. Div. Intelligence Summary No. 15 is attached; also a copy of GRO.5104 announcing that the Continental system of time would be adopted throughout the British Armies in France from midnight Septr. 30th/1st Octr.	Appx.LXVIII & LXIX.
			G.C.54 (with reference to Divl. Instructions No. 6, para. 7) described an example of a German booby trap recently discovered.	Appx. LXX.
			Div. Order No. 208 was issued at 9.15 p.m. This was to the effect that, owing to the defeats sustained by the enemy on various points of the Western Front, it was possible that he intended either still further reducing his forces opposite us, or contemplated a withdrawal to the DOUAI LILLE Canal and the LILLE DEFENCES. In order to ascertain whether either of these surmises was correct, 184 Inf.Bde. would carry out a minor operation, in accordance with instructions already issued, for the capture of JUNCTION POST and enemy trenches in H.32.a,b,& c. as far N.E. as RUE DES BASSIERES; Zero hour to be notified later. Vigorous and organized patrolling to be carried on to test the strength of the enemy opposite the whole Divl. front; all forward troops to be prepared to commence advanced guard actions immediately the enemy showed signs of weakness or retirement.	Appx. LXXI.

Army Form C. 2118.

WAR DIARY
-- INTELLIGENCE-SUMMARY.--
(Erase heading not required.)

Instructions regarding War Diaries and Intelligence Summaries are contained in F. S. Regs., Part II. and the Staff Manual respectively. Title pages will be prepared in manuscript.

Place	Date	Hour	Summary of Events and Information	Remarks and references to Appendices
RILL WORKS L.33.b.3.7 (Sht.36A)	SEPTR. 1918. 28th (ctd)		Reliefs according to Divl. Order No. 207 (see Appx.XLVII) were reported complete about midnight, and attached list shows dispositions and locations after relief.	Appx. LXXII.
	29th		Fine until evening, when heavy rain commenced, lasting some hours. Throughout the hours of darkness the Divl. front was energetically patrolled, and it was definitely established that the enemy was in normal strength and giving no indication of immediate withdrawal. One of our patrols was bombed from the vicinity of BARTLETTE'S FARM. Hostile artillery fire during the night was intermittent, and scattered over a wide area. By day our artillery fired many concentration shoots, and, together with H.T.Ms., continued to cut and damage the enemy's wire. From dawn onwards hostile aircraft were extremely active at various heights; this activity decreased in the afternoon. Our machines, in face of heavy A.A. & M.G. fire, repeatedly crossed the enemy lines, and reported much train activity eastward from LILLE. German wireless stations were working from a good distance further back than yesterday. FORT ROMPU was heavily shelled towards evening. Shortly after dusk, a fighting patrol operated in the vicinity of BARTLETTE'S FARM; 3 enemy M.Gs. were located, and the sentry of one of them was shot; the enemy gave the alarm by loud shouting, and, heavy M.G. fire opening, our patrol withdrew. Divl. Intelligence Summary No. 16 is attached.	Appx. LXXIII
	30th		Rain during the night and early morning; afterwards dull and cold. Despite the bad weather conditions our patrols kept the closest liaison with the enemy's posts all along the Divl. front throughout the hours of darkness, gaining much valuable information, and capturing 1 prisoner of '49 I.R. M.G. fire on the part of the enemy was heavy from most of the previously reported positions. The number of lights sent up was reported to be normal. Hostile artillery was inactive. At 5.45 a.m., under cover of an artillery, M.G., and T.M. barrage, troops of 2/5th Gloucestershire Regt. attacked and captured JUNCTION POST after fierce fighting. At 7.30 a.m. the situation was as follows :- Left Coy. had reached road junction at H.26.d.1.1, after a hand-to-hand fight; the Centre Coy. was held up in front of the orchard at H.32.a.7.5 by M.Gs., which were being dealt with by left and centre coys; the right coy. was believed to be on the line from H.32.c.5.5 N.E. along the trench to H.32.b.7.7; several prisoners	

(A7091) Wt. W12859/M1293. 75,000. 1/17. D. D. & L., Ltd. Forms/C2118/4.

Army Form C. 2118.

WAR DIARY
or
INTELLIGENCE SUMMARY.
(Erase heading not required.)

Instructions regarding War Diaries and Intelligence Summaries are contained in F.S. Regs., Part II. and the Staff Manual respectively. Title pages will be prepared in manuscript.

Place	Date	Hour	Summary of Events and Information	Remarks and references to Appendices
RILLE WORKS, L.33.b.3.7. (Sht.36A).	SEPTR.1918.	30th(ctd)	of 102 R.I.R. captured, but number not yet known. At 9 a.m. it was reported that we held JUNCTION POST and the orchard at H.32.a.7.5, but not quite up to the line of the RUE DE BASSIERES; the enemy was then making bombing attacks. It transpired later that the enemy had forced the left coy. slightly back by a strong counterstroke; we held the trenches in H.32.a,b,& c; number of prisoners still uncertain. Throughout the day hard fighting continued, especially in the orchard at H.32.a.7.5, which changed hands several times till finally secured by us. At 5.30 p.m. our line ran H.32.c.5.6 - H.32.a.95.35 - JUNCTION POST (incl.) - Orchard H.32.a.7.5 (incl.) - H.26.c.5.0 - H.26.c.5.2 - H.26.c.0.5. A hostile M.G. in a concrete emplacement at H.26.c.60.25 was then still in action and bombing on both sides continued. Captures during the operation: 16 O.R. of 102 R.I.R. (2 wounded), 1 T.M., and 6 M.Gs. - the latter being used against the enemy with good effect. Shelling during the day was scattered, but heavy, chiefly on roads, and enclosure in H.31; FORT ROMPU also received attention. E.A. were conspicuous by their entire absence. Our contact aeroplanes could not co-operate with our attack owing to rain, but later, despite the high wind, were active, and were engaged by hostile field guns. Our forward troops reported enemy holding CROIX BLANCHE and trenches N.E. of that place in strength. Towards evening the situation became much quieter, and at dusk our line remained unchanged. A large fire near CHAPELLE D'ARMENTIERES was observed. The attached wires of congratulation were received from the Corps Commander, and sent by the Divisional Commander, respectively, regarding today's operations. Div. Intelligence Summary No. 17 is attached; also list showing locations of units at the close of the month. - Appendices attached :- Appx. LXXVII - 1/20,000 map, showing progress made during Septr. by 61st Division. Appx. LXXVIII - Total captures during Septr. by 61st Division.	Appx.LXXIV. Appx.LXXV & LXXVI.

signature

Major-General,
Commanding 61st Division.
2nd October, 1918.

SECRET   (Copy)   APPENDIX I

61st DIVISION.

Locations of Units at 6 a.m., 1.9.18.

DIV. H.Q. "G"   CROIX MARRAISSE, J.21.c.
   do.   "A" & "Q".   I.20.a.6.1.

182 Inf.Bde. (RESERVE BDE.), H.Q., STEENBECQUE.
   2/6 Warwicks,   VILLORBA CAMP, J.15.c.
   2/7 Warwicks,   STEENBECQUE.
   2/8 Worcesters,   LA LACQUE.
   L.T.M.B.   STEENBECQUE.

183 Inf.Bde. (M.L.R.BDE.), H.Q., J.4.c.7.5.
   11th Suffolks   (Line Bn.) CHAPELLE BOOM.
   1st E.Lancs,   (Reserve Bn.) SPRESIANO CAMP, J.14.b.
   L.T.M.B.   K.7.b.9.1.

184 Inf.Bde. (ADVANCED GUARD BDE.) H.Q., FACTORY, K.23.c.7.5.
   2/5 Glosters,   (Left Bn.) L.7.c.9.3.
   2/4 R.Berks.   (Right Bn.) L.27.a.0.4.
   2/4 Oxfords,   (Left Support), HUTTON MILL, K.18.b.
* 9th North.Fus.   (Right Support) SACHET FM., K.23.a.
   L.T.M.B.   K.28.b.5.9.

     * (183 Inf.Bde., under orders of G.O.C. Adv.Guard Bde.).

C.R.A.   J.21.c.
   306 Bde.RFA.   K.23.d.6.9 (Adv.Guard Group).
   307   do.   J.21.a.2.6 (Rear Group).
   D.A.C.   I.8.c.5.0.
   D.T.M.O.   D.30.c.8.6.

C.R.E.   J.21.c.
   476 Field Co.R.E.   K.14.c.
   478   do.   K.14.c.
   479   do.   K.7.d.

1/5 D.C.L.I.(P).   H.Q. & 3 Coys. J.11.b.

61 Bn.M.G.C.   H.Q., HAVERSKERQUE.
   "A" Coy.   HAVERSKERQUE.
   "B" Coy.   HAVERSKERQUE.
   "C" Coy.   ICHEN FM. (M.L.R.).
   "D" Coy.   L.13.d.5.5 (Adv.Guard Bde.).

A.D.M.S.   I.19.d.1.9.
   2/1 Field Amb.   I.17.c.5.1.
   2/2   do.   STEENBECQUE.
   2/3   do.   J.28.d.2.6.

61 Div.Train.   PONT DE THIENNES, I.21.a.7.0.
   No. 1 Coy.   STEENBECQUE, I.4.d.6.5.
   No. 2 Coy.   BOESEGHEM, I.8.b.0.4.
   No. 3 Coy.   I.9.b.5.9.
   No. 4 Coy.   I.22.c.8.4.

D.G.O.   )
Anti-Gas Depot)   THIENNES, I.16.c.3.2.

Div. P. of W. Cage,   J.11.b.9.7.

                                                     (Sd.) E.G.BATES, Lt.
31.8.18.   for G.S. 61 Div.

Appendix II

SECRET.   Copy No.

                61st DIVISION ORDER No. 199.   1.9.18.

1.   The following moves and reliefs will take place tonight,
     1st/2nd Septr. 1918 :-

     (a) One battalion of 182 Inf.Bde. will relieve one battalion of
         183 Inf.Bde. now attached to 184 Inf.Bde., and will come
         under the orders of G.O.C. 184 Inf.Bde. on completion of
         relief.
            On completion of above relief, the battalion of 183 Inf.
         Bde. will rejoin its Brigade.

     (b) 182 Inf.Bde. (less one battalion) will move forward and
         occupy the general line CRINQUETTE LOTTE (L.25.d.) - FULLET
         FARM (L.13.d.) - COCHIN CORNER (L.7.c.).

     (c) On completion of above move, the 183 Inf.Bde. will withdraw
         to Divisional Reserve and will be located as follows :-

                 Brigade Headquarters - STEENBECQUE.
                 One battalion   - STEENBECQUE.
                 One battalion   - VILLORBA CAMP.
                 One battalion   - SPRESIANO CAMP.
                 T.M.B.   - STEENBECQUE.

2.   The M.L.R. will remain as at present.
        The Intermediate Brigade (182 Inf.Bde.) will be responsible
     for defence of the M.L.R. in the event of a serious enemy counter-
     attack.
        The Company of 61st Bn. M.G.C. now in the M.L.R. will be
     prepared to move forward to positions covering the crossings of
     the BOURRE River and PLATE BECQUE in the event of a counter-
     attack.
        The Company of 61st Bn. M.G.C. now in reserve at HAVERSKERQUE
     will be prepared to move forward to the M.L.R. and replace the
     Company which will have moved to cover crossings.

3.   Reconnaissances for above must be carried out at once.

4.   All further details will be arranged between Commanders
     concerned.

5.   Command will pass on completion of relief or move, which will
     be notified to Division H.Q.

6.   ACKNOWLEDGE.

                                              C.H. Dowden Maj
Issued at 12 noon.   for
                                                   Lieut.-Col.,
                                                   G.S., 61st Divn.

              Distribution :-
     Copy No. 1 - A.D.C. for G.O.C.   12 - Div.Train.
              2 - Div.Signals.   13 - D.A.P.M.
            3-4 - Div. Arty.   14 - D.A.D.O.S.
              5 - C.R.E.   15-16 - XI Corps.
              6 - 61 Bn. M.G.C.   17 - 28 Bde.R.G.A.
              7 - 1/5 D.C.L.I.   18 - 42nd Sqn.R.A.F.
              8 - 182 Inf.Bde.   19 - 40th Divn.
              9 - 183 Inf.Bde.   20 - 59th Divn.
             10 - 184 Inf.Bde.   21-22 - "Q".
             11 - A.D.M.S.   23 - "G".

"A" Form
MESSAGES AND SIGNALS.

Army Form C. 2121 (in pads of 100).

APPENDIX 11a

TO: C.R.A.   183 Inf. Bde.   M.G. Bn.   A.D.M.S.
    XI Corps   184 Inf. Bde.   Div. Sigs. 40 Div.
                                             56 Div.

Sender's Number: 182 Inf. Bde.
G.592

AAA

Brigade of 61st Divisional Artillery what located West of and covering Main Line of Retention will move forward tomorrow 2nd inst to position of readiness about LES HURESBECQUES under orders of C.R.A. aaa adisd C.R.A. reptd all concerned

Place: 61 Div.
Time: 11.15 p.m.

(sd) O.H. BOLDEN

SECRET.   G.C. 79.

61st DIVISION.
Locations of Units at 6 a.m. 2.9.18.

DIV. H.Q. "G".   CROIX MARRAISSE, J.21.c.
    do. "A" & "Q".   TANNAY, I.22.d.3.1.

182 Inf.Bde. (LINE BDE.); H.Q. K.22.b.75.80.
   2/7 Warwicks,   (Left Bn.) SINBAD FARM, K.17.b.
   2/8 Worcesters,   (Right Bn.) K.24.a.4.3.
   L.T.M.B.   K.22.b.75.80.

183 Inf.Bde. (RESERVE BDE.); STEENBECQUE.
   9th North. Fus.   SPRESIANO CAMP, J.14.b.
   11th Suffolks,   VILLORBA CAMP, J.15.c.
   1st E. Lancs.,   STEENBECQUE.
   L.T.M.B.   STEENBECQUE.

184 Inf.Bde. (ADVANCED GUARD BDE.); H.Q. FACTORY, K.23.c.7.5.
   2/5 Glosters.   (Left Bn.), L.16.a.8.8.
   2/4 R. Berks.   (Right Bn.); L.27.a.0.3.
   2/4 Oxfords.   (Left Support), HUTTON MILL, K.18.b.
   * 2/6 Warwicks.   (Right Support), CARE CROSS, K.30.b.
   L.T.M.B.   K.28.b.5.9.

   * (182 Inf.Bde; under orders of G.O.C. Advanced Guard Bde.).

C.R.A.   J.21.c.
   306 Bde. R.F.A.   K.23.d.6.9 (Advanced Guard Group).
   307   do.   J.21.a.2.6 (Rear Group).
   D.A.C.   I.8.c.5.0.
   D.T.M.O.   D.30.c.8.6.

C.R.E.   J.21.c.
   476 Field Co. R.E.   K.14.a.
   478   do.   K.14.a.
   479   do.   K.7.d.

1/5 D.C.L.I.(P).   H.Q. & 2 Coys., J.11.b.
                        1 Coy., K.22.a.

61 Bn. M.G.C.   H.Q., HAVERSKERQUE.
   "A" Coy.,   HAVERSKERQUE (Reserve Coy.).
   "B" Coy.,   J.31.d.8.2.)
   "C" Coy.,   ICHEN FM.) Line Coys.
   "D" Coy.,   L.13.d.5.5 (Advanced Guard Bde.Coy.).

A.D.M.S.   I.20.d.1.1.
   2/1 Field Amb.   I.17.c.5.1.
   2/2   do.   STEENBECQUE I.5.d.4.8.
   2/3   do.   HAVERSKERQUE, J.28.d.2.8.

61 Div. Train.   PONT DE THIENNES, I.21.a.7.0.
   No. 1 Coy.,   STEENBECQUE, I.4.d.6.5.
   No. 2 Coy.,   BOESEGHEM, I.8.b.0.4.
   No. 3 Coy.,   I.9.b.5.9.
   No. 4 Coy.,   I.22.c.8.4.

D.G.O.   )
Anti-Gas Depot)   HAVERSKERQUE.

Div. P. of W. Cage,   J.11.b.9.7.

1.9.18.   *E.P.Bates.* Lieut
                                          for G.S., 61st Divn.

APPENDIX IV

SECRET.

Copy No. 25

61st DIVISION ORDER NO.200.

2.9.1918.

1. The 182 Inf. Bde. will relieve the 184 Inf. Bde. on the 2nd/3rd inst., and will take over the duties of Advanced Guard Brigade from the hour of relief.

2. On completion of relief the 184 Inf. Bde. (Intermediate Brigade) will be responsible for the defence of the M.L.R. in the event of a serious counter-attack and will be located as follows :-

    Two Battalions   about the area CRINQUETTE LOTTE - PULLET Farm - CHCHIN CORNER.

    One Battalion   about LES FURESBECQUES.

3. The 184 Inf. Bde. will however be prepared to move forward to the area -
    CHAPPELLE DUVELLE - RUE MONTIGNY
    and will carry out the necessary reconnaissance re movement and accommodation as early as possible.

4. The following troops which form part of the Advanced Guard will come under the orders of G.O.C., 182 Inf. Bde. on completion of relief :-

    1 Brigade, R.F.A.
    2 Sections Field Coy., R.E.
    2 Coys 61st Bn.M.G.C.
    1 Troops K.E.H.

5. Command will pass on completion of relief which will be notified to D.H.Q.

6. All further details will be arranged between Commanders concerned.

7. ACKNOWLEDGE.

Issued at 7 a.m.

C.H.Dowden Maj
for Lieut. Col.,
G.S., 61 Division.

DISTRIBUTION

Copy No. 1 - A.D.C. for G.O.C.
        2 - 61 Div. Signals.
      3-4 - 61 Div. Arty.
        5 - C.R.E.
        6 - 61 Bn.M.G.C.
        7 - 1/5 D.C.L.I.
        8 - 182 Inf. Bde.
        9 - 183 Inf. Bde.
       10 - 184 Inf. Bde.
       11 - A.D.M.S.
       12 - 61 Div. Train.
       13 - D.A.P.M.
       14 - D.A.D.O.S.
    15-16 - XI Corps.
       17 - 28 Bde., R.G.A.
       18 - 42 Squadron R.A.F.
       19 - 40th Division.
       20 - 59th Division.
    21-22 - "Q"
       23 - "G".

APPENDIX V

"A" Form
MESSAGES AND SIGNALS.

Army Form C. 2121
(in pads of 100).

Sender's Number.	Day of Month.	In reply to Number.	AAA
C.306	2		

Reference Div. Order No. 200 para 3 aaa

RUTU on relief will be located with 2 Bns.

about the line CHAPELLE DUVELLE - RUE MONTIGNY

and one Bn. about NEUF BERQUIN aaa Addsd

RUTU reptd all concerned

From: MEDO
Time: 12 noon.

(Copy)   APPENDIX VI.

    182 Bde.   Div. Signals.
    183 Bde.   Q.
    184 Bde.   61 Bn. M.G.C.
    C.R.A.   28 Bde. R.G.A.
    C.R.E.

        G.598.   2nd

Objective today for Advanced Guard Bde will be G.35.c.6.3 -
road junction G.35.a.8.8 - SAILLY STA. G.29.b.2.5 - G.23.centr
- line of road to G.17.c.2.7 and thence north and along
STILLBECQUE to northern boundary aaa Southern boundary of Divn
will now be from G.25.d.6.3 - road junction G.26.c.2.2 (excl)
and in straight line to G.34.d.3.2 and thence due eastwards aa
Addsd 184 Bde reptd 182 183 Bdes CRA CRE Bde.RGA Signals Q
Bn.MGC.

    61 Div.   (Sd.) C.H.Dowden, Maj.
    10.25 am.

(Copy)　　　　　　　　　　　　　　　APPENDIX VII.

184 Bde.

    G.602.　2nd.

40 Div wire begins aaa Liaison on right flank is unsatisfactory aaa Detail a special platoon to form a lisiaon party with a platoon being detailed by 61 Div aaa This party will work on the south Div boundary and be responsible for keeping touch between both Divs aaa Senior officer of both platoons to take command and should report frequently to battalion commanders on flanks direct aaa Similar orders are being issued by 61 Div aaa 121 Inf.Bde to acknowledge aaa Addsd 121 Inf.Bde. reptd tl Div aaa Ends.

    61 Div.
    2.10 pm.　　　　　　　　　　　　　　　　　(Sd.) E.S.Bates, Lt.
    　　　　　　　　　　　　　　　　　　　　　　　　for G.S.

(Copy)　　　　　　　　　　　　　　　　　APPENDIX VIII.

182 Bde
59 Div.

    G.616.　　2nd.

A detachment of about 2 companies of infantry with machine gun
will be detached by you to operate along the south side of the
LYS Canal early tomorrow morning crossing by the MEUSE and LYS
bridges aaa This detachment will be reinforced as the crossin
E and NE of Pt.LEVIS are cleared of the enemy, by troops now
along the Pt.LEVIS - FM on BRETAGNE road aaa The objective of
the Advanced Guard Bde tomorrow will be CROIX DU BAC excl. -
BAC ST.MAUR and line of railway south-west to G.34.d.2.2 aaa
Addsd 182 Bde reptd 59 Div.

   61 Div.
   10.55 pm　　　　　　　　　　　　　　(Sd.) W.Whetherly, Lt.Col
   　　　　　　　　　　　　　　　　　　　　　　　　G.S.

(Copy)   APPENDIX IX.

H.Q. 61 Div.

    F.771.   2nd.

Thank you for kind message of sympathy which I greatly
appreciate from my old Divn aaa My son's condition now gives
good hopes of recovery aaa I regret I cannot manage to visit
you aaa

   (N.B: In reply to message from General Duncan sympathising
          on General Mackenzie's son being wounded).

   Major General Sir Colin Mackenzie.

WAR DIARY APPENDIX X

SECRET.   61st DIVISION.   G.C. 79.
                Locations of Units at 6 a.m. 4.9.18.

DIV. H.Q. "G".   CROIX MARRAISSE, J.21.c.
    do.   "A" & "Q".   TANNAY, I.22.d.3.1.

182 Inf. Bde. (ADVANCED GUARD BDE.); H.Q. L.27.a.0.3.
  2/6 Warwicks,   (Left Bn.), G.8.d.8.6.
  2/7 Warwicks,   (Reserve Bn.) L.16.a.8.5.
  2/8 Worcesters,   (Right Bn.) L.24.c.5.5.
  L.T.M.B.   L.28.d.4.7.

183 Inf. Bde. (RESERVE BDE.); STEENBECQUE.
  9th North. Fus.   SPRESIANO CAMP, J.14.b.
  11th Suffolks,   VILLORBA CAMP, J.15.c.
  1st E. Lancs.   STEENBECQUE.
  L.T.M.B.   STEENBECQUE.

184 Inf. Bde. (LINE BDE.); H.Q. FACTORY, K.23.c.5.4.
  2/5 Glosters.   (Left Bn.) L.7.d.1.3.
  2/4 R. Berks.   (Support Bn.) K.24.a.3.4.
  2/4 Oxfords,   (Right Bn.) K.30.b.5.4.
  L.T.M.B.   K.28.d.7.6.

C.R.A.   J.21.c.
  306 Bde. R.F.A.   L.26.b.8.3 (Advanced Guard Group).
  307 do.   GREVE FM. K.24.d. (Rear Group).
  D.A.C.   J.21.a.2.6.
  D.T.M.O.   J.10.a.6.5.

C.R.E.   J.21.c.
  476 Field Co. R.E.   K.14.a.
  478 do.   K.14.a.
  479 do.   L.27.a.3.0.

1/5 D.C.L.I.(P).   H.Q. & 2 Coys., L.27.d.6.6.
                        1 Coy., K.22.a.7.6.

61 Bn. M.G.C.   H.Q., HAVERSKERQUE.
  "A" Coy.,   J.31.d.8.2 (Line Coy.).
  "B" Coy.,   L.13.d.5.5 (Advanced Guard Bde. Coy.).
  "C" Coy.,   ICHEN FM., (Line Coy.).
  "D" Coy.,   HAVERSKERQUE; (Reserve Coy.).

A.D.M.S.   I.22.d.1.1.
  2/1 Field Amb.   I.17.c.5.1.
  2/2 do.   STEENBECQUE, I.5.d.4.8.
  2/3 do.   HAVERSKERQUE, J.28.d.2.8.

61 Divl. Train.   PONT DE THIENNES, I.21.a.7.0.
  No. 1 Coy.,   STEENBECQUE, I.4.d.6.5.
  No. 2 Coy.,   BOESEGHEM, I.8.b.0.4.
  No. 3 Coy.,   I.9.b.5.9.
  No. 4 Coy.,   I.22.c.8.4.

D.G.O.   )   HAVERSKERQUE.
Anti-Gas Depot)

Div. P. of W. Cage,   J.11.b.9.7.

Police Detachment,   K.24.c.7.1.

                                        E S Bates Lieut.
  3.9.18.   for G.S., 61st Divn.

(Copy) APPENDIX XI.

182 Bde
59 Div
40 Div
C.R.A.
28 Bde.RGA.

G.627.   3rd.

Objective of Advanced Guard Bde tomorrow will be the line ROUGE DE BOUT and RUE BIACHE through G.36.d - H.31.a - H.25.d - H.26.a - H.20.d. to road junction H.21.a. - PORT A CLOUS FM - H.15.central - RUE DORMOIRE - H.9.a.0.0. Left post 59 Div now at M.3.a.8.7 aaa Establish liaison patrol with 59 Div at the road junction G.33.c.8.4 at daybreak tomorrow aaa Addsd 182 Bde reptd 59 40 Divs CRA. Bde.RGA.

61 Div.
11 pm

(Sd.) W.Whetherly, Lt.Col
G.S.

(Copy) APPENDIX XII.

182 Bde
59 Div
40 Div
C.R.A.
28 Bde.R.G.A.

    G.632.   4th.

Corps objective for today 4th inst aaa Road junction H.33.d.5.0 - East of FLEURBAIX - road junction H.16.c.6.8 - H.10.cent., all incl aaa Push on to this line and keep touch with enemy aaa Addsd 182 Bde reptd flank Divs CRA Bde.RGA.

    61 Div.
    11.10 a.m.   (Sd.) C.H.Dowden, Maj.GS

(Copy) APPENDIX XIII.

Major-General Duncan,
    61st Divn.

G.A.269.   4th.

Please convey to Col. BURNAND and all ranks of the 182 Inf.Bde. my appreciation of the progress made today resulting in the capture of LAVENTIE and the advance of your line to FLEURBAIX.

Gen. HAKING,
10 pm.

Appendix XIIIa

SECRET.   Copy No. 26

61st DIVISION ORDER No. 201.   4.9.18.

Ref. Map 36A, 1/40,000.
     36, 1/40,000.

1.   The 184th Infantry Brigade will move forward today, 4th inst., to the general area FAGGOT FARM (L.23.d.) - TROU BAYARD (G.19) - G.9.c. & d.
     Brigade Headquarters to CHAPELLE DUVELLE (L.27.a.0.3).

2.   The 183rd Infantry Brigade will move forward tomorrow, 5th inst., to the area CHAPELLE DUVELLE - RUE MONTIGNY; Brigade Headquarters to the FACTORY (K.23.c.5.4).

3.   All details of the move to be arranged by Commanders concerned.

4.   Completion of moves to be reported to Division Headqrs.

5.   ACKNOWLEDGE.

Issued at 6 p.m.   *C H Dowden Maj*
                              for   Lieut.-Col.,
                                   G.S., 61st Divn.

Distribution :-

Copy No. 1 - A.D.C. for G.O.C.   13 - D.A.P.M.
         2 - 61 Div. Signals.   14 - D.A.D.O.S.
       3-4 - 61 Div. Arty.   15-16 - XI Corps.
         5 - C.R.E.   17 - 28 Bde.R.G.A.
         6 - 61 Bn.M.G.C.   18 - 42nd Sqn.R.A.F.
         7 - 1/5 D.C.L.I.   19 - 40th Divn.
         8 - 182 Inf.Bde.   20 - 59th Divn.
         9 - 183 Inf.Bde.   21-22 - "Q".
        10 - 184 Inf.Bde.   23 - "G".
        11 - A.D.M.S.   24 - D.G.O.
        12 - 61 Div. Train.

APPENDIX XIV

61 Bn.M.G.C. by wire.

61 Bn.M.G.C.
Q.   1/5 D.C.L.I.
C.R.A.   61 Signal Coy.
C.R.E.   A.D.M.S.
182 Inf.Bde.   61 Div. Train.
183 Inf.Bde.   D.A.P.M.
184 Inf.Bde.   D.A.D.O.S.

G.635.   4th.

61 Bn.M.G.C. (less companies in the line) will move to
LA GORGUE 5th inst. under arrangements made by O.C. ada
Added. all concerned

                                       C.W.Dowden
                                           Major,
                                       G.S., 61 Division.
7.45 p.m.

SECRET.

Appendix XV
Copy No. 23

61st DIVISION INSTRUCTIONS No. 1.

OPERATIONS.

1. The enemy's continued withdrawal, and the distance which the Advanced Guard Brigade has now gained, necessitates the following revision of plans for future operations.

Advanced Guard Brigade. 2. The Advanced Guard Brigade will continue to maintain contact with, and act vigorously against, the enemy rearguards, and be prepared to take advantage of opportunities created by success elsewhere.

Objectives. 3. Objectives to be reached by the Advanced Guard Bde. will be given from time to time, but in the event of a very rapid advance, contact will continue to be made, even though the advance is made beyond the objective line laid down by the Division.

Outpost Line of Resistance. 4. An Outpost Line of Resistance, to which the advanced troops of the Advanced Guard Bde. will fall back in event of heavy hostile counter-attack, and upon which the Advanced Guard Bde. and supporting artillery will resist and break up an enemy counter-stroke, will be selected and notified to Divisional Headquarters from time to time

Corps Battle Line. 5. A Corps Battle Line, usually some 3,000 to 5,000 yds. in rear of the objectives to be reached by the Advanced Guard Bde., will be selected and notified to all concerned.

This Corps Battle Line will represent the front of the position on which the Division will stand and fight in the event of a heavy hostile counter-attack, and its selection will therefore regulate the forward movement of the main body of the Division and Heavy Artillery.

Method of holding Corps Battle Line. 6. The Corps Battle Line on this Divisional front will be held with two Infantry Brigades in the line, covered by one Field Artillery Brigade and Heavies.

The Advanced Guard Bde. will be brought into Divisional Reserve on being forced to withdraw.

The inter-Brigade boundary will be notified, together with the publication of the Corps Battle Line.

Dispositions. 7. The above dispositions for defence will, for the future, modify those of the two Infantry Brigades forming the main body of the Division. These two Brigades will now be disposed in depth in three echelons. Each Brigade will be disposed with one battalion forward, on or in close proximity to the existing Corps Battle Line; one battalion within supporting distance in rear of the Corps line, and the third battalion in reserve.

The necessary orders in regard to these dispositions will be issued.

Accommodation of troops. 8. This arrangement will facilitate the question of accommodation, battalions improving the accommodation for the successive moves forward of battalions in rear.

The importance of the improvement of accommodation in the area vacated by the enemy is emphasized. All units will make every endeavour to prepare and repair the houses they may be temporarily occupying, as well as those in the vicinity that can be made habitable.

At the same time, advantage will be taken of the excellent facilities for training in the present area by battalions and other units not operating with the Advanced Guard.

(P.T.O.)

(2)

Defences. 9. Infantry Brigades concerned will be responsible for the siting in detail of the line to be held in case of counter-attack.

It is not the intention to construct new systems of defence until the line stabilizes, but it will be necessary to strengthen localities, and to improve and adapt such defences as exist and are suitable.

In order to save time, and labour, the fullest use will be made of existing wire entanglements.

Machine Guns. 10. Two Companies Machine Gun Bn. will be prepared to occupy the Corps Battle Line, one Company being allotted to the defence of each Brigade sector, and to come under the orders of the G.O.C. Infantry Brigade concerned.

The O.C., 61st Bn. M.G.C. will, on receipt of the notification of the Corps Battle Line, detail one Company to each Infantry Brigade, and will notify all concerned.

These Companies will be accommodated in the area allotted to the forward battalions of Brigades, under arrangements to be made by Brigadiers concerned, and will be in a position to man their battle positions immediately on the receipt of orders.

The Machine Gun Company Commander will carry out the necessary reconnaissances on the Brigade sector of the Corps line under the orders of the G.O.C. Brigade.

Artillery. 11. The Advanced Guard Artillery Brigade will be disposed to cover the Outpost Line of Resistance, and to assist the forward movement of the advanced troops.

The remaining F.A. Brigade will be kept in positions of readiness, and will be prepared to occupy previously reconnoitred positions to cover the Corps Battle Line, under orders of the C.R.A.

Communications. 12. Signal communications will be run upon the lines laid down in SS.191, chapter III. To this end, the XI Corps will determine, in consultation with Divisions, a succession of points on the line of advance of the Division.

These points are to be the most likely positions of Brigade and Divisional Headquarters, and Signals will make all such points communication centres.

All telephone lines will be laid to these communication centres, and very early information as to their positions will be necessary to enable Signals to establish and equip them for Signal traffic as soon as they are needed.

13. ACKNOWLEDGE.

M Wetherly

4.9.18.

Lieut.-Col.,
G.S., 61st Divn.

Distribution :-

Copy No.1 - A.D.C. for G.O.C.	8 - 182 Inf. Bde.	13-14 - XI Corps.
2 - 61 Div. Signals.	9 - 183 Inf. Bde.	15 - 28 Bde. R.G.A.
3-4 - 61 Div. Arty.	10 - 184 Inf. Bde.	16 - 40th Divn.
5 - C.R.E.	11 - A.D.M.S.	17 - 59th Divn.
6 - 61 Bn. M.G.C.	12 - D.A.P.M.	18-19 - "Q".
7 - 1/5 D.C.L.I.		20 - "G".
		21 - D.G.O.

(Copy) APPENDIX XVI.

```
182 Bde    28 Bde.RGA.
184 Bde    40 Div
C.R.A.     59 Div
```

G.638. 4th.

Your objective tomorrow will be the line road junction H.33.d.4.2 - RUE DES LOMBARDS - cross roads H.22.c.95.10 - CANTEEN FARM - LA ROLANDERIE H.11.c aaa Addsd 182 Bde reptd 184 Bde CRA RGA flank Divs

61 Div
11.50 pm

(Sd.) W.Whetherly,
Lt.Col. G.S.

SECRET.

Appendix XVII

Copy No. 25

5.9.18.

61st DIVISION ORDER No. 202.

Ref. Map 36A, 1/40,000.
      36, 1/40,000.

1. The following moves and readjustments will take place tomorrow, 6th inst.

2. (Reference para. 6 of 61st Division Instructions No. 1).
   The two Brigades holding the Corps Battle Line will be located side by side in depth on a one-battalion front in the vicinity of this line as follows :-

   (a) Northern Brigade.
       (i) One battalion in the area:-
           TROU BAYARD (G.19.b.) - G.14.a.5.0 - L.12.d.9.0 - L.18.b.0.0.
       (ii) One battalion in the area:-
           L.11.d.2.2 - L.16.c.9.5 - L.10.c.8.2 - L.11.c.4.8.
       (iii) One battalion in the area:-
           L.16.a.0.4 - L.10.c.0.0 - L.8.d.9.6 - L.14.b.9.5.
       (iv) Brigade Headquarters at FACTORY K.23.c.5.4.

   (b) Southern Brigade.
       (i) One battalion in the area:-
           L.30.b.8.5 - L.24.b.9.0 - L.23.b.3.4 - L.29.b.0.4.
       (ii) One battalion in the area :-
           L.29.b.0.4 - L.22.d.2.8 - L.28.d.5.0.
       (iii) One battalion in the area :-
           L.27.c.8.4 - L.21.d.2.1 - L.26.b.5.5 - L.26.d.1.6.
       (iv) Brigade Headquarters, L.27.a.0.3.

   (c) Machine Guns.
       One Company of 61st Bn. M.G.C. is allotted to each Brigade on the Corps Battle Line, and will be located in the area of the Brigade, except that the Company allotted to the southern Brigade which is now located in the vicinity of RILL WORKS, will not move into the Brigade area for the present.

3. The 183 Inf. Bde. will be located in the Northern Brigade Area.
   The 184 Inf.Bde. will be located in the Southern Brigade Area.
   The boundary between Brigade areas is as follows :-
       The grid line between L.13 and L.19 Eastward to L.17.d.0.0, thence in a straight line G.22.central.

4. The above moves and readjustments to be completed by 7.0 p.m. tomorrow, 6th inst., and completion reported to Div. Headqrs.

5. The following reliefs will take place on the nights 6th/7th and 7th/8th inst :-

   (a) One battalion of 183 Inf.Bde. will relieve one battalion of 182 Inf.Bde. in the Advanced Guard Bde. area on the night 6th/7th inst., and will come under orders of G.O.C. 182 Inf. Bde. until completion of relief on night 7th/8th inst.

       Similarly, relieved battalion of 182 Inf.Bde. will come under orders of G.O.C. Northern (183rd) Brigade.

(P.T.O.)

(2)

    (b) 183rd Inf.Bde. (less one battalion) will relieve 182nd Inf. Bde. (less one battalion) on the night 7th/8th inst., and will take over the duties of Advanced Guard Brigade from the hour of relief.

6.   The following troops which form part of the Advanced Guard Brigade will come under the orders of G.O.C. 183rd Inf.Bde. on completion of relief :-

        1 Brigade R.F.A.
        1 Field Coy. R.E.
        2 Coys. 61st Bn.M.G.C.
        1 Troop K.E.H.

7.   On relief, the 182nd Inf. Bde. will withdraw to the Corps Battle Line, and will be located in the Northern Brigade area.

8.   Command will pass on completion of relief, which will be reported to Divisional Headquarters.

9.   All further details of moves and reliefs will be arranged by Commanders concerned.

10.   ACKNOWLEDGE.

Issued at 6.0 p.m.

C H Dowden Ma

for Lieut.-Col.,
G.S., 61st Divn.

Distribution :-

Copy No.		Copy No.	
1	A.D.C. for G.O.C.	13	D.A.P.M.
2	61 Div. Signals.	14	D.A.D.O.S.
3-4	61 Div. Arty.	15-16	XI Corps.
5	C.R.E.	17	28 Bde. R.G.A.
6	61 Bn. M.G.C.	18	42 Sqn. R.A.F.
7	1/5 D.C.L.I.	19	40th Divn.
8	182 Inf.Bde.	20	59th Divn.
9	183 Inf.Bde.	21-22	"Q".
10	184 Inf.Bde.	23	"G".
11	A.D.M.S.	24	D.G.O.
12	61 Div. Train.	25-26	War Diary.

(Copy) APPENDIX XVIII.

XI Corps (I).
40 Div
59 Div
182 Bde

GS.364.   6th

Preliminary examination of prisoners of 14 IR captured in H.14 this afternoon aaa 14 IR appears to hold newly constructed line running through H.15, H.9, and has outpost screen of 3 groups and 2 MGs per coy about 500 yds in advance of that line aaa Dispositions 2 coys each of 2nd and 3rd Bn in front aaa 1st Bn believed to be in reserve around G.22.b. aaa Men of following regts seen in LILLE 2 days ago 169 170 80 FAR. aaa 77 Regt stated to have left LILLE area for ARRAS during last few days aaa 14 IR relieved outpost screen of 140 IR night Sept 5/6 aaa Prisoners generally very poor material and moral appears low aaa No information as to enemy intentions or order of battle aaa Any counter attack by enemy considered improbable aaa Addsd XI Corps I reptd flank Divs 182 Bde.

61 Div
10.40 pm

(Sd.) P. Hicks, 2/Lt.
for G.S.

(Copy) APPENDIX XVIIIa

```
C.R.A
C.R.E.          Train
182 Inf.Bde     D.A.P.M.
183 Inf.Bde.    28 Bde.RGA
184 Inf.Bde.    40 Div
Div.Signals     Q.
A.D.M.S.        D.G.O.
```

G.660.   6th

Corps Battle Line is now advanced to line NOUVEAU MONDE - West bank of LYS - West bank of STILBECQUE aaa No movement of troops responsible for the defence of the line will be necessa aaa Addsd all concerned.

61 Div.
9.30 pm

(Sd.) W.Whetherly,
Lt.Col. G.S.

APPENDIX XIX.

(Copy)

182 Inf.Bde.

       G.658.   6th.

Very glad you have had a success, please congratulate battalion concerned aaa Keep up the pressure.

    GENERAL DUNCAN.

                                      (Sd.) C.H.Dowden,
                                                Maj.G.S.

"A" Form.
MESSAGES AND SIGNALS.

Army Form C. 2121.
(In pads of 100.)

APPENDIX XX

Sender's Number.	Day of Month.	In reply to Number.	
G 679	8		AAA

Advanced Div.H.Q. will close at CROIX MARRAISSE at 10 a.m. tomorrow 9th inst. and open at RILL WORKS L.33.b.3.7 at that hour aaa Added all concerned.

Distribution :-

Signals	D.A.P.M.
C.R.A.	D.A.D.O.S.
C.R.E.	XI Corps
61 Bn.MGC.	28 Bde.RGA
1/5 DCLI	42 Sqn. RAF.
182 Bde	40th Div.
183 Bde	59th Div.
184 Bde	"Q"
A.D.M.S.	Camp Cdt.
Div.Train.	D.G.O.

From 61 Div
Place
Time 12 noon

(Sd).C.H.DOWDEN, Maj.GS.

SECRET.　　　　　　　　　　61st DIVISION.　　　　　　　　　　G.C. 79

Locations of Units at 6 a.m., 9.9.18.

Ref.Shts.36A
& 36.

DIV. H.Q. "G".　　　　CROIX MARRAISSE, J.21.c.
 "　　"A" & "Q",　　TANNAY, I.22.d. (Billet 31).

182 Inf.Bde. (LEFT BDE. C.B.L.); H.Q. G.8.a.8.1.
  2/6 Warwicks, (Support Bn.); L.16.a.8.5.
  2/7 Warwicks, (Line Bn.); L.18.a.5.0.
  2/8 Worcesters, (Reserve Bn.); L.7.d.25.30.
  L.T.M.B.　　L.8.c.3.0.

183 Inf.Bde. (ADVANCED GUARD BDE.); H.Q. G.14.a.2.1.
  9th North.Fus. (Support Bn.) G.9.d.1.1.
  11th Suffolks, (Left Bn.) G.23.a.8.3.
  1st E. Lancs., (Right Bn.) G.34.c.7.3.
  L.T.M.B.　　G.14.c.55.95.

184 Inf.Bde. (RIGHT BDE. C.B.L.); H.Q. L.27.a.0.3.
  2/4 Oxfords, (Line Bn.)- L.23.d.4.6.
  2/5 Glosters, (Support Bn.) L.28.b.8.8.
  2/4 R. Berks, (Reserve Bn.) YAM FM., L.22.a.
  L.T.M.B.　　FELT FM., L.27.b.

C.R.A.　　　　CROIX MARRAISSE, J.21.c.
  307 Bde. R.F.A. (Advanced Bde. Group), G.13.b.6.4.
  306　do.　(Rear Group), L.11.d.25.75.
  D.A.C.　　K.7.d.9.0.
  D.T.M.O.　　J.10.a.9.3.
  28 Bde.R.G.A.　L.32.a.75.75.

61 Bn. M.G.C.,　　H.Q., L.34.d.3.9.
  "A" Coy. (Left Coy. C.B.L.),　L.6.c.5.3.
  "B" Coy. (Advanced Guard Coy.), G.27.d.5.5.
  "C" Coy. (Advanced Guard Coy.), G.27.b.8.5.
  "D" Coy. (Right Coy. C.B.L.),　L.34.d.3.6.

C.R.E.　　　　RILL WORKS, L.33.b.
  476 Field Co.RE. L.23.b.3.7.
  478　do.　L.29.a.6.6.
  479　do.　L.26.b.1.2.

1/5 D.C.L.I.(P).　L.30.c.95.80.
  1 Coy.,　　L.27.c.3.6.
  1 Coy.,　　L.27.d.2.9.
  1 Coy.,　　L.29.d.2.7.

A.D.M.S.　　　TANNAY, I.22.d.1.1.
  2/1 Field Amb. L.27.c.2.6 (Main Dressing Station).
  2/2　do.　STEENBECQUE, I.5.d.4.8.
  2/3　do.　L.22.c.2.3.

61 Div. Train.　PONT DE THIENNES, I.21.a.7.0.
  No. 1 Coy.,　K.14.b.5.4.
  No. 2 Coy.,　K.11.b.5.5.
  No. 3 Coy.,　J.22.c.4.7.
  No. 4 Coy.,　K.23.a.2.4.

D.G.O. & ANTI-GAS DEPOT, MERVILLE, K.29.a.80.55.
Advanced Depot,　L.22.c.0.9.
Div. P. of W. Cage, L.29.b.1.1.

E.S.Bates Lieut.
for G.S., 61st Divn.
8.9.18.

SECRET.

Appendix XXII

61st DIVISION INSTRUCTIONS No. 2.

INTELLIGENCE.

1. During the present phase of mobile fighting, the collection and transmission of every kind of information regarding the enemy are of supreme importance.
    It is increasingly important now :-

    (a) To identify continually the hostile troops opposed to us,

    (b) To report regularly, and as soon as possible, all hostile shelling,

    (c) To report the degree and nature of the resistance offered by the enemy during the different stages of the operations.

2. The systematic collection of information during active operations, and, if it is to be of value, its quick transmission to higher authority, has for one of its main objects the assistance that can be given to the fighting troops by ensuring the most effective use of all our weapons.
    It must also be impressed upon all ranks that much of the information obtained by the fighting troops, although not always of immediate tactical value to themselves, is nevertheless essential to the Higher Commands to enable the enemy plans to be foreseen by means of an accurate knowledge of his dispositions.
    It is the duty, therefore, of all ranks of fighting troops to co-operate in obtaining information regarding the enemy.

3. The principal sources from which information can be obtained are :-
    (a) Reports from fighting troops.
    (b) Ground observation of movement, aerial and anti-aircraft activity, fires, explosions, etc.
    (c) Prisoners and dead.
    (d) Captured documents and material.
    (e) Air photographs.

4. The Intelligence personnel at Brigade and Battalion Headquarters must be properly reorganised in sections, and made full use of.
    This personnel will consist of :-

    Brigade   - The Brigade Intelligence Officer.
                  1 N.C.O.
                  3 O.Rs. per battalion.

    Battalion - The Battalion Intelligence Officer.
                  1 N.C.O.
                  2 O.Rs. per Company.

    The above sections under the Intelligence Officers will be specially selected men qualified to observe, recognise troops, transport, etc. frame reports, read a map correctly, and to read an air photograph. Both Brigade and Battalion Sections should all be efficient snipers and scouts.

5. The Intelligence Sections of Brigades and Battalions in the line will be primarily responsible for the collection of information by observation and by other means for a distance up to 3,000 yards behind the enemy's front line.

(P.T.O.)

Their duties will comprise :-

(a) The rapid transmission of identifications made by the fighting troops from prisoners and dead.

Brigade and Battalion Intelligence Officers will take all precautions to satisfy themselves that these identifications are accurate, and especially, in cases when an identification points to the presence of new troops in their area, that the evidence is complete and convincing.

They will know the presumed order of battle of the enemy troops opposite this front, and will make themselves acquainted with any unusual marks by which those troops may be identified.

Small forms made out in German will be provided, on which prisoners will be asked to write the number of their regiment and of that on either flank.

All identifications will be communicated direct by Infantry Brigade Headquarters to Intelligence, Fifth Army, the message being repeated to Divisional and Corps Intelligence. These messages should only contain the following information, viz., prisoners (or men killed) - their regiment - approximate location of capture. The message will be valueless if the last item is omitted.

All identification messages will be franked "URGENT OPERATION PRIORITY", and the senior Staff Officer of every formation is responsible that these messages are regarded as second only in importance to Operation Orders and Tactical Reports of an urgent nature.

Notes on Identification, for the guidance of all concerned, are being issued.

(b) Observation of enemy movement.

Brigade and Battalion Sections will be trained to move in bounds as the line is advanced or retired.

Their duties will consist almost entirely in reporting the actual progress of the battle, though in some cases they may be able to observe the movement of hostile bodies of troops in rear of the enemy's advanced troops. They must be trained to act on their own initiative, and to transmit their information to someone with the greatest possible rapidity.

At each bound it will be their duty to reconnoitre and get in touch at once with the nearest Infantry H.Q. and the nearest Battery.

Having thus ensured that immediate action can be taken on any information they may obtain, they will next endeavour to get into communication with Brigade or Battalion H.Q. This may be difficult, or impossible, but the commander of the section will despatch periodically a report stating his position and summarising the information obtained. Even though this arrive late, it may still be of considerable value.

Where the country admits of Visual signalling, it will be possible for observers, though not trained signallers, to report the most vital features in the progress of the battle by pre-arranged signals denoting that such and such a locality has been captured or lost.

(c) Reporting of hostile shelling.

Under existing conditions, reports of hostile shelling, even if incomplete as to certain details, are essential if any accurate estimate of hostile artillery strength is to be made. If this information is not forthcoming, hostile batteries cannot be located and their zones of fire fixed, so as to ensure that neutralization is effective during our minor operations, or in event of an enemy counter-attack in force.

Reports will be sent direct to the nearest Infantry Headqrs., whether Battalion or Brigade, and the Artillery Liaison Officer attached to the Headquarters concerned will be responsible for the rapid transmission of the information to Corps Counter Battery Staff.

(Reports

(3)

Reports should give the following particulars :-
    (i) Srea shelled.
    (ii) Time and duration.
  (iii) Calibre.
    (iv) Number of guns firing.
     (v) Direction - to be given in grid bearing, or true sound bearing.

The headings (i) and (ii) are of chief importance, but all should be given when possible. Even single rounds should be reported, and may give all the information required.

(d) **Special Reconnaissance.**
When called upon, Brigade and Battalion Intelligence Sections will be prepared to carry out scouting reconnaissances, with the object of obtaining information of a special nature, such as the confirmation of enemy wire reported in a certain locality; its extent and strength; enemy dispositions; river corssings, or approaches to the enemy's positions, etc.

6. The Intelligence Sections of Brigades and Battalions out of the line will be primarily responsible for the collection of information immediately in rear of the advanced troops in the line.
Their duties will comprise :-

(a) **Identifications** wherever the enemy has vacated defences or billets. Regiments of Infantry and Artillery can usually be identified in this way as the result of careful search for small clues. Captured letters and documents should be sent to Divisional H.Q. as rapidly as possible. In the case of maps and orders, where neighbouring units may be affected, it is especially essential that all necessary information be extracted, and the documents must therefore be forwarded by the quickest means possible.

(b) **Intelligence Police duties.**
It is probable that German agents disguised as French peasants have been left behind, and it is the duty of all ranks to arrest civilians who cannot satisfactorily explain their movements. Thorough search is required to find any German soldiers who may have been purposely left behind and provided with means of communication with enemy forces by telephone or signal.
Signal cable running towards the enemy lines should be sought for, and the Signal Service immediately informed.

7. The above duties of the Intelligence organization of Brigades and Battalions in no way absolves the troops themselves, of all ranks, from being responsible for securing, by patrols, scouts, and reconnaissances, all the information which is required.
Officers, N.C.Os., and men will be instructed so that they may know the numbers and monograms signifying the German regiments that may be opposed to them. They will also be instructed in the importance to themselves of reporting at once the presence, from either prisoners or dead, of strange units opposite their front, which they will readily detect from the shoulder-badges. Timely information on this point may thus find our troops prepared against an impending attack by fresh enemy forces.

M.Metherly
Lieut.-Col.,
G.S., 61st Divn.

8.9.18.

Distribution :-

C.R.A.	61 Bn. M.G.C.
C.R.E.	1/5 D.C.L.I.
Div.Signals.	28 Bde. R.G.A.
182 Inf.Bde. (4)	D.A.P.M.
183 Inf.Bde. (4)	"Q".
184 Inf.Bde. (4)	Copy to XI Corps (I).

WAR DIARY

APPENDIX XXIII
G.C.79.

SECRET.   61st DIVISION.
                Locations of Units at 6 a.m., 10.9.18.

Ref. Shts. 36A
    & 36.

    DIV. H.Q. "G",   RILL WORKS, L.33.b.
      do. "A" & "Q",   CROIX MARRAISSE, J.21.c.

    182 Inf. Bde. (LEFT BDE. C.B.L.);   H.Q. G.8.a.8.1.
      2/6 Warwicks,   (Support Bn.) L.16.a.8.5.
      2/7 Warwicks,   (Line Bn.)   G.8.b.0.2.
      2/8 Worcesters,   (Reserve Bn.) L.7.d.25.30.
      L.T.M.B.   L.8.a.6.7.

    183 Inf. Bde. (ADVANCED GUARD BDE.), H.Q. G.14.a.2.1.
      9th North. Fus., (Support Bn.) G.9.d.1.1.
      11th Suffolks,   (Left Bn.)   G.23.a.8.3.
      1st E. Lancs.,   (Right Bn.)   G.34.c.7.3.
      L.T.M.B.   G.14.c.55.95.

    184 Inf. Bde. (RIGHT BDE., C.B.L.) H.Q. L.27.a.0.3.
      2/4 Oxfords,   (Line Bn.)   L.23.d.4.6.
      2/5 Glosters,   (Support Bn.) L.28.b.8.8.
      2/4 R. Berks.,   (Reserve Bn.) YAM FM., L.22.a.
      L.T.M.B.,   FELT FM., L.27.b.

    C.R.A.   RILL WORKS, L.33.b.
      307 Bde. R.F.A.   (Advanced Bde Group) G.13.b.6.4.
      306   do.   (Rear Group) L.11.d.25.75.
      D.A.C.   K.7.d.9.0.
      D.T.M.O.   J.10.a.9.3.
      28 Bde. R.G.A.   L.32.b.75.75.

    61 Bn. M.G.C.   H.Q., L.34.d.3.9.
      "A" Coy.,   (Advanced Guard Coy.) G.27.b.8.5.
      "B" Coy.,   (Right Coy., C.B.L.)   L.34.d.3.6.
      "C" Coy.,   (Left Coy., C.B.L.)   L.6.c.5.3.
      "D" Coy.,   (Advanced Guard Coy.) G.27.d.5.5.

    C.R.E.   RILL WORKS, L.33.b.
      476 Field Coy. R.E. L.23.b.3.7.
      478   do.   L.29.a.6.6.
      479   do.   L.26.b.1.2.

    1/5 D.C.L.I. (P).   L.30.c.95.80.
      1 Coy.,   G.8.a.6.7.
      1 Coy.,   L.27.d.2.9.
      1 Coy.,   L.29.d.2.7.

    A.D.M.S.   TANNAY, I.22.d.1.1.
      2/1 Field Amb.,   L.27.c.2.6 (Main Dressing Station).
      2/2   do.   STEENBECQUE, I.5.d.4.8.
      2/3   do.   L.22.c.2.3.

    61 Div. Train,   J.27.a.7.7.
      No. 1 Coy.,   K.14.b.5.4.
      No. 2 Coy.,   K.11.b.5.5.
      No. 3 Coy.,   J.22.c.4.7.
      No. 4 Coy.,   K.23.a.2.4.

    D.G.O. & ANTI-GAS DEPOT, MERVILLE, K.29.a.80.55.

    Advanced Depot,   L.22.c.0.9.
    Div. P. of W. Cage, L.29.b.1.1.

E.G. Bates Lieut.
for G.S. 61 Divn.
9.9.18.

APPENDIX XXIV.

(Copy)

183 Inf.Bde.
184 Inf.Bde.

G.697.   10th.

One battalion of 184 Bde will relieve one battalion of 183 Bde tonight aaa Remainder tomorrow aaa Orders follow aaa Addsd 183 & 184 Bdes

61 Div.

(Sd.)   C.H.Dowden, Maj.G.

APPENDIX XXV

SECRET.

61st DIVISION ORDER No. 203.

Copy No. 21
10.9.18.

Ref. Map 36, 1/40,000.
     36A, 1/40,000.

1. 184th Infantry Bde. will relieve the 183rd Infantry Bde. as Advanced Guard Brigade on the nights 10th/11th and 11th/12th inst. as follows :-

   (a) On night 10th/11th inst., one battalion of 184th Infantry Bde. will relieve one battalion of 183rd Infantry Bde., and will come under orders of G.O.C. 183rd Infantry Bde. until completion of relief on the night 11th/12th inst.
   Similarly, the relieved battalion of 183rd Infantry Bde. will come under the orders of G.O.C. 184th Infantry Bde.

   (b) On the night 11th/12th inst. the 184th Infantry Bde. (less one battalion) will relieve 183rd Infantry Bde. (less one battn.) and will take over the duties of Advanced Guard Bde. from the hour of relief.

2. The following troops, which form part of the Advanced Guard, will come under orders of G.O.C. 184th Infantry Bde. on completion of relief :-

       1 Brigade R.F.A.
       1 Field Coy. R.E.
       2 Coys. 61st Bn. M.G.C.
       1 Troop K.E.H.

3. On relief, the 183rd Infantry Bde. will withdraw to, and be responsible for, the defence of the Southern Area of the Corps Battle Line, and will take over accommodation vacated by the 184th Infantry Brigade.

4. Command will pass on completion of relief, which will be notified to D.H.Q.

5. All further details of relief and moves will be arranged by Commanders concerned.

6. ACKNOWLEDGE.

                                            C H Dowden Maj
Issued at 12 noon.   for   Lieut.-Col.
                                            G.S., 61st Division.

Distribution :-

Copy No. 1 - A.D.C. for G.O.C.   12-13 - XI. Corps.
       2 - 61 Div. Signals.   14 - 28 Bde. R.G.A.
     3-4 - 61 Div. Art.   15 - 40th Divn
       5 - C.R.E.   16 - 59th Divn
       6 - 61 Bn. M.G.C.   17-18 - "Q".
       7 - 1/5 D.C.L.I.   19 - D.G.O.
       8 - 182 Inf. Bde.   20 - "G".
       9 - 183 Inf. Bde.   21-22 - War Diary.
      10 - 184 Inf. Bde.   23 - D.A.P.M.
      11 - A.D.M.S.

SECRET.   Copy No. **21**

Appendix XXVI

61st DIVISION INSTRUCTIONS No. 3.

ANTI-AIRCRAFT DEFENCE.

(To be read in conjunction with G.H.Q. letter A.A.25 dated 13.4.18
(Revised) as amended by A.A.25 of 25.8.18).

1. The Commander of every Field Unit, wherever located, is responsible at all times for the defence of his unit against hostile aircraft flying below 3,000 feet.

2. The British Zone is divided into two areas for the purpose of Anti-Aircraft defence:-
   (a) the FORWARD Area,
   (b) the INTERMEDIATE and BACK Areas.

   These areas are divided by a line which joins up the Headquarters of Divisions holding the front.

3. (i) In the FORWARD Area: the defence will be organised in four lines :-

   (a) First Line.
       About 500 yards in rear of our most forward line.
       Personnel and guns found by the two forward battalions and M.G. Companies of the Advanced Guard or Outpost Brigade.

   (b) Second Line.
       About 1,500 yards in rear of our most forward line.
       Personnel and guns found by the reserve battalion, Machine Guns, and the forward batteries of artillery of the Advanced Guard or Outpost Brigade.

   (c) Third Line.
       On the line of the leading battalions manning the Corps Battle Line.
       Personnel and guns furnished by those battalions, and by batteries of artillery in the vicinity of this line.

   (d) Fourth Line.
       On the line of the battalions in support and reserve, to the Corps Battle Line.
       Personnel and guns furnished by these battalions and the M.G. Coys. and Batteries of Artillery in the vicinity.

   (The positions of above lines and Forward Area will move forward automatically with the advance).

   (e) Maps showing locations of Anti-aircraft guns will be maintained by all formations and units, and handed over on relief.

   (ii) In the INTERMEDIATE and BACK Areas:
        Anti-aircraft Lewis or Vickers guns will be mounted for the protection of all billets, camps, and wagon or transport lines.
        These guns will be manned by personnel of the unit in occupation
        Guns should be placed about 400 - 500 yards outside the locality to be defended.

   (iii) Orders:
        A copy of the orders, which are attached to these Instructions as Appendix "A", will be posted in all Anti-aircraft Lewis and Vickers gun positions.
                                                                    (P.T.O.)

(2)

4. In order that the work of the Searchlight Sections is not interfered with unnecessarily, A.A. Lewis or Vickers guns should not be located within 1,000 yards of any Searchlight Emplacement.
Searchlight Emplacements are located as under :-

    FORT AVAGNAIN (36A - H.6.d.6.2).
    RINCQ   (36A - H.20.b.8.8).
    LAMBRES (36A - N.12.d.5.9).
    HARTE VENT (36A - F.2.b.1.4).
    ST.MARTIN (36A - H.22.b.8.5).
    ISBERGUES (36A - O.2.d.3.3).
    BERGUETTE (36A - O.16.b.7.4).
    LILLERS   (36A - O.9.b.2.8).

5. During stationary warfare, defence against E.A. flying above 3,000 ft. is controlled by Army H.Q.
"B" Anti-aircraft Battery is affiliated to the Corps for this purpose.
Gun Sections are located as under :-

    MERVILLE   (36A - K.29.c.).
    LESLAURIERS (36A - K.15.c.).
    LA PIERRIERE (36A - O.24.d.6.8).
    MOLINGHEM (36A - O.13.a.3.8).
    ST.QUENTIN (36A - H.32.b.2.5).

Each A.A. Section is affiliated, for purposes of laaison, to the nearest Brigade R.F.A.

6. ACKNOWLEDGE.

                C.H.Dowden Maj
               for Lieut.-Col.,
10.9.18.   G.S., 61st Divn.

Distribution :-

Copy No.				
1	- A.D.C. for G.O.C.		12	- 28 Bde.R.G.A.
2	- Div. Signal Co.		13	- Div. Train.
3-4	- 61 Div.Art.		14	- Camp Comdt.
5	- "Q".		15	- "G".
6	- C.R.E.		16-17	- XI Corps.
7	- 61 Bn.M.G.C.		18-24	- Spare.
8	- 1/5 D.C.L.I.		25	- 40th Divn.
9	- 182 Inf.Bde.		26	- 59th Divn.
10	- 183 Inf.Bde.			
11	- 184 Inf.Bde.			

Appendix XXVI

APPENDIX "A" TO 61st DIVISION DEFENCE INSTRUCTIONS No. 3,
ANTI-AIRCRAFT DEFENCE.

ORDERS FOR A.A. LEWIS AND VICKERS GUN POSITIONS.

1. A sentry will always be on duty at each A.A. gun.

2. On the approach of suspected hostile aircraft, the sentry will warn the N.C.O. in charge of the gun, and will prepare the gun for firing.

3. No fire will be opened without the orders of the N.C.O. in charge of the gun.

4. By day, fire will not be opened on hostile aircraft unless the markings or struts can be clearly seen with the naked eye.

5. By night, fire will not be opened on aircraft unless they clearly demonstrate their hostility by dropping bombs or opening M.G. fire, or their identity is clearly identified in the beam of a searchlight.
    Note :- As a general rule, it may be taken that at night an aeroplane is within range of small arms fire -
    (a) if the aeroplane can be seen against the sky.
    (b) if the struts can be seen when the aeroplane is in the beam of a searchlight.

6. Long bursts of fire will be used.

7. Guns will be kept mounted except in wet or foggy weather, but will not be loaded until the approach of hostile aircraft.

8. A.A. sights will, when possible, be used on all Vickers and Lewis guns mounted for A.A. defence.

61 Div. H.Q.
10.9.18.

APPENDIX XXVII.

(Copy)

```
59 Div      Div.Signals
40 Div      C.R.E.
182 Bde     C.R.A.
184 Bde     61 Bn.MGC.
            Q.
```

G.719   11th.

A minor operation by troops of the Advanced Guard Bde will be carried out with arty support at an early hour tomorrow morning aaa The 59 Div.Arty are assisting with smoke and shell in the neighbourhood of the objective aaa 61 Signals will arrange to synchronize the time at 9 pm tonight direct with the Advanced ~~Eurd~~ Guard Bde, 61 Div.Art., and 59 Div aaa Addsd all concerned.

61 Div.
3.45 pm

(Sd.) C.H.Dowden,
Maj.G.S.

APPENDIX XXVIII.

(Copy)

183 Bde
C.R.A.

G.732   11th

Intercepted message indicates that enemy will attempt a raid with artillery support between ERQUINGHEM & FAUQUISSART (M.18. tonight aaa Addsd 183 Bde CRA.

61 Div.
9.35 pm.   (Sd.) C.H.Dowden, Maj.G.S

APPENDIX XXIX.

(Copy)

11 Corps
40 Div
59 Div
184 Bde

G.747.   12th.

The Outpost line of resistance for tonight and until further orders will be as follows aaa H.31.c.9.0 along trench to H.31.d.60.85 - H.25.d.4.4 - H.25.b.8.7 - NW along road to H.19.c.7.7 - NE to H.14.a.5.2 - H.14.a.4.8 - H.8.c.3.7 - H.7.b.8.4 aaa Addsd all concerned.

61 Div.
9.45 pm

(Sd.)   C.H.Dowden, Maj.G.S

WAR DIARY   APPENDIX XXX

S E C R E T.   61st DIVISION.   G.C. 79.
                    Locations of Units at 6 a.m. 13.9.18.

Ref.shts.36A
    & 36.

        DIV.H.Q. "G"   RILL WORKS, L.33.b.
           do. "A" & "Q"   CROIX MARRAISSE, J.21.c.

        182 Inf.Bde. (LEFT BDE., C.B.L.), H.Q., G.8.a.8.1.
           2/6 Warwicks,   (Support Bn.) L.16.a.8.5.
           2/7 Warwicks,   (Line Bn.),   G.8.b.0.2.
           2/8 Worcesters, (Reserve Bn.) L.7.d.25.30.
           L.T.M.B.   G.1.d.9.5.

        183 Inf.Bde. (RIGHT BDE, C.B.L.), H.Q., L.27.a.0.3.
           9th North.Fus., (Reserve Bn.), YAM FM., L.22.a.
           11th Suffolks,   (Support Bn.), L.28.b.8.8.
           1st E. Lancs.,   (Line Bn.), L.23.d.4.6.
           L.T.M.B.,   FELT FM., L.27.b.

        184 Inf.Bde. (ADVANCED GUARD BDE.), H.Q., G.14.a.2.1.
           2/4 Oxfords,   (Right Bn.), G.34.c.7.3.
           2/5 Glosters,   (Left Bn.), G.18.a.15.15.
           2/4 R. Berks.,   (Support Bn.), G.9.d.1.1.
           L T.M.B.,   G.14.c.55.95.

        C. R. A.   RILL WORKS, L.33.b.
           307 Bde.R.F.A., (Advanced Bde. Group), G.13.b.6.4.
           306   do.   Rear Group), L.11.d.25.75.
           D.A.C.   L.20.c.7.0.
           D.T.M.O.   L.17.b.75.10.
           28 Bde.R.G.A.   L.32.b.75.75.

        61 Bn. M.G.C.   H.Q., L.34.d.3.9.
           "A" Coy.,   (Advanced Guard Coy.), G.27.b.8.5.
           "B" Coy.,   (Right Coy., C.B.L.), L.34.d.3.6.
           "C" Coy.,   (Left Coy., C.B.L.),   L.6.c.5.3.
           "D" Coy.,   (Advanced Guard Coy.), G.27.d.5.5.

        C. R. E.   L.27.d.8.4.
           476 Field Co.R.E., G.14.c.5.3.
           478   do.   L.29.a.6.6.
           479   do.   L.26.b.7.3.

        1/5 D.C.L.I. (P)   L.30.c.95.80.
           1 Coy.,   G.8.a.6.7.
           1 Coy.,   L.30.c.7.9.
           1 Coy.,   L.29.d.2.7.

        A. D. M. S.   TANNAY, I.22.d.1.1.
           2/1 Field Amb., L.27.c.2.6 (Main Dressing Stn.).
           2/2   do.   STEENBECQUE, I.5.d.4.8.
           2/3   do.   L.22.c.2.3.

        61 Div. Train.   J.27.a.7.7.
           No. 1 Coy.,   K.14.b.5.4.
           No. 2 Coy.,   K.11.b.5.5.
           No. 3 Coy.,   J.22.c.4.7.
           No. 4 Coy.,   K.23.a.2.4.

        D. G. O.   RILL WORKS, L.33.b.
           Anti-Gas Depot, L.27.c.1.5.
           Advanced Depot, G.27.b.6.5.

        Div. P. of W. Cage, L.29.a.5.6.

                                          E.S Bates Lieut.
                                       for G.S., 61st Divn.
                                               12.9.18.

SECRET.

Copy No: 22

APPENDIX XXXI

61st DIVISION INSTRUCTIONS No. 4.

OPERATIONS.

Advanced Guard Brigade.   1.   The continued resistance to our further advance by the enemy rearguards during the past few days necessitate an increase in our activity in order to ascertain the strength, dispositions, and intentions of the enemy.

The Advanced Guard Brigade will therefore maintain a vigorous system of fighting and reconnoitring Patrols along the front, both by day and night, with the object of taking prisoners, and to discover his dispositions. This system will be properly organised and coordinated by Battalion and Brigade Commanders, and schemes for these and any other minor enterprises along their fronts will be prepared and handed over by Battalion Commanders to relieving battalions from time to time, to assist the latter to continue the policy without interruption.

Harassing fire by the Advanced Guard Artillery and Machine Gun Companies will be maintained by day and night

Any sign of his continued withdrawal on any portion of the front will be reported at once, and preparations should always be ready to resume the advance, so that no delay is caused in following up his retirement and maintaining contact.

Raids by the enemy will be guarded against by extreme vigilance and by the frequent changing of the location of advanced posts.

Plans will be made, and handed over to relieving unit for counter-attacks by reserve platoons and companies for the re-capture of any important point lost in a hostile raid or minor enterprise.

Objective.   2.   In event of the enemy continuing his withdrawal at any moment, the objective to be reached by the Advanced Guard Brigade will be the line CROIX BLANCHE - FLEURBAIX ERQUINGHEM (H.4.d.9.7).

Corps Battle Line.   3.   The Divisional Sector of the Corps Battle Line will remain the line MUDDY LANE POST (exclusive) - NOUVEAU MONDE - thence line of LYS to G.16.b.8.7 and line of STILBECQUE to G.10.b.6.0, and will be known as the Left Divisional Sector.

The Divisional Sector will be sub-divided into Sections as follows :-

    Right Brigade - Nau MONDE Section.
    Left Brigade - SAILLY Section.

The inter-Brigade boundary will remain as already given in 61st Div. Order No. 202.

Nucleus Garrison Posts.   4.   Nucleus garrisons, strength 1 section to 1 platoon, with machine guns, will be provided to cover the following important points and main lines of approach :-

Nau MONDE Section:
  (i) MUDDY LANE POST (G.33.c.1.5 and G.33.c.1.7) - Road
       Mixed platoon of 61st and 59th Divisions.
  (ii) NOUVEAU MONDE (G.27.c.7.2) - 2 roads.
  (iii) G.27.c.4.5 - Road Bridge.
  (iv) On high ground immediately East of Canal at
      G.21.d.7.0 - this post to be responsible for
      footbridge at G.27.a.9.3 and road bridge at
      G.21.d.5.2 (PONT DE LA JUSTICE).   (P.T.O.)

(2)

    (v) G.21.d.8.8 - 2 road bridges. Post also to be
         responsible for foot-bridges at G.21.d.7.6 and
         G.21.b.95.60 respectively.
         Mixed platoon of Right and Left Brigades.

    (vi) G.16.c.8.6 (Pt. TOURNANT) - road bridge.

    (vii) G.16.b.6.6 - road bridge. Post also to be responsibl
         for footbridge at G.16.b.35.35 and for road bridge
         at G.16.b.85.85.

    (viii) G.10.d.75.45 - road bridge. Post also to be
         responsible for footbridge at G.10.d.80.15.

    (ix) House G.10.b.0.1. Mixed platoon of 61st and 40th
         Divisions.

Nucleus garrisons (except machine guns) may, when the tactical situation admits, be withdrawn during the daytime for training with their units. When not required for training, they should be allotted definite tasks for the maintenance and improvement of their posts.

5.   The above posts will be established on receipt of these Instructions, and a report will be made to Division as soon as they are in position, and repeated to flank Divisions in the case of Liaison Posts (i) and (ix).

    The Advanced Guard Brigade will supply the officer to command the Right Liaison Post; the 40th Division will supply the officer for the Left Liaison Post.

6.   ACKNOWLEDGE.

[signature]

13.9.18.

                         Lieut.-Col.,
                       G.S., 61st Division.

Distribution :-

Copy No.			
1	A.D.C. for G.O.C.	11	A.D.M.S.
2	61 Div. Signals.	12	D.A.P.M.
3-4	61 Div. Arty.	13-14	XI Corps.
5	C.R.E.	15	28 Bde.R.G.A.
6	61 Bn.M.G.C.	16	40th Divn.
7	1/5 D.C.L.I.	17	59th Divn.
8	182 Inf.Bde.	18-19	"Q".
9	183 Inf.Bde.	20	"G".
10	184 Inf.Bde.	21	D.G.O.

APPENDIX XXXII

SECRET.   Copy No. 21

                   61st DIVISION ORDER No. 204.   13.9.18.

Ref, Map 36, 1/40,000.
     36A, 1/40,000.

1.   182 Infantry Bde. will relieve the 184 Infantry Bde. as
Advanced Guard Bde. on the nights 14th/15th and 15th/16th inst.
as follows :-

   (a) On night 14th/15th inst. one battalion of 182 Infantry Bde.
       will relieve one battalion of 184 Infantry Bde., and will
       come under orders of G.O.C. 184 Infantry Bde. until
       completion of relief on night 15th/16th inst.
          Similarly, the relieved battalion of 184th Infantry Bde.
       will come under the orders of G.O.C. 182 Infantry Bde.

   (b) On the night 15th/16th inst. the 182nd Infantry Bde. (less
       one battalion) will relieve 184th Infantry Bde. (less one
       battalion) and will take over the duties of Advanced Guard
       Brigade from the hour of relief.

2.   The following troops, which form part of the Advanced Guard,
will come under orders of G.O.C. 182nd Infantry Bde. on
completion of relief :-

           1 Brigade, plus 1 battery, R.F.A.
           1 Field Coy. R.E.
           2 Coys. 61st Bn. M.G.C.
           1 Troop K.E.H.

3.   On relief, the 184th Infantry Bde. will withdraw to, and be
responsible for, the defence of the Northern Area of the Corps
Battle Line, and will take over accommodation vacated by the
182nd Infantry Bde.

4.   Command will pass on completion of relief, which will be
notified to D.H.Q.

5.   All further details of relief and moves will be arranged by
Commanders concerned.

6.   ACKNOWLEDGE.

Issued at 6 p.m.
                                                     Lieut.-Col.,
                                                     G.S., 61st Division.
                   Distribution:-

        Copy No. 1 - A.D.C. for G.O.C.   12-13 - XI Corps.
                 2 - 61 Div. Signals.   14 - 28 Bde. R.G.A.
               3-4 - 61 Div. Art.   15 - 40th Divn.
                 5 - C.R.E.   16 - 59th Divn.
                 6 - 61 Bn. M.G.C.   17-18 - "Q".
                 7 - 1/5 D.C.L.I.   19 - D.G.O.
                 8 - 182 Inf. Bde.   20 - "G".
                 9 - 183 Inf. Bde.   21-22 - War Diary.
                10 - 184 Inf. Bde.   23 - D.A.P.M.
                11 - A.D.M.S.   24 - Div. Train.

Appendix XXXIII

SECRET.   Copy No. 18

61st DIVISION INSTRUCTIONS No. 5.

DEFENCE AGAINST GAS.

1.   The general instructions regarding defence against gas are contained in S.S. 534 - "Standing Orders for defence against Gas". Attention is also called to the instructions contained in 61st Divn. G.C. 17/3 of 23.8.18, paras. 4 & 5.
   The following instructions are supplementary to, or in amplification of, above instructions.

2.   The ALERT ZONE will be the area forward (Eastward) of a line running approximately 6,000 yards West of the most advanced troops.
   The location of this zone will be determined by the positions of the advanced troops, and any alteration of its western boundary will be notified from time to time.
   The present western boundary is as follows :-

   G.25.d.8.8 - G.19.b.7.7 - G.8.d.8.5.

   (The Divisional Gas Officer will ensure that the western limit of the ALERT Zone is marked by notice-boards where crossed by roads).

3.   The READY ZONE will consist of the area between the Western edge of the ALERT ZONE and a line about 10,000 yards West of that Zone.
   Its location will move automatically with the movement of the ALERT ZONE.
   The Western limits, which are marked by notice-boards, will be notified from time to time.
   The present Western limit of the READY ZONE is :-

   The general line RIEZ DU VINAGE - RUE DES VACHES - CALONNE CHURCH - PT.TOURNANT (K.15.d.) - ARREWAGE - CAUDESCURE (all inclusive).

4.   Box respirators will always be worn in the "ALERT" position by everyone in the ALERT ZONE.
   Box respirators will be carried by everyone when in the READY ZONE.

5.   Attention is drawn to S.S. 212, which deals with YELLOW CROSS GAS and measures to be taken to counteract its effect.

6.   A large percentage of casualties from gas shelling are due to either carelessness or ignorance, and are preventable.
   Casualties can be reduced to a minimum by :-

(a) Rigid gas discipline.

(b) Giving all ranks a thorough knowledge of the properties of the various gasses, their effect, and the measures which must be taken to counteract them, with special reference to the persistency of YELLOW CROSS GAS, and its habit of reappearing after dawn under the influence of the sun. The imparting of this knowledge should be the duty of all officers.

7.   In order to reduce casualties to a minimum, all Commanders will ensure that the responsibilities of all concerned for successful anti-gas measures are fully realised and acted upon.
   All gas casualties will be investigated by C.Os. as soon as possible after they occur, in order to ascertain that all reasonable precautions were taken by officers, N.C.Os., or men, either for their own protection or for that of the men under their charge. Neglect of these precautions will be severely dealt with.
                                                                (P.T.O.)

Results of these investigations, together with any suggestions, will be forwarded to D.H.Q. through the usual channels, in order that as much information as possible may be available on the subject to assist the troops in the Division.

Formations and Units will make such arrangements that will ensure that all who become "gas casualties" are not evacuated before their cases are investigated, and that evidence be taken on oath at the Dressing Stations or Field Ambulances, from men whose condition permits.

8. The following arrangements should be made previous to bombardment

(a) Every formation and unit must have a scheme ready for the evacuation of a gassed area should the tactical situation permit. These evacuations will not take place down wind.

(b) Supplies of spare clothing and stocks of chloride of lime and bi-carbonate of soda will be held by all batteries and aid posts, and as far as possible by all other units.

(c) The A.D.M.S. will make such arrangements that will enable any men who may become splashed with the liquid of YELLOW CROSS GAS to wash immediately with soap and water, or bathe affected parts with solution of soda bi-carbonate.

(d) Orders will be issued to prevent dugouts, or other protected places, from becoming contaminated during bombardments by anyone who has been in contact with gas entering and bringing in gas on their clothing, etc.

This especially refers to YELLOW CROSS GAS, as the presence of dangerous quantities of GREEN or BLUE Cross can be noticed.

9. Action to be taken at the commencement of a bombardment :-
The alarm will be spread as laid down in S.S. 534.

(a) All instances of gas shelling will be reported to the Divisional Gas Officer immediately, giving location and approximate number of rounds fired.

(b) Should the bombardment exceed approximately 500 rounds, all units within 2,000 yards of the affected area will be warned by the formation or unit in whose area the shelling occurs, giving area affected. The next higher formation will be informed by wire, stating area affected, nature of gas, and approximate number of rounds.

The affected area will be picqueted in order to prevent other troops entering the gassed area.

When informing Division, the wire will be repeated to the Divisional Gas Officer, who will proceed, or cause a representative of the Gas Services to proceed, to the scene of the bombardment, and advise formations and units as to the protective measures to be adopted, and if possible to diagnose the gas or gasses.

(c) Plans for evacuating affected areas will be put into practice if necessary and possible.

(d) Divisional Artillery will notify Counter-Battery Officer, in order that Heavy Artillery may deal with offending enemy batteries.

10. Formations and units, in whose area gas shells have fallen, are responsible that the contaminated area is plainly marked with notices and picqueted to prevent other troops entering it until free of gas, and that the very earliest opportunity is taken to fill in all gas shell holes.

11.   The Divisional Gas Officer is responsible that a sufficient supply of material for neutralising gassed areas is located at convenient points and known to all concerned.
        He will visit all formations and units periodically, and ensure that their arrangements for gas defence are in order, and report results to the General Staff of the Division.

12.   In order to assist Commanders in Anti-Gas measures :-

(a) The C.R.A. and each Infantry Bde. will appoint an officer to act as "Temporary Gas Officer" to the Divisional Artillery and Infantry Bdes. respectively. This officer will be attached to and located at the headquarters of the formation concerned, and will be employed on anti-gas duties only.

(b) Definite orders will be issued that Battalion, Company, and Battery Gas N.C.Os. are not to be detailed for any other than Anti-gas duties when their unit is in the ALERT ZONE.

13.   CLOUD GAS ATTACK.
        Attention is directed to S.S. 534, Appendix IV, Section 5, the provisions of which will be strictly adhered to.
        Formations or units will arrange to warn :-
                (a) all troops in their area,
                (b) troops on their flanks,
                (c) Div. H.Q., repeating to Divl. Gas Officer.

14.   The "Cloud Gas" warning message will be kept ready made out in all Signal offices of the Advanced Guard or Outpost Brigade, and will be in the following form :-

(a) G.A.S. (name of part of the front from which the message originates).
    (Strombos horns will be sounded).

(b) It will only be sent by order of an officer, and will be signed by him.

(c) It will be timed.

(d) It will be sent without preamble, or address "to" or "from".

(e) It will take precedence over all messages except S.O.S., and will interrupt messages in course of transmission.

(f) It will be sent by all available means.

(g) It will be sent to the next station in rear and to each flank, except that the Divisional Signal office will not repeat the message until ordered by the General Staff.

14.9.18.

C H Dowden Maj
for Lieut.-Col.,
G.S., 61st Divn.

Distribution :-

Copy No. 1 - C.R.A.   9 - A.D.M.S.
         2 - C.R.E.   10 - Div. Train.
         3 - 182 Inf.Bde.   11 - "Q".
         4 - 183 Inf.Bde.   12 - D.A.P.M.
         5 - 184 Inf.Bde.   13 - D.A.D.O.S.
         6 - 61 Bn. M.G.C.   14 - D.A.D.V.S.
         7 - 1/5 D.C.L.I.   15 - D.G.O.
         8 - Div. Signals.   16 - Camp Comdt.

(Copy)   S E C R E T   APPENDIX XXXIV.

AMENDMENT No. 1
to 61 DIV. INSTRUCTIONS No. 4.

Para. 5.

For "Advanced Guard Brigade",

read "Brigade holding N^{au} MONDE Section".

(Sd.) C.H. Dowden, Maj. GS.
for Lt.-Col.,
G.S., 61st Divn.

14.9.18.

To all recipients
of above Instructions.

Appendix XXXV
I.G.44/2.

182 Inf. Bde.
183 Inf. Bde.
184 Inf. Bde.
C.R.A. (for information).
61 Bn.M.G.C.(for information).

1. The necessity and importance of sending in early information of events as they occur and the consequent discontinuance of the Daily Intelligence Summary was pointed out in 61st Division I.G.44/2 dated 9.9.18.

2. A considerable improvement has already been effected in the service of Intelligence, especially with regard to reports upon hostile shelling, and it is hoped that this will continue.

3. At the same time it is considered that a record of the information gained should again be kept daily and that the Daily Intelligence Summary should be revived.
   The necessity for this arises from the fact that Brigades out of the line at the present time possess no record of events and that when they relieve the Advanced Guard Brigade they are out of touch with recent events and the information gained along their front. They are also unable to appreciate "Normal" or "Abnormal" conditions after having taken over.

4. A Daily Intelligence Summary covering a period of 24 hours (6 a.m. to 6 a.m.) will therefore be kept by the Advanced Guard Brigade and forwarded to reach Division every day by 2 p.m. The usual Summary from Divisional Artillery and M.G.Bn. will continue to be forwarded by the same time.
   A Divisional Summary will be issued to all concerned every night by 6 p.m. This will enable units out of the line to appreciate the present situation and to be in touch with events when resuming their duties with the Advanced Guard Brigade.
   The reproduction of Intelligence Summaries will, however, in no way alter the present procedure of reporting all events as early as possible and as they occur.

Wetherly
Lieut.Col.,
G.S., 61 Division.

14.9.18.

War Diary   APPENDIX XXXV^a

S E C R E T :- NOT TO BE TAKEN BEYOND BATTALION H.Q. IN THE LINE.

61st Division Intelligence Summary
No. 1.

Period covered - 12 midnight 13th - 12 noon 14th Sept.
Visibility - Fair to bad.

Infantry.
Despite difficult progress, owing to the muddy state of the ground, our patrols were active between dusk and dawn. Our advanced post line remains unchanged.

Artillery.
Registration and bursts of fire on selected targets.
9 concentration shoots on hostile forward positions.
Normal harassing fire on enemy's communications.

M.Gs.
Special shoot in co-operation with artillery, 12 midnight to 5 a.m. 56,000 rounds expended. Targets: cross-roads & enclosures in H.33.a.
Roads & enclosures between H.26.b.8.0 & H.27.a.80.95.

Aerial.
Our machines were active from dawn to 9.30 a.m., when weather conditions prevented further flying.

ENEMY ACTIVITY.

Infantry.
No hostile patrols encountered.

Artillery.
Harassing fire decreased during the period. 10.5cm. guns active, firing single shots on roads W. of LYS. No concentrations reported. Gas shelling below normal. A.A. fire particularly heavy.
(Note: Details of hostile shelling forwarded to Corps Counter-Battery Office).

M.Gs.
Active throughout the night, sweeping across our front; this was especially heavy during our M.G. shoot.
Presence of several guns at BARTLETTE FM. again demonstrated.
A.A. very active, even when our machines were some distance in rear of our lines.

Aerial.
One machine at 2,000 ft. crossed our lines twice, at 6.15 a.m. and 6.30 a.m; driven off by A.A. and small arms fire. 12 machines patrolled our lines at 9.15 a.m., flying a fair height; this formation came from the direction of FLEURBAIX and departed towards ARMENTIERES after being some time over our positions.

Work and Defences.
H.20.a.85.40 - enemy working with picks.
H.21.c; H.27.a. - new earth outside old trench running through these.

Hostile T.Ms. and snipers inactive.
No E.O.Bs. up.
No hostile movement observed.

General.
Explosions - 11.40 a.m: house in ESTAIRES.

14.9.18.

E g Bates Lieut.
for G.S., 61st Divn.

(P. T. O.)

(Appendix to 61 Div. Int. Summary No. 1).

NOTES ON AIR PHOTOGRAPHS OF 13.9.18.

Photos. of this date, covering the areas H.11, 12, 16, 17, 18, 22, and I.1, 2, 7, 8, show very few signs of any enemy work on existing defences in these localities.

The following are the chief features :-

Bridges at I.7.b.5.5 and I.7.c.94.88 appear to be well used in conjunction with tracks shown on 36.NW. Ed. 9a.

Shallow C.T. in course of construction from I.1.d.80.25 fo I.2.c.60.30.

Recently constructed C.T. from H.12.c.80.90 running on S. side of light railway to H.12.d.8.2 - thence in a N.E. direction across the railway to about I.7.d.4.2, thence it runs in a S.E. direction crossing the railway again at I.7.c.45.10.

(Copy) S E C R E T Appendix XXXVI
G.C. 40/5.

XI Corps.

1. The information so far gained as to the enemy's strength and dispositions along the front of the Division during the past 4 or 5 days, does not point to any change in his tactical methods, strength, or intentions, at the present moment.

2. I attach a map showing the location of all enemy outposts, machine guns, and trench mortars, reported since the 12th inst.

3. Attempts at various times to penetrate this screen by means of patrols have not added materially to already existing information. These operations have disclosed, however, that the enemy now exercises extreme vigilance, and to a greater extent than usual. This increase in the enemy's observation and vigilance is for the moment the outstanding feature of his attitude. The slightest movement in our advanced posts, activity of our machine guns and trench mortars, appear to draw his immediate attention.

   On the other hand, his attitude has been entirely a passive defence, and no attempt has so far been made to raid our posts, and hostile patrols are seldom if ever encountered.

4. The enemy holds his present line by means of a screen of mutually supporting posts, closely supported and covered by both heavy and light machine guns, sited to sweep the front of his line, which is everywhere flat and open.

   The positions of his posts and machine guns frequently change. Our patrols have reached several of his posts, which have been found unoccupied, and have been caught by machine gun fire from his alternative positions on either flank.

   During the wet weather of the past few days, attempts to approach his posts have been made still more difficult owing to the ditches - which in most cases afford the only cover for approach - being filled with water, and the silent movement of patrols is almost impossible.

5. After one or two attempts to penetrate and capture JUNCTION POST, a raid with artillery support was carried out on the early morning of 12th inst., with the object of establishing posts astride the trench system in H.32.a.& b. The known enemy positions at BARTLETT'S FARM and TWO TREE FARM were kept under heavy fire with smoke and H.E. during the operation, but, owing to the unfortunate weather conditions, the operation was unsuccessful. It did, however, establish useful information that the enemy was in stronger force here than at other portions of his line further north, and his active defence of this part of his line showed that he was probably fighting here to retain his outpost line of resistance.

6. Observation beyond his present front line is difficult in this flat country, so that it is not possible to say whether his line to the north of BARTLETT'S FARM is an outpost screen, or his outpost line of resistance, or whether his outpost line of resistance runs from JUNCTION POST - FLEURBAIX - ERQUINGHEM SWITCH. The latter seems the most probable.

   A great deal of information on this point will no doubt be possible when recent photographs of this area are compared.

7. In the meantime, I do not consider that any value can be gained by making further local attempts on small frontages to penetrate his defence. These operations must prove too costly against his present system of holding his front. If it is desired to force the enemy to withdraw further, then I think a more serious operation on our part will be required.

8. The enemy, however, is being given no rest. Both fighting patrols to secure prisoners, and reconnoitring patrols to maintain the closest contact and further discover his strength and dispositions, have been continuously active on my whole front, and harassing fire by artillery, machine guns, trench mortars, is being carried out by day and night.

(Sd.) F.J. DUNCAN,
Major-General,
Commanding 61st Division.

15.9.18.

War Diary. Appendix XXXVII

SECRET — NOT TO BE TAKEN BEYOND BATTALION H.Q. IN THE LINE.
61st Division Intelligence Summary No.2.

Period covered: 12 noon 14th to 6 a.m. 15th Septr.
Visibility - Rain interfered considerably; fair at times.

OUR ACTIVITY.

Infantry.
Patrols continued their activity along the Divisional front.

Artillery.
Shoots were carried out on selected targets in H.20 and H.27; also FLEURBAIX Church; good results were observed in each case. Harassing fire and concentrations on H.16, FLEURBAIX & eastern outskirts, CROIX DE ROME, and area between CROIX BLANCHE & CROIX LESCORNE; BOIS GRENIER & ERQUINGHEM also engaged.

Machine Guns.
8,000 rounds fired on cross roads H.33.a., road running N. & S. through H.27.b., and FLEURBAIX.

Trench Mortars.
L.T.M.B. fired 97 rounds on suspected M.G. emplacements. M.Gs. in JUNCTION POST were effectively silenced.

Aerial.
Scouts and artillery machines were active.

ENEMY ACTIVITY.

Infantry. No hostile parties seen.

Artillery.
Slight increase on forward positions; corresponding decrease on rear area. G.36.c, G.33.d, G.11.d, G.12.c, G.22.a, & G.23.c were favourite targets. LAVENTIE, BAC ST. MAUR, & SAILLY heavily engaged. 200 gas shells on G.34.c.
(Note: Details of hostile shelling forwarded to Corps Counter-Battery Office).

Machine Guns. Active at intervals.
Guns located at JUNCTION POST, H.32.a.75.60, H.32.a.4.8, H.32.c.6.6, H.20.b.65.60, H.20.c.40.45, H.20.c.4.3, and H.32.c.40.25; the last-mentioned is a night position only.

Trench Mortars. Slightly increased.
6 rounds M.T.M. in rear of post H.32.c.9.1.
6 rounds L.T.M. on H.25.b.5.5.
30 rounds L.T.M. on road junction H.25.d.95.95 (fired from direction of BARTLETT'S FARM).

Aerial. Considerable activity, both in evening and early morning, but A.A. fire kept them in check. One suspected registration on G.11.d.

Work & Defences.
1. Posts located at H.20.c.2.7, H.20.c.3.5, & H.20.c.1.3; wire in front of these not strong or continuous.
2. JUNCTION POST is strongly protected by 5 or 6 strong belts, double apron; no recent work on fence.
3. Wire between H.20.c.5.5 to H.20.a.9.3 weak.
4. Wire in front of BARTLETT'S FM. is good.
5. Small breastwork 60 yds. W. of BARTLETT'S FM.

Movement. Movement seen at the windows of house at H.27.b.25.65 - at once fired on by a 4.5"; no further movement observed.

General.

1. Abnormal number of hostile Very lights during the night.
2. Further explosions caused by enemy mines occurred during the period - at G.14.d.4.7 (house), G.18.d.35.80 (house), G.29.d.4.0 (house), and G.29.d.6.8 (cross-roads); at the latter place a crater 12 feet deep was made and the roads temporarily rendered impassable.
3. A dump of 9 mines found at G.8.a. (description and sketch forwarded to units).
4. 2 escaped Portuguese prisoners came into our lines in H.31.c. at 11 p.m.

15.9.18.

E.G. Bates Lieut
for G.S., 61st Divn.

APPENDIX XXXVIII

SECRET.   61st DIVISION.   G.C. 79.
Locations of Units at 6 a.m. 16.9.18.

Ref. Shts. 36A & 36.

  DIV. H.Q. "G". RILL WORKS, L.33.b.
   do. "A" & "Q", CROIX MARRAISSE, J.21.c.

  182 Inf. Bde. (ADVANCED GUARD BDE.), H.Q., G.14.a.2.1.
   2/6 Warwicks, (Left Bn.) G.18.a.15.15.
   2/7 Warwicks, (Right Bn.) G.34.c.7.3.
   2/8 Worcesters, (Support Bn.) G.9.d.1.1.
   L.T.M.B. G.14.c.55.95.

  183 Inf. Bde. (RIGHT BDE., C.B.L.), H.Q. L.27.a.0.3.
   9th North. Fus., (Reserve Bn.) YAM FM., L.22.a.
   11th Suffolks, (Support Bn.) L.28.b.9.9.
   1st E. Lancs., (Line Bn.) L.23.d.4.6.
   L.T.M.B. FELT FM., L.27.b.

  184 Inf. Bde. (LEFT BDE., C.B.L.), H.Q., G.8.a.8.1.
   2/4 Oxfords, (Line Bn.), G.8.b.0.2.
   2/5 Glosters, (Support Bn.), L.16.a.8.5.
   2/4 R. Berks, (Reserve Bn.) L.7.d.25.30.
   L.T.M.B., G.1.d.9.5.

  C.R.A. RILL WORKS, L.33.b.
   307 Bde. R.F.A., (Advanced Bde. Group), G.13.b.6.4.
   306 do. (Rear Group), L.11.d.25.75.
   D.A.C. L.20.c.7.0.
   D.T.M.O. L.17.b.75.10.
   28 Bde. R.G.A. L.34.d.1.5.

  61 Bn. M.G.C. H.Q., L.34.d.3.9.
   "A" Coy., (Left Coy. C.B.L.), L.6.c.5.3.
   "B" Coy., (Advanced Guard Coy.) G.27.d.5.5.
   "C" Coy., (Advanced Guard Coy.) G.23.a.8.3.
   "D" Coy., (Right Coy., C.B.L.), L.34.d.3.6.

  C.R.E. L.27.d.8.4.
   476 Field Co. R.E., K.23.c.6.3.
   478 do. G.14.a.5.3.
   479 do. L.26.b.7.3.

  1/5 D.C.L.I.(P), H.Q. & 2 Coys., L.30.c.95.80.
    1 Coy., G.8.a.6.7.

  A.D.M.S. TANNAY, I.22.d.1.1.
   2/1 Field Amb., L.27.c.2.6 (Main Dressing Stn.).
   2/2 do. STEENBECQUE, I.5.d.4.8.
   2/3 do. L.22.c.2.3.

  61 Div. Train. J.27.a.7.7.
   No. 1 Coy., K.14.b.5.4.
   No. 2 Coy., K.11.b.5.5.
   No. 3 Coy., J.22.c.4.7.
   No. 4 Coy., K.23.a.2.4.

  D.G.O. RILL WORKS, L.33.b.
   Anti-Gas Depot, L.27.c.1.5.
   Advanced Depot, G.27.b.6.5.

  Div. P. of W. Cage, L.29.a.5.6.

         E.G. Bates Lieut.
        for G.S., 61st Divn.
         15.9.18.

(Copy) APPENDIX XXXIX.

G.O.C., 5th Divn.

    P.61.   16th.

Many congratulations on your great mention.

    Maj.-Gen. DUNCAN,
    61st Divn.

                          (Sd.) E.J.Bates, Lt.,
                                  for G.O.C.

(Copy)　　　　　　　　　　　　　　　　　　　　　APPENDIX XL.

61 Div.

    T.647.　　16th.

Where road ditches enter drains in front of houses built close up to roads look for charges pushed into the drain aaa This probably caused demolition at G.16.b.2.8 this morning.

    C.R.E., 61 Div.

(Copy) APPENDIX XLI.

```
182 Bde    61 Bn.MGC.
183 Bde    1/5 DCLI.
184 Bde    28 Bde.RGA.
C.R.A.     40 Div
C.R.E.     59 Div
```

G.793.   16th.

Ref Div Instructions No.1 para 4 of 4th inst aaa During present stationary period outpost line of resistance will be selected by Divn aaa Line will run ROUGE DE BOUT - enclosures G.36.a. - enclosures G.30.a. - road junction G.24.d.0.1 - G.24.central - railway to BAC ST.MAUR - old British defences G.18.b. & 12.d. aaa Establish liaison posts with flank Brigades aaa Acknowledge aaa Addsd 182 Bde reptd all concerned.

61 Div.
10.20 pm

(Sd.) W.H.Dowden,
Maj.G.S.

War Diary APPENDIX XLII

S E C R E T - NOT TO BE TAKEN BEYOND BATTALION H.Q. IN THE LINE.

61st Division Intelligence Summary No.3.

Period covered: 6 a.m. 15th to 6 a.m. 16th Septr.
Visibility: Good.

OUR ACTIVITY.

Infantry.
Continued patrol activity throughout the night.

Artillery.
Enemy's forward area repeatedly harassed. Special shoots on H.10.d.20.25 and H.15.d.9.2. A.A. batteries kept well employed.

Machine Guns.
21,500 rounds expended on selected targets.

Trench Mortars.
6" Newtons fired 30 rounds on H.3.d.9.2; good shooting observed.

Aerial.
Much increased, both by day and night. A heavy bomb dropped in enemy's front system 9.30 p.m. An R.E.8 was driven down by a hostile machine and landed in G.7.d.

ENEMY ACTIVITY.

Infantry.
No patrols encountered. H.15.a.6.8 strongly garrisoned. Working party near here dispersed by L.G. fire.

Artillery.
Slightly decreased. Shelling was reported at various times in G.11, 12, 17, 18, 21, 22, 23, 24, 27, 28, 29, 33, 34, 35, 36; also in H.8, 13, 14, & 31.
Gas shelling was confined to 100 rounds on G.22, 23, 36.d; H.13.b. and 14.c. H.V. guns were inactive.
A.A. batteries were energetic, and their barrages well placed. (Note: Details of hostile shelling forwarded to Corps Counter-Battery Office).

Machine Guns.
Usual intermittent activity, especially from JUNCTION POST, BARTLETT'S FARM, H.15.c.6.8, & H.32.b.5.6.

Trench Mortars. (G)
10 rounds on H.32.c.1.1; otherwise quiet. Emplacement suspected H.26.d.

Aerial.
Much increased. Our lines crossed several times at various altitudes. One low-flyer fired into our forward posts. One E.A. driven down behind enemy lines during afternoon.

Observation Balloons.
Several in position. 1 was shot down in flames at 5.30 p.m.

Work & Defences.
Knife-rests across road at H.9.c.5.1. Double apron fence, two belts, either side of this point.

Miscellaneous.
1. Abnormal number of hostile Very lights during the night again reported.
2. Horse transport heard fairly close behind enemy lines.
3. No hostile movement observed.
4. Further enemy mines exploded during the period at houses in G.16.b, G.17.b.& c, G.18.d, L.29.b, H.15.a, & H.21.a., the two latter being in front of our lines. 2 men were killed in the first-named explosion, but no other casualties have been sustained.

(P.T.O.)

(2)

Identification.
A deserter of the 3rd M.G.Coy., 100 Reserve Grenadier Regt., 23rd Res. Div., gave himself up to the Divn. on our right in N.1.b. yesterday afternoon; he is unintelligent, and knows nothing of enemy intentions.

General.

1. Another escaped Portuguese prisoner came into our lines in H.31. this morning.

2. From the examination of those reported in yesterday's Summary:
Captured on April 9th, they were marched to LILLE, where they were left for 6 weeks in the CITADEL. They were then taken to BEAUCHAMPS, and employed there for a further 6 weeks on drains. Moved again, they proceeded to LAVENTIE, doing fatigues in that area for 40 days. Once again they were moved, this time to SANTES, from which place they eventually escaped.
They state there is a rumour current that all civilians are being evacuated from LILLE and all towns W. of there.
A considerable amount of artillery has been withdrawn to the E. of LILLE.
All German troop movement Eastwards took place at night.
No identifications could be given.
Roads in FOURNES, LATTRE, and MARQUILLES are said to be mined.
The large R.E. and ammunition dumps in SANTES have been withdrawn.

Air Photos.
Air photos. of 15th show additional work on the enemy's new trench line between ERQUINGHEM & FLEURBAIX. This line is now continuous between these two points, and is wired throughout; an extension in a southerly direction through FERRET POST to CROIX BLANCHE appears to be in course of construction.
The enemy's Outpost Line now runs through H.9.b.& d, H.15.a, H.14.d, H.20.b,& c, to BARTLETT FARM; from the latter point short lengths of trench have been dug to link up with JUNCTION POST.

16.9.18.

Bowden Maj
G.S., 61st Divn.

"A" Form.
MESSAGES AND SIGNALS.

Army Form C. 2121.
(In pads of 150.)

APPENDIX XLIII

TO	184 Bde.
	Q

Sender's Number.	Day of Month.	In reply to Number.	A A A
G.792	16		

Detail one battalion to proceed to LINGHEM by march route tomorrow aaa will be accommodated in huts aaa probable stay 4 days aaa To work under orders issued by 11 Corps Q aaa No restrictions as to time or route aaa addsd 184 Bde. reptd Q

From 61 Div.
Place
Time 10.20 p.m.

(sgd) C.H. DOWDEN, Maj.

(Copy) APPENDIX XLIV.

G.O.C., 61st Divn.

(In reply to)
P.61

Many thanks.

G.O.C., 5th Divn.

War Diary APPENDIX XLV

S E C R E T — NOT TO BE TAKEN BEYOND BATTALION H.Q. IN THE LINE.

61st Division Intelligence Summary No. 4.
Period covered: 6 a.m. 16th – 6 a.m. 17th, Septr.
Visibility: Fair at first, & gradually improving.

OUR ACTIVITY.

Infantry.
Although much hampered by storms, our patrols succeeded in keeping constant touch with the enemy's posts, and carrying out thorough reconnaissance of NO MAN'S LAND.
A liaison post with Div. on our left has been established at H.3.c.3.7.

Artillery.
The enemy's forward area, roads and buildings, were continuously harassed. A.A. batteries had plenty of shooting, and drove off many hostile machines.

Machine Guns.
Inactive, reliefs being in progress during the night.

Trench Mortars.
BARTLETT'S FARM was engaged by 6" Newtons.

Aerial.
Great activity maintained.

ENEMY ACTIVITY.

Infantry.
Patrols found the enemy very alert, and holding his line in strength. Several small wiring parties were seen in front of BARTLETT'S FARM, but entire absence of hostile patrols was again reported.

Artillery.
Increased. BAC ST.MAUR, SAILLY, and the vicinity of the road between those places received most attention; much of the shooting was preceded by air-burst registration; remainder of shelling was slight and very scattered. 4.2" & 5.9" H.V. guns shelled L.29.b. and the road in L.3.b.& d. with 40 rounds. 100 rounds of BLUE CROSS on roads in G.36, and fumes were detected over a large area. A battery is suspected in H.5.d. (S.E. of railway).

Machine Guns.
The BARTLETT'S FARM guns were again active, and guns were located firing from the huts at H.3.d.6.6 & 6.3.
A L.M.G. was brought in from a forward position by our troops.

Trench Mortars.
30 rounds on Farm at H.31.a.50.65 from direction of JUNCTION POST.

Aerial.
Continued above normal. Single machines patrolling our lines were covered by protective flights flying higher in rear of the enemy lines.
A photographic machine was over our battery positions for half an hour just after noon.
E.O.Bs: None observed.

Work & Defences.
Wire running S.W. from JUNCTION POST consists of 2 belts of double apron fence.

Transport.
Transport heard about H.26.d.1.1 during the night.

(P.T.O.)

Explosions.
Further explosions have occurred - mostly in houses; old enemy shelters have also gone up.   A pill-box at G.25.b.0.7 exploded, killing 1 officer and wounding several men.

Identification.
4th Coy., 1st Bn., 100th Res. Grenadier Regt. (23rd Res. Div.); man killed on the 15th at N.13.b.7.7.
From this it appears that the 100th Res. Gren. Regt. has extended its front southwards.
(From the Div. on our right).

General.
Air observers report that ARMENTIERES is apparently evacuated.

Air Photographs.
Photos. of 15th inst. show further trench work on the ERQUINGHEM - FLEURBAIX System in H.5.a.& c. and H.11.a.

17.9.18.

E.G. Baker Lieut.
for
G.S., 61st Divn.

Appendix XLVI

S E C R E T.

61st DIVISION ORDER No. 205.

Copy No. 21
17.9.18.

Ma Ref. map 36, 1/40,000.
36A, 1/40,000.

1. 183rd Infantry Bde. will relieve the 182nd Infantry Bde. as Advanced Guard Bde. on the nights 20th/21st and 21st/22nd inst., as follows :-

(a) On night 20th/21st inst. one battalion of 183rd Infantry Bde. will relieve one battalion of 182nd Infantry Bde., and will come under orders of G.O.C. 182nd Infantry Bde. until completion of relief on night 21st/22nd inst.
Similarly, the relieved battalion of 182nd Infantry Bde. will come under the orders of G.O.C. 183rd Infantry Bde.

(b) On the night 21st/22nd inst. the 183rd Infantry Bde. (less one battalion) will relieve 182nd Infantry Bde. (less one battalion), and will take over the duties of Advanced Guard Bde. from the hour of relief.

2. The following troops, which form part of the Advanced Guard, will come under orders of G.O.C. 183rd Infantry Bde. on completion of relief :-

    1 Brigade, plus 1 battery, R.F.A.
    1 Field Coy. R.E.
    2 Coys. 61st Bn. M.G.C.
    1 Troop K.E.H.

3. On relief, the 182nd Infantry Bde. will withdraw to, and be responsible for, the defence of the Southern Area of the Corps Battle Line, and will take over accommodation vacated by the 183rd Infantry Bde.

4. Command will pass on completion of relief, which will be notified to D.H.Q.

5. All further details of relief and moves will be arranged by Commanders concerned.

6. ACKNOWLEDGE.

Issued at 6 p.m.

for Lieut.-Col.,
G.S., 61st Division.

Distribution :-

Copy No. 1 - A.D.C. for G.O.C.	12-13 - XI Corps.
2 - 61 Div. Signals.	14 - 28 Bde. R.G.A.
3-4 - 61 Div. Art.	15 - 40th Div.
5 - C.R.E.	16 - 59th Div.
6 - 61 Bn. M.G.C.	17-18 - "Q".
7 - 1/5 D.C.L.I.	19 - D. O.
8 - 182 Inf. Bde.	20 - "G".
9 - 183 Inf. Bde.	21-22 - War Diary.
10 - 184 Inf. Bde.	23 - D.A.P.M.
11 - A.D.M.S.	24 - Div. Train.

APPENDIX XLVII

SECRET.   AMENDMENT No. 1
                    to 61st Div. Instructions No. 3.

ANTI-AIRCRAFT DEFENCE.

1. Para. 4.   Delete last 8 lines, and substitute :-
                    GUARBECQUE (36A), O.18.a.3.5.
                    HARTE VENT (36A), P.2.b.1.4.
                    TANNAY   (36A), I.30.c.1.6.

2. Para. 5.   Delete last 5 lines, and substitute :-
                    LAVENTIE   (36), G.33.d.3.8.
                    SAILLY SUR LA LYS,
                                  (36), G.17.a.7.3.
                    MERVILLE   (36A), L.25.c.6.4.
                    TANNAY   (36A), I.29.a.2.9.
                    MOLINGHEM (36A), O.13.a.3.8.
                    ST. QUENTIN (36A), H.32.b.2.5.

3. ACKNOWLEDGE.

18.9.18.

                                    for Lieut.-Col.,
                                    G.S., 61st Divn.
To all recipients of 61 Div. Instructions No.3.

War Diary   Appendix XLVIII

S E C R E T — NOT TO BE TAKEN BEYOND BATTALION H.Q. IN THE LINE.

61st Division Intelligence Summary No. 5.
Period covered: 6 a.m. 17th – 6 a.m. 18th Sept.
Visibility – Fair to very good.

OUR ACTIVITY.

Infantry.
Patrols maintained close touch with the enemy, and found him alert and still holding his line in strength.

Artillery.
Harassing fire was increased from the afternoon onwards on forward roads and enclosures, particular attention also being paid to ERQUINGHEM SWITCH in H.16.b. & d.
A concentration shoot on FLEURBAIX took place in the morning.

Machine Guns.
17,500 rounds expended on selected targets.

Trench Mortars.
6" Newtons fired 15 rounds on the "HOSPITAL" in H.15.c., and 20 rounds on the Copse and house at H.15.b.1.2; several direct hits were obtained on the house, good shooting being also observed on the first-named target.
3" Stokes engaged a hostile M.G. at H.3.d.6.4.

Aerial.
Great activity throughout the period. The enemy's line was frequently crossed by day, and bombing machines were active at night.

ENEMY ACTIVITY.

Infantry.
Two working parties out at H.26.a.2.6 and H.3.d.6.5; no patrols encountered.

Artillery.
Considerable during the morning, then quieter until night, when it became brisker again. SAILLY & BAC ST. MAUR were again the favourite targets, also G.10, 11, & 12. Other shelling was scattered over a wide area E. of the LYS. H.V. guns were inactive.
A few phosgene gas shells fell on road in G.35.a., and some mustard gas shells in H.13.c.

Machine Guns.
Increased activity, especially opposite our right subsector.
The guns in ERQUINGHEM and H.15.c. were also kept well employed.

Trench Mortars - Inactive.

Aerial.
Considerably less, only two machines crossing our lines during the day. Bombs were dropped near LAVENTIE shortly after midnight.
E.O.Bs: 3 in position towards evening.

Work & Defences.
The enemy's wire at H.32.c.5.6 and H.32.c.6.8 is very thick, consisting of our old wire reinforced with angle-irons and much loose wire thrown in.

Lights & Signals.
Again a great many Very lights were fired from hostile positions, including some single and double red, also double green.
Hostile searchlights were active against our bombing machines.

(P.T.O.)

Explosives.
    Houses went up at L.9.d.7.1, G.16.d.45.00, and G.13.c.1.5.
    Loud explosions some distance behind the enemy lines were heard on a 91° T.B. from H.13.b.15.50, at 4.30 p.m. and 4.45 p.m.

German summer time.   (From 5th Army Summary).

    German summer time, which commenced at 2 a.m. on April 15th, ceased at 3 a.m. Septr. 16th.
    Consequently, Franco-British time will now be the same as German time until Franco-British summer time ceases - when German time will again be one hour in advance of Franco-British time.

E.S. Bates Lieut.
for G.S., 61st Divn.

18.9.18.

Appendix XLIX

SECRET. NOT TO BE TAKEN BEYOND BATTALION H.Q. IN THE LINE.

61st Division Intelligence Summary No. 6.
Period covered - 6 a.m. 18th - 6 a.m. 19th Septr.
Visibility - Good, with one poor period.

OUR ACTIVITY.

Infantry.
A fighting patrol, which proceeded along the S. bank of the LYS, reached a wide, stagnant ditch at H.3.d.8.4, forming an impassable obstacle; they therefore worked south along the ditch, striking the main road at H.3.d.5.0, where a barricade of trees was found. Heavy hostile M.Gs. opened from both sides of the main road, and the patrol withdrew, after bringing their Lewis gun into action.

All patrols report progress much hampered by the intensity of the enemy's M.G. fire, and his extreme alertness.

Artillery.
Active harassing fire maintained, and 40 targets engaged in the enemy's forward zone. A successful shoot was carried out on buildings at H.20.d.60.65, and a concentration, in co-operation with H.A., was fired on a hostile battery position at H.23.a.8.8.

Machine Guns.
30,000 rounds expended on selected points in hostile territory.

Trench Mortars.
6" Newtons and 3" Stokes engaged BARTLETTE FM. & JUNCTION POST respectively.

Aerial.
Activity very pronounced all day.

ENEMY ACTIVITY.

Infantry.
Towards dawn, a hostile party, about 20 strong, wearing soft caps and greatcoats, were observed near our southern boundary; they were vigorously engaged by small-arms fire and scattered. Casualties are believed to have been inflicted, but increasing daylight prevented investigation.

Artillery.
Activity slight during the morning, but increased towards evening. Night firing was normal. A considerable amount of air-burst ranging was reported. Many enemy guns appeared to be firing at very long, and even extreme, ranges.

Shelling was, as usual, very scattered, and practically the whole area between our outpost line and the LYS received attention during the period, also the usual targets E. of the STILBEKE.

An intense concentration was carried out at 6.15 p.m. on G.17.a.&.b. (77mm. and 4.2").

Machine Guns.
Very active in retaliation to our M.G. fire; also against our aircraft. M.G. located at H.3.d.7.1.

Guns all along front very active against our patrols.

A hostile M.G. engaged a tree O.P. close up to our line, with success; this gun was silenced by our artillery fire.

Trench Mortars.
Except for a few rounds on G.31.d.5.6, inactive.

(P.T.O.).

Aerial.
Only one E.A., which retreated on our machines approaching, was observed during the period.

E.O.Bs. Two in position at 105° and 143° T.B. from G.34.d.53.43 respectively. A third, 71° from G.29.c.15.50, was brought down in flames at 4.50 p.m.

Explosions.
House at G.17.c.95.95 went up at 6 p.m.
Explosions were observed in the direction of ARMENTIERES.

- - - - - - - - - - - - - - - - -

Disbanded German Divisions.

The 235th German Division has been disbanded.
On April 23rd & 24th this Division suffered very severe casualties when opposed to the 61st Division in the ROBECQ sector, losing 200 prisoners.
The 109th German Division has also been disbanded.

19.9.18.

E.G. Bates Lieut.
for G.S., 61st Divn.

APPENDIX L

SECRET.   61st DIVISION.   G.C. 79.
                    Locations of Units at 6 a.m. 20.9.18.
Ref.Shts.36A & 36.

DIV. H.Q. "G"   RILL WORKS, L.33.b.
   do. "A" & "Q",   CROIX MARRAISSE, J.21.c.

182 Inf.Bde. (ADVANCED GUARD BDE.), H.Q. G.14.a.05.05.
   2/6 Warwicks,   (Support Bn.) G.20.b.4.8.
   2/7 Warwicks,   (Left Bn.) G.18.a.15.15.
   2/8 Worcesters,   (Right Bn.) G.34.d.60.45.
   L.T.M.B.   G.14.c.65.90.

183 Inf.Bde. (RIGHT BDE., C.B.L.), H.Q. L.27.a.0.3.
   9th North.Fus.   (Reserve Bn.) YAM FM., L.22.a.
   11th Suffolks,   (Support Bn.) L.28.b.9.9.
   1st E. Lancs.   (Line Bn.) L.23.d.4.6.
   L.T.M.B.   FELT FM., L.27.b.

184 Inf.Bde. (LEFT BDE, C.B.L.), H.Q., G.8.a.8.1.
   2/4 Oxfords,   (Line Bn.) G.8.b.0.2.
   2/5 Glosters,   (Support Bn.) L.16.a.8.5.
   2/4 R. Berks,   (Reserve Bn.) L.7.d.25.30.
   L.T.M.B.   G.1.d.9.5.

C.R.A.   RILL WORKS, L.33.b.
   306 Bde. R.F.A.   (Rear Group) L.10.d.7.3.
   307   do.   (Advanced Bde. Group) G.13.b.6.3.
   D.A.C.   L.20.c.7.0.
   D.T.M.O.   L.17.b.75.10.

61 Bn. M.G.C.   H.Q., L.34.d.3.9.
   "A" Coy.,   (Left Coy. C.B.L.) L.6.c.5.3.
   "B" Coy.,   (Advanced Guard Coy.) G.27.d.5.5.
   "C" Coy.,   (Advanced Guard Coy.) G.23.a.8.3.
   "D" Coy.,   (Right Coy. C.B.L.) L.34.d.3.6.

C.R.E.   L.27.d.8.4.
   476 Field Co. R.E.   K.23.c.6.3.
   478   do.   G.14.a.5.3.
   479   do.   L.26.b.7.3.

1/5 D.C.L.I.(P),   H.Q. & 2 Coys., L.30.c.95.80.
                               1 Coy., G.8.a.6.7.

A.D.M.S.   CROIX MARRAISSE, J.21.c.
   2/1 Field Amb.,   L.27.c.2.6 (Main Dressing Stn.).
   2/2   do.   J.27.d.8.7.
   2/3   do.   L.22.c.2.3.

61 Div. Train.   J.27.a.7.7.
   No. 1 Coy.,   K.14.b.5.4.
   No. 2 Coy.,   K.24.d.3.6.
   No. 3 Coy.,   J.22.c.4.7.
   No. 4 Coy.,   K.23.a.2.4.

D.G.O.   RILL WORKS, L.33.b.
   Anti-Gas Depot,   L.27.c.1.5.
   Advanced Depot,   G.27.b.6.5.

Div. P.of W. Cage,   L.29.a.5.6.

                                          E.S.Bates Lieut.
19.9.18.   for G.S., 61st Divn.

Appendix LI

S E C R E T - NOT TO BE TAKEN BEYOND BATTALION H.Q. IN THE LINE.

61st Division Intelligence Summary No. 7.
Period covered: 6 a.m. 19th - 6 a.m. 20th Sept.
Visibility: Good.

OUR ACTIVITY.

Infantry.
Patrols were active throughout the night, and established the fact that the enemy was still holding his line in strength, and keenly combating any attempt to penetrate his wire. Bright moonlight hindered our patrols very much, and increased the enemy's alertness correspondingly.

Artillery.
The usual harassing fire was maintained on the enemy's forward positions during the period.

Machine Guns.
37,000 rounds expended on selected targets, particular attention being paid to tracks and roads.

Trench Mortars.
6" Newtons engaged suspected hostile M.G. emplacements in ERQUINGHEM. 3" Stokes fired on the strong point in H.9.b, H.32.a.8.8, and houses at H.3.d.8.2.

Aerial.
Activity slightly decreased until evening, when the enemy's lines were crossed several times.

HOSTILE ACTIVITY.

Infantry.
No patrols or working parties seen.
It is believed that listening posts were pushed forward from hostile posts, to take full advantage of the moonlight in detecting the approach of our patrols.
Enemy post at H.26.a.0.4 was held strongly.

Artillery.
Artillery slightly increased. After being registered in the early morning, G.11 was subjected to harassing fire throughout the period. Much attention was also given to G.12, 17, & 18.
Night firing was of the usual scattered description in the area E. of the LYS, especially in the vicinity of all roads.
Blue Cross gas shelling was reported on G.31.a.& b, G.36.d, and G.25.d. H.V. guns were inactive.

Machine Guns.
Much activity, especially against our patrols.

Trench Mortars.
Slightly increased. 30 rounds M.T.M. on H.25.d, and a few bursts of L.T.M. fire on our advanced posts in the right subsector.
3 incendiary T.M. bombs burst over WINTER'S NIGHT POST.

Aerial.
One flight of 6 machines, and 2 single 'planes, crossed our line towards evening, but did not penetrate far.
E.O.Bs: Only one in position (139° G.B. from G.28.d.75.30).

Explosions.
House at G.36.d.85.65 went up; the road was undamaged.

(P.T.O.)

Lights & Signals.
 A considerable number of single red lights throughout the night, without apparent action resulting.

Work & Defences.
 Wire at H.15.a.3.9 and H.9.d.3.7 - also 300 yds. south of the latter point - forms a strong obstacle, and is covered by M.Gs.

- - - - - - - - - - - - - - -

Foot Artillery Regts.
 Shoulder-straps bearing Nos. 11 and 21 have been found on old German tunics in G.36.a.

20.9.18.

E.G. Bates Lieut.
for G.S., 61st Divn.

(Copy)   APPENDIX LIa.

G.O.C., 182 Inf.Bde.

    G.841.   21st.

Will you please congratulate Lieut. THOMAS, 2/8 WORCESTER Regt. and his patrol on their excellent work.

    G.O.C., 61st Divn.

                                          (Sd.) G. Bates, Lt.

War Diary   Appendix LII

S E C R E T.   61st DIVISION.   G.C. 79.
Locations of Units at 6 a.m., 22.9.18.

Ref. Shts. 36A & 36.

DIV.H.Q. "G"	RILL WORKS, L.33.b.	
do. "A" & "Q",	CROIX MARRAISSE, J.21.c.	

182 Inf. Bde. (RIGHT BDE., C.B.L.), H.Q. L.27.a.0.3.
- 2/6 Warwicks, (Support Bn.) L.28.b.9.9.
- 2/7 Warwicks, (Reserve Bn.) YAM FM., L.22.a.
- 2/8 Worcesters, (Line Bn.) L.23.d.4.6.
- L.T.M.B., FELT FM., L.27.b.

183 Inf. Bde. (ADVANCED GUARD BDE.), H.Q. G.14.a.05.05.
- 9th North.Fus., (Left Bn.) G.18.a.15.15.
- 11th Suffolks, (Support Bn.) G.20.b.4.8.
- 1st E. Lancs., (Right Bn.) G.34.d.60.45.
- L.T.M.B., G.14.c.65.90.

184 Inf. Bde. (LEFT BDE., C.B.L.), H.Q., G.8.a.8.1.
- 2/4 Oxfords, (detached).
- 2/5 Glosters, (Support Bn.) L.16.a.8.5.
- 2/4 R. Berks, (Line) G.8.b.0.2.
- L.T.M.B., G.1.d.9.5.

C.R.A. RILL WORKS, L.33.b.
- 306 Bde. R.F.A., (Advanced Bde. Group) G.13.b.6.3.
- 307 do. (Rear Group) L.10.d.7.3.
- D.A.C. L.20.c.7.0.
- D.T.M.O. L.17.b.75.10.

61 Bn. M.G.C. H.Q., L.34.d.3.9.
- "A" Coy., (Left Coy., C.B.L.) L.6.c.5.3.
- "B" Coy., (Advanced Guard Coy.) G.27.d.5.5.
- "C" Coy., (Advanced Guard Coy.) G.23.a.8.3.
- "D" Coy., (Right Coy., C.B.L.) L.34.d.3.6.

C.R.E. L.27.d.8.4.
- 476 Field Co. R.E. K.23.c.6.3.
- 478 do. G.14.a.5.3.
- 479 do. L.26.b.7.3.

1/5 D.C.L.I. (P), H.Q. & 2 Coys., L.30.c.95.80.
                           1 Coy., G.8.a.6.7.

A.D.M.S. CROIX MARRAISSE, J.21.c.
- 2/1 Field Amb., L.27.c.2.6 (Main Dressing Stn.).
- 2/2 do. J.27.d.8.7.
- 2/3 do. L.22.c.2.3.

61 Div. Train. J.27.a.7.7.
- No. 1 Coy., K.14.b.5.4.
- No. 2 Coy., K.24.d.3.6.
- No. 3 Coy., J.22.c.4.7.
- No. 4 Coy., K.23.a.2.4.

D.G.O. RILL WORKS, L.33.b.
- Anti-Gas Depot, L.27.c.1.5.
- Advanced Depot, G.27.b.6.5.

Div. P. of W. Cage, L.29.a.5.6.

21.9.18.

                                           E.S. Bates Lieut.
                                         for G.S., 61 Div.

APPENDIX LIII

S E C R E T — NOT TO BE TAKEN BEYOND BATTALION H.Q. IN THE LINE.
61st Division Intelligence Summary No. 8.
Period: 6 a.m. 20th – 6 a.m. 21st Septr. 1918.
Visibility: Good.

OUR ACTIVITY.

Infantry.
Determined patrolling was carried out between dusk and dawn, and close touch maintained with enemy posts.
A fighting patrol, operating in the vicinity of BARTLETTE FM., encountered heavy opposition, which prevented the enemy wire being penetrated; our patrol, having sustained casualties, was reinforced, and continued to observe the hostile position; finally, after being in close contact with the enemy for two hours, our patrol withdrew, after having gained much information.

Artillery.
Orchards, roads, and tracks in the enemy's forward area were harassed, and three special shoots carried out.

Machine Guns.
18,000 rounds expended on selected targets.

Trench Mortars.
6" Newtons engaged BARTLETTE FM. and adjacent hedges, good shooting being observed.

Aerial.
Activity maintained.

ENEMY ACTIVITY.

Infantry.
The enemy attitude remains exceedingly alert, and it is evident that the BARTLETTE FM and JUNCTION POST areas are both held very strongly still. Our patrol at the former place encountered two hostile parties; the first engaged a section of our patrol near H.26.a.3.4 with rifle fire; the other, which was very strong, moved towards our patrol from the road between H.20.c.5.5 & H.20.c.9.0; this was engaged by rifle and L.G. fire with success. The enemy was heard shouting for reinforcements. Throughout the period our troops were in contact with him, the hostile fire was extremely severe.
An attempt to outflank a small party of ours near JUNCTION POST forced our patrol to withdraw in face of heavy enemy fire.

Artillery.
Rather quieter, and no registration during the period. A certain amount of retaliation to our heavies. The BAC ST.MAUR – SAILLY area, H.31, and the ROUGE DE BOUT cross-roads, received most attention, from all calibres. No gas shelling is reported.
A.A. batteries very active against our machines.

Machine Guns.
Extremely heavy shooting, both against our patrols and with long-range overhead fire. The   patrol at JUNCTION POST was engaged by at least 5 guns with great intensity.
Guns located at H.20.c.9.1, H.26.a.8.6; the former covers the hostile wire at H.26.a.3.4.

Trench Mortars.
T.M. firing from near BARTLETTE FM., dropped several rounds near our post at H.25.b.7.2.

(P.T.O.)

(2)

Aerial.
Slightly increased.
5 single machines crossed our line during the day.
E.O.Bs: 3 in position, at respective G.Bs. of 90°, 105°, and 130° from G.34.d.5.4.

Work & Defences.
1. Post at H.25.b.90.55 unoccupied, and showing no signs of recent use; this is an earth mound, with a M.G. loophole.
2. Strong rifle post suspected in southern corner of enclosure in H.20.c. Posts about H.32.b.4.5 not occupied. A large quantity of loose wire strewn about near this place.
3. Suspected pill-box in orchard at about H.32.a.7.5.
4. There is a barricade across the road at H.26.a.15.15, and wire across the ditches at each side of this point.

Explosions and Fires.
MOULIN FOURNEAUX (G.22.b.) and the cross-roads in SAILLY (G.22.a.) both blew up, a very large crater being formed at the latter place.
Two large fires in the vicinity of ARMENTIRES are reported.

- - - - - - - - - - - - -

Identifications.
140 I.R., 40 Div. A pigeon, which was shot down in our lines yesterday evening, carried a message dated 16th Septr. from the 3rd Coy. of 140 I.R.

100 Res. Gren. Regt. - TWO TREE FARM. Shoulder-strap identification obtained in course of this morning's raid by Divn. on our right.

Operation by Divn. on our right.
At 4.36 a.m. this morning the Division on our right carried out an attack, in conjunction with an oil-drum projection, on TWO TREE FM.
Strong opposition was encountered, and, after inflicting casualties on the enemy and obtaining an identification, the raiding party was forced to withdraw.

21.9.18.

E.S. Bates Lieut.
for G.S., 61st Divn.

APPENDIX LIV

S E C R E T — NOT TO BE TAKEN BEYOND BATTALION H.Q. IN THE LINE.

61st Division Intelligence Summary No. 9.

Period covered: 6 a.m. 21st - 6 a.m. 22nd Septr.
Visibility: Good.

OUR ACTIVITY.

Infantry.
Our patrols reconnoitred the enemy's positions throughout the night, and again had complete command of NO MAN'S LAND.

Artillery.
Active harassing fire maintained on the enemy's forward positions. 3 concentration shoots carried out on H.22.c. in co-operation with H.A.

Machine Guns.
12,000 rounds expended on selected targets.

Trench Mortars.
6" hows. fired on the wire at H.26.a.20.55 and H.26.a.3.2, with good results. Buildings at H.15.c.4.2 were also engaged; also BARTLETTE FM., one end of which we demolished.
3" Stokes carried out shoots on H.3.d.8.2 and H.9.b.6.6, obtaining several direct hits on the latter target.

Aerial.
Great activity throughout the period. Hostile machines were engaged, but retired hastily. One of our 'planes forced to land about G.29.a.

ENEMY ACTIVITY.

Infantry.
Attitude remains alert, but somewhat quieter. No hostile parties were encountered, but voices were heard in enemy post at H.25.b.9.5.

Artillery.
Normal. G.10.c was heavily shelled after air-burst registration. BAC ST.MAUR, G.27, and G.11 were favourite targets, 50 rounds of gas shell falling in the latter vicinity. Other shelling was, as usual, scattered over a wide area E. of the LYS. H.V. guns remained inactive.

Machine Guns.
Very active all night, and against our aeroplanes by day. Guns located at H.26.a.5.5, H.26.a.9.9, H.3.b.8.2, H.15.c.6.8, and H.9.b.9.3 - the last-mentioned in a tree.

Trench Mortars.
L.T.Ms. fired on H.13, H.9.a.& c, and H.25.b. Emplacement suspected at H.33.a.5.1.

Aerial.
Slightly increased; heavily engaged, both from the air and ground.

Work & Defences.
Thick belt of wire, double-apron, with loose wire thrown in, at H.32.c.55.50.
Digging proceeded between H.20.c.9.0 to H.26.a.5.5.
Stakes being driven in N. of railway in H.15.a.

Movement.
2 men seen in JUNCTION POST.
Individual movement in trench between H.15.c.2.6 - H.15.c.8.8.

(P.T.O.)

Lights & Signals.
    Again a large number of single and double red lights went up from the enemy lines without apparent action resulting.

Explosions.
    Explosions due to enemy mines occurred at the LEVEL CROSSINGS at G.29.b.30.48, the house at G.17.central, and a house in G.16.b.

    Fires in the direction of ARMENTIERES were again reported.

Pigeons.
    Several pigeons have been seen near LAVENTIE, where the enemy used to have a loft.

22.9.18.

E.G. Bates Lieut
for G.S., 61st Divn.

(Copy) APPENDIX LV.

Commanding Northumberland Fusiliers.

22nd.

I have heard of death of Major EBBSWORTH with the deepest regret.

(Sd.) F.J. DUNCAN.

General Duncan.

Appendix LVI

S E C R E T — NOT TO BE TAKEN BEYOND BATTALION H.Q. IN THE LINE.

61st Division Intelligence Summary No. 10.

Period covered: 9 a.m. 22nd - 9 a.m. 23rd Septr.
Visibility: Fair until afternoon, when spoilt by rain.

OUR ACTIVITY.

Infantry.
The Divisional front was patrolled throughout the night, the enemy's posts being consistently harassed, and his wire reconnoitred.

Artillery.
Active harassing fire during the period on roads and trenches in the enemy's forward zone.
Goods results were observed from special shoots on BARTLETTE FM., houses in H.21.d., and hospital in H.15.c.
A section of 18-pdrs. went forward in daylight and fired 200 rounds on selected targets.
The main road in H.20.d. and the cross-roads at H.22.b.95.10 were kept under constant 4.5" How. fire.

Machine Guns.
10,000 rounds expended on roads and tracks in H.20.b. and H.21.a: also on FLEURBAIX and approaches to that place.

Trench Mortars.
6" Newtons fired on wire in H.32.a. and H.9.b: also on the JUNCTION POST and BARTLETTE FM. wire.
3" Stokes were very active, and fired 130 rounds on various targets.

Aerial.
Much in evidence during the early part of the period. One was forced down in G.28.a. by hostile fighters, but effected a good landing.

ENEMY ACTIVITY.

Infantry.
No patrols were encountered. The garrison of a post at H.9.b.2.2 was alert, and bombed one of our patrols, who replied by revolver shots into the post. Rifles were fired from H.32.c.7.5.

Artillery.
Rather less active. G.11 was very heavily shelled in the afternoon and evening, and BAC ST. MAUR in the early morning. Other shelling was much decreased.
H.V. guns fired a few rounds on L.34.a.
Blue Cross gas shells fell in G.33.d.

Machine Guns.
A certain amount of harsssing fire, but the guns opposite our right subsection were kept much quieter by the great activity of our M.Gs. and L.Gs.
3 guns fired from BARTLETTE FM. on our patrols.
Other guns located at approximately H.21.a.2.3, H.15.c.1.4, and H.9.b.2.2.
Very active against our aircraft.

Trench Mortars.
Retaliated to our H.T.Ms., and fired on H.25.b.5.4.
Emplacement suspected about H.10.c.1.9.

(P.T.O.)

(2)

Aerial.
Increased, but no low flying. Fighters engaged our 'planes several times. Our R.E.8s were attacked by hostile scouts and pursued, but none were brought down.

Work & Defences.
Thick belt of high wire at corner of enclosure H.32.a.55.65. Belt of wire 3 ft. high at H.9.b.2.0. A second belt, apparently new, 5 ft. high, 10 ft. thick, at H.9.b.6.1; good condition, and no gaps.

Movement.
2 men seen in trench at H.21.a.25.30.
Movement again reported in trench about H.15.a.7.8.
Our patrols heard sound of movement about H.32.a.6.5.

Explosion.
An explosion occurred 41° G.B. from G.28.d.95.30 (8.35 p.m.).

- - - - - - - - - - - - -

Air Photographs.
Photos. taken 22nd show shallow trench between H.36.b.35.70 and H.30.d.31.27, and another shallow trench at H.20.b.85.20.

E G Bates Lieut
for G.S., 61st Divn.

23.9.18.

(Copy)   APPENDIX LVII.

182 Bde.	C.R.A.	28 Bde.RGA.
183 Bde.	C.R.E.	"Q".
184 Bde.	61 Bn.MGC.	Div.Signals.

G.870.   24th.

Corps Intelligence reports that the forward wireless stations of 4th and 23rd Res. Divs. opposite to us have been silent for the last 24 hours aaa The utmost vigilance must be exercised to dete any signs of enemy withdrawal aaa Addsd all concerned.

61 Div.

2.55 p.m.

(Sd.) E.G.Bates, Lt.
for G.S.

SECRET.   G.C. 79.
                          61st DIVISION.
                  Locations of Units at 6 a.m., 25.9.18.

Ref.Shts.36A & 36.

    DIV. H.Q. "G"   RILL WORKS, L.33.b.
       do.   "A" & "Q".   CROIX MARRAISSE, J.21.c.

    182 Inf.Bde. (RIGHT BDE., C.B.L.), H.Q. L.27.a.0.3.
       2/6 Warwicks,   (Line Bn.) L.23.d.4.6.
       2/7 Warwicks,   (Reserve Bn.) YAM FM., L.22.a.
       2/8 Worcesters,   (Support Bn.) L.28.b.9.9.
       L.T.M.B.,   FELT FM., L.27.b.

    183 Inf.Bde. (ADVANCED GUARD BDE.), H.Q. L.12.c.8.3.
       9th North.Fus.   (Left Bn.) G.18.a.15.15.
       11th Suffolks,   (Support Bn.) G.20.b.4.8.
       1st E. Lancs.   (Right Bn.) G.34.d.60.45.
       L.T.M.B.   G.14.c.65.90.

    184 Inf.Bde. (LEFT BDE., C.B.L.), H.Q. G.8.a.8.1.
       2/4 Oxfords,   (Reserve Bn.) L.12.c.7.7.
       2/5 Glosters.   (Support Bn.) L.16.a.8.5.
       2/4 R.Berks.   (Line Bn.) G.8.b.0.2.
       L.T.M.B.   G.1.d.9.5.

    C. R. A.   RILL WORKS, L.33.b.
       306 Bde. R.F.A.   (Advanced Bde. Group) G.13.b.6.3.
       307   do.   (Rear Group) L.10.d.7.3.
       D.A.C.   L.20.c.7.0.
       D.T.M.O.   L.17.b.75.10.

    61 Bn. M.G.C.   H.Q., L.34.d.3.9.
       "A" Coy.   (Left Coy., C.B.L.) L.6.c.5.3.
       "B" Coy.   (Advanced Guard Coy.) G.27.d.5.5.
       "C" Coy.   (Advanced Guard Coy.) G.23.a.8.3.
       "D" Coy.   (Right Coy., C.B.L.) L.34.d.3.6.

    C. R. E.   L.27.d.8.4.
       476 Field Co. R.E.   K.23.c.6.3.
       478   do.   G.14.a.5.3.
       479   do.   L.26.b.7.3.

    1/5 D.C.L.I.(P),   H.Q. & 2 Coys. L.30.c.95.80.
                                1 Coy. G.8.a.6.7.

    A. D. M. S.   CROIX MARRAISSE, J.21.c.
       2/1 Field Amb.   L.26.c.8.7 (Main Dressing Stn.).
       2/2   do.   J.27.d.8.7.
       2/3   do.   L.22.c.2.3.

    61 Div. Train.   J.27.a.7.7.
       No. 1 Coy.   K.14.b.5.4.
       No. 2 Coy.   K.24.d.3.6.
       No. 3 Coy.   L.28.c.3.6.
       No. 4 Coy.   K.23.a.2.4.

    D. G. O.   RILL WORKS, L.33.b.
       Anti-Gas Depot,   L.27.c.1.5.
       Advanced Depot,   G.27.b.6.5.

    Div. P.of W. Cage,   L.29.a.5.6.

24.9.18.   G.S., 61st Divn.

Appendix LIX

S E C R E T — NOT TO BE TAKEN BEYOND BATTALION H.Q. IN THE LINE.

61st Division Intelligence Summary No. 11.

Period covered: 6 a.m. 23rd – 6 a.m. 24th Septr.
Visibility: Fair to good.

OUR ACTIVITY.

Infantry.
Our patrols continued their activity between dusk and dawn, repeatedly gaining touch with hostile posts and examining the enemy's wire.

Artillery.
Roads, tracks, and fences in enemy's forward zone were severely harassed. Several special shoots were carried out, and excellent shooting reported. Between midnight and 1 a.m. an area shoot, in co-operation with H.A., took place on BARTLETTE FM. and vicinity.

Machine Guns.
25,000 rounds on roads, tracks, and trenches; also on suspected enemy M.G. emplacements.

Trench Mortars.
6" Newtons fired 113 rounds on wire at JUNCTION POST, BARTLETTE FM: also on H.9.b. and H.14.d. Good results were observed, in each case the wire was badly damaged.
3" Stokes fired 134 rounds, also with good effect, on various targets.

Aerial.
Normal until evening, when very great activity was noticed.
An R.E.8 was brought down in flames by a hostile scout at 5.15 p.m., falling in the enemy's lines 171° G.B. from H.13.d.8.2.

ENEMY ACTIVITY.

Infantry.
No hostile parties encountered.
Posts at H.9.b.45 53, H.3.d 36.17, H.3.d.38.32, all occupied by enemy Snipers were active from BARTLETTE FM.

Artillery.
Active throughout period.
Considerable number of small area shoots, and much high shrapnel.
Two shoots carried out on NOUVEAU MONDE by 8".
H.8, G.27, G.11, BAC ST MAUR, SAILLY, and the road between these two places, were heavily fired on.
Gas shelling is reported in G.24.a. and G.23.a.
Other shelling was intermittent, and scattered over the usual areas E. of the LYS.

Machine Guns.
Active along whole Divisional front throughout the night, replying vigorously to our M.G. fire.

Trench Mortars.
Inactive, except for a few rounds on H.25.d. – a usual target.

Aerial.
Some activity of high-flying machines.
E.O.Bs. 2 in position, 141° and 111° G.B. respectively from G.35.a.8.6.

(P.T.O.)

Work & Defences.
    Wire at H.9.b.45.65 double belt of apron fence on screw pickets;
    good condition, and no gaps.
    Wire round JUNCTION POST at H.32.a.5.6 still <u>uncut</u> - gaps have been
    filled in with loose wire.
    4 belts of thick wire protecting BARTLETTES FM. 20 - 25 yds. thick.

Movement.
    2 men at H.15.c.1.4 waved a black flag, and disappeared when fired
    on.   Movement at BARTLETTES FM., TREF O.P., and H.20.d.3.1 (hostile
    observer suspected at latter point) ceased on being engaged.

Fires & Explosions.
    Explosion in C.29.a. (3 p.m.).
    Fire observed in FLEURBAIX (3.30 p.m.).
    Fire on 78° G.B. from H.3.c.75.40.

Lights & Signals.
    White parachute light dropped over BAC ST. MAUR 11.30 p.m.
    Double white rocket every 6 minutes on 100° G.B. from G.35.a.8.6.

                                            EG Bates Lieut.

24.9.18.
                                            for G.S., 61st Divn.

Appendix LX

S E C R E T — NOT TO BE TAKEN BEYOND BATTALION H.Q. IN THE LINE.

61st Division Intelligence Summary No. 12.
Period covered: 6 a.m. 24th – 6 a.m. 25th Septr.
Visibility: Fair to good.

OUR ACTIVITY.

Operations.
At 11.5 p.m. 460 gas projectors and 40 smoke projectors were discharged on JUNCTION POST & BARTLETTE FM.

Infantry.
Our patrols showed great activity, and ascertained that the enemy was still holding his line.

Artillery.
Registration and harassing fire on enemy's forward zone. Suspected M.G.Es. included in the targets. Bombardment in co-operation with gas projection was carried out.

Machine Guns.
28,000 rounds expended, including a special shoot in conjunction with artillery during gas projection.

Trench Mortars.
6" Newtons continued wire cutting in the neighbourhood of BARTLETTE FM., JUNCTION POST, and H.9.b. Road and houses in H.15.a. also fired on.
3" Stokes fired 120 rounds on various targets, very good shooting being observed. Casualties were probably caused in hostile post at H.32.a.8.4.

Aerial.
Scouts and artillery machines showed continued activity.

ENEMY ACTIVITY.

Infantry.
The garrisons of BARTLETTE FM. & JUNCTION POST were very quiet for a long while after our projection discharge, and fired no lights.
A hostile patrol, 9 strong, among their own wire about H.9.b.50.45, bombed one of our patrols.
An enemy party of 10, apparently carrying wire at H.9.c.8.2, was engaged with bombs and rifle grenades, and withdrew.
Hostile wiring party at H.15.c.05.65 dispersed by rifle grenade fire.
Post at H.9.b.7.3 was held.

Artillery.
Fairly active. No retaliation forthcoming to our gas projection. BAC ST.MAUR, SAILLY cross-roads, G.10.a, and FORT ROMPU vicinity, were favourite targets. NOUVEAU MONDE & ESTAIRES received attention also.
Gas shelling is reported on NOUVEAU MONDE & G.25.
H.8.d.3.7 was shelled, apparently in reply to enemy red lights.
The usual amount of scattered intermittent shelling is reported.

Machine Guns.
Decreased activity. BARTLETTE FM. guns silent. Guns located H.32.a.4.4, H.9.b.6.6 (2).

(P.T.O.)

(2)

Trench Mortars.
L.T.Ms. shelled H.14, and H.T.Ms. H.8.c. slightly; otherwise inactive.

Aerial.
Considerable throughout the period, and several determined attempts to cross our line - generally prevented by our machines and A.A.fire.
At 5.20 p.m. 4 E.As. penetrated our defence, but were soon turned back; 2 of these carried German markings, but 2 carried no markings.
E.O.Bs: Only one in position, a long way behind the enemy lines.

Work & Defences.
Double apron fence at JUNCTION POST uncut.
Wire at BARTLETTE FM. cut in two places, but otherwise still very strong.
Thin belt of wire at H.9.b.3.6.
Work proceeding in posts at H.9.d.20.45.
Post at H.9.b.6.6 protected by a double apron fence.

Movement.
No movement was observed during daylight.

Lights.
During our bombardment at 11.50 p.m. white and red Very lights were sent up in quick succession.
20 orange Very lights were observed at 3.25 a.m. on our right.

Explosions & Fires.
Large clouds of smoke in enemy back areas 142° G.B. from G.35.a.8.4.
Large explosion caused in enemy's lines by our bombardment (11.10 pm).

O.Ps.
Tree at H.20.d.50.55.

Searchlight.
Active, 128° G.B. from G.28.d.95.30.

Railways.
Column of smoke from an engine seen 128° G.B. from G.28.d.95.30.

25.9.18.

E.G.Bates Lieut.
for G.S., 61st Divn.

Addenda.

Identification: 2nd Guard Res.Div. N. of VIOLAINES. Prisoner of 77 R.I.R. captured this morning on ESTAIRES - LA BASSEE road. 9th Res.Div., which occupies the sector immediately S. of 23rd Res.Div., appears to be in process of relief by 2nd Guard Res.Div., which was withdrawn from the ARRAS Sector during the last week of August.

Operation by Divn. on Left: Posts were established last night at B.24.a.1.1 B.23.b.8.2, B.23.b.7.3, B.17.d.6.4, B.17.d.1.9. Considerable opposition met with in establishing posts in B.17.d. Enemy hold line road from B.17.d.6.6 - B.17.d.3.7 with M.G. B.17.d.4.6.

Operation by Corps on Right: Corps on Right report 10.20 a.m. that they have taken line of East side of LA BASSEE Road from S.11.a.5.4 - the DISTILLERY - SHEPHERD'S REDOUBT and PIONEER DUMP, all inclusive. Prisoners estimated 60 and our casualties slight.

APPENDIX LXI

S E C R E T.   Copy No. 21

              61st DIVISION ORDER No. 206.   25.9.18.

Ref. Map 36, 1/40,000.
     36A, 1/40,000.

1. 184 Infantry Bde. will relieve 183 Infantry Bde. as Advanced Guard Bde. on the nights 26th/27th and 27th/28th inst., as follows :-

   (a) On night 26th/27th inst. one battalion of 184 Infantry Bde. will relieve one battalion of 183 Infantry Bde., and will come under orders of G.O.C. 183 Infantry Bde. until completion of relief on night 27th/28th inst.
       Similarly, the relieved battalion of 183 Infantry Bde. will come under the orders of G.O.C. 184 Infantry Bde.

   (b) On the night 27th/28th inst. the 184 Infantry Bde. (less one battalion) will relieve 183 Infantry Bde. (less one battalion) and will take over the duties of Advanced Guard Bde. from the hour of relief.

2. The following troops, which form part of the Advanced Guard, will come under orders of G.O.C. 184 Infantry Bde. on completion of relief :-

        1 Brigade, plus 1 Battery, R.F.A.
        1 Field Coy. R.E.
        2 Coys. 61st Bn. M.G.C.

3. On relief, the 183 Infantry Bde. will withdraw to, and be responsible for, the defence of the Northern Area of the Corps Battle Line, and will take over accommodation vacated by the 184 Infantry Bde.

4. Command will pass on completion of relief, which will be notified to D.H.Q.

5. All further details of relief and moves will be arranged by Commanders concerned.

6. ACKNOWLEDGE.

Issued at 6 p.m.

                                                for Lieut.-Col.,
                                                G.S., 61st Division.

Distribution :-

Copy No. 1 - A.D.C. for G.O.C.   12-13 - XI Corps.
       2 - 61 Div. Signals.   14 - 28 Bde. R.G.A.
     3-4 - 61 Div. Art.   15 - 40th Div.
       5 - C.R.E.   16 - 59th Div.
       6 - 61 Bn. M.G.C.   17-18 - "Q".
       7 - 1/5 D.C.L.I.   19 - D.G.O.
       8 - 182 Inf. Bde.   20 - "G".
       9 - 183 Inf. Bde.   21-22 - War Diary.
     10 - 184 Inf. Bde.   23 - D.A.P.M.
     11 - A.D.M.S.   24 - Div. Train.

S E C R E T.

Appendix LXII

Copy No. 17

61st DIVISION INSTRUCTIONS No. 6.

OPERATIONS.

Information. 1. There are still indications of a possible further withdrawal of the enemy on the XI Corps front.
In order to ascertain at short notice whether the enemy is withdrawing, the Advanced Guard Brigade Commander will be prepared to carry out the necessary reconnaissance in force, in the form of an operation with (approximately) one battalion on a selected portion of the front. Preparation will be made to carry out this operation at 48 hours notice.

Intention. 2. Information as to the actual withdrawal of the enemy as a result of the above operation, or from other sources, will be immediately followed by a vigorous renewal of our advance

Objectives. 3. The Objectives to be reached will be :-
1st Objective: CROIX BLANCHE - FLEURBAIX - ERQUINGHEM.
2nd Objective: LA BOUTILLERIE (exclusive) - BOIS GRENIER - RUE MARLE (exclusive).

Dispositions for an advance. 4. In order to ensure greater vigour to our further advance, the Division will be prepared to operate on a front of two Brigades, thereby facilitating command and control by Brigade and Battalion Commanders.
Twenty-four hours' notice of such a change will, however, be given; it being undesirable to alter the present dispositions until further information of the enemy's intention to withdraw is obtained.

5. Orders will accordingly be issued at the time for the Southern or Northern Brigade to move forward and take up the advance on the right or left of the Infantry Brigade forming the Advanced Guard, relieving troops of the Advanced Guard Brigade on its right or left battalion sector.
The two Infantry Brigades in the line will then become the "Right and Left" Brigades. Each will operate on a two-battalion front, without at first necessarily placing greater strength than at present in the front line.
The necessary artillery will be allotted to each of the above Infantry Brigades, and a reserve of artillery will be retained in the hands of the Divisional Commander.
One Company Machine Gun Battalion, one Field Section of R.E. & 1 platoon Pioneers, will be allotted to each Brigade.
The inter-Brigade boundary will be the grid line running East and West through H.19.central.

Position of Brigade and Battn. H.Q. 6. Headquarters of Brigades in the line, and of the Artillery Brigades supporting them, will be located in close proximity to one another, the Artillery and Infantry Brigade Headquarters being situated at the same spot in each case.
The bounds forward of these Headquarters will be laid down by Division.
The Headquarters of Infantry Battalions in the line on each Brigade front will similarly be situated close together as far as possible.

Accommodation in area vacated by enemy. 7. There is every reason to expect that the enemy has elaborated his system of mining dugouts, buildings, and cross-roads in the area over which the advance will take place. It is, therefore, important that the troops are

(P.T.O.)

(2)

warned beforehand to avoid any places likely to be mined. Headquarters of Brigades, Battalions, Companies, and Units of Divisional Troops will not occupy dugouts or buildings in the area vacated by the enemy. Accommodation must be taken forward or improvised, and arrangements made accordingly beforehand.
The Section Field Co. R.E. and Pioneers attached to Brigades will be employed to examine and mark enemy dugouts, shelters, etc. and to make the initial improvements of communications in forward area.

Brigade Forward Stations. 8. To ensure uniformity in the system of the collection and transmission of information during the advance, Brigade Forward Stations will be in charge of the Brigade Intelligence Officer with the Brigade Observer.
His duties will consist of :-
(a) Informing all Company and Battalion Commanders in front line as to the position of the Brigade Forward Station by means of his observers.
(b) Obtaining through his Observers information both as to the situation of our own troops and of the enemy.
(c) Transmitting all messages and information received to Brigade Headquarters, deciding on the priority of the messages as they are sent.
(d) Carrying out any instructions received from Brigade Headquarters, and so acting as the link between the Brigade Staff and fighting troops.
(e) Keeping the Artillery Liaison Officer or Artillery Commander at Brigade Headquarters constantly informed as to the line to which our infantry have advanced. The supporting artillery will thus be kept in touch with the situation at all times.

Communication. 9. Emphasis is again laid upon the importance of fully utilizing every alternative means of communication possible.
Lucas lamps must be more extensively used than has formerly been the case. There is no restriction to the use of the lamp in a forward direction.

10. Close touch will be maintained on the flanks of Brigades during the advance by means of liaison units composed under arrangements to be made between Brigades concerned.
Lateral communication and liaison between Brigades and Battalions in the line is essential to mutual cooperation, and will receive special consideration.

11. All details discussed at the Conference at Divisional Headquarters today, in reference to the organization, equipment, and mobility within formations and units, and other points of a similar nature, will be carefully considered and preparations made.

12. ACKNOWLEDGE.

25.9.18.

Lieut.-Col.,
G.S., 61st Division.

Distribution :-

Copy No. 1 - A.D.C. for G.O.C.
2 - 61 Signal Co.
3 - C.R.A.
4 - C.R.E.
5 - 61 Bn.M.G.C.
6 - 1/5 D.C.L.I.
7 - 182 Inf.Bde.
8 - 183 Inf.Bde.
9 - 184 Inf.Bde.
10 - A.D.M.S.
11 - XI Corps.
12 - 28 Bde.R.G.A.
13 - 40 Divn.
14 - 59 Divn.
15 - "Q".
16 - "G".
17-18 - War Diary.

SECRET.

Appendix LXIII
G.C. 31/1

AMENDMENT No. 1
to 61st Division Order No. 206.

All dates are postponed 24 hours.

26.9.18.

W.B. Dowden Maj.
for Lieut.-Col.,
G.S., 61st Divn.

To all recipients
of above Order.

Appendix LXIV

SECRET - NOT TO BE TAKEN BEYOND BATTALION H.Q. IN THE LINE.

61st Division Intelligence Summary No. 13.
Period covered: 6 a.m. 25th – 6 a.m. 26th Septr.
Visibility: Good, with one poor interval.

OUR ACTIVITY.

Infantry.
Our patrols maintained a thorough command of NO MAN'S LAND, and actively reconnoitred enemy wire.

Artillery.
Active harassing fire throughout the period on the enemy's forward area. A 4.5" how. battery was employed in cutting wire round BARTLETTE FM.

Machine Guns.
12,500 rounds expended.

Trench Mortars.
6" Newtons were engaged on wire-cutting in the vicinity of BARTLETTE FM. & JUNCTION POST. At the former place wire was badly damaged, and at the latter a gap appears to have been made at H.32.a.5.8.
Wire in H.9.b. and roads and houses in H.15.a. were also fired on.
3" Stokes were active on selected targets.

Aerial.
Much activity, especially by large fighting formations.
A good deal of night flying was carried out.

ENEMY ACTIVITY.

Infantry.
No hostile patrols seen.
A covering party, to a working party, were firing Very lights from H.15.a.20.75. The enemy was very alert, and his attitude showed signs of nervousness.

Artillery.
Rather below normal. G.10.b.& d, G.11.central, G.13.c, G.18, G.28, and G.34.a, were heavily shelled at times.
An increase of gas shelling is reported – LAVENTIE, G.31, G.34.a, H.8 & 9, being the areas affected. 200 rounds on LAVENTIE between 2 & 3 a.m. was the heaviest concentration.

Machine Guns.
Active, continually harassing our patrols. A gun was located about H.32.a.6.3, and another gun was firing from a screened position 121° G.B. from H.3.c.70.05.

Trench Mortars.
Increased slightly. WINTER'S NIGHT POST was a target, and H.13.d. and H.19.b. also received attention.

Aerial.
Below normal; only one machine penetrated our line.
E.O.Bs: 3 in position – 1 on G.B. of 135° from G.28.a.95.30.

Snipers.
Active from ruins in H.3.d.

(P.T.O.)

Work & Defences.
(1) Hostile working parties were heard at H.15.a.2.7 and H.32.a.5.6. Sounds of hammering proceeded from both these places.
(2) A line of old posts between BARTLETTE FM. and Farm at H.32.c.42.40 were unoccupied.
(3) Wire at H.32.a.5.6 is damaged, but still forms an obstacle.
(4) Wire at H.32.a.5.2 consists of 3 belts, practically intact. Between this point and H.32.a.5.5 wire is <u>not</u> passable, and there is much loose wire about.
(5) Wire at H.26.a.2.6 is badly damaged in one place only, and otherwise is very thick indeed.

Lights & Signals.
Green rockets and golden rain were sent up, without apparent action following.
Strings of white lights went up when our night-flying aircraft crossed the enemy lines.

Fires & Explosions.
Large flare in direction of ARMENTIERES (8.20 p.m.).
Mine exploded at G.24.a.5.5 (11.40 p.m.).
Railway running through H.14.a.& b. blew up in several places during the period.

Searchlights.
Active on G.Bs. 60°, 63°, 80°, & 84°, from G.28.d.95.30 (9.50 p.m.).

. . . .

Air Photographs.
42 HAB 210 of 25th shows following :-
Short trenches at H.9.d.7.7 and H.9.d.95.70.
Railway blown up where it crosses roads at H.10.c.10.65 and H.10.b.25.30.
Shell-holes worked on at H.16.a.1.7, H.16.a.15.78, and H.16.a.21.85.

E.G.Bates Lieut.

26.9.18.

For G.S., 61st Divn.

Appendix LXV

S E C R E T - NOT TO BE TAKEN BEYOND BATTALION H.Q. IN THE LINE.
61st Division Intelligence Summary No. 74.
Period covered: 6 a.m. 26th - 6 a.m. 27th Septr.
Visibility: Good.

OUR ACTIVITY.

Infantry.
At 10.10 p.m. a fighting patrol of the 1st East Lancs. Regt. attacked and captured BARTLETTE FM. (H.26.a.45.45.) and JUNCTION POST (H.32.a.9.3.) under cover of smoke and harmless gas projection, and with artillery, T.M. and M.G. support. A number of the enemy were killed and 9 prisoners (1 wounded) and 1 M.G. were taken.
About 6 a.m. a strong hostile counter-attack developed and our troops were forced to withdraw. It is reported that the counter-attack was made by about 300 of the enemy and accompanied by a barrage.

Later Report
We have established posts at the following points :-
H.19.b.60.25.   H.19.d.35.35.   H.19.d.77.75.

Artillery.
A box barrage was put down round JUNCTION POST at 7.10 a.m.
Harassing fire was directed on selected targets in the enemy's forward zone during the day and evening. Barrages were fired later in conjunction with operations.

Machine Guns.
40,000 rounds expended, including co-operation with our attack.

Trench Mortars.
6" Newtons continued wire cutting during the day and fired in support of subsequent operations.
3" Stokes fired 79 rounds on suspected M.G.E's and 44 rounds during our attack on hostile M.G. at H.26.c.25.40.

Aerial.
Very active. Our fighting machines repeatedly chased hostile planes and energetically prevented any patrolling on their part.
One of our machines was attacked by 8 hostile scouts but succeeded in driving them off one after another.

ENEMY ACTIVITY.

Artillery.
Considerable activity over a wide area.
Retaliation to our barrage was intense on H.25., otherwise not marked. H.13., G.18.a., G.12.a. and b., G.27.d. and BAC ST. MAUR were the principal targets during the period.
Some gas shell were put down on main road in G.17.c. and a Bridge in G.18.a. was registered with aeroplane registration and afterwards intermittently shelled.
H.V. guns were active against the ESTAIRES balloon.

Machine Guns.
Very active opposite Right Subsector between 10 and 11.30 p.m., otherwise unusually quiet.

Trench Mortars.
30 rounds on H.9.c.35.35. and 8 air bursts over H.9.c.5.4.
From 10 p.m. to 11 p.m. our Stokes Mortars were engaged in reply to their activity. From midnight onwards our front line in H.25.b. and H.32.a. was harassed.

Aerial.
Many attempts to cross our line were frustrated by our A.A. defences. This activity was most marked between 4.30 and 6 p.m.

(P. T. O.)

E.O.B's.
11 in position at various times.

Movement.
Individual movement at H.32.a.50.45. during the day.

Lights and Signals.
A great variety of coloured lights were sent up by the enemy during our barrage. Red, green, yellow, white, single and double, are reported, also a few golden rain rockets.

Fires and explosions.
An enemy mine exploded on the railway at G.29.c.15.15. Fires observed in FLEURBAIX, probably caused by our artillery.

Pigeons.
2 pigeons were released from enemy post at N.3.a.2.8. at 4.30 p.m. A pigeon caught near SAILLY bears the following marks :-
419 VL 158/18 on wing, 108 01962/18 on ring.

G.S. 61st Division.

27.9.18.

Identifications. (49 I.R. (BARTLETTE FARM).
100 Res.Gren.Regt. (JUNCTION POST.)
Prisoners captured last night in course of our attack on BARTLETTE FARM and JUNCTION POST comprise 6 O.R. of 49 I.R. 4th Div. at the former place, and 2 O.R. of 100 Res.Gren.Regt. 23rd Res.Div. at the latter. One wounded prisoner was also captured.

Order of Battle.
N. to S. appears to be 14 I.R., 49 I.R., 100 Res.Gren.Regt., 102 R.I.R. The boundary between 4th Divn. and 23rd Res. Divn. is stated to be at H.26.a.1.1. which would also be the boundary between the 4th and 6th German Armies.

Enemy Intentions.
Nothing definite known, but 4th Divn. appears to have orders to retake immediately any ground which may be lost. No work has been done recently on the front line.
49 I.R. relieved the 140 I.R. about a week ago. The latter is now in rest at LOMME. Two Bns. of 49 I.R. beliebed to be in front line with one in support. 7th Coy. has had considerable reinforcements and is stated to be 90 strong with 6 light M.Gs, and 2 heavy. Coy. front about 400 yards. Two coys. of 2nd Battn. stated to be in front with one or two in support (statements vary as to whether there are 3 or 4 coys. in the Battn.)
7th Coy. was to have been relieved at midnight last night by support Coy. and the stocks of ammunition and bombs had been reduced to a minimum.

Portugese.
Two escaped Portugese prisoners came into our lines during the night.

From Div. on our left.
The following wire timed 1.30 p.m. has been received from the Divn. on our left :- "Preliminary examination of prisoners of I.R.88 and I.R.186. Order of battle N. to S. I.R.186, 1st Bn. I.R.186 1st Bn. I.R.88. I.R.88 holds line West of LYS with 3 Coys. forward (N. to S. 4th, 3rd, 1st) 3rd Bn. in support on line through LE BIZET. 2nd Bn in rest near FRELINGHIN. Reliefs 1st Bn. I.R.88 relieved 2nd Bn. in front line on night 22/23. 1st Bn. I.R.186 relieved 3rd Bn. yesterday. All Bns. of I.R.186 and I.R.88 now reduced to 3 Coys. 56th Divn. received draft of 500 on 21st Recruit Depot at ALTER. Average Coy. strengths now about 80. Prisoners know of no intentions of further withdrawals. H.Q. of I.R.88 at ST. ANDRE. Light signals in force Red lengthen range, green barrage. Ends.

(Copy) APPENDIX LXVI.

183 Inf.Bde.

G.908.   27th

Following message from GEN. HAKING aaa Please ask Brig.Genl. ANLEY to tell Lt.Col. EARLE that I am very pleased to hear that troops of his battalion under Lt. LEYTON and 2/Lt. WEBSTER captured BARTLETT'S FARM and JUNCTION POST last night aaa timed 9.0 a.m.

61 Div.

(Sd.) E.C.Bates, Lt.

- - - - - - - - - -

Commanding 183 Bde.

Best congratulations your success aaa Am so glad success has come so soon to you aaa I have wired E. Lancs direct.

(Sd.) General DUNCAN.

- - - - - - - - - -

Commanding East Lancashires.

Best congratulations you and your brave men.

(Sd.) General DUNCAN.

Appendix LXVII

S E C R E T.

Copy No. 21

61st DIVISION ORDER No. 207

27th Sept. 1918.

Ref. Maps 36A. 1/40,000
36. 1/40,000

1. All moves ordered in Division Order No. 206 to take place on 28th/29th inst. are cancelled.

2. In accordance with 61st Division Instructions No. 6 dated 25th inst., preparations to renew an advance will immediately be made and the Divisional front will be re-organised on a two Brigade front, each Brigade being disposed in depth on a frontage of two Battalions, with one Brigade in Divisional Reserve.

3. The following moves and reliefs will accordingly be carried out on the night 28th/29th inst:-

    (a) 184 Inf. Bde. will relieve all units of 183 Inf. Bde. South of the inter-Brigade boundary given in the above-quoted instructions by 4 a.m. on 29th inst., and will become the Right Brigade.
    Brigade H.Qrs. will be established at L.12.c.8.3.
    Command of the Right Brigade Sector will pass to G.O.C. 184 Inf. Bde. on completion of relief.

    (b) The 182 Inf. Bde. will relieve all units of 183 Inf. Bde. North of the inter-Brigade boundary by the same hour and will become the Left Brigade,
    Brigade H.Qrs. will be established at G.8.a.8.1.
    Command of the Left Brigade Sector will pass to G.O.C. 182 Inf. Bde. on completion of relief.

    (c) The 183 Inf. Bde. on relief will move into Divisional Reserve into the area vacated by 182 Inf. Bde. with Headquarters at CHAPELLE DUVELLE, and battalions located in the areas MAURIANNE FM., YAM FARM and KENNET CROSS.

    (d) Reserve Battalions of Brigades in the Line will then take over the accommodation at present occupied by leading Battalions of Brigades in Corps Battle Line.

    (e) The Inf. Bde. in Divisional Reserve will be responsible for the defence of the Corps Battle Line and will relieve the present nucleus garrisons by 6 p.m. on 28th inst.

4. Divisional troops are allotted to the Right and Left Brigades as follows and will come under the orders of Brigade Commanders on completion of above reliefs :-

    1 F.A. Bde. (less 1 18-pdr. and 2 Sections 4.5" How. Battery)
    1 Coy. 61 Bn. M.G.C.
    1 Section Field Coy. R.E.
    1 Platoon 1/5 D.C.L.I. (Pioneers).

5. All further details of reliefs and moves will be arranged by Commanders concerned.

6. Completion of reliefs and moves will be wired to Div. H.Q.

7. ACKNOWLEDGE.

Lieut.Col.,
G.S., 61st Division.

Issued at 9.15 pm.

P.T.O.

DISTRIBUTION 61 DIVISION ORDER No.207.

```
Copy No. 1.  A.D.C. for G.O.C.
        2.  61 Div. Signals.
      3-4.  61 Div. Art.
        5.  C.R.E.
        6.  61 Bn. M.G.C.
        7.  1/5 D.C.L.I.
        8.  182 Inf. Bde.
        9.  183 Inf. Bde.
       10.  184 Inf. Bde.
       11.  A.D.M.S.
    12-13.  XI Corps.
       14.  28th Bde., R.G.A.
       15.  40th Division.
       16.  59th Division.
    17-18.  "Q"
       19.  D.G.O.
       20.  "G"
    21-22.  War Diary.
       23.  D.A.P.M.
       24.  61 Div. Train.
```

Appendix LXVIII

S E C R E T. — NOT TO BE TAKEN BEYOND BATTALION H.Q. IN THE LINE.

61st Division Intelligence Summary No. 15
Period covered: 8 a.m. 27th - 8 a.m. 28th.
Visibility: Good throughout.

OUR ACTIVITY.

Artillery.
Roads, houses and tracks behind the enemy line were harassed during the day, and a forward section of 4.5" Hows. carried out special shoots on houses in H.21.a. and H.20.d. and on BARTLETTE FM. and JUNCTION POST at regular intervals.
In the night firing programme particular attention was paid to enemy relief routes.

Machine Guns.
8,500 rounds expended.

Trench Mortars.
6" Newtons shot on Trenches H.26.a.8.6., H.32.b.5.6., H.32.b.30.25 and H.14.d.8.2.
3" Stokes fired on M.G.E. at H.3.d.6.2. and post at H.9.b.65.65.

Aerial.
Constant activity by artillery and fighting machines.
A night flying machine - nationality unknown - brought down by A.A. fire behind enemy lines at 1 a.m.
At 12.50 p.m. a hostile balloon was attacked and observer forced to descend in a parachute: Balloon was again attacked at 1.45 p.m. and another observer descended by parachute.

ENEMY ACTIVITY.

Infantry.
Two Germans approaching one of our posts in H.14. were fired on and one badly wounded, was brought into our lines.
It has been established that the captured man was a prisoner of war attempting to escape into the enemy's lines. He belonged to I Pioneer Bn. 15 (normally attached 30th German Div.)

Artillery.
Below normal. G.34.c., Road in G.35.a., G.24., G.29 and H.13 received most attention. Some gas shelling in H.18.b. and d. and on LAVENTIE.
Our right subsector front line was bombarded at 4 p.m. by 15 cm. Hows. H.E. and 10.5 cm. Gas.
15 cm. Hows. fired on BAC ST.MAUR and NOUVEAU MONDE.
H.V. gun active against ESTAIRES Balloon (2.30 p.m.)
A.A. fire only moderately active.

Machine Guns.
Renewed activity during the night, especially opposite the Left Subsector.

Trench Mortars.
Active on H.14.c.15.60.

Aerial.
4 attempts to penetrate our lines by single high flying machines were prevented by our A.A. defence and hostile 'planes retired without having made much progress.

K.C.Bs.
Were in position 66°, 110°, 127°, 147°, and 163° G.B. from H.13.c.60.96. also 100°, 117°, and 140° G.B. from G.23.b.45.85.

P.T.O.

Works and Defences.
    Working heard at H.9.d.10.25.

Lights and Signals.
    A good many single Red, double Orange and Golden Rain rockets during the hours of darkness.

Explosions.
    In H.26. G.B. 164° from H.13.c.60.36 (caused by our artillery).

....

Air Photos.
    Photo 42 HAB 233 taken yesterday shews wire from H.15.d.05.42 to H.15.b.6.3. with several posts behind.

E G Bates Lieut.

28.9.18.   G.S., 61 Division.

ADOPTION OF   CONTINENTAL SYSTEM OF TIME.

G.R.O. 5104 dated 26.9.18.

Continental System of Time, Adoption of, throughout the British Army.

    The Continental system of time - i.e., the 24 hour clock - will be brought into use throughout the British Army from midnight, 30th September/1st October, 1918.
    The "time of origin" that is, the time at which a message or despatch is signed by the originator, will always be represented by four figures, the first two figures, 01 to 23, representing the hours from midnight to midnight, and the second two figures, 01 to 59 representing the minutes of the hour.   For example :-

```
            12.10 a.m will be written  0010
             3.25 a.m.   "        "    0325
            11.0  a.m.   "        "    1100
            Noon                       1200
             3.25 p.m.   "        "    1525
            11.40 p.m.   "        "    2340
```

    0000 and 2400 will not be used, but the message or despatch will be timed 2359 or 0001.

(Copy)   APPENDIX LXIX

General Routine Order No. 5104
dated 26.9.18.

5104 - Continental System of Time - Adoption of, throughout the British Army. -

The Continental system of time - i.e., the 24 hour clock - will be brought into use throughout the British Army from midnight, 30th September/1st October, 1918.

The "time of origin" that is, the time at which a message or despatch is signed by the originator, will always be represented by four figures, the first two figures, 01 to 23, representing the hours from midnight to midnight, and the second two figures, 01 to 59, representing the minutes of the hour.   For example:-

        12.10 a.m. will be written 0010
         3.25 a.m.   "   "   0325
        11.0 a.m.   "   "   1100
        Noon   "   "   1200
         3.25 p.m.   "   "   1525
        11.40 p.m.   "   "   2340

0000 and 2400 will not be used, but the message or despatch will be timed 2359 or 0001.

(Authority:- A.O. IX, dated 17.9.18.)
(5781/O.)

Appendix LXX

G.S.84.

With reference to 61st Division Instructions No. 6 dated 25th inst. para. 7; an example of an enemy booby trap recently discovered is the following :-

Grenades, bombs, or boxes of perdite are placed under the floors of Nissen Huts, dug-outs, etc., and the striker mechanism attached by means of a wire to old clothes, rubbish, or odd articles on the floor. Any attempt to clear out the floors of these huts without careful inspection results in the wire being pulled and the explosive fired.

M Wetherby

Lieut.Col.,
G.S., 61 Division.

28.9.18.

To all recipients of 61 Div. Instructions No. 6.

APPENDIX LXXI

SECRET.

Copy No. 21
28.9.18.

61st DIVISION ORDER No. 208.

1. (a) The attack of American and French Armies between the MEUSE and SUIPPE Rivers is making good progress.
   The British offensive between the SCARPE and the SOMME still continues, and the First and Third British Armies attacked successfully North of HAVRINCOURT WOOD yesterday.
   The Belgian Army, assisted by the British Second Army and French troops, are attacking successfully East of the YSER.

   (b) As a result of the above operations, it is possible that the enemy forces opposed to us may be still further reduced, or that the German withdrawal may be continued to the DOUAI - LILLE Canal and the LILLE Defences.

2. In order to ascertain whether the enemy forces opposed to us have been weakened or are withdrawing, the 184 Infantry Bde. will carry out the minor operation, in accordance with instructions already issued, for the capture of JUNCTION POST and enemy trenches in H.32.a. b. & c. as far North-East as the RUE DES BASSIERES.
   Zero hour for this operation will be notified later.

3. In addition to the above, Brigades in the line will constantly test the strength of the enemy on their respective fronts by vigorous and carefully organized patrol work.
   Companies in the line will be prepared, on their own initiative, to act immediately on receipt of information that the enemy has withdrawn, and to make good the objectives already allotted to them, informing their battalion and companies on their flanks.

4. On the enemy retiring, the leading companies will form advanced guards to each Brigade, and will be directed to gain the most important tactical localities during the advance, and will not necessarily advance in lines or waves.
   The great necessity for vigour and boldness of all units in the advance, and the initiative of platoon, company, and battalion commanders, cannot be too strongly emphasized.

5. Brigade Commanders will carefully consider the necessity of the early relief of advanced units that have been engaged in continuous operations, so that the fatigue and strain occasioned by operations in the open may not tell too strongly on the men.

6. The Left Brigade will arrange for the protection of its left by means of a flank guard, until such time as the 40th Division of the XV Corps can gain the East side of ARMENTIERES. For this purpose, a second Machine Gun Company will be allotted to the Left Brigade.

7. Attention is again drawn to previous instructions as to the use of all means of inter-communication, and to the great importance of a constant flow of information from front to rear at all times in addition to the system of reports at stated times.

8. ACKNOWLEDGE.

Issued at 9.15 p.m.

Lieut.-Col.,
G.S., 61st Divn.

(P.T.O.)

Distribution :-

Copy No. 1 - A.D.C. for G.O.C.	12-13 - XI Corps.
2 - 61 Div. Signals.	14 - 28 Bde. R.G.A.
3-4 - 61 Div. Art.	15 - 40th Divn.
5 - C.R.E.	16 - 59th Divn.
6 - 61 Bn.M.G.C.	17-18 - "Q".
7 - 1/5 D.C.L.I.	19 - D.G.O.
8 - 182 Inf.Bde.	20 - "G".
9 - 183 Inf.Bde.	21-22 - War Diary.
10 - 184 Inf.Bde.	23 - D.A.P.M.
11 - A.D.M.S.	24 - 61 Div. Train.

SECRET.

61st DIVISION
Locations of Units at 6 a.m. 29.9.18.

G.C. 79

Ref. Shts. 36A & 36.

61 DIV.H.Q. "G"	RILL WORKS, L.33.b.
do. "A" & "Q"	CROIX MARRAISSE, J.21.c.

182 Inf.Bde. (LEFT BRIGADE), H.Q. G.8.a.8.1.
- 2/6 Warwicks,   (Left Bn.) G.12.c.
- 2/7 Warwicks,   (Reserve Bn.) G.8.b.0.2.
- 2/8 Worcesters,   (Right Bn.) G.18.a.15.15.
- L.T.M.B.   G.2.a.0.5.
                      (C.B.L.)

183 Inf.Bde. (RESERVE BDE.) H.Q. L.27.a.0.3.
- 9th North. Fus.   L.22.a.40.98.
- 11th Suffolks,   L.28.b.9.9.
- 1st E. Lancs.   G.35.a.20.25.
- L.T.M.B.   L.27.b.1.6.

184 Inf.Bde. (RIGHT BDE.), H.Q. L.12.c.8.3.
- 2/4 Oxfords,   (Right Bn.) G.25.a.10.15.
- 2/5 Glosters,   (Reserve Bn.) L.23.c.4.9.
- 2/4 R. Berks.   (Left Bn.) G.23.c.00.95.
- L.T.M.B.   Line.

C. R. A.
- 306 Bde. R.F.A.   RILL WORKS, L.33.b.
- 307   do.   (Rear Group) L.10.d.7.3.
- D.A.C.   (Advanced Group) G.13.b.6.3.
- D.T.M.O.   L.20.c.7.0.
                     L.17.b.75.10.

61 Bn. M.G.C.   H.Q., L.34.d.3.9.
- "A" Coy.,   (Right Bde. Coy.) G.23.a.8.3.
- "B" Coy.,   (Right Coy. C.B.L.) L.34.d.3.6.
- "C" Coy.,   (Left Coy. C.B.L.) L.6.c.5.3.
- "D" Coy.,   (Left Bde. Coy.) G.27.d.5.5.

C. R. E.   L.27.d.8.4.
- 476 Field Co.R.E. K.23.c.6.3.
- 478   do.   G.14.a.5.3.
- 479   do.   L.26.b.7.3.

1/5 D.C.L.I.(P),
- H.Q., L.30.c.95.80.
- 1 Coy., G.8.a.6.7.
- 2 Coys. L.30.a.7.5.

A. D. M. S.   CROIX MARRAISSE, J.21.c.
- 2/1 Field Amb.   L.26.c.8.7 (Main Dressing Stn.).
- 2/2   do.   J.27.d.8.7.
- 2/3   do.   L.22.c.2.3.

61 Div. Train.
- No. 1 Coy.   J.27.a.7.7.
- No. 2 Coy.   K.14.b.5.4.
- No. 3 Coy.   K.24.d.3.6.
- No. 4 Coy.   L.28.c.3.6.
                     K.23.a.2.4.

D. G. O.   RILL WORKS, L.33.b.
- Anti-Gas Depot,   L.27.c.1.5.
- Advanced Depot,   G.27.b.6.5.

Div. P. of W. Cage,   L.29.a.5.6.

28.9.18.

E.G. Bates Lieut.
for G.S., 61st Divn.

APPENDIX LXXIII

S E C R E T. - NOT TO BE TAKEN BEYOND BATTALION H.Q. IN THE LINE

61st Division Intelligence Summary No. 16

Period covered: 9 a.m. 28th - 9 a.m. 29th September.

Visibility: Very poor at first, afterwards improving.

OUR ACTIVITY.

Infantry.
Throughout the hours of darkness the Divisional front was energetically patrolled and it was definitely established that the enemy was in normal strength and giving no indication of immediate withdrawal.

Artillery.
Concentration shooting was carried out on BARTLETTE Fm., JUNCTION POST Buildings at H.10.d.2.3., H.29.c.30.65, H.23.c.25.30, H.33.d.4.3, Bridge at H.16.b.6.8, suspected T.M.E. at H.33.a.4.2, Shelters at H.28.b.4.5 and new work at H.27.c.4.5.

A house at H.15.a.80.75 from which smoke was seen rising was shot at with good results.

A forward section of 4.5" Hows. was engaged in wire-cutting around BARTLETTE Fm.

A short test 4.5" How. barrage put down on a line H.21.c - H.26.cent. (3 p.m.)

Harassing fire maintained on roads and tracks in enemy's forward area.

Machine Guns.
8,000 rounds expended on selected targets.

Trench Mortars.
6" Newtons engaged wire at JUNCTION POST, and in H.14.d.

Aerial. Heavy rain in the early part of the period prevented any flying but later when conditions became better there was much activity by all types of machines.

An E.O.B. was brought down in flames this morning.

ENEMY ACTIVITY.

Infantry.
BARTLETTE Fm., and JUNCTION POST was found to be strongly held and one of our patrols was bombed from the vicinity of the former place.

The hostile post at H.26.c.2.7 was unoccupied. 2 newly dug posts at H.9.d.0.5 and H.9.d.2.7 were held.

Enemy attitude was alert.

Artillery. Decreased activity.

FORT ROMPU, and BAC ST. MAUR were heavily shelled from 4.30 a.m. to 6 a.m. with 200 rounds 4.2.

The BAC ST. MAUR - SAILLY road and adjacent enclosures were intermittently harassed during early morning with 4.2 and 5.9

G.16.a, G.17, G.12.c and the road running N.E. through G.24.d., H.13.a., and H.13.d all received considerable attention. Blue cross gas being reported on the last named target.

Other shelling was scattered and fairly light and practically all from 105 and 150 mm. hows.

A number of gas shells were included in the shoots on FORT ROMPU, BAC ST. MAUR and G.17.

A.A. Batteries extremely active and making good practise.

Machine Guns.
Much activity especially from BARTLETTE Fm., and JUNCTION POST vicinity. Guns located at H.26.c.7.5., H.32.c.6.6., H.9.c.75.15 H.9.central, and H.20.d.2.7. At least 5 guns were reported firing simultaneously from the edge of the orchard between H.32.a.50.65 and H.32.a.7.5.

A great deal of fire against our aircraft and our M.G. positions were also engaged.

P.T.O.

- 2 -

Trench Mortars.
Several rounds L.T.M. on H.25.c. containing gas.
30 rounds on our Post in H.13.b.
L.T.M. fired on Road through H.25.b. and on H.31.c.9.2.
T.M.E. suspected at H.33.a.4.2.

Aerial.
Active all day without penetrating far across our lines although one machine carried out a 15 minute reconnaissance at 12,000 feet.
2 E.O.Bs. only were up yesterday opposite the Divisional Sector.

Movement.
Two men left farm at H.20.d.2.2 and entered Trench at H.20.d.2.7
Individual movement subsequently at the latter point was fired on.

Fires and explosions.
Fires were seen in the direction of ARMENTIERES, and an explosion took place at 5.50 p.m. 140° G.B. from G.29.b.45.45.

Lights.
The normal number observed, a particular large number being from JUNCTION POST.

Flashes. At 4.30 p.m. 4 distinct flashes, 120° G.B. from H.13.c.68.96.

Work and Defences.
New posts at H.9.d.0.5 and H.9.d.2.7.
New work has been done at H.27.c.4.5.

E.G. Cates Lieut

29th September, 1918. for G.S., 61st Division.

.. ..

TELEPHONE MESSAGE FROM CORPS. 3.30 p.m.

We hold NAUROY, S.W. edge of GOUY, GONNELIEU, and LA VACQUERIE.

From bend in Canal E. of FONTAINE - NOTRE DAME, line now runs due N. to SAILLY, W. edge of TILLOY along railway to BLECOURT (incl.) West of ABANCOURT thence to AUBENCHEUL.

In Flanders our troops are entering WATERDAMNOEK and PASSCHENDAELE.

(Copy) APPENDIX LXXIV.

61st Divn.

    GA.165.   30th.

The Corps Commander congratulates Lt.Col. CHRISTIE-MILLER and the 2/5 Gloucester Regt. on the success of their operation this morning.

    XI Corps.

Copy.

Brigadier General PAGAN, 184th Infy. Brigade.

G. 948.   30.

Please accept my best congratulations on your good work today aaa I have wired CHRISTIE MILLER direct my appreciation of his fine fight

General DUNCAN.

Copy.

Lieut. Colonel CHRISTIE MILLER, Commanding 5th Gloucesters.

G.948.   30.

Best congratulations to you and your Battalion on your fine
fight today aaa I fully realise your difficult conditions of
weather and enemy resistance

General DUNCAN.

APPENDIX LXXV

S E C R E T. - NOT TO BE TAKEN BEYOND BATTALION H.Q. IN THE LINE.

61st Division Intelligence Summary No. 17

Period covered: 9 a.m. 29th - 9 a.m. 30th September.

Visibility: Fairly good at first; afterwards poor.

OUR ACTIVITY.

Infantry.

Despite heavy rain, patrols were active in keeping close touch with the enemy's posts all along the Divisional front. Daylight patrols had previously been a considerable distance out.

One patrol leader penetrated the wire W. of BARTLETTE FM.

Much valuable information was gained by all patrols, and one prisoner captured.

At 5.45 a.m., under cover of an artillery, M.G., and T.M. barrage, troops of the 2/5th Gloucesters - of the Right Brigade - attacked and captured JUNCTION POST and the enclosures at H.32.a.7.5, advancing the line to approximately H.32.e.7.7 - H.32.b.7.7 - H.32.b.0.7 - H.32.a.5.7.

At 8 a.m. the enemy made a bombing counter-attack, and our left was forced slightly back to the line given above; fighting has continued all day.

We captured, during the operation, 16 prisoners (2 wounded), several M.Gs., and 1 T.M. (See Identifications).

Artillery.

Concentrations were fired by field artillery on selected areas in the enemy's forward system, and harassing fire continuously maintained. Barrages were fired at 5.45 a.m. in support of operations, and were reported to be extremely good.

Machine Guns.

41,000 rounds expended in co-operation with our attack.

Trench Mortars.

6" Newtons, after a successful wire-cutting programme had been carried out in H.9.b, H.14.d, & H.32.a., fired in conjunction with operations.

3" Stokes fired 235 rounds during our operations, silencing an enemy M.G.

Aerial.

Considerable activity when weather conditions permitted.

The E.O.B. reported brought down in yesterday's summary was on a G.B. of 156° from H.13.c.60.95.

Contact aeroplanes were prevented from operating this morning by the heavy rain and wind.

ENEMY ACTIVITY.

Infantry.

Patrols heard a good deal of movement, shouting, and talking, in the enemy's positions. The two newly-dug posts reported in yesterday's summary were found unoccupied.

The bombing counter-attack against JUNCTION POST was made along existing trenches only, and was unaccompanied by any movement across the open.

Artillery.

Below normal.

The chief targets were G.30.a.65.00, H.31.a.55.57, H.7.b, G.35, G.28.b, ROUGE DE BOUT, and BAC ST.MAUR.

85 gas shells (4.2") on the BAC ST.MAUR - FORT ROMPU - LYS S. bank area. Retaliation to our bombardment during the attack was not heavy, and mostly came down in the forward area.

A.A. fire very heavy; one gun at H.27.a.4.7 was dealt with by our artillery.

(P.T.O.)

Machine Guns.
Active against aircraft all day, but decreased activity at night.
Heavy fire against our attack.
Guns located at H.15.a.8.4, H.26.a.5.7, H.26.a.6.2, H.20.c.30.35, H.20.d.1.2, H.9.d.8.2, BARTLETTE FM., JUNCTION POST.

Trench Mortars.
Considerable retaliation on our T.M.Es.   Hostile position located at H.20.c.75.20.
L.T.Ms. fired on road running N.E. in H.13.d.

Aerial.
Hostile machines were active, and crossed our lines several times during the day, but were all eventually driven back by A.A. & M.G. fire.
E.O.Bs: 4 in position.

Work & Defences.
Gap in enemy wire at H.9.c.5.0 covered by M.G. at H.15.c.8.4.
New work is visible at H.27.c.4.5.
Wire at H.20.c.4.3 and H.26.a.3.4 is good.

Movement.
A party of 40 men seen near house at H.10.a.05.15.
3 men seen near main road in H.32.a. fired on, one being hit.
A M.G. sentry at H.26.a.5.7 was shot.

Transport.
Much transport movement in rear of enemy lines during the night.

Lights.
Normal during the night. Golden rain and double and single red rockets for 10 minutes after our barrage opened.

Gun Flashes.
G.Bs. from G.29.b.45.45: 138°, 133°, 158°, 169°, 131°, 120°, 144°, 104°, & 162°.
G.Bs. from G.23.d.45.65: 162°, 144°, 101°, 135°, 155°, 169°, 159°, 138°, 133°, 147°, 137°, & 150°.
G.Bs. from H.13.c.60.96: 108°, & 130°.
G.Bs. from H.2.c.25.55: 47° & 92°.

Identifications.
One O.R., 3rd Coy., 49 I.R., 4th Div., (captured in H.19.b. by patrol). Prisoner lost his way and ran into our patrol. He is a Landsturmer, 43 years of age, and had been with 11th Landsturm Bn. Schneidemuhl on Russian frontier since the beginning of the war. He joined the 49th I.R. at LOMME on Septr. 23rd, and came into front line on 26th. He can give no information, but letters on him indicate that the 3rd Coy. has been 12 days in the front line and is expecting relief.

14 O.R., 6th & 8th Coys., 102 R.I.R., 23rd Res.Div. (captured in H.32. during operations). (2 other prisoners, wounded, have been evacuated).
102 R.I.R. stated to have relieved 100 R.G.R. after our attack on JUNCTION POST on the night 26th/27th Septr.   Order of battle - N.to S: 49 I.R. - 102 R.I.R. - 392 I.R.
Prisoners differ as to whether one or two Bns. are in the front line. 2nd Bn. has 6th & 7th Coys. in front with one group of 8th Coy. between them. Remainder of 2nd Bn. is in support in trench 500 yds. behind front line. All prisoners agree that Bn. has still 4 coys. Company strength about 60, with 4 to 6 L.M.Gs.
No work has been done on present positions.
Prisoners know nothing of enemy intentions, or of movements of any other units in their Divn.
(Note: Prisoner captured by Div. on our right today stated 100 R.G.R. was withdrawn from the 23rd Res.Div. and sent north hurriedly. This statement has been verified by the identification of this Regt. on the YPRES front today).

Operations by Divisions on our flanks.
Both Divisions on our flanks have carried out operations today, and have advanced their lines, capturing prisoners.

Latest local situation.
Reports timed 4.45 p.m. from the Right Brigade announces that we hold the whole of the orchard at H.32.a.7.5 (N.W. of JUNCTION POST). N. of this orchard our line has been withdrawn 200 yards. Our line now runs approximately H.32.c.5.6 - H.32.a.95.35 - JUNCTION POST (incl.) - orchard at H.32.a.7.5 (incl.) - H.26.c.5.0 - H.26.c.5.2 - H.26.c.0.5.
Hostile M.G. in concrete emplacement at H.26.c.60.25 still in action. Bombing is still in progress.
Hostile shelling scattered but heavy, chiefly on roads and orchards in H.31.a. (115mm, 105mm, & 77mm).

E.G. Bates Lieut.
for G.S., 61st Divn.

30.9.18.

APPENDIX LXXVI

SECRET.   61st DIVISION   G.C. 79
        Locations of Units at 6 a.m. 1.10.18.

Ref.Shts.36A & 36.

    61 DIV.H.Q. "G"   RILL WORKS, L.33.b.
       do.   "A" & "Q"   CROIX MARRAISSE, J.21.c.

    182 Inf.Bde. (LEFT BRIGADE-, H.Q. G.8.a.8.1.
      2/6 Warwicks,   (Left Bn.) G.12.d.5.3.
      2/7 Warwicks,   (Reserve Bn.) G.8.b.0.2.
      2/8 Worcesters,   (Right Bn.) G.18.a.15.15.
      L.T.M.B.   G.2.a.0.5.

    183 Inf.Bde. (RESERVE BDE., C.B.L.), H.Q., L.27.a.0.3.
      9th North. Fus.   L.22.a.40.98.
      11th Suffolks,   L.28.b.9.9.
      1st E. Lancs.,   L.12.c.8.9.
      L.T.M.B.   L.27.b.1.6.

    184 Inf.Bde. (RIGHT BDE.), H.Q. L.12.c.8.3.
      2/4 Oxfords,   (Right Bn.) G.35.a.10.15.
      2/5 Glosters,   (Advanced Bn.) H.31.c.95.70.
      2/4 R. Berks.   (Left Bn.) G.23.c.00.95.
      L.T.M.B.   Line.

    C.R.A.   RILL WORKS, L.33.b.
      306 Bde. R.F.A.   (Left Group) G.8.b.1.7.
      307   do.   (Right Group) G.13.b.6.3.
      D.A.C.   L.20.c.7.0.
      D.T.M.O.   L.17.b.75.10.

    61 Bn. M.G.C.   H.Q., L.34.d.3.9.
      "A" Coy.   (Right Bde.Coy.) G.23.a.8.3.
      "B" Coy.   (Right Coy. C.B.L.) L.34.d.3.6.
      "C" Coy.   (Left Coy. C.B.L.) L.6.c.5.3.
      "D" Coy.   (Left Bde.Coy.) G.27.d.5.5.

    C.R.E.   L.27.d.8.4.
      476 Field Co.R.E.   L.16.a.8.5.
      478   do.   G.8.c.3.2.
      479   do.   L.26.b.7.3.

    1/5 D.C.L.I.(P),   H.Q., L.30.c.95.80.
                           1 Coy., G.8.a.6.7.
                           2 Coys.,L.30.a.7.5.

    A.D.M.S.   CROIX MARRAISSE, J.21.c.
      2/1 Field Amb.   L.26.c.8.7 (Main Dressing Stn.).
      2/2   do.   J.27.d.8.7.
      2/3   do.   L.22.c.2.3.

    61 Div. Train.   J.27.a.7.7.
      No. 1 Coy.   K.14.b.5.4.
      No. 2 Coy.   K.24.d.3.6.
      No. 3 Coy.   L.28.c.3.6.
      No. 4 Coy.   K.23.a.2.4.

    D.G.O.   RILL WORKS, L.33.b.
      Anti-Gas Depot,   L.27.c.1.5.
      Advanced Depot,   G.27.b.6.5.

    Div. P.of W. Cage,   L.29.a.5.6.

                                                     E S Bates Lieut.
30.9.18.   G.S., 61 Divn.

Appendix
LXXVII.

APPENDIX LXXVIII.

TOTAL CAPTURES DURING SEPTR. 1918 BY 61st DIVISION.

    46   Other Ranks.

     8   Machine Guns.

     1   Trench Mortar.

War Diary.
61st. Divⁿ.
October. 1918.
Vol. XXX.

Confidential

Army Form C. 2118.

WAR DIARY
—or—
—INTELLIGENCE SUMMARY—

VOLUME XXX.

(Erase heading not required.)

Instructions regarding War Diaries and Intelligence Summaries are contained in F. S. Regs., Part II. and the Staff Manual respectively. Title pages will be prepared in manuscript.

Place	Date OCTR. 1918	Hour	Summary of Events and Information	Remarks and references to Appendices
RILL WORKS L.33.b. Sht.36A.	1st		The night was quiet, though there was slight hostile artillery and machine gun activity, the latter being more pronounced than during the preceding night. 60 rounds Blue Cross gas shell fell in LAVENTIE after midnight.	
			Our positions near JUNCTION POST were slightly improved during the early morning by the 2/5 Glosters, in spite of stiff opposition by the enemy.	
			During the day there was some shelling of our outposts W. of BARTLETTE FARM and the vicinity of ROUGE DE BOUT; also FORT ROMPU (H.8.c.) and JUNCTION POST, but on the whole the enemy remained quiet.	Appx.I.
			For locations at 6 a.m., see Appendix I.	
			With a view to still further improving our positions and developing our successes, the 184 Inf.Bde. were ordered to capture BARTLETTE FARM on the morning of 2nd inst.	Appx.II.
			On receipt of orders from XI Corps, 61 Div. Orders Nos. 210 & 211 were issued, relating to the relief of this Division by 59th Division, between the 2nd and 5th inst.	Appx.III & IV.
			Weather - fine, but cold; visibility fair.	
	1/2nd		Hostile artillery was quiet during the night, but machine guns were active.	
	2nd		A successful minor operation was carried out against BARTLETTE FARM at 0545. 4 prisoners belonging to 49 I.R. were captured. As a result of this operation, and one by the Division on the right against TWO TREE FARM (N.2.c.), the enemy was found to be holding his outpost line very thinly, and to have retired to his main line of resistance. Our troops closely followed up this retirement, and at the end of the day the line ran approximately as follows :- (Sht. 36 - 1/40,000) :- H.36.c.0.0 - H.30.central - RED HOUSE POST (H.24.b.1.6) and GUNNER POST (H.18.d.7.5) both inclusive - N. along FLEURBAIX - HOUPLINES line to H.7.a.0.0, thence N. to southern outskirts of ARMENTIERES (RUE MARLE inclusive). Total prisoners during the day, 5; (including 1 wounded), 49 I.R; 1 wounded (since died) from No. 9 M.G. Marksmen Detachment.	
			183 Inf.Bde. withdrew to the STEENBECQUE area during the afternoon, by march route.	
			Brigade Groups were detailed, to come into force on arrival of formations and units in areas as given in D.O. 211.	
			Weather - overcast at times, but generally fine, with good visibility.	
	2/3rd		The night was very quiet; hostile artillery was inactive, and machine guns opposite the left Brigade fired from far back.	
			182 Inf.Bde. were relieved by a Composite Brigade of 59 Div. under G.O.C. 178 Bde. in the Left Section; relief complete at 0600; 182 Bde. on relief occupied billets of the Reserve Bde.,	Appx.V

Army Form C. 2118.

WAR DIARY
— or —
— INTELLIGENCE SUMMARY. —
(Erase heading not required.)

Instructions regarding War Diaries and Intelligence Summaries are contained in F. S. Regs., Part II. and the Staff Manual respectively. Title pages will be prepared in manuscript.

Place	Date OCTR. 1918.	Hour	Summary of Events and Information	Remarks and references to Appendices
RILL WORKS L.33.b. Sht.36A.			prior to entraining for MOLINGHEM area. During the day the advance was continued, with no opposition except that during the afternoon there was some shelling of our forward positions, chiefly by 77mm., and the advance was slightly held up in the centre of the Divisional front by M.G. fire. The line at the end of the day ran approximately as follows:- (Sht. 36, 1/40,000):- I.33.c.0.0 - I.28.central - old British front line I.21.a.4.0 - N.N.W. along road to I.14.b.6.0 - I.9.central. For locations at 0900, see Appendix VI. Copy of congratulatory message from the Army Commander is found in Appendix VII. Weather - fine, cool; visibility good.	Appx. VI. Appx. VII. Map 'A'
	3/4th		A quiet night, with only slight hostile artillery and M.G. fire. 184 Inf.Bde. was relieved in the right section by 177 Brigade; relief complete at 0735. Troops of 184 Inf.Bde. were bussed to the THIENNES area. A troops of 1st K.E.H. was attached to the Right Bde., to send out a strong officers' patrol at dawn. One platoon XI Corps Cyclists were also sent up to follow up above patrol and form relay posts back for rapid transmission of information. The cavalry were, however, unable to make any headway owing to M.Gs.	
LA LACQUE CAMP. I.32.b. Sht.36A.	4th	1000	G.O.C., 59th Divn., took over command of the Left Divisional Sector of the XI Corps. 61 Div.H.Q. closed at RILL WORKS and reopened at LA LACQUE CAMP at the same hour. For locations at 1200 see Appx. VIII. Following on receipt of a wire from Third Army, 61 Div. Order No. 212 was issued, to the effect that the Division would be transferred by strategical trains from XI Corps to XVII Corps, Third Army, commencing at 0900 on 5th inst. Weather - mild, fine.	Appx.VIII. IX Appx.VIII.
	4/5th		61st Div. Artillery was relieved in the line by 59th Div. Artillery.	
	5th		For locations at 0600 today, see Appx. IX. Entraining of the Division for XVII Corps area commenced today, Brigade Groups entraining as follows :- 182 Bde. from BERGUETTE; 183 Bde. STEENBECQUE; 184 Bde. THIENNES; detraining at DOULLENS, ROSEL, and DOULLENS respectively. The Divl. Artillery used all above stations. Appendix XI is a copy of a congratulatory message sent by the Divisional Commander to G.O.C. 184 Inf.Bde. Weather - bright sunshine, but cold.	Appx. IX. Appx. XI.

Army Form C. 2118.

WAR DIARY
—of—
—INTELLIGENCE SUMMARY.—

(Erase heading not required.)

Instructions regarding War Diaries and Intelligence Summaries are contained in F.S. Regs., Part II. and the Staff Manual respectively. Title pages will be prepared in manuscript.

Place	Date OCTR. 1918.	Hour	Summary of Events and Information	Remarks and references to Appendices
DOULLENS.	6th		61 Div. H.Q. closed at LA LACQUE at 0930 and reopened at L'HUILERIE, DOULLENS, at the same hour. Weather - fair; overcast at times.	
	7th		Following receipt of wire from XVII Corps (morning of 6th), orders were sent out with reference to move of the Division to the area S.W. of MOEUVRES (61 D.O. 213 - Warning - Appx. XI, and 61 D.O. 214 - Appx. XII). 61 Div. Artillery and transport of the Division to move by march route, commencing 8th inst: remainder of the Division to move by tactical trains on 9th inst. Move of the Division from XI Corps area completed about 1600. For locations in DOULLENS area, see Appx. XIII. XIV Weather - dull, with passing showers.	Appx. XI & XII. Appx. XIII.
	8th		61 Div. Arty. (less R.A. H.Q.) and transport of the Division left DOULLENS area for area S.W. of MOEUVRES, travelling by road, and spending two nights on the way. Weather - Fine, mild.	Appx. XIV.
LAGNICOURT. C.24.c.4.5. (Sht.57C)	9th	1030	For locations of Units (less transport) at 0600, see Appx. XIV. XV Dismounted personnel of the Division moved by train to area S.W. of MOEUVRES. 61 Div.H.Q. closed at DOULLENS, reopening at LAGNICOURT at the same hour. Weather - Fine, mild.	Appx. XV.
	10th		For locations of units at 0600, see Appx. XVI. 61 D.O. 215 gives the Corps organisation for the advance, and details the 183 Bde. Group as the Advanced Guard of this Division in the event of the Division being ordered to advance through the Leading and Support Groups. Orders were issued (61 D.Os. 216 & 217) for Brigade Groups, less artillery, to move further forward, in order to conform to the rapid advance on the Army front; Div. Arty. to move accordingly during morning of 11th; Advanced Guard, Support, and Reserve Bdes. to be 183, 182, & 184 Inf. Bdes. respectively. For locations after this move, see Appx. XIX. XX	Appx.XVI. Appx.XVII. Appx.XVIII & XVIII XIX Appx.XIX

(A7092). Wt. W12839/M1293. 75,000. 1/17. D. D. & L., Ltd. Forms/C.2118/4.

Army Form C. 2118.

WAR DIARY
or
INTELLIGENCE SUMMARY.
(Erase heading not required.)

Instructions regarding War Diaries and Intelligence Summaries are contained in F. S. Regs., Part II. and the Staff Manual respectively. Title pages will be prepared in manuscript.

Place	Date	Hour	Summary of Events and Information	Remarks and references to Appendices
LAGNICOURT. C.24.c.4.5 (Sht.57C)	OCTR. 1918. 10th	(ctd)	On receipt of a wire from XVII Corps, orders were issued (61 D.O. 218) for 61 Div. Arty. to relieve 40th Div.Arty. in the Leading Group of the Corps during the night 13th/14th inst. Orders were received from XVII Corps, and repeated to the 1/5 D.C.L.I., to the effect that the Pioneer Bn. would be attached for duty to Commandant, CAMBRAI, to assist in putting out fires. This battalion marched off at 1700 hrs. Weather- fine, mild.	Appx. XX.
	11th		61 Div.Art., less R.A. H.Q., moved forward to Brigade Groups as ordered in Div. Orders Nos. 216 & 217 (See Appendices XVII & XVIII9.XIX) For locations at 1200 today, see Appx. XXI. Weather - Overcast, with very slight drizzles during the day; mild.	Appx. XXI.
	12th		A Warning Order (D.O. 219) was issued at 0945, to the effect that the Division be prepared to move at short notice. Weather - overcast, cool.	Appx. XXII.
NOYELLES. L.11. (Sht.57C)	13th		61 Div.H.Q. closed at LAGNICOURT at 1500 hrs., and opened at NOYELLES at the same hour. 2/5 Glosters also moved during the day to PROVILLE. 61st Div. Arty. moved forward during the day, and relieved 40th Div. Arty. in the Leading Group of the Corps during the evening, coming under the orders of G.O.C., 24th Divn. For amendments to locations of units, see Appx. XXIII. Weather - overcast, cold.	Appx. XXIII.
	14th		The Divisional Commander held a conference at 182 Bde. H.Q., at which Brigade Commanders, and Os.C. 1/5 D.C.L.I. and 61 Bn. M.G.C. attended. The chief object of this conference was to have all ranks warned against any slackening of the offensive spirit on account of current rumours of a possible armistice. Weather - fair, becoming overcast and cold.	
	15th		For locations of units at 0600; see Appx. XXIV.	Appx. XXIV.

Army Form C. 2118.

WAR DIARY
INTELLIGENCE SUMMARY.
(Erase heading not required.)

Instructions regarding War Diaries and Intelligence Summaries are contained in F. S. Regs., Part II. and the Staff Manual respectively. Title pages will be prepared in manuscript.

Place	Date OCTR.1918.	Hour	Summary of Events and Information	Remarks and references to Appendices
NOYELLES, L.11. (Sht.57C)	15th (ctd)		Weather - fine, visibility low.	
	16th		61st Div. Instructions No. 7 - Intelligence -, issued. Training continued. Corps Commander called on G.O.C. during the afternoon. 61 Bn. M.G.C. was placed at disposal of 19th Divn. - order issued for move to RIEUX to take place on 17th. Weather - dull, some rain.	Appx.XXV. Appx.XXVI.
	17th		61 Bn. M.G.C. moved to RIEUX, and came under the orders of 19th Divn. 61 Div. Order No. 220 issued at 1200 hrs.(Cancelled by D.O.221 owing to areas allotted to this Division S. of CAMBRAI not being available.) Weather - dull morning, followed by a fine afternoon.	Appx.XXVI-I.
	18th	0600	61 Div. became the Supporting Group of the XVII Corps and in accordance with 61 D.O. 221, the following moves of Bdes. were carried out: 182 and 183 Bdes. to CAMBRAI, 184 Bde. to CANTAING.	Appx.XXVII Appx.XXVIII
		2000	61 D.O. 222 issued - Move of Division to area AVESNES - RIEUX - CAGNONCLES	
RIEUX U.20.c.9.9. (Sh.51A)	19th		Div. H.Q. closed at NOYELLES-sur-L'ESCAUT at 1200 hrs. and opened at RIEUX at the same hour. 182 Bde. Group moved to RIEUX 183 do. do. AVESNES-LEZ-AUBERT 184 do. do. CAGNONCLES. For locations after this move Weather dull - rain in evening.	Appx.XXIX.
	20th		19th Division attacked under heavy barrage at 0200 hrs; 61st Div. Arty. and 61st Bn. M.G.C. were operating under orders of G.O.C. 19th Div. All objectives were taken and patrols pushed out to River HARPIES. Orders received 2130 hrs. that 61st Div. would be prepared to carry out an attack on high ground East of R.ECAILLON about 23rd inst.	

WAR DIARY
or
INTELLIGENCE SUMMARY.
(Erase heading not required.)

Army Form C. 2118.

Place	Date OCTR. 1918	Hour	Summary of Events and Information	Remarks and references to Appendices
RIEUX. U.20.c.9.9. (Sh.51A)	20th (Ctd)		Rain all day.	
	21st		Preliminary Order 223 issued 1030 hrs. – 61 Div. to be prepared to carry out above attack not before 23rd inst. G.O.C's. conference 1200 hrs. – attended by Brigadiers, C.R.A., C.R.E., O.C. M.G.Bn. M.G.Bn. returned to RIEUX.	Appx.XXX
	22nd		Order No. 224 issued 1300 hrs. – Orders for move forward preparatory to attack on 24th inst. G.O.C's. conference 1400 hrs. Very wet day. Order No. 225 issued 2300 hrs. – Orders for attack on high ground E. of River ECAILLON on 24th inst.	Appx.XXXI Appx.XXXII
ST.AUBERT. U.24.b.6.1.	23rd		G.C.40/5 (further details of attack orders) issued 1100 hrs. Adv. Div. H.Q. opened at ST.AUBERT 1430 hrs. 184 Bde. Group moved to ST.AUBERT from CAGNONCLES. 183 Bde. Group moved to ST.AUBERT from AVESNES. 182 Bde. Group moved to MONTRECOURT Wood from RIEUX (H.Q. at Sandpits, V.5.a.) M.G.Bn. moved to ST.AUBERT from RIEUX. 19th Division advanced their line during the day and by 1600 hrs. held line which was to have been 61st Div. first objective of 24th. 61st Div. objectives were therefore extended in depth. Div. order 226 issued at 2030 hrs., giving new final objective and alterations in barrage tables.	Appx.XXXIII Appx.XXXIV
	24th	0400	The Division was disposed as follows at Zero (0400 hours) :- 183 Bde. on the right, with 9th North Fus. on right, 11th Suffolks on left and 1st East Lancs. in Brigade Reserve. 182 Bde. on the left, with 2/6 Warwicks on right, 2/7th Warwicks on left, and 2/8 Worcesters in Bde. Reserve. 184 Bde. in Divisional Reserve.	

WAR DIARY
INTELLIGENCE SUMMARY

(Erase heading not required.)

Army Form C. 2118.

Place	Date	Hour	Summary of Events and Information	Remarks and references to Appendices
ST.AUBERT U.24.b.6.1.	24th (Ctd)		The first reports received indicated that the battle was going fairly well, namely that the hostile barrage was not heavy, that the right Brigade had crossed the River ECAILLON, but that there was heavy M.G. fire from VENDEGIES.	
		0640	182 Bde. reported that they had crossed the river, but that the right Bn. had been driven back by a heavy counter-attack. Meanwhile the 183 Bde. on the right had pushed on about 1000X beyond BERMERAIN though the Suffolks had suffered heavily from the counter barrage and M.G. fire from the eastern outskirts of VENDEGIES.	
		0800	The 2/7 Warwicks, though held up for a time outside SOMAING, captured the village in spite of the Bn. on the right still being held up in front of VENDEGIES by very heavy M.G. fire and thick wire. They were, however, later forced to withdraw by a counter-attack on their right Coy. By this time reports were received from the 2nd Div. on the right that their advance was proceeding well, and from the 4th Div. on the left that they had reached but had not taken MUR COPSE, but were going well on their left. By 0800 hrs. the 9th North Fus. had reached the line LA FOLIE - MILL (Q.16.c.), while owing to the situation in VENDEGIES the Suffolks had been obliged to form ~~a defensive flank from the~~ ~~rising~~ MILL (Q.16.c.) back to the original line in Q.26.	
		0900	The Support and Reserve Coys. of the 2/6 Warwicks were ordered to effect a crossing in Q.13.b., and outflank VENDEGIES from the north; at this time the left Coy. of the 2/7 Warwicks held the CHAPEL Q.7.c.9.7., and were working up the sunken road in Q.7.c. and b.	
		1115	The Divisional Commander visited Bdes. and gave instructions as regards further operations to clear up the situation in the afternoon. During the morning the 183 Bde. moved up the 1st E.Lancs. to take over the ~~Northern~~ flank N. of BERMERAIN from the Suffolks owing to the losses of the latter.	
		1145	Orders were issued to 183 Bde. to push out and hold the high ground in Q.17.a. and b., in order to prepare the way for 184 Bde., who received orders direct from the Divisional Commander to move forward south and east of BERMERAIN and attack across to the north of VENDEGIES.	
		1200	61 Div. Adv. H.Q. opened at MONTRECOURT (V.14.a.0.8.)	Appx.XXXV
MONTRECOURT (V.14.a.0.8.)		1630	By noon 6 Officers and 234 O.R. had passed through the Divisional Cage. At 1630 hrs. the situation was as follows :- 183 Bde. was in touch with the 2nd Div. about R.7.c.0.0., their line running roughly south of and parallel to the CHAUSSEE BRUNEHAUT to LARBLIN (Q.16.a.), thence back to the river at about Q.21.d.0.7. On the left there was no change in the situation in front of VENDEGIES, but SOMAING was clear of the enemy except for a	

WAR DIARY
INTELLIGENCE-SUMMARY

Army Form C. 2118.

Place	Date	Hour	Summary of Events and Information	Remarks and references to Appendices
MONTRECOURT (V.14.a.O.8.)	24th(Ctd)		post at Q.7.d.8.2., and the 2/7 Warwicks had 2 platoons north of the river from Q.7.d.8.8. - Q.7.b.6.2. - Q.7.b.O.4. - MUR COPSE, where they were in touch with the 4th Division. In addition to the operation by the 184 Bde., which comprised directing 1 Bn. from about LA FOLIE on to the high ground in Q.12.b. - Q.11.a. and b., and 1 Bn. across the ROGNEAU stream on to the spurs in Q.9.a., the 182 Bde. were ordered to cooperate with the right Bde. of the 4th Div. from the N.W. and take the high ground in Q.1.c. and sunken roads in Q.7.b. and d., Q.8.b. and d.	
		1730	184 Bde. started going through outpost line of 183 Bde. As soon as it got dark the enemy evacuated his positions round VENDEGIES, which he had been so stubbornly defending all day, fearing our outflanking movement, VENDEGIES being clear of the enemy at 1800 hrs.	
		2012	2/4 Oxfords reported 2 Coys. on high ground in Q.12.c., Q.11.d; Support Coy. along the stream Q.17; Reserve Coy. at LA FOLIE (Q.23.a.), and in touch with 2nd Div.	
		2205	2/4 R.Berks. had 1 Coy. in Q.15.d. and 21.b., remainder of the Bn. being in Q.26.d. and 32.a. 2/8 Worcesters reported along line Limekiln (Q.8.c.) - Q.8.cent. - Q.7.b.7.5. Locations of Bde. H.Q. at 2200 hrs. were as follows :- 182 Bde. P.30.c.2.1. 183 & 184 Bdes. MAISON BLEUE, Q.31.b.9.9. Prisoners captured by the Div. during the day numbered 10 officers and nearly 400 O.R. Prisoners were taken from 9 different infantry regiments, representing 5 different German Divisions, elements of different units being put in as reinforcements. The following divisions, were represented in the battle opposite the 61 Div. during the day:- 111 Div., 48 Res. Div., 21 Res. Div., 25 Res. Div.(elements attached to 48 R.D.), 113 Div.(brought up in support). Weather: Fine and cold throughout the day, but poor visibility.	
	24/25th	0105	Orders were issued ordering 184 Bde., with 2 Bdes. R.F.A. and 1 M.G.Coy. to resume the advance as Advance Guard Bde. after taking over the whole Divisional front. 182 and 183 Bdes. were ordered to re-organise in depth and continue the advance in their respective areas in support of 184 Bde. - 183 Bde. on right, 182 Bde. on left. Hostile artillery was active during the night especially on BERMERAIN.	Appx.XXXVI
	25		For locations at 0000 hrs. see	Appx.XXXVII

Army Form C. 2118.

WAR DIARY
or
INTELLIGENCE SUMMARY.
(Erase heading not required.)

Instructions regarding War Diaries and Intelligence Summaries are contained in F.S. Regs., Part II. and the Staff Manual respectively. Title pages will be prepared in manuscript.

Place	Date	Hour	Summary of Events and Information	Remarks and references to Appendices
MONTRECOURT (V.14.a.0.8.)	25th	0700	By 0700 hrs. patrols of the 2/4 Ox. & Bucks. L.I. had proceeded down the road from Q.11.d.1.2. to the railway line in Q.6. without meeting opposition, while the 2/4 R.Berks. had secured the high ground N.W. of LA JUSTICE.	
		0900	2/4 Ox. & Bucks. had patrols along whole line of railway and reported SEPMERIES clear of the enemy, who were holding high ground N.W. of MARESCHES.	
		1100	By 1100 hrs. our advanced troops were in touch with both flank Divisions.	
VENDEGIES (Q.14.a.1.7.)		1700	184 Adv. Bde. H.Q. moved to LARBLIN (Q.16.a.). 61 Adv. Div. H.Q. opened at VENDEGIES. Further objectives were given as follows:- PRESSAU - VILLERS POL road, and G.O.C. 184 Bde. gave his commanders the following orders: Right Bn./to secure slopes in L.31 and 32 and seize and secure crossings over the RHONELLE River, then to secure high ground in L.26. and 27: Left Bn. to secure high ground in K.24., L.19. This advance started in conjunction with 99 Inf. Bde. on the right at 1600 hours but made little headway owing to M.G's from ARTRES and MARESCHES, and at 1830 hrs. our line ran approximately along road in Q.4.b. - Q.5.a. and c. round outskirts of SEPMERIES (incl.) - thence to about K.32.d.0.0. where we were in touch with 2nd Div, and patrols in front of this line along railway near ARTRES. For locations at 1800 hours see	Appx.XXXVIII
			183 and 182 Bdes. were consolidating the main line of resistance along the high ground Q.18.a. - Q.10.b. - LES COPSE. The 2nd Div. on the right were along the line of the railway and were not in touch with the enemy. Orders issued for 184 Bde. to continue the advance tomorrow, but if unable to establish bridgeheads without heavy fighting they were to confine themselves to reconnoitring enemy's dispositions and RHONELLE River. Weather: Fine, mild.	Appx.XXXIX
	25/26th	2050	During the night patrols reconnoitred LA RHONELLE River and encountered M.G. fire from the crossings and MARESCHES. SEPMERIES was heavily shelled and there was scattered shelling of forward and back areas. At 0500 there was no change in the situation. We were in touch with the 2nd Div. at R.2.a.8.9., and patrols had been sent out along the railway in K.28.c. to get in touch with the 4th Div.	
	26th		For locations at 0600 hours see	Appx.XL.

Army Form C. 2118.

Instructions regarding War Diaries and Intelligence Summaries are contained in F.S. Regs., Part II. and the Staff Manual respectively. Title pages will be prepared in manuscript.

WAR DIARY
of
INTELLIGENCE SUMMARY.
(Erase heading not required.)

Place	Date	Hour	Summary of Events and Information	Remarks and references to Appendices
VENDEGIES (Q.14.a.1.7.)	26th (Ctd.)	1100	During the morning the 4th Div. attacked ARTRES; our patrols co-operating from the south and east entered the village but found it unoccupied. Line reported as follows :- Oxfords in touch with 2nd Div. at R.2.b.2.8., thence L.32.d.0.4. - L.32.c.15.85., - L.31.d.5.9. - L.31.c.9.7. - K.36.b.5.4. - K.36.c.4.7. - K.35.d.9.8. - K.29.c.3.2. - K.28.c.5.0., where the R.Berks were in touch with 4th Div.	
		1210	Orders issued for 183 Bde. to relieve 184 Bde. as Advance Guard Bde. during night 26/27th.	Appx.XLI.
		1510	Information received from 4th Div. that they had established a bridgehead over the RHONELLE at FME. de L'HOTEL DIEU (K.29.a.), and that they had patrols on the high ground in K.24.c. (N.W. of MARESCHES). 184 Bde. were informed and ordered to push 2 companies over the bridge and work round to MARESCHES from the north-west. These moved forward at 1600 hrs., but about 1615 the 4th Div. troops in K.24.c. were counter-attacked and forced to withdraw to the bridgehead.	
		1600	Our line was unchanged on the right, and on the left we had 2 coys. of the R.Berks across the river in K.29.a. and b.	
		1730	Weather - fine and mild.	
	26/27th		183 Bde. relieved 184 Bde. as Advance Guard Bde., relief complete at 0635 hours. Hostile artillery active on forward and back areas.	
	27th	0830	For locations at 0600 hours see At dawn the 183 Bde. made an attempt to extend the bridgehead in K.29., but the opposition was too strong. A second attempt was made under a barrage, and patrols were pushed forward along the whole of the Divisional front. Hostile M.G. fire proved too heavy, though the bridgehead was extended as far as Q.30.a.5.0. One Coy. E. Lancs. was established E. of the river here, and the remainder of the Bn. was withdrawn to positions on the W. bank; the right flank of the bridgehead was withdrawn slightly. The enemy was holding the line of the river in great strength, and heavy fire from artillery, T.Ms. and M.Gs. was directed on any movement. The vicinity of the railway and the RHONELLE valley heavily shelled with gas shells. 66 prisoners were taken by the 1st E. Lancs. during this operation belonging to 76 I.R., 111 Div. Arrangements were made for the relief of any troops of the 4th Div. who were in our area in the neighbourhood of the bridgehead.	Appx.XLII

WAR DIARY
INTELLIGENCE SUMMARY

(Erase heading not required.)

Army Form C. 2118.

Instructions regarding War Diaries and Intelligence Summaries are contained in F.S. Regs., Part II. and the Staff Manual respectively. Title pages will be prepared in manuscript.

Place	Date	Hour	Summary of Events and Information	Remarks and references to Appendices
VENDEGIES (Q.14.a.1.7.)	27th (Ctd.)		As a result of the two reconnaissances this morning it was decided to make no further attempt to advance until the position had been dealt with by artillery. G.O.C. 183 Bde. was instructed to cover the bridgehead by M.G. and rifle fire, and maintain his dispositions there, but to withdraw all other troops as far back as possible while giving them complete observation of the valley.(See D.O.227)	Appx. XLIII.
		1250	The artillery and T.Ms. swept the valley on both banks of the river and heavily shelled MARESCHES, while M.Gs. carried out harassing fire. During the morning considerable hostile movement was seen on the high ground between MARESCHES and PRESAU; this was engaged by our artillery. S.O.S. sent up. The enemy (estimated by R.A.F. at about 200) advanced against the bridge-head in two waves in open formation. They were, however, caught in our artillery and M.G. barrage and dispersed after suffering very heavy casualties, none succeeding in reaching our line. The rest of the day passed quietly. Weather: Fine, mild.	
	27/28th		There was considerable retaliation to our shoots during the night, and searching fire on the high ground S.W. of SEPMERIES. Three footbridges were constructed over the RHONELLE between K.29.a.6.1. and K.29.d.0.5.	
	28th		For locations at 0600 hours see Appx. XLIV. During the morning LA JUSTICE, BERMERAIN and VENDEGIES, also river crossings near the two latter were shelled by 15 cm. H.V. guns. E.A. flew over back areas during the morning. At 1200 the situation was unchanged, although there had been local fighting round the bridgehead.	
	28/29th		The enemy was very active on forward and back areas, with H.E. and gas shell. VENDEGIES and BERMERAIN were continuously shelled by 15 cm. and 13 cm. Yellow Cross gas shell. 9th North Fus. relieved 11th Suffolks on the right of the Advance Guard Bde. Patrols report south bank of RHONELLE clear of the enemy, who held the N bank in strength.	
	29th	1600	During the morning the bridgehead was extended E. as far as K.29.d.4.7. 13th Sqn. R.A.F. reported that our machines had flown low over MARESCHES several times without being fired on. 1st E.Lancs. pushed out 2 strong patrols on receiving this intelligence;	

Army Form C. 2118.

WAR DIARY
or
INTELLIGENCE-SUMMARY.

(Erase heading not required.)

Instructions regarding War Diaries and Intelligence Summaries are contained in F.S. Regs., Part II. and the Staff Manual respectively. Title pages will be prepared in manuscript.

Place	Date	Hour	Summary of Events and Information	Remarks and references to Appendices
VENDEGIES (Q.14.a.1.7)	29th	(ctd)	one towards high ground in K.24.c., the other eastwards towards MARESCHES between the road and river. The first patrol had only proceeded about 300x when it was heavily engaged by M.G. fire; on which it withdrew under a smoke barrage which was put down on a pre-arranged signal. This smoke barrage was mistaken by the enemy for an indication of an attack, the result being heavy counter-preparation along the Divisional front for half an hour.	
		1730	61 Div. Order No. 228 issued - Orders for an attack, in conjunction with 4th Div, the objective of 61 Div. being MARESCHES and the high ground between this village and PRESEAU. The attack to take place on 31st Oct., zero 0515 hours.	See Appx. I for November.
	29/30th		Hostile artillery was much quieter during the night. There was some shelling of VENDEGIES and crossings over the ECAILLON by 15 and 13 cm. H.V. guns; about 25 rounds 15 cm. were fired into BERMERAIN.	
	30th		For locations at 0600 hours see 61 Div. Order 229 was issued at 0700 hours. - orders for necessary reliefs and changes in distribution of Brigades prior to attack on MARESCHES. 182 Bde. to become Advance Guard Bde. and carry out the attack. Owing to the failure of troops of the XXII Corps (on the left) to seize and hold MONT HOUY (K.2.), operations on this Divisional front were put off 48 hours in all, (as the attack had been planned for Oct. 30) and all dates in Div. Orders 228 and 229 were postponed 24 hours. The 183 Bde. had been holding the line a long time, but it was decided to keep them in till the 182 Bde. attacked, as otherwise there would be no fresh troops in Divisional Reserve. G.C.45/7 was issued at 1200 hours - Defence Instructions. During the morning there was intermittent shelling of our forward areas, especially of SEPMERIES. Increased movement in L.20 and L.25 was dealt with by our artillery. No change in our dispositions.	Appx. XLIV. Appx. XLVI Appx. XLVII.
	30/31st		During the night there was heavy shelling of ARTRES and SEPMERIES, and a few H.V. shells on VENDEGIES and BERMERAIN. 183 Bde. made an attempt to capture M.G. at the MILL (L.25.d.O.3.), but the enemy was very alert and brought heavy M.G. fire to bear on our patrol from MARESCHES.	

Army Form C. 2118.

WAR DIARY
—or—
INTELLIGENCE-SUMMARY.
(Erase heading not required.)

Instructions regarding War Diaries and Intelligence Summaries are contained in F. S. Regs., Part II. and the Staff Manual respectively. Title pages will be prepared in manuscript.

Place	Date	Hour	Summary of Events and Information	Remarks and references to Appendices
VENDEGIES (Q.14.a.1.7.)	31st	1545 1600	E.A. brought down by L.G. fire of 9th North Fus. The Commander-in-Chief visited Div. H.Q. Orders were received for relief of 61 Div. by 19 and 24 Divs. Captures during the month include 10 Officers, 475 502 O.R. 108 M.Gs. (heavy and light), 8 Trench Mortars, 1 4.5" How., 1 77mm. gun. Map "B" attached shews the jumping off line at zero 24th and general dispositions on Oct. 31st. 5.11.18.	

F. J. Duncan
Major-General,
Commanding 61st Division.

APPENDIX I

SECRET.   61st DIVISION   G.C. 79
                Locations of Units at 6 a.m. 1.10.18.

Ref.Shts.36A & 36.

    61 DIV.H.Q. "G"   RILL WORKS, L.33.b.
        do.   "A" & "Q"   CROIX MARRAISSE, J.21.c.

    182 Inf.Bde. (LEFT BRIGADE-, H.Q. G.8.a.8.1.
      2/6 Warwicks,   (Left Bn.) G.12.d.5.3.
      2/7 Warwicks,   (Reserve Bn.) G.8.b.0.2.
      2/8 Worcesters,   (Right Bn.) G.18.a.15.15.
      L.T.M.B.   G.2.a.0.5.

    183 Inf.Bde. (RESERVE BDE., C.B.L.), H.Q., L.27.a.0.3.
      9th North. Fus.   L.22.a.40.98.
      11th Suffolks,   L.28.b.9.9.
      1st E. Lancs.,   L.12.c.8.9.
      L.T.M.B.   L.27.b.1.6.

    184 Inf.Bde. (RIGHT BDE.), H.Q. L.12.c.8.3.
      2/4 Oxfords,   (Right Bn.) G.35.a.10.15.
      2/5 Glosters,   (Advanced Bn.) H.31.c.95.70.
      2/4 R. Berks.   (Left Bn.) G.23.c.00.95.
      L.T.M.B.   Line.

    C. R. A.   RILL WORKS, L.33.b.
      306 Bde. R.F.A.   (Left Group) G.8.b.1.7.
      307   do.   (Right Group) G.13.b.6.3.
      D.A.C.   L.20.c.7.0.
      D.T.M.O.   L.17.b.75.10.

    61 Bn. M.G.C.   H.Q., L.34.d.3.9.
      "A" Coy.   (Right Bde.Coy.) G.23.a.8.3.
      "B" Coy.   (Right Coy. C.B.L.) L.34.d.3.6.
      "C" Coy.   (Left Coy. C.B.L.) L.6.c.5.3.
      "D" Coy.   (Left Bde.Coy.) G.27.d.5.5.

    C. R. E.   L.27.d.8.4.
      476 Field Co.R.E.   L.16.a.8.5.
      478   do.   G.8.c.3.2.
      479   do.   L.26.b.7.3.

    1/5 D.C.L.I.(r),   H.Q., L.30.c.95.80.
                               1 Coy., G.8.a.6.7.
                               2 Coys.,L.30.a.7.5.

    A. D. M. S.   CROIX MARRAISSE, J.21.c.
      2/1 Field Amb.   L.26.c.8.7 (Main Dressing Stn.).
      2/2   do.   J.27.d.8.7.
      2/3   do.   L.22.c.2.3.

    61 Div. Train.   J.27.a.7.7.
      No. 1 Coy.   K.14.b.5.4.
      No. 2 Coy.   K.24.d.3.6.
      No. 3 Coy.   L.28.c.3.6.
      No. 4 Coy.   K.23.a.2.4.

    D. G. O.   RILL WORKS, L.33.b.
      Anti-Gas Depot,   L.27.c.1.5.
      Advanced Depot,   G.27.b.6.5.

    Div. P.of W. Cage,   L.29.a.5.6.

                                        E S Bates Lieut.
30.9.18.   G.S., 61 Divn.

APPENDIX II

S E C R E T.

Copy No.

61st DIVISION ORDER No. 209

1.10.18.

1. In face of considerable opposition our positions at JUNCTION POST have been improved this morning. Our line now runs from H.26.c.10.10 - H.26.c.95.00 - H.32.b.4.5 - trenches running South West through JUNCTION POST to our outpost line.

2. The Right Brigade will carry out the following minor operations tomorrow 2nd October, with a view to still further improving our positions and developing our success:-

   (a) An attack at dawn by not less than 1 Company will be made for the capture of BARTLETTE FARM.
   The capture of BARTLETTE FARM is necessary to the further development of our operation to the North East of JUNCTION POST.

   (b) During the day our success at JUNCTION POST will be developed along the enemy trench system and enclosures to the North East in the direction of FLEURBAIX and particularly along the trenches running South East from JUNCTION POST through H.32.b.4.3 and H.32.d.65.95.
   The latter operation will assist operations by the Division on our right from the direction of TWO TREES FARM.

3. The Zero hour for the above operations will be fixed by G.O.C. 184 Inf. Bde. and will be communicated to all concerned as early as possible.

4. Arrangements for artillery and machine gun cooperation will be made direct by Right Brigade with C.R.A. and 61st Bn. M.G.C.
   307 F.A. Bde. will only be available for the operation (a); after 9 a.m. both Field Artillery Brigades will be available for operation (b).

5. 42nd Squadron R.A.F. are arranging for a machine to be in the air at dawn and about 12 noon to attack any counter-attack ground targets observed in the neighbourhood of the above operation.
   The machine will be recognised by a black square patch on the rear edge of the lower planes.
   A copy of 184 Inf. Bde. orders will be forwarded through Divisional H.Qrs. for transmission to 42nd Squadron R.A.F.

6. ACKNOWLEDGE.

Issued at 2 p.m.

Lieut. Col.,
G.S., 61st Division.

Distribution:

Copy No.		Copy No.	
1	A.D.C. for G.O.C.	11	A.D.M.S.
2	61 Div. Signals.	12	D.A.P.M.
3-4	61 Div. Art.	13-14	XI Corps.
5	C.R.E.	15	28 Bde. R.G.A.
6	61 Bn. M.G.C.	16	40 Div.
7	1/5 D.C.L.I.	17	59 Div.
8	182 Inf. Bde.	18	Q.
9	183 Inf. Bde.	19	G.
10	184 Inf. Bde.	20-21	War Diary.

SECRET.

Copy No. 21

APPENDIX III

61st DIVISION ORDER NO.210.

WARNING ORDER.

1st October, 1918.

1. The 59th Division is relieving the 61st Division during the period 2nd/5th October, 1918.

2. (a) 183 Inf. Bde. will move by March Route to THIENNES tomorrow, 2nd inst.

   (b) Bde. of 59th Div. will relieve 182 Inf. Bde. on night 2nd/3rd inst. 182 Inf. Bde. will withdraw to the accommodation vacated by 183 Inf. Bde. in the Reserve Bde. area on relief.

   (c) 183 Inf. Bde. will march to STEENBECQUE on 3rd inst..

   (d) 182 Inf. Bde. will move to THIENNES by Train and thence to MOLINGHEM by March Route on 3rd inst.

   (e) Bde. of 59th Div. will relieve 184 Inf. Bde. on night 3rd/4th inst. 184 Inf. Bde. will withdraw to THIENNES by Train on relief.

   (f) D.A.C. will be withdrawn on 4th inst.

   (g) Div. Artillery will be relieved by 59 Div. Arty. on 4th/5th inst.

3. Detailed orders will be issued later.

4. ACKNOWLEDGE.

C.S. Dowden Maj.
for Lieut. Col.,
G.C., 61st Division.

Issued at 6 p.m.

DISTRIBUTION.

Copy No. 1 - A.D.C. for G.O.C.
2 - 61 Signal Coy.
3-4 - 61 Div. Artillery.
5 - C.R.E.
6 - 61 Bn. M.G.C.
7 - 1/5 D.C.L.I.
8 - 182 Inf. Bde.
9 - 183 Inf. Bde.
10 - 184 Inf. Bde.
11 - A.D.M.S.
12 - 13 - "Q"
14 - D.G.O.
15 - D.A.P.M.
16 - 61 Div. Train.
17 - D.A.D.O.S.
18 - D.A.D.V.S.
19 - Camp Commandant.
20 - "G"
21 - 22 - War Diary.

SECRET G.S. 31/1/1

APPENDIX IV

Reference D.O. 211 of 1.10.18.

Divisional Headquarters (less "A & Q" Branch) will go to LA LACQUE and not to NORRENT FONTES.

"A & Q" Branch will remain at CROIX MARRAISSE.

3.10.18.   To all recipients of D.O. 211.

C A Dowden
Major,
G.S., 61st Divn.

SECRET.

APPENDIX IV

61st DIVISION ORDER No. 211.

Copy No. 2
1.10.18.

Ref. Maps HAZEBROUCK 1/100,000,
36A, 1/40,000.
36, 1/40,000.

1. The 61st Division will be relieved by the 59th Division, and withdrawn to an area E. of AIRE, between 2nd and 5th inst., in accordance with attached Movement Table.
   After relief, the Division will be in G.H.Q. Reserve at 24 hours' notice, and ready to entrain if ordered on or after 5th inst.

2. The following distances will be maintained between units on the line of march :-
   (i) Between Batteries, Sections D.A.C., Companies, Units and their transport, and transport of units when brigaded . . . . 100 yds.
   (ii) Between Arty. Bdes. and Battalions . . . . 500 yds.
   (iii) Between groups of 6 vehicles . . . . 25 yds.

3. All documents relating to the area, trench maps, defence schemes and instructions, aeroplane photographs, and current intelligence summaries, will be handed over to relieving formations and units, and receipts taken.

4. In every case, command will pass on completion of relief, which will be reported to Div. H.Q.

5. All formations and units of 59th Division arriving in the Divl. area before 10.00 on 4th inst. will come under the orders of G.O.C. 61st Divn. until that hour.
   Command of the Left Divl. Sector will pass to G.O.C. 59th Divn. at 10.00 on 4th inst.

6. In order to give assistance to the incoming formations and units regarding local details of administration and intelligence, etc., the following personnel will be left in the line with 59th Divn. for a period of 24 hours :-

   With each Bde.H.Q. in the line - Intelligence Officer and 2 O.R. of Signal Service.
   With each Battalion in the line - 1 officer and 2 N.C.Os. with each battalion H.Q. 2 N.C.Os. with each Company H.Q.
   M.G. Battalion . . . . - 1 officer with each Company,
   1 N.C.O. with each Section,
   1 O.R. with each gun.
   R. A. . . . . - 1 officer per Brigade H.Q.
   1 officer & 2 signallers per Battery.
   R. E. . . . . - As arranged by C.R.Es.

7. All further details of reliefs and moves will be arranged by commanders concerned.

8. H.Q., 61st Division, will close at RILL WORKS and open at NORRENT FONTES at 10.00 on 4th inst.

9. Administrative instructions and details re trains will be issued by "Q".

(P.T.O.)

(2)

10. Definite locations will be notified as soon as possible.

11. Brigade Schools will rejoin units on arrival in the new area.

12. ACKNOWLEDGE.

Issued at 23.30.

A.H.Dowden, D.A.J.
for
Lieut.-Col.,
G.S., 61st Division.

Distribution :-

Copy No.				
1	- A.D.C. for G.O.C.		16	- 40th Divn.
2	- Div. Signals.		17	- 59th Divn.
3-4	- Div. Arty.		18-19	- "Q".
5	- C.R.E.		20	- "G".
6	- 61 Bn. M.G.C.		21-22	- War Diary.
7	- 1/5 D.C.L.I.		23	- 42nd Sq. R.A.F.
8	- 182 Inf. Bde.		24	- Div. Train.
9	- 183 Inf. Bde.		25	- D.A.D.O.S.
10	- 184 Inf. Bde.		26	- D.A.D.V.S.
11	- A.D.M.S.		27	- Mob. Vet. Sec.
12	- D.A.P.M.		28	- D.G.O.
13-14	- XI Corps.		29	- Camp Comdt.
15	- 28 Bde. R.G.A.		30-36	- Spare.

S E C R E T.   MOVEMENT TABLE TO ACCOMPANY 61st DIVISION ORDER No. 211., dated 1.10.18.
(Amended)

Ser. No.	Date Octr.	Formation or unit.	From	To	Route	Relieved by	Remarks
1	2nd	183rd Inf.Bde.Group. 183 Inf.Bde. No.3 Coy.Div.Train.	Reserve Bde.Area	STEENBECQUE area.	Any	-	To march at 09.00. Nucleus garrisons in the Corps Battle Line to be taken over by 182 Inf.Bde.
2	Night 2/3rd	182nd Inf.Bde.	Left Front.	Reserve Bde.Area.	-	178 Inf.Bde.	To relieve nucleus garrisons of 183 Inf.Bde. in Corps Battle Line on morning of 3rd inst. Relief of Bde. to be complete by 04.00 on 3rd inst.
3	3rd	H.Q. 61 Bn.M.G.C.	LA GORGUE	HAM EN ARTOIS	MERVILLE ST.VENANT GUARBECQUE	H.Q. 200th M.G.Bn.	Under orders of O.C.M.G.Bn. Dismounted personnel by rail to THIENNES.
4	"	2 Coys.61st Bn.MGC.	Reserve Area	do.	do.	2 Coys. 200th MG.Bn	Transport by march route to march at 11.00.
5	"	1/5 D.C.L.I. (Pioneers)	Present Areas	HAM EN ARTOIS	MERVILLE ST.VENANT GUARBECQUE	Pioneer Bn. 59th Divn.	Transport by march route to march at 08.30. Dismounted personnel by rail to THIENNES, thence by march route.
6	"	182 Inf.Bde.Group. 182 Inf.Bde. No.2 Coy.Div.Train.	do.	MOLINGHEM - ISBERGUES - TREIZENNES Area.	MERVILLE THIENNES LA LACQUE	177 Inf.Bde	Transport by march route to march at 09.00. Dismounted personnel by rail to THIENNES, thence by march route.
7	"	2/3(SM)Field Amb.	L.22.c.2.3	STEENBECQUE.	MERVILLE LA RUE DES MORTS LE PARC.	Field Amb. 59th Div.	To march at 10.30.
8	"	I.Q. Div.Engrs.	L.27.d.8.4.	NORRENT FONTES	-	H.Q. 59 Div. Engrs.	-
9	"	476 Fd.Coy.R.E.	L.16.a.8.5.	MOLINGHEM.	MERVILLE ST.VENANT	Fd.Coy. 59 Div.	To march at 08.30 - To follow 1/5 D.C.L.I. from MERVILLE.

(P.T.O.)

(2)

Ser. No.	Date	Formation or Unit	From	To	Route	Relieved by	Remarks
10	Octr. 3rd	478 Field Co.RE.	G.8.c.3.2.	STEENBECQUE	NEUF BERQUIN - MERVILLE - LA RUE DES MORTS - LE PARC.	Fd.Coy.59 Div.	To march at 09.00.
11	"	479 Field Co.RE.	L.26.b.7.3.	THIENNES.	MERVILLE - TANNAY	Fd.Coy.59 Div.	To march at 09.00.
12	Night 3/4th	1 Coy.61 Bn.M.G.C.	Left Front.	HAM EN ARTOIS	Any	1 Coy.200th M.G.Bn.	Transport by march route. Dismounted personnel by rail to THIENNES, thence by march route.
13	"	1f 4 Inf.Bde.Group. 1f 2 Inf.Bde. No.4 Coy.Div.Train	Right Front.	THIENNES - TANNAY - LA LACQUE Area.	MERVILLE - TANNAY	177 Inf.Bde.	Train Coy. may move on afternoon of 3rd inst. Dismounted personnel by rail. Transport by march route. Relief to be complete by 04.00 on 4th inst.
14	4th	D.A.C.	L.20.c.7.0.	LAMBRES - MAZINGHEM - FONTES area.	ST.VENANT - GUARBECQUE.	D.A.C.59 Div.	Relief to be complete by 12.00. 59 D.A.C.to assume responsibility for supply of all ammunition from 12.00 on 4th inst.
15	"	61 Div. H.Q.	RILL WORKS	NORRENT FONTES	-	59 Div. H.Q.	To march at 10.00.
16	"	61 Div.Signals	do.	do.	-	59 Div.Signals	To march at 10.15.
17	"	2/2 Field Amb.	J.27.d.8.7.	MOLINGHEM	MERVILLE - THIENNES - LA LACQUE	Fd.Amb. 59 Div.	
18	"	2/1 Field Amb.	L.26.c.8.7.	THIENNES	MERVILLE - TANNAY	do.	
19	"	Mob.Vet.Sec.	ROUSSEL FARM	LAMBRES	-	-	To march at 09.30.
20	Night 4/5th	61 Div.Arty. No.1 Coy.Div.Train	Line	LAMBRES - FONTES - MAZINGHEM area	ST. VENANT - GUARBECQUE.	59 Div.Art.	Relief to be completed by 04.00 on 5th inst.
21	"	1 Coy.61 Bn.M.G.C.	Line Right.	HAM EN ARTOIS	-	One Coy. 200th MG.Bn.	ditto.

(Copy)   S E C R E T.   APPENDIX V

G.C. 31/1/2

61 Div.Art.
61 Div.Eng.
182 Inf.Bde.   A.D.M.S.
183 Inf.Bde.   61 Div. Train.
184 Inf.Bde.   "Q".

On arrival of formations and units in the areas detailed in D.O. 211 dated 1.10.18, Divl. Artillery and Brigade Groups will be composed as under, and will come under the orders of C.R.A. and G.Os.C. Brigades concerned :-

Div.Arty.Group.	182nd Brigade Group.
61st Div.Arty.	182nd Infantry Bde.
61st D.A.C.	476 Field Co.R.E.
No.1 Coy.Div.Train.	No.2 Coy.Div.Train.
	2/2 (S.M.) Field Amb.

183rd Brigade Group.	184th Brigade Group.
183rd Infantry Bde.	184th Infantry Bde.
478 Field Co.R.E.	479 Field Coy.R.E.
No.3 Coy.Div.Train.	No.4 Coy.Div.Train.
2/3 (S.M.) Field Amb.	2/1 (S.M.) Field Amb.

2.10.18.

(Sd.) C.H. DOWDEN,
Major,
for Lieut.-Col.,
G.S., 61st Divn.

WAR DIARY   APPENDIX VI

S E C R E T.   61st DIVISION.   G.C. 79
                       Locations of Units at 09.00, 3.10.18.

   61st DIV. H.Q. "G"   RILL WORKS, L.33.b.
      do.   "A" & "Q".   CROIX MARRAISSE, J.21.c.

  182 Inf.Bde. H.Q.   L.27.a.0.3.
    2/6 Warwicks,   L.12.c.8.9.
    2/7 Warwicks,   L.22.a.40.98.
    2/8 Worcesters,   L.29.b.9.9.
    L.T.M.B.   FELT FM., L.27.b.

  183 Inf.Bde. H.Q.   MAIRIE, STEENBECQUE.
    9th North.Fus.   LES CISEAUX.
    11th Suffolks.   BOESEGHEM.
    1st E. Lancs.   STEENBECQUE.
    L.T.M.B.   do.

  184 Inf.Bde. H.Q.   (RIGHT BDE.), H.Q. L.12.c.8.3.   G.29.a.8.6
    2/4 Oxfords,   (Right Bn.) G.35.a.10.15.   H.31.a.3.0
    2/5 Glosters.   L.23.d.4.8.   G.25.a.10.15
    2/4 R. Berks.   (Left Bn.) G.23.c.00.95.   H.29 (Command Post)
    L.T.M.B.   Line,

  C. R. A.   RILL WORKS, L.33.b.
    306 Bde. R.F.A.   (Left Group) G.8.b.1.7.   G.29.a.95.65
    307   do.   (Right Group) G.13.b.6.3.   G.23.a.0.9
    D.A.C.   L.20.c.7.0.
    D.T.M.O.   L.17.b.75.10.

  61 Bn. M.G.C.   H.Q., L.34.d.3.9.
    "A" Coy.   (Right Bde.Coy.) G.23.a.8.3.
    "B" Coy.   (Right Coy. C.B.L.) L.34.d.3.6.
    "C" Coy.   (Left Coy. C.B.L.) L.6.c.5.3.
    "D" Coy.   (Left Bde. Coy.) G.27.d.5.5.

  C. R. E.   L.27.d.8.4.
    476 Field Coy. R.E.   L.16.a.8.5.
    478   do.   G.8.c.3.2.
    479   do.   L.26.b.7.3.

  1/5 D.C.L.I. (P),   H.Q., L.30.c.95.80.
                                 1 Coy., G.8.a.6.7.
                                 2 Coys. L.30.a.7.5.

  A. D. M. S.   CROIX MARRAISSE, J.21.c.
    2/1 Field Amb.   L.26.c.8.7 (Main Dressing Stn.).
    2/2   do.   J.27.d.8.7.
    2/3   do.   L.22.c.2.3.

  61 Div. Train.   J.27.a.7.7.
    No. 1 Coy.   K.14.b.5.4.
    No. 2 Coy.   K.24.d.3.6.
    No. 3 Coy.   L.28.c.3.6.
    No. 4 Coy.   K.23.a.2.4.

  D. G. O.   RILL WORKS, L.33.b.
    Anti-Gas Depot,   L.27.c.1.5.
    Advanced Depot,   G.27.b.6.5.

  Div. P.of W. Cage,   L.29.a.5.6.
  Advanced   do.   G.22.c.2.1.

2.10.18.

A.D. Stephenson Capt.
G.S., 61st Divn.

Appendix VII

(Copy)

Fifth Army G.A. 186/3.
1st Octr., 1918.

XI Corps.
x x x x

The Army Commander wishes to thank Corps and Divisional Commanders, all officers and men, for the spirited and successful minor operations effected on the Fifth Army front on the 30th September.

In the great operations now in progress it was important to ascertain clearly the situation on this front and to influence the moral of the enemy. In this we were successful, and the Army Commander welcomes this further proof of the high moral and gallantry of the troops of the Fifth Army.

(Sd.) C.B.B. WHITE,
Major-General,
G.S.

----

(2)

61st Division.
x x x x x x

XI Corps G.S. 68/18

For information, and communication to all concerned.

(Sd.) J.D. BOYD, Major,
for B.G.G.S.

XI Corps,
2.10.18.

----

(3)

	Copies		Copies	
C.R.A.	16			G.C. 77
C.R.E.	4	1/5 D.C.L.I.	18	
182 Inf.Bde.	65	A.D.M.S.	4	
183 Inf.Bde.	65	61 Signal Coy.	1	
184 Inf.Bde.	65	"Q"	1	
61 Bn. M.G.C.	5	28 Bde. R.G.A.	6	

For information, and communication to all ranks.

Sufficient copies are forwarded for issue down to Platoons, Batteries, M.G. Companies, and Field Companies R.E.

Wetherby
Lieut.-Col.,
G.S., 61st Divn.

3.10.18.

WAR DIARY Appendix VIII

SECRET G.C. 79

61st DIVISION.
Locations of Units at 12.00, 4.10.18.

61st DIV. H.Q. "G"	LA LACQUE CAMP.
do. "A & Q".	CROIX MARRAISSE, J.21.c.
182 Inf. Bde. H.Q.	MOLINGHEM.
2/6 Warwicks,	TREIZENNES.
2/7 Warwicks,	ISBERGUES.
2/8 Worcesters,	MOLINGHEM.
L.T.M.B.	do.
183 Inf. Bde. H.Q.	MAIRIE, STEENBECQUE.
9th North. Fus.	LES CISEAUX.
11th Suffolks,	BOESEGHEM.
1st E. Lancs.,	STEENBECQUE.
L.T.M.B.	do.
184 Inf. Bde. H.Q.	THIENNES.
2/4 Oxfords,	do.
2/5 Glosters,	LA LACQUE & LA ROUPIE.
2/4 R. Berks,	PECQUEUR & HOULERON.
L.T.M.B.	THIENNES.
C.R.A.	RILL WORKS, L.33.b.
306 Bde. R.F.A.	(Left Group) G.99.a.95.65.
307 do.	(Right Group) G.23.c.0.9.
D.A.C.	L.20.c.7.0.
D.T.M.O.	L.17.b.75.10.
61 Bn. M.G.C.)	
& all Coys.)	HAM-EN-ARTOIS.
C.R.E.	LA LACQUE.
476 Field Coy. R.E.	MOLINGHEM.
478 do.	STEENBECQUE.
479 do.	THIENNES.
1/5 D.C.L.I. (P).	HAM-EN-ARTOIS.
A.D.M.S.	CROIX MARRAISSE, J.21.c.
2/1 Field Amb.	THIENNES.
2/2 do.	MOLINGHEM.
2/3 do.	STEENBECQUE.
61 Div. Train.	J.27.a.7.7.
No. 1 Coy.	K.14.b.5.4.
No. 2 Coy.	MOLINGHEM.
No. 3 Coy.	STEENBECQUE.
No. 4 Coy.	THIENNES.

3.10.18.

A.D. Stephenson.
Capt.,
G.S., 61st Divn.

Appendix IX

S E C R E T.

Copy No. 28

61st DIVISION ORDER No. 212.

4.10.18.

1. 61st Division will be transferred by rail from XI Corps, Fifth Army, to XVII Corps, Third Army, commencing at 09.00 on 5th inst.

2. Details of the moves will be issued by "Q".

3. ACKNOWLEDGE.

Issued at 07.00

(signed) A Dowden Major
for
Lieut.-Col.,
G.S., 61st Divn.

Distribution :-

Copy No.1 - A.D.C.for G.O.C.	13-14 - XI Corps.
2 - Div. Signals.	15-16 - "Q".
3-4 - Div. Arty.	17 - "G".
5 - C.R.E.	18-19 - War Diary.
6 - 61 Bn.M.G.C.	20 - Div.Train.
7 - 1/5 D.C.L.I.	21 - D.A.D.O.S.
8 - 182 Inf.Bde.	22 - D.A.D.V.S.
9 - 183 Inf.Bde.	23 - Mob.Vet.Sec.
10 - 184 Inf.Bde.	24 - D.G.O.
11 - A.D.M.S.	25 - Camp Comdt.
12 - D.A.P.M.	

WAR DIARY   APPENDIX IX

S E C R E T   G.C. 79

                    61st DIVISION.
                 Amendment to Locations.

        No. 1 Coy. Div. Train   -   LA BEFORE F., LAMBRES.
        H.Q., 61 Div. Arty.   -   FONTES.
        306 Bde. R.F.A.   -   FONTES.
        307 Bde. R.F.A.   -   LAMBRES.
        D.A.C.   -   MAZINGHEM.
        T.M.B'ties   -   FONTES.
        1/5 D.C.L.I.(P).   -   BOURECQ.

                                              A.B. Stephenson Capt.
4.10.18.   G.S. 61 Div.

SECRET   Copy No. 21

61st DIVISION ORDER No. 213
WARNING ORDER.   7.10.1918.

1. The 61st Division will be prepared to move to the forward area as follows :-

   (a) Divisional Artillery and other transport by march route, commencing on the 8th inst., staging at :-
       1st night - BRETONCOURT and BAILLEULMONT.
       2nd night - BOISLEUX AU MONT and BOYELLES.

   (b) Remainder of Division by tactical train from DOULLENS and AUTHIEULE on the 9th inst.

2. Details will be issued.

3. ACKNOWLEDGE.

Issued at 0700
                                                   Lieut.-Col.,
                                              G.S., 61st Division.

Distribution :-

Copy No. 1 - A.D.C. for G.O.C.   13 - Camp Comdt.
       2-3 - 61 Div.Art.   14 - D.A.D.O.S.
         4 - Div. Eng.   15 - D.A.P.M.
         5 - 182 Inf.Bde.   16 - D.A.D.V.S.
         6 - 183 Inf.Bde.   17 - Mob.Vet.Sec.
         7 - 184 Inf.Bde.   18 - D.G.O.
         8 - 61 Bn. M.G.C.   19 - "Q".
         9 - 1/5 D.C.L.I.   20 - "G".
        10 - A.D.M.S.   21-22 - War Diary.
        11 - 61 Div. Train.
        12 - 61 Div.Signals.

SECRET.

Appendix XIII

AMENDMENT No. 1
to
61st Division Order No. 214.

Para 1

for "Area about MOEUVRES - GRAINCOURT (Area D)"

read "Area South West of MOEUVRES".

8.10.18.

[signature] Dowden
Major,
G.S., 61 Division.

to all recipients of 61 Div. Order No. 214.

APPENDIX XIII

S E C R E T.   61st DIVISION ORDER No. 214.   Copy No. 19
                                                                        7.10.18.

Ref. Maps LENS 1/100,000,
VELENCIENNES 1/100,000.

1. The 61st Division will move from the DOULLENS area to an area about MOEUVRES - GRAINCOURT (Area "D"), commencing on 8.10.18 as follows :-

    (a) Divl. Artillery and transport of Division (less transport carried on omnibus trains) will move by march route in accordance with Movement Table attached.

    (b) Remainder of Division by tactical trains on 9th inst.

2. The following distances will be maintained :-
    (i)   Between Batteries, Sections of D.A.C., Companies, Field Ambulances, Units & their transport, transport of units, and similar bodies of troops or transport .... 100 yds.

    (ii) Between Artillery Brigades & Battalions .... 500 yds.

    (iii) Between groups of 6 vehicles, either mechanical or horse-drawn .... 25 yds.

3. Os.C. Groups will send forward daily parties to reconnoitre positions to halt for the night within the areas shown in the March Table.

4. Roads as shown on the maps do not always exist. An officer from each Group should be sent forward to reconnoitre routes for the following days.

5. Train arrangement and transport for omnibus train will be notified by "Q".

6. Advance parties will be held ready to proceed to the forward area on the 8th inst. One lorry per Brigade and Artillery Group will report for this purpose at 0700 hours tomorrow. Lorries will return empty on same day.

7. All further details will be arranged by Commanders concerned.

8. ACKNOWLEDGE.

Issued at 12 noon.

                                                    C.H.Dowden Major
                                              for   Lieut.-Col.,
                                                    G.S., 61st Divn.

                        Distribution :-
            Copy No.1 - A.D.C. for G.O.G.   14-15 - XVII Corps ADV.
                   2 - Div. Signals.   16 - XVII Corps Rear.
                 3-4 - 61 Div. Art.   17 - "Q".
                   5 - C.R.E.   18 - "G".
                   6 - 61 Bn.M.G.C.   19-20 - War Diary.
                   7 - 1/5 D.C.L.I.   21 - Mob.Vet.Sec.
                   8 - 182 Inf.Bde.   22 - D.A.D.O.S.
                   9 - 183 Inf.Bde.   23 - D.A.P.M.
                  10 - 184 Inf.Bde.   24 - D.A.D.V.S.
                  11 - A.D.M.S.   25 - D.G.O.
                  12 - 61 Div.Train.   26-30 - Spare.
                  13 - Camp Comdt.

SECRET.

MOVEMENT TABLE to accompany 61 Div. Order No. 214 dated 7.10.18.

Serial No.	Date Oct.	Formation or Unit.	From	To	Route	Remarks
1	8	Div.Art.Group Div.Arty. D.A.C. Mob.Vet.Sect. No.1 Coy.Train	AMPLIER - SARTON area	BRETONCOURT	MONDICOURT - LA BELLE VUE - X roads S.E. of BEAUMETZ	To be clear of cross roads North of M in MONDICOURT by 0930 hrs.
2	8	Div.Troops Group 61 Bn. M.G.C. 1/5 D.C.L.I. Div. H.Qrs. Div. Signals Div. Engrs.H.Q. Div. Train H.Q.	DOULLENS area	BRETONCOURT	MONDICOURT - LA BELLE VUE - X roads S.E. of BEAUMETZ	To march in order as shown under orders of O.C. 61 Bn. M.G.C. Not to reach above cross roads before 0930 hrs and to be clear of same by 1015 hrs
3	8	183 Bde. Group. 183 Inf. Bde. 478 Fd.Coy.R.E. No. 3 Coy.Train 2/3 Field Amb.	POMMERA area	BRETONCOURT BAILLEUL MONT area	MONDICOURT - LE BAC DU SUD (Main Road)	Not to reach above cross roads before 1030 hrs and to be clear of same by 1115 hrs.
4	8	182 Bde. Group 182 Inf. Bde. 476 Fd.Coy.R.E. No. 2 Coy.Train 2/2 Field Amb.	DOULLENS area	BRETONCOURT BAILLEUL MONT area	DOULLENS - ARRAS Road	Not to reach above cross roads before 1130 hrs. and to clear same by 1215 hrs.
5	8	184 Bde. Group 184 Inf. Bde. 479 Fd.Coy.R.E. No. 4 Coy.Train 2/1 Field Amb.	BEAUVAL area	BAILLEUL MONT area	DOULLENS - ARRAS Road	Not to reach above cross roads before 1230 hrs
6	9	Div.Arty.Group	BRETONCOURT	BOYELLES	BLAIRVILLE - FICHEUX - BOISLEUX	To be clear of FICHEUX by 1000 hrs.
7	9	Div.Troops Group	BRETONCOURT	BOYELLES	BLAIRVILLE - FICHEUX - BOISLEUX	Not to arrive at FICHEUX before 1000 hrs and to be (R.T.O.) clear by 1100 hrs

(2)

Serial No.	Date	Formation or Unit	From	To	Route	Remarks
8	Oct. 9	183 Bde. Group	BRETONCOURT - BAILLEUL MONT area	BOYELLES - BOISLEUX area	BRETONCOURT - BLAIRVILLE - FICHEUX	Not to arrive at FICHEUX before 1100 hrs. and to be clear by 1200 hrs.
9	9	182 Bde. Group	BRETONCOURT - BAILLEUL MONT area	BOYELLES - BOISLEUX area	BRETONCOURT - BLAIRVILLE - FICHEUX	Not to arrive at FICHEUX before 1200 hrs. and to be clear by 1300 hrs.
10	9	184 Bde. Group	BRETONCOURT - BAILLEUL MONT area	BOYELLES - BOISLEUX area	BRETONCOURT - BLAIRVILLE - FICHEUX	Not to arrive at FICHEUX before 1300
11	10	Div. Arty. Group	BOYELLES	MOEUVRES - GRAINCOURT area	HENIN - CROISILLES - LAGNICOURT - X roads ½ mile N.W. of DOIGNIES	To be clear of HENIN by 0800 hrs.
12	10	Div. Troops Group	BOYELLES	MOEUVRES - GRAINCOURT area	HENIN - CROISILLES - LAGNICOURT - X roads ½ mile N.W. of DOIGNIES	Not to arrive at HENIN before 0800 hrs. and to be clear by 0900 hrs.
13	10	183 Bde. Group	BOYELLES - BOISLEUX area	MOEUVRES - GRAINCOURT area	HENIN - CROISILLES - LAGNICOURT - X roads ½ mile N.W. of DOIGNIES	Not to arrive at HENIN before 0900 hrs. and to be clear by 1000 hrs.
14	10	182 Bde. Group	BOYELLES - BOISLEUX area	MOEUVRES - GRAINCOURT area	HENIN - CROISILLES - LAGNICOURT - X roads ½ mile N.W. of DOIGNIES	Not to arrive at HENIN before 1000 hrs and to be clear by 1100 hrs.
15	10	184 Bde. Group	BOYELLES - BOISLEUX area	MOEUVRES - GRAINCOURT area	HENIN - CROISILLES - LAGNICOURT - X roads ½ mile N.W. of DOIGNIES	Not to arrive at HENIN before 1100 hrs.

Final destination will be notified by "Q".

WAR DIARY APPENDIX XIV

SECRET.
61st DIVISION.
Locations of Units at 1800, 7.10.18.

G.C. 79

61st DIV. H.Q.	DOULLENS.
182 Inf.Bde.H.Q.	½ mile S. of D in DOULLENS.
2/6 Warwicks,	GEZAINCOURT.
2/7 Warwicks,	CITADELLE, DOULLENS.
2/8 Worcesters,	do.
L.T.M.B.	GEZAINCOURT.
183 Inf.Bde.H.Q.	POMMERA.
9th North.Fus.	do.
11th Suffolks,	HALLOY.
1st E. Lancs.,	AUTHIEULE.
L.T.M.B.	POMMERA.
184 Inf.Bde.H.Q.	BEAUVAL.
2/4 Oxfords,	do.
2/5 Glosters,	do.
2/4 R. Berks,	do.
L.T.M.B.	do.
C.R.A.	AMPLIER.
306 Bde. R.F.A.	SARTON.
307 do.	~~DEVILLE~~ ORVILLE.
D.A.C.	AMPLIER.
D.T.M.O.	~~DEVILLE~~ ORVILLE
61 Bn. M.G.C.) & all Coys.)	TERRAMESNIL.
C.R.E.	DOULLENS.
476 Field Coy.	GEZAINCOURT.
478 do.	AUTHIEULE.
479 do.	BEAUVAL.
1 5 D.C.L.I.(P).	CITADELLE, DOULLENS.
A.D.M.S.	DOULLENS.
2/1 Field Amb.	BEAUVAL.
2/2 do.	FRESCHEVILLERS.
2/3 do.	BEAUREPAIRE.
61 Div. Train.	DOULLENS.
No. 1 Coy.	SARTON.
No. 2 Coy.	BRETEL.
No. 3 Coy.	BEAUREPAIRE.
No. 4 Coy.	BEAUVAL.

7.10.18.

E S Bates Lieut.
for G.S., 61st Divn.

SECRET.

APPENDIX XV

G.C. 79.

LOCATIONS OF 61st DIVISION at 0600, 9.10.18.

Serial No.	Unit.	Location.	Moves within 24 hours.
1	DIV. H.Q.	DOULLENS.	LAGNICOURT.
2	61 Div. Art. H.Q.	AMPLIER.	
3	306 Bde.R.F.A.)		
4	307 do.)	BRETONCOURT	
5	D.A.C.)	AREA.	
6	D.T.M.O.)		
7	61 Div.Eng.H.Q.	DOULLENS.	
8	478 Field Co.RE.	GEZAINCOURT.	
9	478 do.	AUTHIEULE.	
10	479 do.	BEAUVAL.	
11	61 Bn. M.G.C. H.Q.) & all Coys.)	TERRAMESNIL.	AREA WEST OF MONCHY-VERRES.
12	182 Inf.Bde.H.Q.	½ mile S. of D in DOULLENS.	
13	2/6 Warwicks,	GEZAINCOURT.	
14	2/7 Warwicks,	CITADELLE, DOULLENS.	
15	2/8 Worcesters,	do.	
16	182 T.M.Bty.	GEZAINCOURT.	
17	183 Inf. Bde.H.Q.	POMMERA.	
18	9th North.Fus.	do.	
19	11th Suffolks,	HALLOY.	
20	1st E. Lancs,	AUTHIEULE.	
21	183 T.M.Bty.	POMMERA.	
22	184 Inf.Bde.H.Q.	BEAUVAL.	
23	2/4 Oxfords,	do.	
24	2/6 Glosters,	do.	
25	2/4 R. Berks,	do.	
26	184 T.M.Bty.	do.	
27	1/5 D.C.L.I.(P).	CITADELLE, DOULLENS.	
28	A.D.M.S.	DOULLENS.	
29	2/1 Field Amb.	BEAUVAL.	
30	2/2 do.	FRESCHEVILLERS.	
31	2/3 do.	BEAUREPAIRE.	
32	61 Div. Train.	DOULLENS.	
33	No. 1 Coy.	SARTON.	
34	No. 2 Coy.	BRETEL.	
35	No. 3 Coy.	BEAUREPAIRE.	
36	No. 4 Coy.	BEAUVAL.	

8.10.18.

Captain,
G.S., 61st Divn.

SECRET.   APPENDIX XVI

Sheet 57c.
                          61st DIVISION.
                 Locations of Units at 0600, 10.10.18.

            61 DIV.H.Q.   LAGNICOURT.

            182 Inf.Bde.H.Q.   E.28.b.5.3.
              2/6 Warwicks,   E.28.b.7.0.
              2/7 Warwicks,   E.29.c.central.
              2/8 Worcesters,   E.29.c.8.3.
              182 L.T.M.B.   E.28.b.5.3.

            183 Inf.Bde.H.Q.   E.21.a.05.20.
              9th North.Fus.)
              11th Suffolks.)
              1st E. Lancs.   )   E. of MOEUVRES.
              183 L.T.M.B.   )

            184 Inf.Bde.H.Q.   J.6.c.8.8.
              2/5 Glosters.   K.3.a.9.9.
              2/4 Oxfords.   K.2.a.5.9.
              2/4 R. Berks.   K.1.a.9.5.
              184 L.T.M.B.   K.1.a.9.5.

            C. R. A.   LAGNICOURT.
              306 Bde.RFA.   C.30.c.5.2.
              307   do.   C.30.a.7.3.
              D.A.C.   C.30.b.3.7.
              D.T.M.O.   D.25.a.2.9.

            61 Bn.M.G.C.   E.20.a.5.1.

            C. R. E.   LAGNICOURT.
              476 Field Co.RE.   E.29.central.
              478   do.   E. of MOEUVRES.
              479   do.   D.30.b.1.8.

            1/5 D.C.L.I.(P).   D.15.b.5.9.

            A. D. M. S.   LAGNICOURT.
              2/1 Field Amb.   J.6.a.4.6.
              2/2   do.   E.27.d.9.8.
              2/3   do.   J.7.c.central.

            61 Div. Train.   LAGNICOURT.
              No.1 Coy.   J.6.a.0.5.
              No. 2 Coy.   E.25.d.0.0.
              No. 3 Coy.   S. of MOEUVRES.
              No. 4 Coy.   J.6.a.5.9.

            XXXXXXX
            9.10.18.

APPENDIX XVII

S E C R E T.

Copy No. 16

61st DIVISION ORDER No. 215.

10.10.18.

1. From all information to hand, the enemy is carrying out a retirement on a large scale. A vigorous pursuit has been ordered along the whole Army front.

2. The pursuit by the XVII Corps is to be carried out with the utmost determination. The hostile rearguards are to be attacked as soon as located. The one aim and object of all ranks will be to get at the enemy's main forces and bring them to battle.

3. The attached map shows the Corps boundaries for the advance.

4. The organisation for the advance will be, for the present, as follows:
   (a) <u>Leading Group.</u>
      24th Division.
      Corps Mounted Troops.
      5 Brigades Field Artillery - Brig.Genl. PALMER (acting)
      1 Brigade Heavy Artillery.
                                       C. R. A.
   (b) <u>Support Group.</u>
      19th Division.
      4 Brigades of Field Artillery - Brig.Genl. RUDKIN (acting)
                                           C. R. A.
   (c) <u>Reserve Group.</u>
      61st Division.
      61st Divisional Artillery.
   (d) <u>Corps Group.</u>
      3 Brigades of Heavy Artillery.

The grouping of Artillery will be adjusted by the Corps from time to time to conform to the relief of Divisions, but the principle will remain the same as regards the amount of artillery allotted to each Group.
The position of the Artillery of the Support and Reserve Groups will always be well forward in these formations, in order that it can move up to supplement the artillery of the leading Group when required.

5. One section of Tunnellers is allotted by Corps to accompany the leading Group for the purpose of searching for and removing mines and "booby traps" in the villages, and to report when the latter are safe for occupation. Attention is called to 61st Division G.C. 54 of 7.10.18 publishing the various markings to be made on all buildings, dugouts, etc., after examination.

6. In accordance with the above detail, the Division will be prepared to move forward at short notice. In the meantime, every advantage will be taken, by all units in the Division while in Reserve Group, of the excellent facilities and ground in their neighbourhood for training purposes.

7. The strictest march discipline of all arms will be enforced. Troops will move off the roads to halt whenever possible.

8. The main cable route through Corps area will be as follows :-
MT. SUR L'OEUVRE - the railway to A.18.central - main road to B.20.b. - CAUROIR - AVESNES by the CAMBRAI - SOLESMES road - ST. AUBERT.
Divisional and Brigade H.Q. will always be situated in or near to this route.

(P.T.O.)

(2)

9.   In the event of the Division being ordered to advance through the Leading and Support Groups, the following troops will form the Advanced Guard of the Division :-

   Commander - Brig.Gen. B.D.L.G. ANLEY, C.M.G., D.S.O.
   183 Inf.Bde:
   306 F.A.Bde.
   1 Coy. 61 Bn. M.G.C.
   478 Field Coy. R.E.

Officers commanding the above units will get into touch with B.G.C. 183 Inf.Bde.

10.   ACKNOWLEDGE.

Issued at 1300

             Lieut.-Col.,
            G.S., 61st Division.

    Distribution :-
 Copy No. 1 - A.D.C. for G.O.C.
    2 - 61 Signal Coy.
   3-4 - C.R.A.
    5 - C.R.E.
    6 - 182 Inf. Bde.
    7 - 183 Inf. Bde.
    8 - 184 Inf. Bde.
    9 - 61 Bn. M.G.C.
   10 - 1/5 D.C.L.I.
   11 - A.D.M.S.
   12 - "Q"
   13 - XVII Corps (Adv.)
   14 - 19th Division.
   15 - "G"
  16-17 - War Diary.

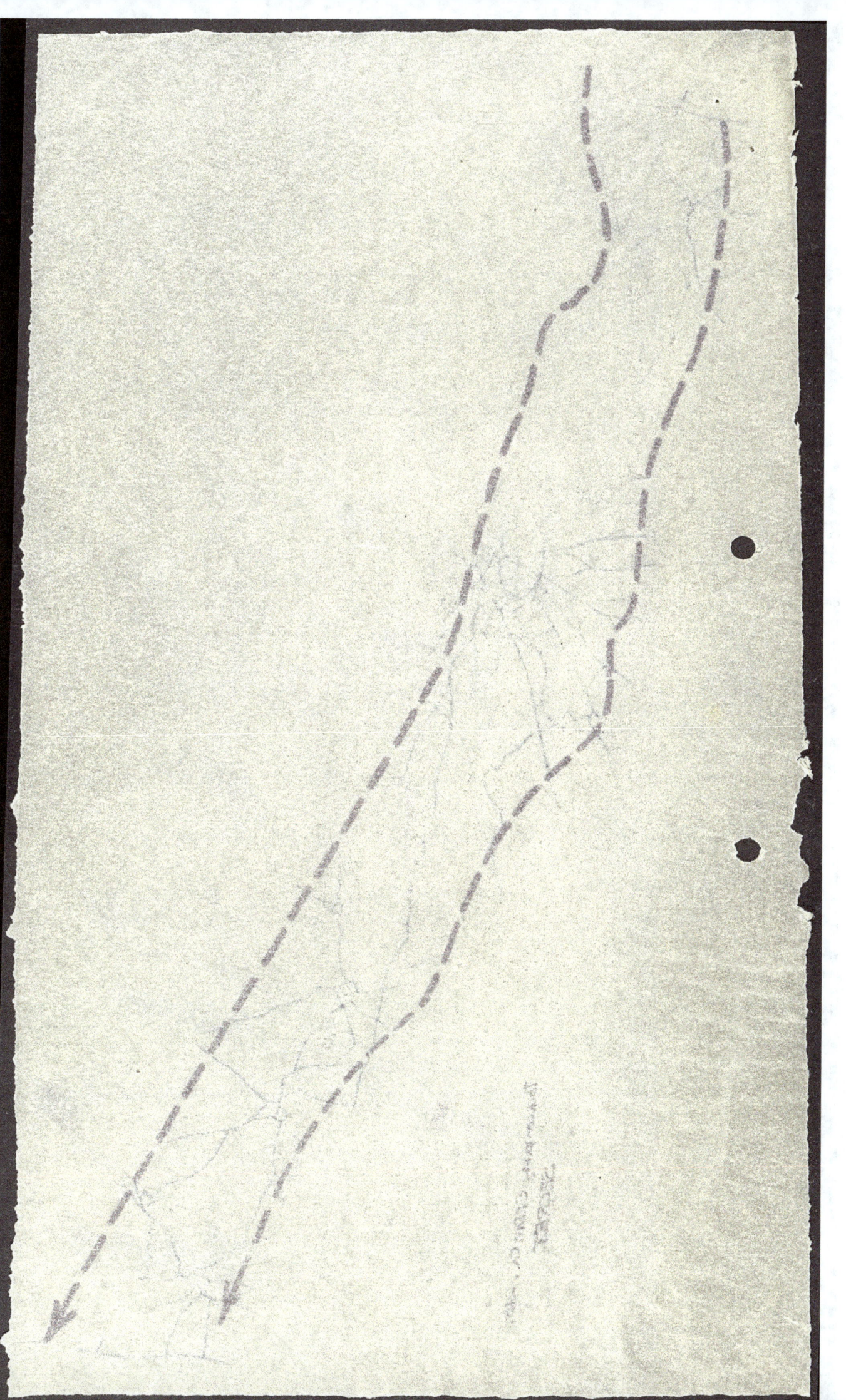

Appendix XVIII

SECRET.

Copy No. 17

61st DIVISION ORDER No. 216.
WARNING ORDER

10.10.18.

Reference Map 57^C. 1/40,000.

1. In order to conform to the rapid advance this morning the Division will be prepared to move to areas as shown below and complete moves by dusk today.

    (a) Advanced Guard Brigade Group.
        Consisting of 183rd Bde. Group, plus 306 Bde. R.F.A., and one Company 61st Bn. M.G. Corps, to an area in squares L.2., 3., and 4.

    (b) Support Brigade Group.
        Consisting of 182nd Bde. Group, plus 307 Bde. R.F.A., and one Company 61st Bn. M.G. Corps, to an area in squares F.25., and 26.

    (c) Reserve Brigade Group.
        Consisting of 184th Bde. Group, plus D.A.C., 61st Bn. M.G. Corps (less two companies), No. 1 Coy. Div. Train, to an area in squares E.22., 28., and 29 and K.4., and 5.

2. The above areas should be reconnoitred and allotted at once.

3. Div. H.Qrs. will remain at LAGNICOURT for the present.

4. ACKNOWLEDGE.

Issued at 1300

Dowden Maj.
for Lieut.Col.,
G.S., 61 Division.

Distribution:

    Copy No. 1 - A.D.C. for G.O.C.
            2 - 61 Signal Coy.
          3-4 - 61 Div. Arty.
            5 - 182 Inf. Bde.
            6 - 183 Inf. Bde.
            7 - 184 Inf. Bde.
            8 - 61 Bn. M.G.C.
            9 - 1/5 D.C.L.I.
          10 - C.R.E.
          11 - A.D.M.S.
          12 - 61 Div. Train
          13 - Q.
          14 - A.P.M.
          15 - Camp Comdt.
          16 - G.
       17-18 - War Diary.

APPENDIX XIX

SECRET.

61st DIVISION ORDER No. 217.

Copy No. 22
10.10.18.

Ref. Map 57C, 1/40,000.

1. 61st Division (less Artillery) will move into the areas laid down in Div. Order No. 216 of today, as follows :-

    (a) <u>Advanced Brigade Group</u>:
        Commence at once, and to be completed by 1630 hrs.

    (b) <u>Support Brigade Group</u>:
        Move at 1630 hrs: move to be completed by 1730 hrs.

    (c) <u>Reserve Brigade Group</u>:
        Move at 1730 hrs: move to be completed by 1830 hrs.

2. Artillery and D.A.C. will join Groups on the morning of 11th inst., under orders issued by C.R.A. 61st Division; move to be completed by 1200 hrs.

3. Location of all Headquarters will be forwarded to D.H.Q. as soon as possible after the move is complete.
    Completion of move to be notified to D.H.Q.

4. Administrative Instructions are issued herewith.

5. ACKNOWLEDGE.

Issued at 1545.

Lieut.-Col.,
G.S., 61st Divn.

Distribution :-

Copy No. 1 - A.D.C. for G.O.C.
       2 - 61 Signal Coy.
       3 - 61 Div. Engrs.
     4-5 - 61 Div. Arty.
       6 - 182 Inf. Bde.
       7 - 183 Inf. Bde.
       8 - 184 Inf. Bde.
       9 - 1/5 D.C.L.I.
      10 - A.D.M.S.
      11 - 61 Div. Train.
      12 - 61 Bn. M.G.C.
      13 - "Q".
      14 - D.A.P.M.
      15 - Camp Comdt.
      16 - "G".
   17-18 - XVII Corps Adv.
      19 - 19th Divn.
      20 - D.A.D.O.S.
      21 - D.A.D.V.S.

SECRET.

Appendix XX

Copy No. 18

61st DIVISION ORDER No. 218.

10.10.18.

1.   61st Divisional Artillery and 61st D.A.C. (less S.A.A. Section) will relieve 40th Divisional Artillery in the Leading Group of the Corps on the night 13th/14th inst.
No. 1 Company Divisional Train will accompany 61st Divl. Artillery.

2.   C.R.A., 61st Division, will take over command of the Artillery of the above Group on the night 13th/14th inst.

3.   All arrangements for the relief will be made by C.R.A. 61st Division and 40th Divl. Artillery.

4.   61st Divl. Artillery will report completion to H.Q., 24th and 61st Divisions.

5.   61st Divl. Artillery to acknowledge.

Issued at 2215 hrs.

C.W. Dowden, Maj.
for Lieut.-Col.,
G.S., 61st Division.

Distribution :-

Copy No.1 - A.D.C. for G.O.C.	8 - 61 Div. Train.
2 - 61 Div. Signals.	9 - A.D.M.S.
3-4 - 61 Divl. Arty.	10 - D.A.D.V.S.
5 - 182 Inf. Bde.	11 - D.A.D.O.S.
6 - 183 Inf. Bde.	12-13 - XVII Corps Adv.
7 - 184 Inf. Bde.	14 - "Q".

WAR DIARY   APPENDIX XXI

SECRET.   G.C. 79
                          61st DIVISION.
            Locations of Units at 1200, 12.10.18.

   61st DIV. H.Q.   LAGNICOURT.   Moves before
                                                   0600,14.10.18.
   61 DIV. ART.H.Q.   LAGNICOURT.)
     306 Bde.R.F.A.   L.2.a,b,c.   )   Moving during morning
     307   do.   F.25.a.3.8.)   13th to 24th Div.
     D.T.M.O.)   )   Area.
     D.A.C.   )   E.28.a.& b.)

   C.R.E.   LAGNICOURT.
     476 Field Coy.R.E.   F.25.a.8.5.
     478   do.   L.3.d.3.7.
     479   do.   E.29.b.1.5.

   182 Inf.Bde.H.Q.   F.19.c.6.2.
     2/6 Warwicks,   F.26.a.1.1.
     2/7 Warwicks,   F.26.a.9.1.
     2/8 Worcesters,   F.25.b.5.3.
     182 L.T.M.B.   F.25.a.6.9.

   183 Inf.Bde.H.Q.   F.27.d.8.0.
     9th North.Fus.   L.3.a.5.1.
     11th Suffolks,   L.3.b.7.2.
     1st E. Lancs.,   L.3.a.3.6.
     183 L.T.M.B.   L.3.b.6.7.

   184 Inf.Bde.H.Q.   Lock, E.21.a.
     2/5 Glosters,   E.22.b.7.3.
     2/4 Oxfords,   E.22.b.5.1.
     2/4 R.Berks,   E.29.c.5.9.
     184 L.T.M.B.   E.23.c.3.3.

   61 Bn. M.G.C.   SUCRERIE, E.29.a.75.75.
     "A" Coy.,   F.25.a.4.7.
     "B" Coy.,   E.23.c.15.10.
     "C" Coy.,   L.2.d.0.9.
     "D" Coy.,   E.29.c.0.0.

   1/5 D.C.L.I.(P),   COLLEGE, CAMBRAI, A.16.a.

   61 Div. Train H.Q.   LAGNICOURT.
     No. 1 Coy.,   K.3.b.8.8. .... ditto.
     No. 2 Coy.,   K.1.a.9.6.
     No. 3 Coy.,   E.27.b.cent.
     No. 4 Coy.,   K.3.b.8.7.

   A.D.M.S.   LAGNICOURT.
     2/1 Field Amb.   L.3.b.5.6.
     2/2   do.   E.28.c.1.9.
     2/3   do.   J.7.c.cent. (Corps Rest Stn.).

                                            A.S. Stephenson.
                                                 Capt.,
12.10.18.   G.S., 61 Divn.

SECRET.
Copy No. 15
APPENDIX XXII

61st DIVISION ORDER No. 219.
WARNING ORDER.

12.10.18.

1. Division will be prepared to move forward at short notice today.

2. Orders for move will be issued.

3. ACKNOWLEDGE.

Issued 0945.

                                                                           Lieut.-Col.,
                                                        G.S., 61st Division.

Distribution :-

Copy No.		Copy No.	
1	A.D.C. for G.O.C.	10	A.D.M.S.
2	61 Signal Coy.	11	Div. Train.
3-4	61 Div. Arty.	12	"Q".
5	61 Div. Eng.	13	Camp Comdt.
6	61 Bn. M.G.C.		
7	182 Inf. Bde.		
8	183 Inf. Bde.		
9	184 Inf. Bde.		

S E C R E T

		G.C. 79
61 Div.Art.	61 Bn.M.G.C.	
182 Inf.Bde.	1/5 D.C.L.I.	
183 Inf.Bde.	D.A.D.O.S.	Appendix XXIII
184 Inf.Bde.		

----

61 Division. 0600
Locations of Units at ~~1200~~, 14.10.18.

As given in location list for 1200, 12.10.18, except as under :-

```
                61 DIV..H.Q.      )
                C. R. E.          )   NOYELLES.
                61 Div. Train H.Q.)
                A. D. M. S.       )

                61 Div.Art.       ) under 24th Divn.
                No.1 Co. Train    )
```

2/5 GLOSTERS   PROMILLE

(signed) D. Stephenson

Captain,
G.S., 61st Divn.

13.10.18

WAR DIARY   APPENDIX XXIV

SECRET.   G.C. 79

61st DIVISION.
Locations of Units at 0600, 15.10.18.

61st DIV.H.Q.	NOYELLES.
61 Div.Art.H.Q.)	
306 Bde.R.F.A.)	AVESNES LEZ AUBERT,
307 do.)	
D.T.M.O.)	with 24th Divn.
D.A.C.)	
C.R.E.	NOYELLES.
476 Field Co.RE.	F.25.a.8.5.
478 do.	L.3.d.3.7.
479 do.	E.29.b.1.5.
182 Inf.Bde.H.Q.	F.19.c.6.2.
2/6 Warwicks,	F.26.a.1.1.
2/7 Warwicks,	F.26.a.9.1.
2/8 Worcesters,	F.25.b.5.3.
182 L.T.M.B.	F.25.a.6.9.
183 Inf.Bde.H.Q.	F.27.d.8.0.
9th North.Fus.	L.3.a.5.1.
11th Suffolks,	L.3.b.7.2.
1st E. Lancs.,	L.3.a.3.6.
183 L.T.M.B.	L.3.b.6.7.
184 Inf.Bde.H.Q.	Lock, E 21.a.
2/5 Glosters,	PROVILLE, A.20.b.3.7.
2/4 Oxfords,	E.22.b.5.1.
2/4 R.Berks.	E.29.c.5.9.
184 L.T.M.B.	E.23.c.3.3.
61 Bn. M.G.C.	SUCRERIE, E.29.a.75.75.
"A" Coy.,	F.25.a.4.7.
"B" Coy.,	E.23.c.15.10.
"C" Coy.,	L.2.d.0.9.
"D" Coy.,	E.29.c.0.0.
1/5 D.C.L.I.(P),	CAMBRAI, A.17.a.7.9.
61 Div.Train,H.Q.	NOYELLES.
No. 1 Coy.	B.4.a.9.9 (Sht.57B).
No. 2 Coy.	ANNEUX Area.
No. 3 Coy.	CANTAING Area.
No. 4 Coy.	K.3.b.8.7.
A.D.M.S.	NOYELLES.
2/1 Field Amb.	L.3.b.5.6.
2/2 do.	E.28.c.1.9.
2/3 do.	J.7.c.cent. (Corps Rest Stn.).
S.A.A.Sect., D.A.C.	E.28.a.1.1.

A.D. Stephenson
Capt. G.S., 61st Divn.

15.10.18.

SECRET.

War Diary
App XXV

61st DIVISION INSTRUCTIONS No.7.
INTELLIGENCE.

Divisional Observation Group.   1.   In order to supplement the means already existing of obtaining and rapidly transmitting every kind of information on the Divisional front, a Divisional Observation Group is being formed.
    This unit, under the command of Lieut. E.G. BATES, Northumberland Fusiliers, will consist of two sections -

    Mounted Section   - 1 sergt., 2 corpls., & 9 O.R.
    Dismounted Section - 1 sergt., 2 corpls., & 9 O.Rs.

Object in the Moving Battle.   2.   The main object of the Divisional Observation Group in the Moving Battle will be the observation and reporting of the progress of the fighting, chiefly in regard to the position of our own and neighbouring troops, and the degree of opposition with which they are meeting on the various portions of the front.
    Information as to observed enemy movement, dispositions, etc., will at the same time be sent in as far as it is possible to obtain it.

Object in the Stationary Phases.   3.   As soon as movement ceases, and the battle assumes a stationary phase, the main object of the Divisional Observation Group will be the observation and reporting of enemy movement, dispositions, activity, etc. opposite our own front and that of neighbouring troops.

Means of Communication.   4.   A Wireless Set will be detailed by O.C. Divisional Signals to accompany the Divisional Observation Group, and will be erected at its H.Q. The Divisional Observation Officer will also make himself acquainted with the position of the nearest point from which he can telephone.
    The Wireless Set will move forward with the H.Q. of the Divisional Observation Group, where the Divisional Observation Officer will receive messages, from whatever source, and will decide the order of priority of the despatch of messages.

5.   The Mounted Section will be specially trained as Visual Signallers and Despatch Riders. A proportion of them will also be trained in patrol duties and observation.
    Their duties during active operations will be -

(a) To carry information from sub-groups of the Dismounted Section back to the Group H.Q. or beyond as necessary.

(b) To act as Vedettes, or Ground Scouts.

(c) To establish a Visual Station, if necessary.

(d) To act as guides to relieving or reinforcing troops to any part of the line held by the Division.

Location of Group H.Q.   6.   The Divisional Observation Officer will notify Company and Battalion Commanders, as far as possible, the location of his H.Q. by means of his observers, who will periodically collect from troops in the line information as to the situation.

(P.T.O.)

(2)

Observation Posts. 7. At the same time he will select one or two good O.Ps., to each of which he will send an Observation Sub-Group of 2 or 3 observers.
These Sub-Groups will move forward by bounds from high ground to high ground, keeping progress with the advancing troops, and will act as laid down in 61st Division Instructions No. 2, para. 5 (b) & (c).

Transmission of messages. 8. Messages received from his own Group will be transmitted by the Divisional Observation Officer addressed to Infantry Brigades in the line. Messages received at Brigades will be repeated to Div. H.Q.

Assistance to fighting troops. 9. The Divisional Observation Group will thus exist for the general advantage of the fighting troops, and will provide another source for obtaining, and another channel for transmitting information.
The Group should be in a position, also, to take a detached and comprehensive view of the operations - a view which cannot be taken by troops actually engaged in the fighting.
It will not in any way be regarded as a substitute for any existing method, or as absolving the fighting troops and their observers from producing information by all the means at their disposal, as has already been emphasized in the above-quoted Divisional Instructions.

Dissemination of important information to fighting troops. 10. The Divisional Observers, therefore, will consider it one of their primary duties to transmit, on their own initiative, any information of an urgent nature to the nearest body of troops with the greatest possible rapidity, and thus ensure that immediate action be taken on this information.
For this reason, they will invariably find at once and get into touch with the nearest Infantry H.Q. and the nearest Battery.

Distinctive Badge. 11. All ranks of the Divisional Observation Group will wear a distinctive badge on the right arm, consisting of a green brassard with the Divisional sign in white.
Officers commanding units in the front line, and all ranks engaged, will, on recognising the Divisional Observers, give them all the information they possess as to the situation, and such facilities for observation and movement within their formations as will enable these observers to carry out their duties.

M. Wetherly.
Lieut.-Col.,
G.S., 61st Division.

16.10.18.

Distribution :-

182 Inf.Bde.	(4)	1/5 D.C.L.I.	(1)
183 Inf.Bde.	(4)	D.A.P.M.	(1)
184 Inf.Bde.	(4)	"Q"	(1)
61 Bn.M.G.C.	(5)	Div. Signals	(1)
C.R.A.	(3)	D.A.D.V.S.	(1)
C.R.E.	(1)	A.D.M.S.	(4)
61 Div.Train	(4)		

SECRET

G.C. 51/3

War Diary.

App XIII

182 Inf.Bde.
183 Inf.Bde.
184 Inf.Bde.
61 Bn.M.G.C.

1. The 61st Bn. M.G.C. is placed at the disposal of 19th Division and will march to RIEUX tomorrow, 17th inst., under orders of the Officer Commanding.

2. Moves to be completed by 1700 hrs.
   No restrictions as to route.

3. 61st Bn. M.G.C. will send an officer to meet a representative of 19th Division at RIEUX (U.19.d.9.8) at 1030 hrs. on 17th inst., to arrange accommodation.

4. Completion of moves will be reported to Headquarters, 19th and 61st Divisions.

5. ACKNOWLEDGE.

16.10.18.

for C H Dowden Maj
Lieut.-Col.,
G.S., 61st Division.

Copy to 19th Division.
         "Q".

Copy. G.C.31/1.

S E C R E T.

App XXVIII

C.R.E.
182 Inf. Bde.   61 Signal Coy.
183 Inf. Bde.   61 Div. Train.
184 Inf. Bde.   A.D.M.S.
61 Bn. M.G.C.   61 Div. "Q".

Reference D.O. 222 of 18.10.18.

It is possible that all moves except D.H.Q. may be postponed until the following day.

The necessary reconnaissance, billeting arrangements, etc. will, however, be carried out tomorrow morning.

                                (Signed) C. H. DOWDEN,
                                          Major,
18th October, 1918.   G.S., 61st Division.

SECRET.   Copy No.

                    61st DIVISION ORDER No. 221.
                    ─────────────────────────────
                                                                   17.10.18.

Reference Maps   57B. 1/40,000.
      "   57C. 1/40,000.
      ─────────

1.   61st Division Order No. 220 dated 17.10.18 is cancelled.

2.   61st Division will become the Supporting Group of XVII Corps
     from 0600 hours on 18th inst. Order of Groups will then be :-

                    Leading Group   - 19th Division.
                    Supporting Group - 61st Division.
                    Reserve Group   - 24th Division.

3.   The Division (less D.H.Q., Div. Arty., and 61 Bn.M.G.C.)
     will march to the area CANTAING - Southern outskirts of CAMBRAI
     on 18th inst. in accordance with attached movement table.

4.   The following distances will be maintained between units
     on the line of march :-

     (i)   Between Sections D.A.C., Companies, Units and
           their transport, and transport of units when Brigaded -100^x

     (ii) Between Battalions ... ... - 500^x

     (iii) Between Groups of 6 vehicles. ... ... - 25^x

5.   All further details of the move will be arranged by Commanders
     concerned.

6.   Completion of moves, and locations of Brigade Headquarters, will
     be wired to Div. H.Q. as early as possible.

7.   ACKNOWLEDGE.

                                                    Lieut. Col.,
     Issued at 1800 hrs.   for G.S., 61st Division.

                              DISTRIBUTION.

     Copy No. 1 - A.D.C. for G.O.C.   14 - D.A.D.O.S.
             2 - 61 Div. Signal Coy.   15 - D.A.D.V.S.
           3-4 - 61 Div. Arty.   16 - "Q"
             5 - C.R.E.   17 - "G"
             6 - 61 Bn. M.G.C.   18 - D.G.O.
             7 - 1/5 D.C.L.I.   19 - Camp Commandant.
             8 - 182 Inf. Bde.   20 - S.A.A.Sect., D.A.C.
             9 - 183 Inf. Bde.   21 - Mob. Vet. Sect.
            10 - 184 Inf. Bde.   22-23 - XVII Corps Adv.
            11 - A.D.M.S.   24 - 19th Division.
            12 - 61 Div. Train.   25 - 24th Division.
            13 - D.A.P.M.   26 - 13th Sqn., R.A.F.
                        27 - 28 War Diary.

                                                              P.T.O.

MOVEMENT TABLE ISSUED WITH 61st DIV. ORDER No. 221,
dated 17.10.18.

Serial No.	Date	Formation or Unit	From	To	Route	Remarks
1	13.10.18	Advanced Guard Group. 183 Inf.Bde. 478 Field Co.R.E. No.3 Coy.Div.Train. 2/1(SM) Field Amb.	CANTAING Area	Area about A.22 A.23.a.& c.	NOYELLES - Bridge L.6.c.2.3 cross-roads G.15.a.1.3 - A.22.a.0.0.	To be clear of Bridge L.6.c.2.3 by 1100 hrs.
2	do.	Support Group. 182 Inf.Bde. 476 Field Co.R.E. No.2 Coy.Div.Train. Mob.Vet.Sec.	ANNEUX Area	Area about A.21 A.16.c.& d.	NOYELLES - Bridge L.6.c.2.3	Not to arrive at Bridge L.6.c.2.3 before 1130 hrs. To be clear of CANTAING by 1300 hrs.
3	do.	Reserve Group. 184 Inf.Bde. 479 Field Co. R.E. No.4 Coy.Div.Train. 2/2(SM) Field Amb. SAA.Sect. D.A.C.	Area N.W. of GRAINCOURT	CANTAING Area		Not to arrive at CANTAING before 1400 hours. Dismounted troops to keep clear of the roads where possible. Move to be completed by 1700 hrs.

War Diary
Appendix XXVIII

SECRET.   Copy No. 2?

61st DIVISION ORDER No. 222.

18.10.1918.

Reference 57^B 1/40,000.
    "   57^C 1/40,000.

1. The Division will move forward by march route tomorrow in accordance with attached Movement Table.

2. The following distances will be maintained between units on the line of march :-
   (i) Between Sections of D.A.C., Companies, Units and their transport, and the transport of Units when Brigaded .... 1??
   (ii) Between Battalions 500x
   (iii) Between Groups of 6 vehicles 25x

3. Dismounted Troops will move across country as far as this is possible.
   Brigade Staffs will reconnoitre suitable routes for this.

4. Division H.Qrs. will close at NOYELLES sur L'ESCAUT at 1200 hrs. and open at RIEUX at that hour.

5. All further details of move will be arranged by Commanders concerned.

6. Completion of moves and location of Headquarters of Brigades will be wired to D.H.Q. early as possible.

7.   ACKNOWLEDGE.

Issued at 2000 hrs.

                                              C.H. Dowden Major
                                                    Lieut.Col.,
                                          for G.S., 61st Division.

DISTRIBUTION.

Copy No.		Copy No.	
1	A.D.C. for G.O.C.	14	D.A.D.O.S.
2	61 Div. Signals.	15	D.A.D.V.S.
3-4	61 Div. Arty.	16	"Q"
5	C.R.E.	17	"G"
6	61 Bn. M.G. Corps.	18	D.G.O.
7	1/5 D.C.L.I.	19	Camp Commandant.
8	182 Inf. Bde.	20	S.A.A.Sec., D.A.C.
9	183 Inf. Bde.	21	Mob. Vet. Sec.
10	184 Inf. Bde.	22-23	XVII Corps Adv.
11	A.D.M.S.	24	19th Division.
12	61 Div. Train.	25	24th Division.
13	D.A.P.M.	26	13th Sqn., R.A.F.
	27-28	War Diary.	

P.T.O.

MOVEMENT TABLE ISSUED WITH 61st DIV. ORDER No. 222, dated 18.10.18.

Serial No.	Date	Formation or Unit.	From	To	Route	Remarks
1	19.10.18	Support Bde.Group. 182 Inf.Bde. 476 Field Coy. R.E. No.2 Coy.Div.Train. Mob.Vet.Sec.	Area about A.21	RIEUX	Southern outskirts of CAMBRAI - road junction A.18.b.2.3 - cross-roads B.20.b.8.4 - cross-country tracks B.4.d.1.1 - cross-roads C.1.c.8.8.	Dismounted troops to march clear of roads & by cross-country tracks where possible. Not to arrive at RIEUX before 1230 hrs. To be clear of cross-roads B.4.d.1.1 by 1300 hrs.
2	do.	Div. H.Q.	NOYELLES	RIEUX	Bridge L.6.d.2.3 - southern outskirts CAMBRAI - road junction A.18.b.2.3 - cross-roads B.20.b.8.4 - cross-roads B.4.d.1.1. - cross-roads C.1.c.8.8.	To march at 1000 hrs.
3	do.	Div. Signals.	do.	do.	do.	To follow Div. H.Q.
4	do.	Reserve Bde. Group. 184 Inf.Bde. 479 Field Coy. R.E. No.4 Coy.Div.Train. 2/2(SM) Field Amb.	CANTAING Area	CAGNONCLES.	Bridge L.6.d.2.3 - southern outskirts CAMBRAI - road junction A.18.b.2.3 - cross-roads B.20.b.8.4 - CAUROIR.	Dismounted troops to march off the roads and by cross country tracks where possible. Not to arrive at bridge L.6.d.2.3 before 1200 hrs. Not to arrive at CAGNONCLES before 1530 hrs. To be clear of outskirts of CAMBRAI by 1800 hrs.
5	do.	Advanced Guard Bde. Group. 183 Inf.Bde. 478 Field Coy. R.E. No.3 Coy.Div.Train. 2/1(SM) Field Amb. SAA.Sec. D.A.C.	area about A.22	AVESNES LEZ AUBERT	Southern outskirts CAMBRAI - road junction A.18.b.2.3 - cross-roads B.20.b.8.4 - cross-roads B.4.d.1.1 - cross-roads C.3.a.8.4.	Dismounted troops to march off the roads where possible. Not to arrive at AVESNES before 2230 hrs.

SECRET.   G.C. 79.

Locations of 61st Division, at 0600 hours, October 20th, 1918.

Serial No.	Unit.	Location.
1	DIV. H.Q.	RIEUX, U.20.c.9.9.
2	Div. Arty. (under 19th Div.)	AVESNES-LEZ-AUBERT.
3	C. R. E.	RIEUX.
4	61st Bn. M.G.C. (under 19th Div.),	U.20.c.1.8.
5	1/5 D.C.L.I.	A.11.c.1.6.
6	182 Inf.Bde.	RIEUX, U.19.d.1.8.
7	2/6 Warwicks,	" U.20.a.1.3.
8	2/7 Warwicks,	" U.20.c.2.6.
9	2/8 Worcesters,	" U.20.c.0.8.
10	182 L.T.M.B.	" U.19.d.7.4.
11	476 Field Co. R.E.	" U.19.b.7.2.
12	No. 2 Coy. Div. Train	" U.25.central.
13	183 Inf.Bde.	AVESNES-LEZ-AUBERT.
14	9th North. Fus.	do.
15	11th Suffolks,	do.
16	1st E. Lancs.,	do.
17	183 L.T.M.B.	do.
18	478 Field Coy.R.E.	do.
19	No. 3 Coy. Div.Train,	THE BREWERY, AVESNES-LEZ-AUBERT.
20	2/1 Field Amb.	THE CINEMA, do.
21	184 Inf.Bde.	CAGNONCLES, T.28.d.4.3.
22	2/5 Glosters.	do. T.28.d.4.5.
23	2/4 Oxfords,	do. T.28.d.5.6.
24	2/4 R. Berks,	do. T.28.d.4.6.
25	184 L.T.M.B.	do. T.28.d.2.1.
26	479 Field Co.R.E.	do. T.28.d.3.2.
27	2/2 Field Amb.	do. B.4.b.6.8.
28	No. 4 Coy.Div.Train,	do. T.28.d.6.6.
29	S.A.A. Sec. D.A.C.	C.3.a.7.4.
30	Mob.Vet.Sec.	U.19.d.8.7.
31	2/3 Field Amb. (C.R.S.)	COLLEGE, CAMBRAI, A.16.a.8.2.

E.J. Stokesbury Capt
for G.S., 61st Divn.

19.10.18.

Appendix XXX
War Diary

SECRET

61st DIVISION
(PRELIMINARY) ORDER No. 223.

Copy No. 20

21.10.18.

1. The 61st Division is to be prepared to carry out an attack on the high ground East of the River ECAILLON, i.e., approximately line Q.17 - Q.10 - Q.3.

2. Provided the enemy does not retire beforehand, the earliest date on which this attack will take place is the 23rd inst. All arrangements will be made for that date.

3. The Division will be prepared, therefore, to relieve the 19th Division just before the attack, or, more probably, pass through that Division to attack.

4. The attack will be carried out by the 183rd Infantry Brigade on the right, and 182nd Infantry Brigade on the left. The 184th Infantry Brigade will be in Divisional Reserve.

5. The 19th Division will continue to hold the line until relieved by the 61st Division, and will ascertain the enemy's dispositions and the nature of any obstacles between his front and the objective mentioned in para. 1.

6. ACKNOWLEDGE.

Issued at 1030.

M Wetherly
Lieut.-Col.,
G.S., 61st Divn.

Distribution :-

Copy No. 1 - A.D.C. for G.O.C.
2 - 61 Signals.
3-4 - 61 Div. Arty.
5 - C.R.E.
6 - 61 Bn. M.G.C.
7 - 1/5 D.C.L.I.
8 - 182 Inf. Bde.
9 - 183 Inf. Bde.
10 - 184 Inf. Bde.
11 - A.D.M.S.
12 - 61 Div. Train.
13 - D.A.P.M.
14 - D.A.D.O.S.
15 - D.A.D.V.S.
16 - "Q".
17 - Camp Comdt.
18 - S.A.A. Sec. D.A.C.
19 - 19th Division.
20-21 - War Diary.

SECRET.   Copy No.

61st DIVISION ORDER No. 224.

22.10.1918.

Reference Map 57^B 1/40,000.
          51^A 1/40,000.

1. The Division will move forward on the 23rd inst. preparatory to operations to take place on 24th inst., in accordance with the attached movement table.

2. The usual distances will be maintained by units and transport on the line of march.

3. All dismounted troops will march off the roads wherever possible, and in view of the congested and bad state of the roads, the most strict march discipline must be maintained.

4. Accommodation forward will be extremely limited.

5. Advanced Division Headquarters will close at RIEUX at 1430 hrs. and open at the same hour at ST. AUBERT.
   Rear H.Q. will move to ST. AUBERT on the 24th inst.

6. Completion of moves and location of H.Qrs. will be wired to D.H.Qrs. as early as possible.

7. All further details of move will be arranged by Commanders concerned.

8.   ACKNOWLEDGE.

Issued at 1300.

                                                    Lieut. Col.,
                                                G.S., 61st Division.

DISTRIBUTION.

Copy No. 1 - A.D.C. for G.O.C.	14 - D.A.D.O.S.
2 - 61 Signal Coy.	15 - D.A.D.V.S.
3-4 - 61 Div. Arty.	16 - "Q"
5 - C.R.E.	17 - "G"
6 - 61 B^n. M.G. Corps.	18 - D.G.O.
7 - 1/5 D.C.L.I.	19 - Camp Commandant.
8 - 182 Inf. Bde.	20 - S.A.A. Sec., D.A.C.
9 - 183 Inf. Bde.	21 - Mob. Vet. Sec.
10 - 184 Inf. Bde.	22-23 - XVII Corps ADV.
11 - A.D.M.S.	24 - 19th Division.
12 - 61 Div. Train.	25 - 24th Division.
13 - D.A.P.M.	26 - 13th Squadron, R.A.F.
27 - 28 War Diary.	

P.T.O.

MOVEMENT TABLE TO ACCOMPANY 61st DIVISION ORDER No. 224, dated 22.10.18.

Serial No.	Date	Formation or unit.	From	To	Route	Remarks.
1	23.10.18.	184 Bde. Group. 184 Inf.Bde. 479 Fd.Coy.R.E.	CAGNONCLES & RIEUX	ST. AUBERT	Cross-roads B.5.c.0.1 - cross-roads V.25.c.1.1.	To march at 1230 hrs, and to arrange to take over accommodation in ST.AUBERT as soon as vacated by 183 Inf.Bde.
2	do.	183 Bde. Group. 183 Inf.Bde. 1 Coy.M.G.Bn. 478 Fd.Coy.R.E.	AVESNES & RIEUX	do.	Direct	To march at 0930 hrs.
3	do.	182 Bde. Group. 182 Inf.Bde. 1 Coy.61 M.G.Bn.	RIEUX	MONTRECOURT WOOD or locality to be selected by G.O.C. 182 Inf.Bde.	AVESNES-LEZ-AUBERT - AUBERT	Not to march before 1030 hrs.
4	do.	61 Bn.M.G.C., (less 2 Coys).	RIEUX	ST. AUBERT	AVESNES	Not to arrive at ST. AUBERT before 1030 hrs.
5	do.	Adv. Div.H.Q.	do.	do.	do.	To march at 1400 hrs. Rear D.H.Q. will remain at RIEUX for night 23rd/24th.
6	do.	61 Div.Signals	do.	do.	do.	To follow Adv. D.H.Q.
7	do.	476 Fd.Coy.R.E.	do.	do.	do.	To march at 1430 hrs.
8	do.	Coys.Div.Train, Field Ambces., Mob.Vet.Sec.	will move on 23rd inst., in accordance with 61 Div. Administrative Instructions No. Q.57/7/3 dated 21st inst.			

SECRET.   Copy No. 2

              61st DIVISION ORDER No. 225.   22.10.18.

1.   The 61st Division will attack and capture the high ground East of
the River ECAILLON on the 24th October, at a Zero hour which has been
notified to all concerned.
       The 2nd Division (VI Corps) will be attacking at the same time on
the right, and the 4th Division (XXII Corps) on the left.

2.   Objectives and Boundaries.
       The attack will consist of two phases :-
   (a) The crossing of the rivers HARPIES and ECAILLON and the capture of
       the villages of ST. MARTIN and BERMAIN, VENDEGIES and SOMMAING.
   (b) The capture of the high ground to North-East of the ECAILLON from
       LA FOLIE (Q.23.a.) to L'EPINE (Q.3.a.).

The boundaries and objectives will be as shown on the attached map.

3.   Dispositions.
       The attack will be carried out by the 183 Inf.Bde. on the right
and the 182 Inf.Bde. on the left.
       184 Inf.Bde. will be in Divisional Reserve.

4.   The attacking Brigades will move forward during the night 23rd/24th
October, and will form up along tape lines laid out along previously
laid cable close behind the advanced posts of the 19th Division.
       At Zero hour, the attacking troops will advance in conformity with
a creeping barrage, the general direction of the advance being a
magnetic compass bearing of 58°.
       As the attacking Brigades form up, troops of the 19th Division in
rear will be withdrawn.
       Should it be necessary to withdraw the advanced posts of the 19th
Division before Zero hour, the troops on the forming up line will
protect their own front with outposts.
       Arrangements to be made in this respect, and the hour at which
command will pass to G.O.C. 61st Division, will be notified to all
concerned.

5.   Artillery arrangements.
   (a) The attack will be carried out under a creeping barrage of field
       artillery and machine gun fire.
         The attack will be supported by -
           Right Group: 4 Brigades R.F.A.   Commander, Brig.-Gen. E.J.P
                                                          PEEL, D.S.O.
           Left Group: 5 Brigades R.F.A.
                         Commander - Lt.-Col. SPILLER, D.S.O.
                              and
              XVII Corps Heavy Artillery.

   (b) A creeping barrage of 18-pdrs. and 4.5" hows. will come down at
       Zero hour on a line shown on the barrage map which is being issued
to all concerned.
       It will commence to move forward at the rate of 100 yards in 3
minutes up to the 1st Protective Barrage.
       It will lift off this line at Zero plus 40, and advance at the
rate of 100 yards in 6 minutes up to the 2nd Protective Barrage,
with the exception of batteries firing West of the road Q.7.d.3.5 -
Q.2.c.3.3, which will lift in accordance with barrage map.
       It will lift off the 2nd Protective Barrage line at Zero plus 180,
and will move forward at a rate of 100 yards in 4 minutes up to the
3rd and final Protective Barrage line over the BLUE objective.
       The Final Protective Barrage will remain for 15 minutes and then
cease.
                                                      (P.T.O.)

(2)

(c) 10% of smoke will be fired in the barrage on the Right Brigade front.

(d) Thermite at an increased range of 200 yards will be fired at each lift to mark the flanks of battalions and brigades throughout the advance.
   A salvo of Thermite will also be fired when each Protective Barrage is reached.

(e) One section of 18-pdrs. on each Infy. Bde. front will be detailed to accompany the advanced infantry, and will be pushed well forward on reaching the final objective for the purpose of engaging hostile tanks.

(f) There will be no artillery fire without direct observation within squares K.33 and K.34 (North of "Q" squares) until the final dispositions of the 4th Division on the left are known.

6. **Machine Gun arrangements.**
   61st Bn. M.G.C. and 2 coys. 19th Bn. M.G.C., under the command of the Divisional Machine Gun Officer, will support the attack.
   Details of the Machine Gun barrage for the first phase will be arranged by the D.M.G.O. with C.R.A. and Inf. Bdes.
   One M.G.Coy., 61st Bn.M.G.C., will be detailed to accompany each of the attacking Brigades to act as "Forward Guns".
   The remaining 2 coys. 61st Bn.M.G.C. will, as soon as outranged, be re-grouped in Divisional Reserve and disposed on the high ground West of the R. HARPIES and ECAILLON, one coy. in each Inf. Bde. sector.
   The 2 coys. 19th Bn.M.G.C. will be withdrawn as ordered by the D.M.G.O. on completion of their tasks.

7. **Employment of Field Coys. R.E. and Pioneers.**
   The C.R.E. will be responsible for the construction and placing in position of 10 foot-bridges on each Brigade front.
   For this purpose two sections R.E., and two platoons 1/5 D.C.L.I.(P), will accompany each attacking Brigade.
   These bridges, as soon as placed in position, will be marked by X shaped sign-boards painted white.
   The C.R.E. will also be responsible for the construction of two trestle bridges for use of Field Arty. at Q.7.d.2.3 and Q.28.a.7.9.
   For this purpose, two sections R.E. and one platoon 1/5 D.C.L.I.(P) will accompany each attacking Brigade.
   The remaining Field Coys. R.E. and Pioneers will be in General Reserve about MONTRECOURT WOOD, under the C.R.E.
   Heavy bridges will be constructed under C.E. Corps at Q.14.b.4.9, Q.20.a.3.6, Q.20.a.9.8, and Q.21.d.6.6.

8. **Consolidation.**
   Troops, on reaching the Final Objective, will dig themselves in as rapidly as possible, and Battle Outposts will be pushed forward to command all low ground and approaches from the front.
   A proportion of machine guns with Infy. Bdes. will be pushed well forward to cover the work of consolidation.
   Special officers will be detailed by Brigades to organise this consolidation on the ground.
   It is of special importance that the enemy be denied the village line in event of counter-attack.   Special parties will be detailed to prepare the exits of these villages for defence, and a proportion of machine guns will be detailed to sweep all approaches.

9. **Light Signals.**
   (a) WHITE Very lights will be used by the most advanced troops to denote their position.
   (b) RED flares will be lit by the most advanced troops on or near the Final Objective.
   (c) The S.O.S. Signal is a rifle grenade bursting into RED over GREEN over RED.

(3)

10. Cooperation with R.A.F.
    Contact aeroplanes will call for flares at -
        Zero plus 3½ hours,
        Zero plus 5 hours,
        Zero plus 7 hours.
    A counter-attack machine will be in the air continuously from daylight.

11. Reserve Brigade.
    The 184th Inf.Bde. will move from ST. AUBERT at daybreak on 24th inst. across the SELLE River to about square V.5, to occupy the high ground to the West of the river, with Brigade H.Q. at the SANDPITS (V.5.a.).

12. Reports.
    Advanced Divisional Headquarters will close at ST. AUBERT at Zero hour on 24th October, and will open at MONTRECOURT at the same hour.
    H.Q. of attacking Brigades will be as follows :-
        183rd Inf.Bde. - V.5.c.5.1.
        182nd Inf.Bde. - V.5.a. (SANDPITS).

13. Synchronisation of watches.
    Watches will be synchronised by O.C. Div. Signals at 6 p.m., 23rd October.

14. ACKNOWLEDGE.

Issued at 23.00

Lieut.-Col.,
G.S., 61st Division.

Distribution :-

Copy No. 1 - A.D.C. for G.O.C.   11 - A.D.M.S.
        2 - Div. Signal Coy.   12 - "Q".
      3-4 - Div. Arty.   13 - "G".
        5 - C.R.E.   14 - XVII Corps.
        6 - 61 Bn.M.G.C.   15 - XVII Corps H.A.
        7 - 1/5 D.C.L.I.(P).   16 - 2nd Div.
        8 - 182 Inf.Bde.   17 - 4th Div.
        9 - 183 Inf.Bde.   18 - 19th Div.
       10 - 184 Inf.Bde.   19 - 24th Div.
                                   20 - 13th Sqn. R.A.F.
                                21-22 - War Diary.
                                   23 - 12th Bn. Tank Corps.

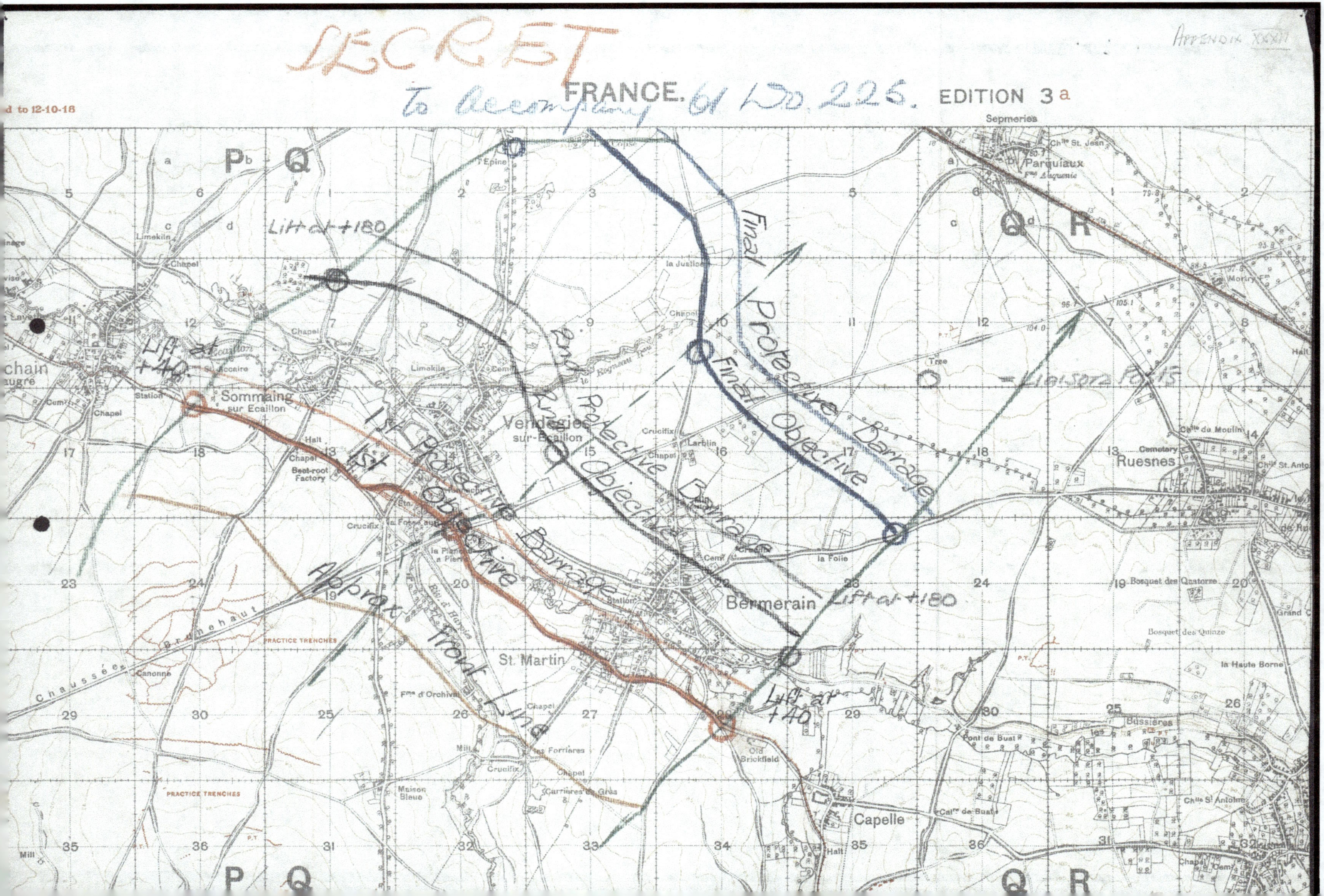

SECRET
Appendix XXXII
To accompany 61 Div. 225.
FRANCE.
EDITION 3a
d to 12-10-18
Final Protective Barrage
Final Objective
2nd Protective Barrage
2nd Objective
1st Protective Barrage
1st Objective
Approx. front line
Lift at +180
Lift at +180
Lift at +40
Lift at +40
Sepmeries
Parquiaux
l'Epine
la Justice
Sommaing sur Ecaillon
Vendegies sur-Ecaillon
Larblin
la Folie
Bermerain
St. Martin
Ruesnes
Bussières
Capelle
Pont de Buat
Old Brickfield
Maison Bleue
Canonne
Chaussée Brunehaut
PRACTICE TRENCHES
Beet-root Factory
Limekiln
Bosquet des Quatorze
Bosquet des Quinze
la Haute Borne
Cemetery
Station
Chapel
Crucifix
Tree
P
Q
R

Rps - XXXII

SECRET.

G.C.40/5.

War Diary
app XXXIII

Reference 61st Division Order No.225 dated 22nd October 1918.

1. **Relief.**
   The advanced posts 19th Division forward of the forming up line will be withdrawn at 0315 hours on the morning of the 24th inst.
   Command of the Divisional front will pass from G.O.C. 19th Div. to G.O.C. 61st Div. at that hour.

2. **Corps Mounted Troops.**
   Two troops Divisional Cavalry and 2 platoons Cyclists will be transferred to the 61st Division from the 19th Division on the passing of the command.
   One section of Cavalry will be attached to each Infantry Bde. H.Q. for communication purposes, and will report at Brigade H.Q. by 0600 hrs. on 24th October as follows :-

   182 Inf.Bde. at SANDPITS, V.5.a.
   183 Inf.Bde. at V.5.c.5.1.
   184 Inf.Bde. at MONTRECOURT.

   One section will be attached for D.R. purposes to Divisional Observation Group, under orders of the Divl. Observation Officer, to be at SANDPITS (V.5.a.) by 0600 hrs. The Divl. Observation Officer will send orders to this section as to the location he has selected for them.
   Remaining troop Divisional Cavalry will remain at Adv. Div. H.Q., MONTRECOURT, reporting there at 0700 hrs. on 24th Octr.
   The two platoons Cyclists will be attached to Divl. Signal Coy. for Despatch Riding; to report to O.C. Divl. Signals at MONTRECOURT at 0600 hrs. 24th October.

3. **Reserve Brigade.**
   Brigade H.Q. will be established at MONTRECOURT, and not as stated in Divl. Order No. 225.

4. **Consolidation.**
   The C.R.E. will arrange to detail special R.E. parties to assist in and supervise the defence of the village line referred to in para. 8 of Div. Order No. 225. Arrangements will be made by C.R.E. with Infantry Bdes. concerned.
   One company of infantry will be detailed to garrison this line in each battalion sector.

5. **Divisional Cage.**
   The Divisional Cage will be situated at HAUSSY, V.11.b.4.5.

6. **Communications.**
   Attention is called to Divl. Instructions No. 8, and to the importance of sending back frequent and early information.

7. ACKNOWLEDGE.

Lieut.-Col.,
G.S., 61st Division.

23.10.18.

Distribution :-

A.D.C. for G.O.C.	"Q".
Div. Signal Coy.	"G".
Div. Arty.	XVII Corps.
C.R.E.	XVII Corps H.A.
61 Bn. M.G.C.	2nd Div.
1/5 D.C.L.I.(P.)	4th Div.
182 Inf.Bde.	19th Div.
183 Inf.Bde.	24th Div.
184 Inf.Bde.	13th Sqn. R.A.F.
A.D.M.S.	12th Bn. Tank Corps.

War Diary.

(2)

Distribution :-

Copy No. 1 - A.D.C. for G.O.C.
       2 - Div. Signal Coy.
    3-4 - Div. Arty.
       5 - C.R.E.
       6 - 61 Bn. M.G.C.
       7 - 1/5 D.C.L.I.(P).
       8 - 182 Inf. Bde.
       9 - 183 Inf. Bde.
     10 - 184 Inf. Bde.
     11 - A.D.M.S.
     12 - "Q".
     13 - "G".
     14 - XVII Corps.
     15 - XVII Corps H.A.
     16 - 2nd Div.
     17 - 4th Div.
     18 - 19th Div.
     19 - 24th Div.
     20 - 13th Sqn. R.A.F.
     21 - 12th Bn. Tank Corps.
  22-23 - War Diary.

SECRET.   Copy No. XXXIV

61st DIVISION ORDER No. 226.

                                                           23.10.18.

1.   In view of the satisfactory progress made in today's attack, the objective of the XVII Corps for tomorrow's operation has been extended in depth.

2.   After reaching the FINAL OBJECTIVE laid down in 61st Div. Order No. 225 of 22nd October, the attack will be continued to establish the Corps Main Line of Resistance along the general line of high ground Q.12.b. - Q.3.b., whence a strong Outpost Line will be pushed forward towards the village of SEPMERIES.
        If opposition is slight, the village will be included in the Outpost Line.

3.   The 2nd Division on the right has been ordered to continue its attack to capture RUESNES and the high ground to N.E. of it.

4.   The 4th Division on the left will take the village of QUERENAING and high ground about K.26, and exploit forward to SEPMERIES - VALENCIENNES Railway.

5.   The point of junction with 2nd Division on the Main Line of Resistance will be at R.7.a.0.0.
        183 Inf.Bde. will establish a Liaison Post at this point.

6.   The 19th Division have had to conform to the advance of the VI Corps on the right today, and their present front line now runs along the whole of the first objective as marked on the Barrage Map.
        The barrage will now come down on the line of the first Protective Barrage at Zero hour, which will not be altered.
        It will lift from this line at Zero plus 6 minutes, and will continue to lift at the rate as laid down for the remainder of the advance.
        The lifts as marked on the Barrage Table will thus be altered, e.g., for "Lift at plus 40" read "Lift at plus 6"; for "plus 46" read "plus 12"; for "52" read "plus 18", and so on.

7.   It is of great importance, therefore, that attacking troops move forward to form up along the line of the First Objective early.
        Should any troops of 19th Div. be forward of that line, they will be withdrawn before Zero.

8.   After reaching the Third Objective, there will be no pause, and the barrage will continue forward at the rate of 100 yards in 4 mins. up to the Final Objective (Corps Main Line of Resistance) given in para. 2 above, viz., Q.12.b.9.0 - Q.12.b.0.9 - K.6.c.5.5 - K.6.a.0.0 - K.5.b.0.5 - K.4.a.0.9 - back to left of Third Objective.
        It will then lift on to a protective barrage line along railway in R.1 - Q.6 - K.35, where it will remain for 15 minutes and then cease.

9.   Divisional and inter-Corps boundaries forward will prolong the existing boundaries in straight lines, viz., Right boundary to L.28.c.0.5, Left boundary to L.7.c.0.0.
        Inter-Brigade boundary forward will run through Q.10.central - Q.5.central - K.36.central.

10.   Reference para. 12 of 61st Div. Order No. 225.
        Advanced Div.H.Q. will remain at ST.AUBERT until further orders.
        Divisional Report Centre will open at MONTRECOURT at Zero hour, October 24th.

11.   ACKNOWLEDGE.

Issued at 2030.
                                                       Lieut.-Col.,
                                                       G.S., 61st Division.

(Distribution overleaf)

"A" Form.
MESSAGES AND SIGNALS.

Army Form C. 2121.
(In pads of 100.)

APPENDIX **XXXV**

URGENT OPERATIONS PRIORITY.

TO	JUBE	62 Heavies	JUME
	JUPI		17 Corps Adv
	C.R.A.	61 Bn. MGC.	2nd Div

Sender's Number.	Day of Month.	In reply to Number.	
* GS.100	24		AAA

Enemy still hold VENDEGIES aaa Our line Right Bde runs along high ground through Q.18.c. - Q.17.b.& a - Mill Q.16.c. - Q.21.d. - ST.MARTIN aaa Divl Comdr is now forward at JUME HQ MONTRECOURT and is issuing orders for Reserve Bde to move by S.& E. of BERMERAIN and to attack across to N. of VENDEGIES aaa JUPI will at once push out to secure and hold the high ground in Q.17.a.& b. and copse in Q.16.c. to prepare the way for the above operation aaa The attack of JUME is expected to develop about 1530 hrs aaa DMGO will detail one M.G.Coy to move at once and be at MAISON BLEUE at 1330 hrs to accompany Reserve Bde aaa GOC JUME will arrange with Right Group Comdr for necessary arty to accompany and support his movements aaa Addsd JUPI JUME Bn.MGC to acknowledge reptd JUBE CRA 62 Heavies Corps 2nd Div

From **VACA**
Place
Time **1145**

(Z) (Sd.) W.Whetherly, Lt.Col
GS.

"A" Form.
MESSAGES AND SIGNALS.

Army Form C. 2121.
(In pads of 100.)

URGENT
~~PRIORITY~~
~~OPERATIONS~~
PRIORITY.

This message is on a/c of: War Diary

App XXXVI

TO	JUBE	CRA	2 Div.	62 Bde.	RGA
	JUPI	CRE	~~4 Div.~~	17 Corps	
	JUME	61 Bn. MGC	19 Div.	Sig. Coy.	

Sender's Number: G.135. Day of Month: 25   AAA

● is absolutely essential that touch with enemy be maintained aaa JUME with 2 Bdes. RFA and 1 MG.Coy. will be prepared to resume advance as Advance Guard Bde. aaa In accordance with instructions already given to JUME and JUPI JUME will extend front now held by right Bn in Q.12.c. Q.11.d. and Q.11.c. by capturing high ground in Q.11.a and to North of LA JUSTICE Q.10.a.8.9 with one Bn. at 0400 hours aaa JUPI will protect this operation on its left flank against any opposition from West aaa JUBE and JUPI will be prepared to continue advance in their respective Bde. areas in support of JUME aaa Every effort will be made by JUBE and JUPI to reorganise and dispose in depth aaa Patrols to clear up situation in VENDEGIES will be sent forward at dawn by all three Bdes. aaa

*This line, except AAA, should be erased if not required.
Wt. W 3253/P511. 500,000 Pads. 1/18. B. & S. Ltd. (E2359.)

"A" Form.
MESSAGES AND SIGNALS.

Army Form C. 2121.
(In pads of 100.)
No. of Message.........

Prefix...... Code......... m.	Words.	Charge.	This message is on a/c of:	Recd. at...... m.
Office of Origin and Service Instructions.	Sent			Date
	At..... m.		......Service.	From
	To			
	By		(Signature of "Franking Officer.")	By

TO — 2 —

Sender's Number.	Day of Month.	In reply to Number.	AAA

In event of enemy withdrawal touch will be maintained by Corps Mounted Troops supported by Infantry and Arty. of Advance Guard aaa Early information of enemy withdrawal is of utmost importance and will be reported immediately aaa If enemy does not retire Advance Guard Bde. will push enemy back up to distance of 2 to 3 miles aaa Should opposition prove so strong that headway cannot be made without support or only by incurring serious casualties advance will not be pressed without further orders aaa Addsd JUBE JUPI JUME DERU to Acknowledge aaa Reptd. ZONI VABO MILA ZIZO GOVU Corps Heavies and NELO

VAGA

From
Place 0105
Time

The above may be forwarded as now corrected.   (Z)
.... Censor.   Signature of Addressor or person authorised to telegraph in his name.

*This line, except A A A, should be erased if not required.
Wt. W 3253/P511. 500,000 Pads. 1/18. B. & S. Ltd. (E2389.)

S E C R E T.   **61st DIVISION.**   G.C.79.

LOCATIONS OF ADVANCED H.Q. at 0600, 25th OCTOBER, 1918.

App XXXVI

61 DIV.H.Q. ADVANCED.	MONTRECOURT.
do. REAR	ST. AUBERT.
C.R.A.	MONTRECOURT.
C.R.E.	do.
182 Inf.Bde.	P.30.c.2.1.
183 Inf.Bde.	MAISON BLEUE, Q.31.b.8.9.
184 Inf.Bde.	do. do.
61 Bn. M.G.C.	HAUSSY, V.11.a.
1/5 D.C.L.I.(P).	HAUSSY.
478 Field Coy. R.E.	do.
6th Dragoon Guards.	ST. AUBERT.
476 Field Coy. R.E.	MONTRECOURT.
479 do.	do.

24.10.18.

A.O. Stephenson
Capt.,
G.S., 61 Div.

SECRET.
G.C. 79

APPENDIX XXXVIII

61st DIVISION
Sht. 51A.   Locations of Units at 1800 hrs, 25.10.18.

61 DIV.ADV.H.Q.	VENDEGIES, Q.14.d.1.7.
do. REAR,	ST. AUBERT. (To VENDREGIES during 26th).
C.R.A.	VENDREGIES.
C.R.E.	do. Q.14.d.1.8.
182 Inf.Bde.Adv.	Q.8.d.8.7.
2/6 Warwicks,	Q.8.d.25.15.
2/7 Warwicks,	Q.13.a.7.5.
2/8 Worcesters,	Q.14.a.6.7.
182 L.T.M.B.	Q.14.a.6.7. ("D" Coy. only).
183 Inf.Bde.Adv.	Q.22.a.5.5.
9th North.Fus.	Q.23.a.8.6.
11th Suffolks,	Q.27.b.4.9.
1st E. Lancs.,	Q.22.a.4.8.
184 Inf.Bde.Adv.	Q.22.a.5.2.
do. Report Centre,	LARBLIN, Q.16.a.
2/5 Glosters,	Line (Left Bn.).
2/4 Oxfords,	Line (Right Bn.).
2/4 R. Berks,	Support Bn.
61 Bn. M.G.C.	Q.14.a.8.1.
476 Field Coy.RE.	Q.14.a.8.5.
478 do.	Q.22.d.0.3.
479 do.	Q.21.b.8.0.
1/5 D.C.L.I.(P),	ST. MARTIN, Q.27.b.6.5.
61 Div. Train.	ST. AUBERT.
6th D.Gds.	ST. MARTIN.
D.O.O.	PARQUIAUX.
P.O.W. Cage,	Q.14.b.1.4.
2/1 Field Amb.	HAUSSY.
2/2 do.	ST. AUBERT.

"A" Form.
MESSAGES AND SIGNALS.
Army Form C. 2121.
(In pads of 100.)
No. of Message ....

Prefix ...... Code ...... m	Words.	Charge.	This message is on a/c of:	Recd. at ...... m.
Office of Origin and Service Instructions.	Sent		*Opp* ~~XXXIX~~	Date
	At ...... m.		Service.	
	To			From
	By		(Signature of "Franking Officer.")	By

TO	JUBE	C.R.A.	2 Div	24 Div
	JUPI	C.R.E.	4 Div	62 Bde. RGA
	JUMM	61 Bn. MGC.	19 Div	17 Corps Adv Div. Sigs.

Sender's Number.	Day of Month.	In reply to Number.	
G.203	25		AAA

JUBE will continue operations tomorrow as in wire G.183 of today aaa If Adv Gd Comdr unable to establish bridgeheads without heavy fighting he will confine himself to reconnaissance to ascertain enemy dispositions aaa Early information as to nature of crossings and bridging requirements over river as a result of expert reconnaissance to be reported aaa CRE will arrange expert assistance as required by JUMM aaa Addsd JUMM CRE reptd JUBE JUPI CRA 2 Div 4 Div 19 Div 24 Div 62 RGA 17 Corps Adv Div.Sigs 61 Bn.MGC

From VAGA
Place
Time 2050

The above may be forwarded as now corrected. (Z) (Sd.) C.H.Dowden,
C.S.

SECRET

Sht. 51.A.

61st DIVISION.
Locations of Units at 0600 hrs. 26.10.18.

War Diary
G.O. 79.

App XL

61 DIV.H.Q. ADV.	VENDEGIES, Q.14.d.1.7.
do. REAR	ST. AUBERT.
C.R.A.	VENDEGIES.
C.R.E.	do.
182 Inf.Bde.H.Q.	Q.8.d.5.7.
183 Inf.Bde.H.Q.	Q.22.a.5.5.
184 Inf.Bde.H.Q.	Q.22.a.5.2.
do. Report Centre,	LARBLIN, Q.16.a.
61 Bn. M.G.C.	Q.14.a.8.1.
1/5 D.C.L.I.(B),	HAUSSY.
476 Field Coy.R.E.	MONTRECOURT. Q14.a.8.5
478 do.	HAUSSY. Q.22.d.0.3
479 do.	MONTRECOURT. Q.21.b.8.0
Div. P.O.W.Cage,	to open during morning at Q.14.b.1.4.

25.10.18.

R.D. Stephenson
Capt

G.S. 61 Div.

"A" Form.
MESSAGES AND SIGNALS.

Army Form C. 2121.
(In pads of 100.)

Prefix......Code......m	Words.	Charge.	This message is on a/c of:	Recd. at ....m.
Office of Origin and Service Instructions.				Date............
	Sent			From
	At......m.		............Service.	
	To......		*Appendix*	
	By......		(Signature of "Franking Officer.")	By............

TO		W D		

Sender's Number.	Day of Month.	In reply to Number.	AAA
G.218	26		

JUPI relieves JUME as Advanced Guard Bde tonight 26/27 Oct aaa Arrangements for relief to be made between Brigadiers aaa Relief to be completed by 0600 hrs 27 Oct aaa 2 Bdes RFA and 1 MG Coy and Subsec DAC at present with Adv Gd will come under orders of GOC JUPI aaa Relief of MG Coy with Adv Gd will be arranged by DMGO on night 27/28 aaa JUME on relief will become Right Support Bde and will be responsible for defence Corps MLR in Right Bde Sector with 2 Bns in BERMERAIN aaa Essential that touch with enemy maintained and preparations ready to resume advance aaa Active patrolling for this purpose and to gain information as stated in G.203 of 25th will continue to be carried out aaa Relief and location to be reported on completion aaa Acknowledge aaa Addsd all concd

From	V AGA
Place	
Time	1210

The above may be forwarded as now corrected. (Z)

Censor. Signature of Addresser or person authorised to telegraph in his name.

* This line should be erased if not required.

APPENDIX XLII

SECRET.

G.C. 79.

Sht.31A.
61st DIVISION.
Locations of Units at 0600 hrs., 27.10.18.

61st DIV. H.Q.	VENDEGIES (Q.14.d.1.7).	
C. R. A.	VENDEGIES.	
306 Bde. R.F.A.	Q.21.a.8.0.	
307 do.	Q.16.a.3.2.	
C. R. E.	VENDEGIES, Q.14.d.1.8.	
182 Inf.Bde.H.Q.	VENDEGIES (Q.8.d.8.7).	
2/6 Warwicks,	Q.8.d.25.15.	
2/7 Warwicks,	Q.13.a.7.5.	
2/8 Worcesters,	Q.14.a.6.7.	
183 Inf.Bde. H.Q.	(ADVANCED GUARD) BERMERAIN.	Moving during day to
9th North. Fus.	(Bde. Res.) LA FOLIE.	LARBLIN (Q.16.a
11th Suffolks,	(Line Right) LARBLIN.	Q.11.c.8.8.
1st E. Lancs,	(Line Left) LA JUSTICE.	Q.4.c.6.5.
184 Inf.Bde.H.Q.	BERMERAIN (Q.22.a.5.2).	
2/5 Glosters,	do. (Q.22.a.45.70).	
2/4 Oxfords,	do.	
2/4 R. Berks,	do.	
61 Bn. M.G.C.	VENDEGIES (Q.14.a.8.1).	
476 Field Coy. R.E.	Q.14.a.8.5.	
478 do.	Q.22.d.0.3.	
479 do.	Q.21.b.8.0.	
1/5 D.C.L.I.(P),	ST. MARTIN (Q.27.b.6.5).	
61 Div.Train,	VENDEGIES (Q.14.b.3.7).	
No. 1 Coy.	Q.32.b.central.	
No. 2 Coy.	Q.28.a.6.4.	
No. 3 Coy.	Q.28.a.3.7.	
No. 4 Coy.	Q.27.c.2.7.	
D. O. O.	SEPMERIES (Q.6.b.central).	
2/1 Field Amb.	Q.20.a.1.7.	
2/2 do.	P.30.b.	
P.O.W. Cage,	VENDEGIES (Q.14.b.1.4).	

A.D. Stephenson
Capt.,
G.S., 61st Div.

26.10.18.

Appendix XLIII War Diary

SECRET

61st DIVISION ORDER No. 227.

Copy No.
27.10.18.

1. As a result of a reconnaissance in force by the Advanced Guard Brigade this morning, the enemy are found to be holding the RHONELLE Valley and crossings in strength and on both banks of the river.

2. In conjunction with the 4th Division on our left, we still hold a bridge-head across the river at FERME DE L'HOTEL DIEU, which extends above the roadway Eastwards to about K.30.a.5.0.

3. The Advanced Guard Bde. Commander will take the necessary steps to cover the bridge-head with fire and to preserve his present dispositions there. He will, however, withdraw all troops that are at present down the forward slopes on the left (South) bank of the river back as far as will still preserve observation of the valley, and will accurately inform the C.R.A. as early as possible as to the position of his line.

4. As soon as the dispositions of the Advanced Guard Bde. are completed, the C.R.A. will commence to bombard, search and sweep the valley on both banks and the village of MARESCHES with artillery and T.Ms. of all natures until further orders.
   The D.M.G.O. will arrange, in conjunction with the C.R.A. and Advanced Guard Commander, to carry out continuous harassing fire by day and night.

5. The artillery programme will be arranged in series of intense fire at odd periods, the intervals being filled with Machine Gun harassing fire on the village and along river valley.

6. The C.R.A. will inform D.H.Q. the time of commencement and periods of fire arranged for, as early as possible, for communication to all concerned.

7. ACKNOWLEDGE.

Issued at 1400 hrs.

M. Wetherby
Lieut.-Col.,
G.S., 61st Division.

Distribution :-

Copy No. 1 - A.D.C. for G.O.C.
     2 - 182 Inf.Bde.
     3 - 183 Inf.Bde.
     4 - 184 Inf.Bde.
     5 - D.M.G.O.
   6-7 - 61 Div.Art.
     8 - 4th Div.
     9 - 3rd Div.
    10 - 24th Div.
    11 - 62 Bde. R.G.A.
    12 - D.O.O.
    13 - "Q".
    14 - XVII Corps Adv.

War Diary. Appendix XLIV

SECRET. G.C.79.
A
Sheet 51   61st DIVISION
            Locations of Units at 0600 Hrs., 28.10.1918.

61st Division H.Q.	VENDEGIES (Q.14.d.1.7.)
C.R.A.	VENDEGIES.
306 Bde., RFA.	Q.28.b.2.8.
305 Bde., RFA.	Q.16.a.4.2.
C.R.E.	VENDEGIES, Q.14.d.1.8.
182 Inf.Bde.H.Q.	VENDEGIES (Q.8.d.8.7)
2/6 Warwicks.	VENDEGIES and SOMMAING.
2/7 Warwicks.	Q.13.a.7.5.
2/8 Worcesters.	Q.14.a.6.7.
183 Inf.Bde.H.Q.	(ADVANCED GUARD). LA JUSTICE.
9th North'd. Fus.	LINE Right LA FOLIE.
11th Suffolks.	BDE. Reserve. LARBLIN.
1st East Lancs.	LINE Left LA JUSTICE.
184 Inf. Bde.H.Q.	(M.L.R.Bde.) BERMERAIN (Q.22.a.5.2).
2/5 Glosters.	MLR. Right. " (Q.22.a.35.60).
2/4 Oxfords.	MLR. Left Q.8.d.25.15.
2/4 R.Berks.	BERMERAIN.
61 Bn. M.G.Corps.	VENDEGIES (Q.14.a.8.1).
476 Field Coy., R.E.	Q.14.a.8.5.
478 Field Coy., R.E.	Q.22.d.0.3.
479 Field Coy., R.E.	Q.21.b.8.0.
1/5 D.C.L.I. (P).	ST. MARTIN (Q.27.b.6.5).
61 Div. Train.	VENDEGIES (Q.14.b.3.7).
No.1 Coy.	Q.32.b.central.
No.2 Coy.	Q.28.a.6.4.
No.3 Coy.	Q.28.a.3.7.
No.4 Coy.	Q.27.c.2.7.
D.O.O.	SEPMERIES (Q.6.b.central).
2/1 Field Ambulance.	Q.20.a.1.7.
2/2 Field Ambulance.	P.30.b.
P.O.W. Cage.	VENDEGIES (Q.14.b.1.4).

28th October, 1918.

A.D. Stephenson
Capt.
G.S., 61st Division.

War Diary   *Appendix XLV*

SECRET.　　　　　　　　　　　　　　　　　　　　　　　　G.C. 79.

61st DIVISION.
Locations at 0600 hours, 30.10.18.

                                                                           Probable moves
                                                                           during next 24 hrs.

```
61 DIV.  "G"           VENDEGIES (Q.14.d.1.7).
   do.   "Q"              do.    (Q.14.a.8.8).

C.R.A.                    do.    (Q.14.d.4.9).
306 Bde.RFA.           Q.28.b.2.8.
307   do.              Q.16.a.4.2.

182 Inf.Bde.H.Q.       SOMMAING (Q.7.d.5.5).          LA JUSTICE (Q.4.c.6.5)
   2/6 Warwicks,       Q.14.a.9.4.                    ) (Line Brigade)
   2/7 Warwicks,       Q.13.a.7.5.                    ) Line.
   2/8 Worcesters,     Q.14.a.6.7.

183 Inf.Bde.H.Q.       (ADVANCED GUARD) BERMERAIN
                                 (Q.22.a.5.5)
   do. Report Centre,  LARBLIN (Q.16.a.).   La JUSTICE (Q.4.c.6.5)
   9th North.Fus.      (Line Right) LA FOLIE.
   11th Suffolks,      (M.L.R. Left) LARBLIN.
   1st E. Lancs,       (Line Left) LA JUSTICE.

184 Inf.Bde.H.Q.       BERMERAIN (Q.22.a.5.2).        Adv.HQ. F.34.c.
   2/5 Glosters,       (M.L.R. Right) Q.22.a.35.60.
   2/4 Oxfords,        BERMERAIN.
   2/4 R. Berks,           do.
61 Bn. M.G.C.          VENDEGIES (Q.14.a.8.1).

476 Fd.Coy.R.E.        Q.14.a.8.5.
478   do.              Q.22.d.0.3.
479   do.              Q.21.b.8.0.

1/5 D.C.L.I.(P).       ST. MARTIN (Q.27.b.6.5).

61 Div. Train,         VENDEGIES (Q.14.b.3.7).
   No. 1 Coy.          Q.32.b.central.
   No. 2 Coy.          Q.26.c.7.3.
   No. 3 Coy.          Q.25.d.7.2.
   No. 4 Coy.          Q.31.b.5.7.

D.O.O.                 SEPMERIES Chau. (Q.6.b.central).

2/1 Field Amb.         Q.20.a.1.7.
2/2   do.              P.30.b.

P.O.W. Cage,           VENDEGIES (Q.14.b.1.4).
```

                                                                                                     A.D. Stephenson
                                                                                                       G.S., 61 Div.

29.10.18.

"C" Form
MESSAGES AND SIGNALS.

Prefix......Code......Words......	Received From...... By......mm	Sent, or sent out At......m. To...... By......	Office Stamp
£ s. d. Charges to collect			
Service Instructions. J+A			

Handed in at............ Office 1230 m. Received 1300 m.

TO — 4th Divn — 391/

*Sender's Number	Day of Month	In reply to Number	AAA
9567	30		

Ref to Divn orders 228 of 29th aaa 229 of 30th inst aaa postpone all dates 24 hours aaa acknowledge aaa addsd all recipients / Done

1315/

FROM PLACE & TIME — 4th Divn 1300

Appendix XLVI War Diary

SECRET.

61st DIVISION ORDER No.229.

Copy No.

30.10.18.

1. With reference to 61st Div. Order No. 228, dated 29th Octr., para. 13; the operation to take place on the 31st Octr. will entail the following movements and reliefs to take place.

2. 29th Octr:
   One battalion 183 Inf.Bde. will relieve one battalion 184 Inf.Bde. in the Corps Main Line of Resistance on the Left Brigade Sector.
   The battalion 184 Inf.Bde. on relief will be withdrawn into billets in BERMERAIN.

3. Night 30th/31st Octr:
   The garrison (2 coys. 183 Inf.Bde.) at the Bridge-Head FERME DE L'HOTEL DIEU will withdraw under arrangements to be made between Brigadiers 182 & 183 Bdes. at Zero plus 15 mins.

4. 31st Octr:
   At 1800 hrs. the following re-distribution of Brigades will take place :-
   (a) 182 Inf.Bde. will become Advanced Guard Bde., (with Bde.H.Q. at Q.4.c.8.7) and will relieve on night 31st Oct./1st Nov. troops of 183.Inf.Bde. who are holding the objective South of the river.
   Troops of the 183 Inf.Bde., with the exception of 2 coys. to be responsible for the defence of the front South of the river, will, however, be withdrawn, should the situation admit, during the day. Orders for the withdrawal of these will be issued from Div.H.Q.
   (b) 184 Inf.Bde. will become Support Bde., with one battalion South of railway near SEPMERIES, one battalion in the present Corps Main Line of Resistance, and one battalion in BERMERAIN with Bde.H.Q. at BERMERAIN.
   (c) 183 Inf.Bde. will become Reserve Bde., with battalions in VENDEGIES and SOMMAING and Bde.H.Q. in VENDEGIES.

5. All details of reliefs and moves will be arranged between Commanders concerned.

6. Div.H.Q. will remain in VENDEGIES.

7. Completion of moves will be notified to D.H.Q.
8. ACKNOWLEDGE.

Issued at 0700 hrs.

Lieut.-Col.,
G.S., 61st Divn.

Distribution :-

Copy No.1 - A.D.C. for G.O.C.	13 - "G".
2 - Div.Signals.	14 - XVII Corps Adv.
3-4 - 61 Div.Arty.	15 - XVII Corps H.A.
5 - C.R.E.	16 - 3rd Div.
6 - 61 Bn. M.G.C.	17 - 4th Div.
7 - 1/5 D.C.L.I.	18 - 19th Div.
8 - 182 Inf.Bde.	19 - 24th Div.
9 - 183 Inf.Bde.	20 - 13th Sqn. R.A.F.
10 - 184 Inf.Bde.	21 - 62 Bde. R.G.A.
11 - A.D.M.S.	22 - D.O.O.
12 - "Q".	23-24 - War Diary.

Appendix XLVII War Diary

SECRET.

G.C.45/7.

```
182 Inf.Bde.      1/5 D.C.L.I.
183 Inf.Bde.      61 Signal Coy.
184 Inf.Bde.      A.D.M.S.
61 Bn.M.G.C.      61 Division "Q"
C.R.A.            4th Division.
C.R.E.    2nd    3rd Division.
```

1. The postponement of the operations ordered in 61 Division Order No.228 dated 29th inst. and the increased activity shewn by the enemy yesterday, necessitate the constant readiness of all units at all times to meet an attack by the enemy.

2. Inf. Bdes. responsible for the defence of the Corps Main Line of Resistance will warn all units to be alert and Battalions responsible for the defence of the Corps Line of Resistance will continue to stand to from one hour before dawn till daylight until the operation above mentioned has taken place.

3. Support Battalions will have their jumping off places ready reconnoitred from which they can counter-attack to preserve the M.L.R. should the enemy succeed in effecting a break in our line, and guides will be warned ready to lead Battalions to these positions. Plans for counter-attack will be kept ready to hand over on reliefs taking place.

4. Reserve Battalions will assemble as ordered by Brigadiers.

5. In case of attack, the O.C., 1/5 D.C.L.I. will have one Company ready detailed to proceed to and occupy the village line of BERMERAIN and the Battalion (less 1 Coy.) will man the village line N. of VENDEGIES and SOMAING. These Companies will come under the orders of the G.Os.C. Brigades on the alarm.

6. O.C., 61st Bn. M.G.C. will detail one Company for the defence of each Sector of the M.L.R. each with 8 guns in position covering the M.L.R. and 8 guns in Reserve.
   Orders for these dispositions to be taken up will be issued by the D.M.G.C. forthwith.

7. The Alarm will be given by Division by the Order "MAN BATTLE STATIONS", but Battle dispositions will be ordered to be taken up at once by Brigade Commanders should they first receive warning of a sudden attack.

8. ACKNOWLEDGE.

M. Wetherby
Lieut. Col.,
G.S., 61st Division.

30th October, 1918.

Issued at 12.00 hrs.

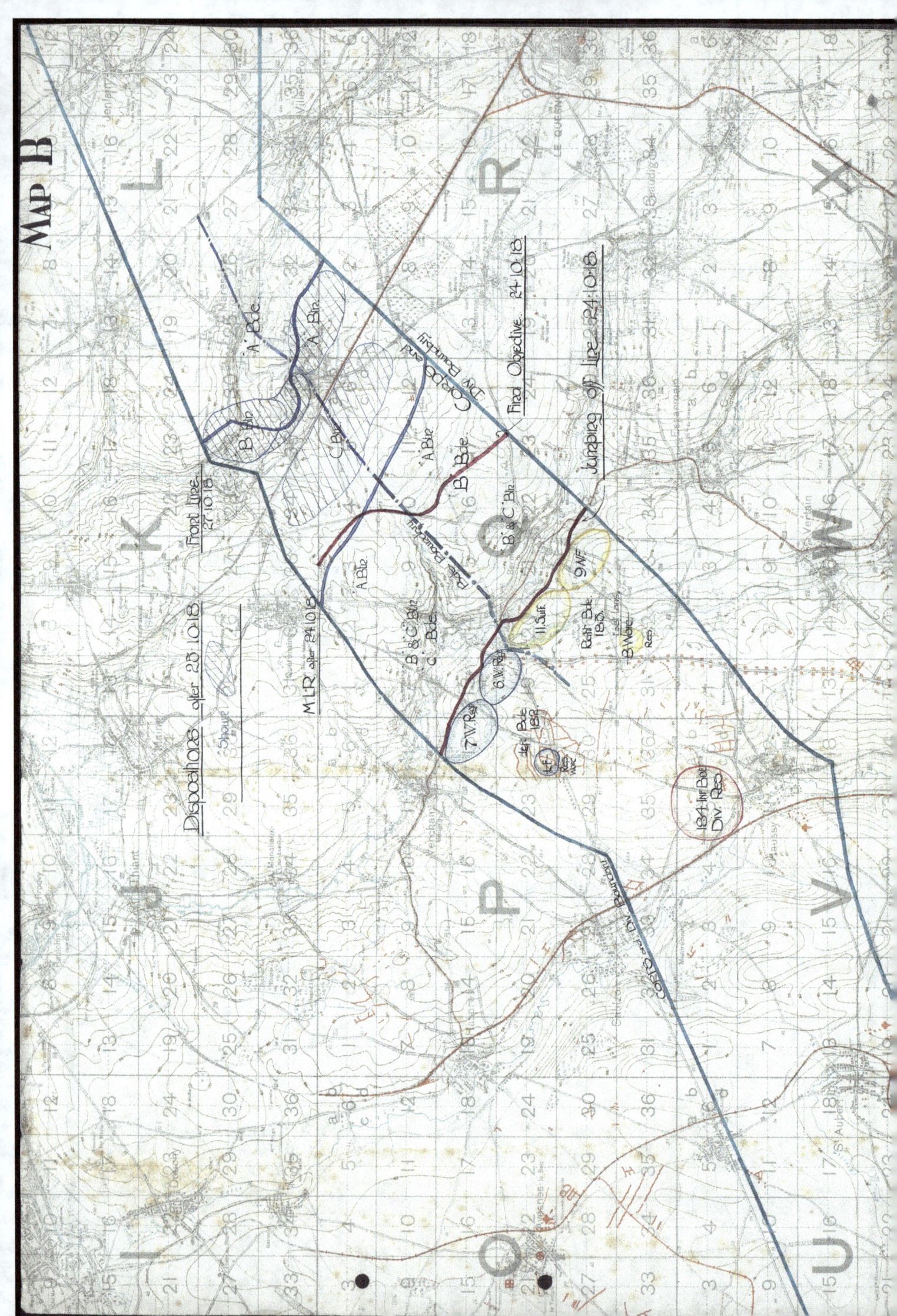

Vol 31

HQ G.S.

61st. Division.
War Diary.
Vol XXXI
November 1918.

Confidential.
14

Army Form C. 2118.

WAR DIARY
*
INTELLIGENCE SUMMARY.

VOLUME XXXI.

(Erase heading not required.)

Instructions regarding War Diaries and Intelligence Summaries are contained in F. S. Regs., Part II. and the Staff Manual respectively. Title pages will be prepared in manuscript.

Place	Date	Hour	Summary of Events and Information	Remarks and references to Appendices
VENDEGIES, Q.14.d.1.7. (Sht.51A).	NOVR.1918. Oct.31/Nov.1st	Night	During the night the two attacking battalions of 182 Inf.Bde. - 2/7 WARWICKS and 2/8 WORCESTERS - assembled at the bridgehead. The assembly was successfully carried out, and was not interfered with by the enemy. At about 0430 hrs. hostile artillery became active, ARTRES being the chief target, but units of 182 Inf.Bde. had already reached their positions. The right bank of the RHONELLE River at the bridgehead E. of ARTRES is very steep, and so provided good cover for the attacking troops while getting into their final positions. For orders for this attack see Appendix I. For locations at 0600 hrs., see Appx. II.	Appx. I. Appx. II.
		0515	The barrage commenced at 0515, and stood on the same line for 15 minutes, during which time the right of the 4th Div. advanced and came up in line with our left.	
		0530	The infantry commenced the advance - 2/8 WORCESTERS on the right, 2/7 WARWICKS on the left, both N. of the river, and 2 coys. 9th North. Fus. working forward S. of MARESCHES. On the barrage coming down, and before the infantry started to advance, it is reported that about 80 Germans ran forward and surrendered.	
		0830	The attack proceeded well, and by 0830 hrs. we had taken all our final objectives except the cross-roads at ST. HUBERT. By 0530 hrs. a bridge for first-line transport and field guns had been completed at K.29.a.4.6 (the enemy having destroyed all old bridges over the river) and also six additional footbridges in K.29.	
		0820	At 0820 hrs. two anti-tank 18-pdr. guns ("B" Bty. 107 Bde.) were advancing through L.24.c., and the remainder of the battery were crossing the river; "C" Bty. 107 Bde. crossed later. At this time the enemy artillery was very active on the RHONELLE Valley, SEPMERIES, and ARTRES.	
		0930	One coy. of the 9th North. Fus. returned to their original positions, according to plan, after mopping up half the village of MARESCHES and gaining touch with 182 Inf.Bde. E. of the village. About 800 prisoners were taken during this operation. At about 0930 hrs. the enemy counter-attacked the troops of the 4th Div. in PRESEAU from the North and East, and succeeded in re-taking the village. This necessitated the throwing back of our left flank, and at 0945 hrs. our line ran approximately as follows :- L.32.d.0.0 - L.20.d.0.5 - L.13.c.0.0, where we were in touch with 4th Div. in the vicinity of the old Mill in L.13.c.	

WAR DIARY
INTELLIGENCE SUMMARY

(Erase heading not required.)

Army Form C. 2118.

Instructions regarding War Diaries and Intelligence Summaries are contained in F. S. Regs., Part II. and the Staff Manual respectively. Title pages will be prepared in manuscript.

Place	Date NOVR. 1918.	Hour	Summary of Events and Information	Remarks and references to Appendices
VENDEGIES, Q.14.d.1.7. (Sht.51A)	1st	1030	At about 1030 hrs. the enemy were counter-attacking along the whole of the 61st Divl. front, supported by four captured British Tanks and units of a Division brought up for the purpose. Two of the Tanks were put out of action by our forward guns, but owing to the weight of the counter-attack and our exposed flank on the left, our line was forced back for a time, and Germans were reported to have re-entered MARESCHES, though not for long. During the counter-attack the RHONELLE Valley and SEPMERIES were heavily shelled with H.E. and gas. After this enemy counter-attack our line was reported to run approximately as follows :- The final objective S. of the river was still held; thence along the river to L.25.d.9.1.- eastern outskirts of MARESCHES to L.19.c.5.1 - L.19.a.3.2 - K.24.b.7.2. Touch was for a time lost with the 4th Div., but their right was still by the MILL in L.13.c.	
		1130	At 1130 hrs. two platoons of the 9th North. Fus. were order to cross the river and hold the N.E. portion of MARESCHES, while one coy. 11th Suffolks was sent to support the 9th North. Fus. in L.31.c. It was originally intended to withdraw the 183 Inf.Bde. as soon as our objectives had been reached, but owing to this counter-attack and consequent obscurity of the situation, it was decided that they should not be withdrawn for the time being.	
		1300	The Divisional Commander spoke to G.O.C. 4th Div. about a second attack to take the final objectives. The 4th Div., however, had decided not to make a further effort during the day, as they intended attacking in conjunction with the 49th Div. on their left in the morning.	
		1355	Instructions were received from XVII Corps to the effect that 61st Div. were to take their final objectives, including the cross-roads at ST. HUBERT, by dawn on the 2nd inst. If the 4th Div. would not cooperate, we were to throw back a defensive flank S. of PRESEAU. It was decided to employ the reserve Brigade (184 Inf.Bde.), and orders were issued to them to attack at 1930 hrs., with two battalions, with artillery support; on reaching the objective, 184 Inf.Bde. would become the Front Brigade, and 182 Bde. the Support Brigade, the latter to reorganize on the N. bank of the river about K.29.b. and K.23.c.	Appx.III
		1700	There was no change in the situation at 1700 hrs., except that our troops had taken the Cemetery (L.25.b.) and were in touch with 11th Brigade at K.24.b.8.6. 184 Inf.Bde. formed up ready for the attack, with 2/5 Glosters on right and 2/4 Oxfords on left, the jumping-off line being the road running through L.25.a. and L.19.c.	
		1930	184 Inf.Bde. started to advance, but owing to M.G. fire from the outskirts of PRESEAU and the darkness of the night, which prevented our troops dealing with such machine guns, it was decided to hold on the for the night and advance with the 4th Div. at dawn.	Appx.IV.

Army Form C. 2118.

WAR DIARY
INTELLIGENCE SUMMARY
(Erase heading not required.)

Instructions regarding War Diaries and Intelligence Summaries are contained in F.S. Regs., Part II. and the Staff Manual respectively. Title pages will be prepared in manuscript.

Place	Date NOVR. 1918.	Hour	Summary of Events and Information	Remarks and references to Appendices
VENDEGIES, Q.14.d.1.7. (Sht.51A)	1st		Weather - fine, mild; visibility good. Appx. V shows the approximate distribution of Brigades at 1800 hrs. 61 Div. Order No. 231 issued - relief of 61 Div. by 19th and 24th Divs. on 2nd and 3rd inst., 61 Div. to march to AVESNES - ST. AUBERT area on relief.	Appx.V Appx.VI
	2nd	0530	184 Inf.Bde. advanced in conjunction with 4th Div. on the left. This attack was a complete success; the objectives were reached everywhere, and our advanced troops consolidated on the general line L.32.b.2.7 - road junction L.27.a.8.8 - FME. DE WULT (L.21.a.0.9) inclusive - L.14.central, with patrols in touch with the enemy, and the total number of prisoners taken by this Division during the operations since Zero, 1st inst., was :- 42 officers and about 1,500 O.R. The following is an estimate of material captured during the same period :- Machine Guns - 140. Lewis guns (from Tanks) 12. Trench Mortars - 13. Field guns - 3. Tanks - 2. Anti-tank rifles - 5. For locations at 0600 hrs. see Appx.VII. The enemy was quiet during the afternoon, and there was little shelling; a few rounds from a H.V. gun were fired at VENDEGIES. The 183 Inf.Bde., less 9th North. Fus., withdrew about noon to VENDEGIES en route for AVESNES-LEZ-AUBERT, by march route. 9th North. Fus. were billeted in SOMMAING for the night and marched to AVESNES on 3rd inst; moves complete by 2000 hrs. The 182 Inf.Bde. commenced withdrawal at 1730 hrs., and marched to ST. AUBERT.	Appx.VII
		2300	Command of Right Section of the Divl. front passed to G.O.C. 73 Bde. (24 Div.), and of Left Section to G.O.C. 56 Bde. (19 Div.) at 2300 hrs. 61 Bn. M.G.C. reported relief complete at 2130 hrs.	
	Night 2/3		There was intermittent shelling of the RHONELLE Valley throughout the night with H.E. and gas.	

Army Form C. 2118.

WAR DIARY
INTELLIGENCE SUMMARY

(Erase heading not required.)

Instructions regarding War Diaries and Intelligence Summaries are contained in F.S. Regs., Part II. and the Staff Manual respectively. Title pages will be prepared in manuscript.

Place	Date NOVR. 1918	Hour	Summary of Events and Information	Remarks and references to Appendices
VENDEGIES, Q.14.d.1.7 (Sht.51A)	Night 2/3		184 Inf.Bde. was relieved by troops of 73 Inf.Bde. on the right and 56 Inf.Bde. on the left, without incident. 184 Inf.Bde. spent the remainder of the night in billets at BERMERAIN, and marched to AVESNES-LEZ-AUBERT on 3rd inst.	
	3rd	0900	For locations at 0600 hrs. see Appx. VIII. Command of the Divisional front passed to G.Os.C. 24th (Right) and 19th (Left) Divs. respectively at 0900 hrs.	Appx.VIII
ST.AUBERT U.24.b.6.1		1000	61 Div. H.Q. opened at ST. AUBERT at 1000 hrs: Rear Div.H.Q. moved back on 2nd inst. Orders issued for moves forward of two Brigades on the 4th, owing to retirement of the enemy; 182 Bde. Group to march from ST.AUBERT to HAUSSY, becoming the Support Bde. of the Div.	Appx.IX
		1800	The move of 184 Bde. to BERMERAIN (Leading Bde.) was postponed for 24 hours, owing to the fact that they were the last to move back and required rest. Weather - dull.	
	4th		For locations at 0600 hrs. see Appx. X. The day was spent by units in cleaning up, etc. Weather - fine, mild; good visibility.	Appx.X
	5th		For locations at 0600 hrs., see Appx. XI. 184 Bde. Group moved to BERMERAIN; other units carried out training. Weather - dull, with some drizzle; mild.	Appx.XI
	6th		The day was spent by units in training. Instructions were issued for the 1/5 D.C.L.I. to be employed under XVII Corps "Q" to clear the battlefield, commencing 7th inst: the battalion to remain billeted at BERMERAIN, and march to and from the work in the neighbourhood of MARESCHES daily. Weather - dull, some light showers; mild.	

Army Form C. 2118.

WAR DIARY
INTELLIGENCE SUMMARY

Instructions regarding War Diaries and Intelligence
Summaries are contained in F.S. Regs., Part II.
and the Staff Manual respectively. Title pages
will be prepared in manuscript.

(Erase heading not required.)

Place	Date NOVR. 1918	Hour	Summary of Events and Information	Remarks and references to Appendices
ST. AUBERT. U.24.b.6.1.	7th		For locations at 0600 hrs. see Appx. XII.	Appx. XII
			Orders issued for the move forward of the whole Division on the 8th inst., to area VENDEGIES - BERMERAIN - SEPMERIES, and MARESCHES.	Appx. XIII
			Weather - dull, but no rain; mild.	
VENDEGIES, (Q.14.d.1.7) Sht.51A.	8th		G.399 (amendment to move orders) issued at 0930 hrs.	Appx. XIV
			Advanced Div.H.Q. moved to VENDEGIES, opening at 1500 hrs.	
			184 Bde. Group moved to SEPMERIES and MARESCHES.	
			182 " " " VENDEGIES and SOMMAING.	
			183 " " " BERMERAIN and ST. MARTIN.	
			Wet day.	
	9th		For locations at 0600 hrs., see Appx. XV.	Appx. XV.
			Rear Div.H.Q. moved to VENDEGIES.	
			Conference of Brigadiers at 1430 hrs.	
			Fine day.	
	10th		VI Corps took over Army front with cavalry and cyclists; XVII Corps to hold MONS - MAUBEUGE - AVESNES line.	
	11th		Wire from Corps received 0718 - "Hostilities to cease at 1100 hours" - repeated to all units 0800 hours.	Appx. XVI
			Fine day.	
	12th		Fine day.	
			Units gave up most of the day to Ceremonial Drill.	

Army Form C. 2118.

WAR DIARY
INTELLIGENCE SUMMARY.

(Erase heading not required.)

Instructions regarding War Diaries and Intelligence Summaries are contained in F.S. Regs., Part II. and the Staff Manual respectively. Title pages will be prepared in manuscript.

Place	Date NOVR. 1918.	Hour	Summary of Events and Information	Remarks and references to Appendices
VENDEGIES, Q.14.d.1.7. (Sht.51A)	13th		Orders received from XVII Corps that 61st Div. (less Arty.) would move to RIEUX area on 14th inst. Orders for move of Division (less Arty.) to RIEUX area on 14th inst. issued. Fine day.	Appx.XVII

	14th		Division (less Arty.) moved in accordance with orders to RIEUX area, and on arrival were billeted as follows :-
			     Div. H.Q. at RIEUX.
			     182 Bde. Group at AVESNES-LEZ-AUBERT.
			     183 Bde. Group at ST. AUBERT.
			     184 Bde. Group at HAUSSY.
			     1/5 D.C.L.I. at AVESNES-LEZ-AUBERT.
			     61st Bn. M.G.C. at ST. AUBERT.	

RIEUX.		1800	Orders for move of Division (less Arty.) to CAMBRAI on 15th and 16th inst. issued.	Appx.XVIII

CAMBRAI.	15th	1100	In accordance with orders, Division (less Arty.) moved as follows :-
			 Div. H.Q. closed at RIEUX and opened at 15, Rue Cantimpre, CAMBRAI.
			     182 Bde. Group moved to CAMBRAI.
			     183 " " " " "
			     184 " " " " CAGNONCLES.
			     1/5 D.C.L.I. " " CAMBRAI.
			     61st Bn. M.G.C. " " "
			 Fine, frosty day.	

	16th		Fine, frosty day. 184 Bde. Group moved to CAMBRAI. 306 & 307 Bdes. R.F.A. and D.A.C. moved from forward area to WARGNIES.	

Army Form C. 2118.

WAR DIARY
INTELLIGENCE SUMMARY

(Erase heading not required.)

Instructions regarding War Diaries and Intelligence Summaries are contained in F.S. Regs., Part II. and the Staff Manual respectively. Title pages will be prepared in manuscript.

Place	Date NOVR. 1918.	Hour	Summary of Events and Information	Remarks and references to Appendices
CAMBRAI.	17th		For locations at 0600 hrs. see Appx. XIX. Div. Arty. moved to BERMERAIN. Orders received from XVII Corps that 315 Army Bde. R.F.A. would be affiliated to 61st Div. from noon, 20th inst. Cold and clear day; hard frost at night.	Appx. XIX.
	18th		306 & 307 Bdes. R.F.A. and D.A.C. moved to ST. VAAST. Frost continued.	
	19th		306 & 307 Bdes. R.F.A. and D.A.C. moved to CAMBRAI. Orders received from XVII Corps that 315 Army Bde. R.F.A. would move, under orders of 61st Div., to NOYELLES-SUR-L'ESCAUT on the morning of 21st inst. Frost less severe, but weather continued bright.	
	20th		Locations of 61 Div. at 0600 hrs. attached. Destination of 315 Army Bde. R.F.A. changed from NOYELLES-SUR-L'ESCAUT to CAMBRAI. Orders for move of 315 Army Bde. R.F.A. on 21st inst. issued by 61st Div. Art. (later cancelled owing to lack of billeting accommodation in CAMBRAI). A heavy mist all day; warmer.	Appx. XX.
	21st		Orders issued that the whole Division would be employed entirely on salvage, on 22nd and 23rd inst., clearing area S. of CAMBRAI. Warning order received from XVII Corps that 61st Div. would be prepared to move by tactical trains and march into the BERNAVILLE area on 23rd, 24th, and 25th; warning order issued to units accordingly. Fine day; slight mist rising in the evening.	Appx. XXI
	22nd		Orders for move to BERNAVILLE area issued. Fine and cold day.	Appx. XXII

Army Form C. 2118.

WAR DIARY

INTELLIGENCE SUMMARY.

(Erase heading not required.)

Instructions regarding War Diaries and Intelligence Summaries are contained in F.S. Regs., Part II. and the Staff Manual respectively. Title pages will be prepared in manuscript.

Place	Date NOVR. 1918.	Hour	Summary of Events and Information	Remarks and references to Appendices
CAMBRAI.	23rd		Div. Artillery (less 315 Army Bde. R.F.A. attached) moved by march route to BEUGNATRE and FAVREUIL. Transport of 182, 183, and 184 Bde. Groups and Div.H.Q. moved by march route to BERTINCOURT and HAPLINCOURT.	
	24th		Div. Arty. Group (less 315 Army Bde. R.F.A.) moved to POMMIER by march route. Transport of 182, 183, & 184 Bde. Groups and Div.H.Q. moved to ALBERT by march route. 315 Army Bde. R.F.A. moved to CAMBRAI. Personnel of Division commenced entraining for AUXI-LE-CHATEAU and CONTEVILLE, whence they were to move by march route to their respective districts in the BERNAVILLE area.	
	25th		Div. Arty. Group (less 315 Army Bde. R.F.A.) moved by march route to WAVANS district of BERNAVILLE area. Transport of 182 Bde. Group moved to MAISON PONTHIEU district. " " 183 " " " " DOMLEGER " " " " " 184 " " " " DOMART " " " " " Div.H.Q. " " " " BERNAVILLE " 315 Army Bde. R.F.A. moved to POMMIER by march route. Div.H.Q. closed at CAMBRAI at 0900 hrs. and reopened at BERNAVILLE at 1500 hrs. Trains, by which personnel were travelling, were very late; only three arrived during the day.	Apx.XXIII.
BERNAVILLE.	26th		315 Army Bde. R.F.A. moved to WAVANS district. Trains from CAMBRAI were still running very late; one train ran off the line at AUXI-LE-CHATEAU, causing casualties (4 killed and 8 injured) to 2/8 WORCESTERS. Locations of Headquarters were as follows :- Div.H.Q. - BERNAVILLE. C.R.A. H.Q. - Chau. de BEAUVOIN. 182 Inf.Bde. - MAISON PONTHIEU. 183 Inf.Bde. - DOMLEGER. 184 Inf.Bde. - DOMART.	

Army Form C. 2118.

WAR DIARY
INTELLIGENCE-SUMMARY.
(Erase heading not required.)

Instructions regarding War Diaries and Intelligence Summaries are contained in F. S. Regs., Part II. and the Staff Manual respectively. Title pages will be prepared in manuscript.

Place	Date NOVR.1918.	Hour	Summary of Events and Information	Remarks and references to Appendices
BERNAVILLE.	27th		Training areas were allotted, but, owing to the number of fields under cultivation, and to the fact that this area had ceased to be a training area, arrangements for training on these parts of uncultivated land in the area had to be made. Arrival of personnel by train continued, but was not completed.	Appx. XXIV
	28th		Last train arrived, being over 60 hours late. Locations of units as per attached list.	
	29th		Organization of Educational and Recreational Training continued.	
	30th		Two lectures on Demobilization were delivered by the Rev. STUDDART KENNEDY ("WOODBINE WILLY") at DOMART to troops of 184 Inf. Bde. Group and 61st Bn. M.G.C.	

C.H.Bowden Maj
for Major-General,
Commanding 61st Division.
3rd Decr. 1918.

SECRET.   *Appendix 1*   G.C. 31/1.

Amendment No. 1 to
to 61st Div. Order No. 228 of 29.10.18.

Para. 7, line 8:

    For "30th/31st October", read "31st Octr/1st Novr.".

Para. 9, line 2:

    For "GREEN" read "WHITE".

                                                       CH Dowden Major

29.10.18.   Lieut.-Col.,
                                              for G.S., 61st Div.

To all recipients of
61st Div. Order No.228.

"A" Form
MESSAGES AND SIGNALS.

Army Form C. 2121 (in pads of 100.)

Sender's Number.	Day of Month.	In reply to Number.	AAA
* GS.667.	30		

Ref. 61 Div. Orders 228 of 29th and 229 of 30th inst aaa Postpone all dates 24 hours aaa Acknowledge aaa Addsd all recipients

Place: VACA
Time: 1200

(Sgd) W. WEATHERLY, Lt.Col.

SECRET.   War Diary

G.O.40/5.

Reference 61st Division Order No.228 dated 29.10.1918.
1. Zero hour will be 0315 hours
2. ACKNOWLEDGE.

                                                           Wetherly

29th October, 1918.   Lieut. Col.,
                                      G.S., 61st Division.

To all recipients of D.O. 228.

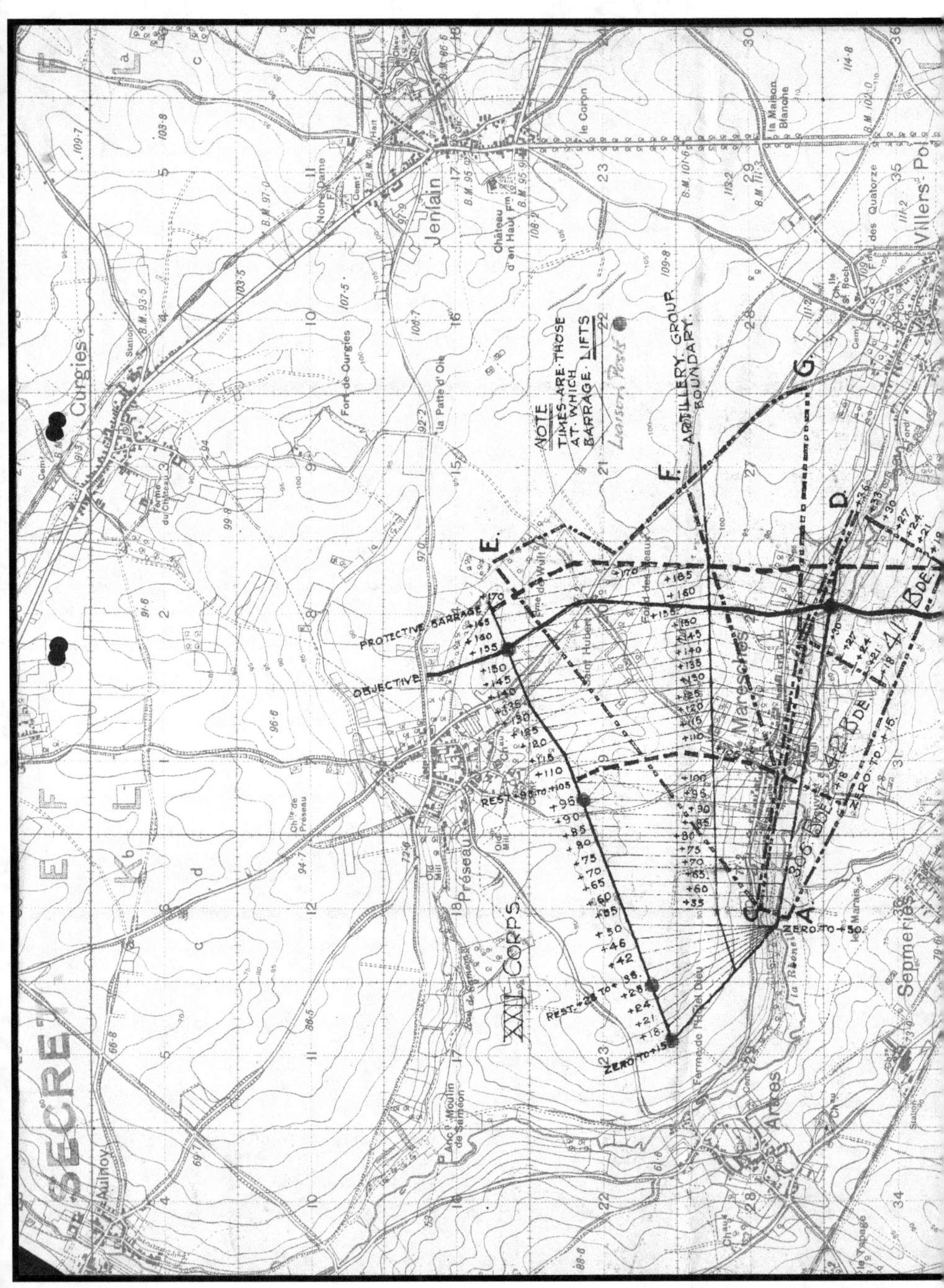

SECRET.
Copy No.
Appendix I

61st DIVISION ORDER No. 228.
29.10.18.

1. On the 31st October, at an hour to be notified separately, the 61st Division, in conjunction with the 4th Division (XXII Corps) will attack and capture the high ground East and North of the RIVER RHONELLE and the village of MARESCHES.

2. **Objective and boundaries.**
   The attack will be made in an Easterly direction from behind the Bridge-Head now held by 183 Inf.Bde. and troops of 4th Division at FME. DE L'HOTEL DIEU.
   Boundaries and objectives will be as shown on the attached barrage map.

3. **Dispositions.**
   (a) The attack will be carried out by the 182 Inf.Bde. with two battalions, and with one battalion in Brigade Reserve about K.34.a.& d.
   (b) That portion of the objective South of the river will be made good by 2 Coys. to be detailed by 183 Inf.Bde., and will be held by them until relieved by the 182 Inf.Bde. Fighting patrols of the 183 Inf.Bde. will cross the river as the barrage lifts, to establish touch with the right of the 182 Inf. Bde. where the objective line crosses the MARESCHES road, and will cooperate in clearing the right bank of the river South of the road as opportunity offers.
   (c) 184 Inf.Bde. will be in Divisional Reserve, and battalions will stand to ready to move from their present positions.

4. The attacking battalions will move across the river on the night 30th/31st October by the bridge at FME. DE L'HOTEL DIEU and the footbridges placed in position in K.29.a.& c., and will form up along the road from the Northern end of FME. DE L'HOTEL DIEU to about K.29.b.8.0, and along the track running between the road and river to about K.29.d.4.5.

5. **Artillery arrangements.**
   (a) The attack will be carried out under a creeping barrage of field artillery and M.G. fire on the North (right) bank of the river. The attack will be supported by :-
   Right Group:
       4 Bdes. R.F.A.   Comdr., Lieut.-Col. E.W.S. BROOKE, D.S.O.
   Left Group: H.Q., sunken road, Q.4.c.6.5.
       3 Bdes. R.F.A.   Comdr. Brig.Gen. H.G.LLOYD, CMG.DSO.
   VI Corps Arty:
       2 Bdes. R.F.A.
   XVII Corps Heavy Arty:
       4 Bdes. (including 62nd (Mixed) Bde. R.G.A. - Lt.Col.ILES.)
   (b) A creeping barrage of 18-pdrs. and 4.5" hows. will come down at Zero hour on a line as shown on the attached barrage map, where it will rest for 15 minutes.
   It will then commence to move forward at the rates shown on the map, that portion of it North of the river pivoting on the river and advancing along the inter-divisional boundary until the barrage line North of the river is approximately North & South. It will then commence to move Eastwards at the rates and with the pauses shown on the barrage map.
   That portion of the barrage South of the river will also commence to lift at Zero plus 15 down to the river, where it will remain searching and sweeping between the road and the river, its left being continuously rolled up as the portion North of the river advances Eastwards.
   (c) 61st Div. Trench Mortars, in action about SEPMARIES, will cooperate in the barrage on North bank of the river, under orders to be issued by C.R.A.
   One Mobile Section, 24th Div. Arty. will accompany 182 Inf. Bde.

(P.T.O.)

(2)

- (d) One round of THERMITE shell will be fired at an increased range of 200 yards at each lift in the barrage, to mark the left flank of the attack along the inter-divisional boundary, also on the inter-battalion boundary along the line K.29.b.7.5 - L.19.c.50.25 - L.20.c.6.0.
One salvo THERMITE will be fired at each halt in the barrage, to show the attacking infantry that a protective barrage is being formed.

- (e) One Bde. R.F.A. will cross the river and commence to advance by batteries at Zero plus 120 minutes, to the close support of the infantry, and will provide two sections for anti-Tank defence.

- (f) From Zero to dawn the Northern flank of the attack South of PRESEAU will be barraged with H.E. and shrapnel.
At dawn, a smoke screen to deny observation from PRESEAU and further smoke-screens, including MARESCHES, VILLERS POL, and the river valley, will be formed under orders to be issued by C.R.A.

- (g) Heavy Artillery:
Intense neutralisation of hostile batteries from Zero to Zero plus 45, every available gun and howitzer that can reach being utilised.
At Zero plus 45 a proportion of guns and howitzers will turn on to strong points, sweeping approaches and bombarding sunken roads.
If the weather is suitable, gas shell will be used in these concentrations.

6. Machine Gun arrangements.
61st Bn. M.G.C. will support the attack.
One M.G.Coy. will move with the attacking battalions under the orders of G.O.C. 182 Inf.Bde., and will act as forward gun and to cover the work of consolidation.
The remaining Coys. will be employed under the Divisional M.G.C. in cooperation with the artillery barrage from positions about SEPMARIES and the spur in L.31.d. and L.32.c., firing by direct fire, one Coy. being ready to move if required to reinforce the Coy. on the North bank of the river.

7. Employment of Field Coys. R.E. and Pioneers.
The C.R.E. will be responsible for the construction and placing in position of additional footbridges across the river in K.29.a.& c. These will be placed in position during the night 30th/31st before Zero hour.
C.R.E. will also arrange to clear the roads in ARTRES and SEPMARIES, and for the collecting of bridging material in SEPMARIES for crossings to be made on the night 30th/31st Octr. in K.30.c.& d., and for foot-bridging required by the 183 Inf. Bde.

8. Consolidation.
As soon as the objective is captured, it will be consolidated and the defence organised in depth.
The objective will then become the MAIN LINE OF RESISTANCE.
Arrangements have been made to fire salvoes of 8" shell with delay action spaced out along the objective line, the craters to be consolidated by the infantry on reaching the objective.
These salvoes will be fired as late as safety will permit.
A proportion of machine guns will be pushed well forward with the attacking infantry to cover the work of consolidation.

9. **Light Signals.**
   (a) GREEN Very lights will be used by the most advanced troops to denote their positions.
   (b) RED flares will be lit by the most advanced troops on or near the objective.
   (c) The S.O.S. Signal is a rifle grenade bursting into RED over GREEN over RED.

10. **Cooperation with R.A.F.**
    (a) Contact aeroplanes will call for flares at -
    Zero plus 1¾ hours,
    Zero plus 2¾ hours,
    Zero plus 3¾ hours.
    (b) A counter-attack aeroplane will be up from daylight onwards.

11. **Reports.**
    Divl. H.Q. will remain at VENDEGIES.
    Advanced H.Q. 182 Inf.Bde. will be in sunken road Q.4.c.6.5.
    Advanced H.Q. 183 Inf.Bde. will be in LARBLIN.
    Advanced H.Q. 184 Inf.Bde. will be in K.34.c.

12. **Synchronisation of watches.**
    Watches will be synchronised by O.C. Div. Signals at 1600 hrs. 30th October.

13. **Reliefs.**
    Troops of the 183 Inf.Bde. will remain in their present positions, and will be relieved under separate orders to be issued.
    Details of movements and reliefs to take place are being issued.

14. ACKNOWLEDGE.

M Metherly.
Lieut.-Col.,
G.S., 61st Divn.

Issued at 1730.

Distribution :-

Copy No.		Maps.
1	A.D.C. for G.O.C.	1
2	Div. Signal Coy.	1
3-4	61 Div. Arty.	
5	C.R.E.	
6	61 Bn. M.G.C.	1
7	1/5 D.C.L.I.	6
8	182 Inf.Bde.	1
9	183 Inf.Bde.	30
10	184 Inf.Bde.	6
11	A.D.M.S.	1
12	"Q".	
13	"G".	1
14	XVII Corps Adv.	1
15	XVII Corps H.A.	
16	3rd Divn.	
17	4th Divn.	1
18	19th Divn.	1
19	24th Divn.	
20	13th Sqn. R.A.F.	
21	62 Bde. R.G.A.	
22	D.O.O.	1
23-24	War Diary.	2

War Diary.   Appendix "

SECRET.

                    61st DIVISION.   G.C. 79.
            Locations of units at 0600, 1.11.18.

    61st DIV.H.Q. "G"   VENDEGIES (Q.14.d.1.7)   Moves during
        do.   "Q"   do.   (Q.14.a.8.8)   next 24 hours.

    C. R. A.   do.
    306 Bde. R.F.A.   Q.28.b.2.8.
    307   do.   Q.23.a.0.5.

    182 Inf.Bde.H.Q.   Q.4.c.6.7 (LA JUSTICE).
        do. Rear H.Q.   SOMMAING (Q.7.d.5.5).
    2/6 Warwicks,   Q.4.c.5.7.
    2/7 Warwicks,   K.35.a.2.1 (Line)(Left).
    2/8 Worcesters,   K.35.a.2.1 (Line)(Right).

    183 Inf.Bde.H.Q.   LARBLIN, Q.16.a.
    9th North.Fus.   Q.6.b.2.3.   VENDEGIES.
    11th Suffolks,   LARBLIN.   do.
    1st E. Lancs,   Q.4.c.6.5.   SOMMAING.
                                                    VENDEGIES.
    184 Inf.Bde.H.Q.   BERMERAIN (Q.22.a.5.2).
        do. Report Centre, K.34.d.4.9.
    2/5 Glosters,   M.L.R. (Q.22.a.35.60).
    2/4 Oxfords,   BERMERAIN.
    2/4 R. Berks,   do. . . . . .Railway near
                                                    SEPMERIES.
    61 Bn. M.G.C.Adv.   Q.4.c.4.8.   VENDEGIES.
                                                    (Q.14.a.8.1)
    476 Field Coy.   Q.14.a.8.5.
    478   do.   Q.22.d.0.3.
    479   do.   Q.21.b.8.0.

    1/5 D.C.L.I.(P),   Q.27.b.6.5.

    D.O.O.   SEPMERIES Chateau (Q.6.b.cent.)

    2/1 Field Amb.   Q.20.a.1.7.
    2/2   do.   P.30.b.

    P.O.W. Cage,   VENDEGIES (Q.14.b.1.4).

                                                A.D.Stephenson
                                                ─────────────
                                                Captain,
                                                G.S., 61 Div.
    31.10.18.

S E C R E T.

G.C.45/7.

182 Inf.Bde.	1/5 D.C.L.I.
183 Inf.Bde.	61 Signal Coy.
184 Inf.Bde.	A.D.M.S.
61 Bn.M.G.C.	61 Division "Q"
C.R.A.	4th Division
C.R.E.	2nd 3rd Division.

1. The postponement of the operations ordered in 61 Division Order No.228 dated 29th inst. and the increased activity shewn by the enemy yesterday, necessitate the constant readiness of all units at all times to meet an attack by the enemy.

2. Inf. Bdes. responsible for the defence of the Corps Main Line of Resistance will warn all units to be alert and Battalions responsible for the defence of the Corps Line of Resistance will continue to stand to from one hour before dawn till daylight until the operation above mentioned has taken place.

3. Support Battalions will have their jumping off places ready reconnoitred from which they can counter-attack to preserve the M.L.R. should the enemy succeed in effecting a break in our line, and guides will be warned ready to lead Battalions to these positions. Plans for counter-attack will be kept ready to hand over on reliefs taking place.

4. Reserve Battalions will assemble as ordered by Brigadiers.

5. In case of attack, the O.C., 1/5 D.C.L.I. will have one Company ready detailed to proceed to and occupy the village line of BERMERAIN and the Battalion (less 1 Coy.) will man the village line N. of VENDEGIES and SOMMAING. These Companies will come under the orders of the G.Os.C. Brigades on the alarm.

6. O.C., 61st Bn. M.G.C. will detail one Company for the defence of each Sector of the M.L.R, each with 8 guns in position covering the M.L.R. and 8 guns in Reserve.
Orders for these dispositions to be taken up will be issued by the D.M.G.C. forthwith.

7. The Alarm will be given by Division by the Order "MAN BATTLE STATIONS", but Battle dispositions will be ordered to be taken up at once by Brigade Commanders should they first receive warning of a sudden attack.

8. ACKNOWLEDGE.

30th October, 1918.

Lieut. Col.,
G.S., 61st Division.

Issued at 12 00 hrs.

GR 12/4
31.10.18

I.G.46/12.

C.R.A.
C.R.E.
182 Inf.Bde.   62 Bde., RGA.
183 Inf.Bde.   XVII Corps ADV)
184 Inf.Bde.   XVII Corps R.A.) For
61 Bn. M.G.C. 2nd Division.) information.
               4th Division.)

Notes on the enemy's counter-preparation in reply to our Smoke Barrage on 29th October.

ON OUR LEFT.

1. Came down on line K.29.central - K.35.b.9.5.

2. Lifted on to Sunken Road running through K.29.c. - K.35.b. from ARTRES to SEPMERIES.
   Particularly strong in front of factory and station in K.35.central.

3. Lifted on to road from CHATEAU K.29.c.0.0 to SEPMERIES.
   Very heavy fire on SEPMERIES and STATION.
   Scattered fire on area S.W. of Railway.

ON OUR RIGHT.

1. Came down on line K.36.b.1.7 - Valley of PRECHELLES RIVER in L.31. R.1.

2. Lifted on to ridge N.E. of Railway and S.E. of SEPMERIES with scattered shelling on area S.W. of Railway.

All the above lasted from ½ hour to 1 hour and consisted chiefly of 5.9.

LIGHTS.

Lights were sent up from forward slope of high ground in front of FME. HOTEL DE DIEU and MARESCHES and repeated further back.
Lights were not sent up from the bottom of the valley.

From G.O.C., 183rd Infantry Brigade, 1000 hours 30.10.1918.

- - - - - -

The enemy's lights went up 5 minutes after our smoke barrage opened and his counter barrage came down about 2 minutes later.

From C.R.A. 1030 hours 30.10.1918.

- - - - - - - - - - - - - - -

30th October, 1918.

Lieut. Col.,
G.S., 61st Division.

(Copy)

C.R.A.
182 Inf.Bde.
184 Inf.Bde.
61 Bn.M.G.C.
----

1. Our present front line runs approximately from K.24.d.8.2 - L.19.a.3.2 - south along road to L.19.c.5.1 - thence along grid line to K.19.d.3.0, and south through cemetery to river about L.26.c.3.0.

2. The 184 Inf.Bde. will recapture the original objective from the River - Mill 100.6 (L.20.c.7.0) - SAINT HUBERT all inclusive, the left flank to be drawn back through L.19.b.& a.

3. 184 Inf.Bde. will attack with 2 battalions behind a creeping barrage which will come down on the Zero plus 115 line of the original barrage in today's attack as far south as the east and west grid line between squares L.19 and L.25.
There will be no barrage put down south of the grid line.
The barrage will open on the above line at 1645 hours, and will remain on that line for 5 minutes, lifting according to original lifts at 100^X in 5 minutes.

4. All troops of 182 Inf.Bde. will be warned not to be East of the road running N. & S. through L.19.c. by 1615 hours, and no troops of that Brigade will be North and South of the grid line between squares L.19 and L.25 at the same hour

5. On reaching the objective given in para. 2 above, the 184 Inf. Bde. will become responsible for the line; the 182 Inf.Bde. will become Support Bde., and will reorganise at dark on the north bank of river about K.29.b. and K.23.c.

6. Acknowledge.
1.11.18.

(Sd.) W.WHETHERLY, Lt.-Col.
G.S., 61st Div.

APPENDIX No.

"A" Form
MESSAGES AND SIGNALS.

Army Form C.2121
(In pads of 100.)

Prefix......Code......m.	Words	Charge	This message is on a/c of:	Recd. at......m
Office of Origin and Service Instructions	Sent			Date
	At ......m		......Service	From
	To			
	By		(Signature of "Franking Officer")	By

TO	JUME	JUPI	62 Bde. RGA
	C.R.A.	61 Bn. MGC.	C.R.E.
	JUBE	Q	Div. Sigs.

| Sender's Number. | Day of Month. | In reply to Number. | AAA |
| G 329 | 1 | | |

4th Div will attack PRESEAU and capture original objective East of it at Zero tomorrow aaa Attack will be carried out behind creeping barrage its southern limit clear of and parallel to Divl. boundary by 100 yds to North aaa Lifts will coincide with those of this morning's barrage aaa Warn all troops to be at least 100 yds south of the Divl. boundary as marked on barrage map before Zero aaa JUME will conform with advance of troops 4th Div on left flank behind barrage and establish touch aaa CRA will arrange protective barrage on line E F to come down at Zero plus 15 mins with smoke at Zero plus 30 mins aaa Heavy arty will bombard southern road through 21.c. and 27.a. same hour aaa Smoke screen will be put down at 0600 hrs on high ground L.9.d. L.16.a.& b. same hour aaa Zero

From
Place
Time

The above may be forwarded as now corrected. (Z)

Censor. Signature of Addressor or person authorised to telegraph in his name
* This line should be erased if not required.

Order No. 1625 Wt. W3253/ P 511 27/2 H. & K., Ltd. (E. 2634)

"A" Form
MESSAGES AND SIGNALS.

Army Form C. 2121
(In pads of 100.)
No. of Message..........

Prefix........Code........m.	Words	Charge.	This message is on a/c of:	Recd. at......m.
Office of Origin and Service Instructions	Sent			Date........
	At........m.		............v.............Service.	From ....
	To			
	By		(Signature of "Franking Officer")	By........

TO		(2)		

Sender's Number.	Day of Month.	In reply to Number.	AAA
G.329	1		

| as notified | aaa Ack | aaa Addsd | JUME | CRA |
| reptd JUBE | JUPI DERU | Q Bde.RGA | CRE | Sigs |

From VAGA
Place
Time 2000

The above may be forwarded as now corrected. (Z) (Sd.) W.H.Dowden, Maj.
G.S.
Censor. Signature of Addresser or person authorised to telegraph in his name
* This line should be erased if not required.

S E C R E T.

Appendix V

61st DIVISION ORDER No.230

Copy No.
31.10.18.

1. With reference to 61st Division Order No.228 dated 29.10.18, para.8 - Consolidation -

   The defence will be organised and consolidated along the lines as shewn in blue on the attached map.

2. With reference to 61st Division Order No.229 dated 30.10.18, para.4 (a) -
   The G.O.C., 184th Inf. Bde. will detail one Company of Infantry to come under the orders of the G.O.C., 182nd Inf. Bde. from 1800 hours on 1st November.

3. At 1800 hours Nov. 1st the approximate distribution of Brigades will be as shewn on the attached map.

4. ACKNOWLEDGE.

Issued at 2230 hrs.

for [signature]
Lieut. Col.,
G.S., 61st Division.

DISTRIBUTION.

Copy No. 1 - A.D.C. for G.O.C.
       2 - 61 Signal Coy.
     3-4 - 61 Div. Arty.
       5 - C.R.E.
       6 - 61 Bn. M.G.C.
       7 - 1/5 D.C.L.I.
       8 - 182 Inf. Bde.
       9 - 183 Inf. Bde.
      10 - 184 Inf. Bde.
      11 - "Q"
      12 - "G"
      13 - XVII Corps ADV.
      14 - 2nd Division.
      15 - 4th Division.
      16 - 19th Division.
      17 - 24th Division.
   18-19 - War Diary.

S E C R E T.   61st DIVISION ORDER No.231.   Copy No. 36
                                                1.11.1918.

Reference Map 51A, 1/40,000.

1. The Division (less Artillery, H.Q. & Nos.1&2 Sections D.A.C. and No.1 Coy. Div. Train) will be relieved on 2nd and 3rd inst. by 19th and 24th Divisions and will march to the AVESNES - ST. AUBERT AREA in accordance with attached movement table.

2. The Boundary between relieving Divisions will be :-
    "The track running N.E. and S.W. through L.26.b.(inclusive to the 24th Division) to bridge over river in L.25.c.8.2 - to junction of roads in SEPMERIES in K.36.d.3.3 to Chapel in Q.10.a. to cross roads at Q.14.d.8.1."
    The 24th Division will be the Right Division - the 19th Division will be the left Division.

3. The following troops of relieving Divisions will arrive in the Divisional Area on 1st inst. -

    One Brigade Group of 19th Division (incl.2 M.G.Coys) to VENDEGIES Area.
    One Brigade Group of 24th Division to ST. MARTIN-BERMERAIN Area.

    Arrangements for their close billeting and accommodation will be made by "Q".
    These two Brigade Groups will be replaced by others of the same Division on the 2nd inst.

4. In order to avoid congestion, Dismounted troops will march across country or on the side of the roads wherever this is possible.
    The usual distances will be maintained on the line of march.
    Accommodation for Infantry and all transport must be carefully arranged before either enters villages so that there is no delay in clearing roads through the villages.
    If necessary Infantry must halt, and transport park off the road clear of the villages until arrangements can be made to receive them Transport will not halt in any village.

5. All Troops of 19th and 24th Divisions arriving in the Divisional Area before 10.00 hrs. on 3rd inst. will come under orders of G.O.C. 61st Division until that hour.
    Command of the Divisional front will pass at the same hour to G.Os.C., 19th and 24th Divisions.

6. All further details of relief and moves will be arranged direct by Commanders concerned.

7. Completion of Reliefs and moves will be reported to D.H.Q. by wire as early as possible.

8. Div. H.Q. will close at VENDEGIES at 10.00 hrs. on 3rd inst., and open at ST. AUBERT at that hour.

                                                P.T.O.

9. Administrative Instructions will be issued

10. ACKNOWLEDGE.

Issued at 1200 hrs.

C.W. Dowden d/Maj
for Lieut.Col.,
G.S., 61st Division.

DISTRIBUTION.

No.1 - A.D.C. for G.O.C.	15 - D.A.D.V.S.
2 - 61 Div. Signal Coy.	16-17 - "Q"
3-4 - 61 Div. Arty.	18 - "G"
5 - C.R.E.	19 - D.G.O.
6 - 61 Bn. M.G.C.	20 - Camp Commandant.
7 - 1/5 D.C.L.I.	21-22 - XVII Corps ADV.
8 - 182 Inf. Bde.	23 - 4th Division.
9 - 183 Inf. Bde.	24 - 2nd Division.
10 - 184 Inf. Bde.	25 - 19th Division.
11 - A.D.M.S.	26 - 24th Division.
12 - 61 Div. Train.	27 - 62 Bde., RGA.
13 - D.A.P.M.	28 - 13 Squadron, R.A.F.
14 - D.A.D.O.S.	29 - Div. Reception Camp.

30 - 31 War Diary.

MOVEMENT TABLE ISSUED WITH 61st DIV. ORDER No. 231, dated 1.11.18.

Serial No.	Date	Formation or Unit	From	To	Route	Remarks
1	2.11.18	183 Bde. Group. 183 Inf.Bde. 478 Fd.Coy. R.E. No.3 Co.Div.Train 2/1 (SM) Fd. Amb. Mob. Vet. Sec.	VENDEGIES area	AVESNES LEZ AUBERT	CHAUSSEE BRUNEHAUT - MONTRECOURT - ST. AUBERT.	To march at 0900 hrs. Field Coy. to march independently, under orders of C.R.E.
2	do.	1/5 D.C.L.I. (P).	VENDEGIES area	ST. AUBERT	CHAUSSEE BRUNEHAUT - MONTRECOURT.	To march at 1200 hrs.
3	Night 2/3.11.18.	184 Bde. Group. 184 Inf.Bde. 479 Fd.Coy. R.E. No.4 Co.Div.Train 2/2 (SM) Fd. Amb.	BERMERAIN and Support area	AVESNES LEZ AUBERT	CHAUSSEE BRUNEHAUT - MONTRECOURT - ST. AUBERT.	To be relieved by 56th Bde. of 19th and a Bde. of 24th Div. Field Coy., Train Coy., and transport may march during the afternoon, remainder march on relief.
4	do.	182 Inf. Bde.	Front	BERMERAIN	Any	To be relieved by 56th Bde. of 19th and a Bde. of 24th Div.
5	3.11.18	61st Bn. M.G.C.	VENDEGIES area	AVESNES LEZ AUBERT	CHAUSSEE BRUNEHAUT - MONTRECOURT - ST. AUBERT.	To march at 0900 hrs.
6	do.	H.Q., 61st Div.	VENDEGIES area	ST. AUBERT	CHAUSSEE BRUNEHAUT - MONTRECOURT.	To march at 1000 hrs.
7	do.	Div. Signals.	do.	do.	do.	To march at 1015 hrs.
8	do.	182 Bde. Group. 182 Inf.Bde. 476 Fd.Coy. R.E. No.2 Co.Div.Train SAA.Sec. D.A.C.	BERMERAIN	do.	do.	To march at 1100 hrs.

(Copy) APPENDIX

183 Inf.Bde. G.C. 31/1
"Q".

Appendix VI

Reference Movement Table issued with D.O. 231 dated 1.11.18.

Serial No. 1:

Cancel "Remarks" and substitute :-

"Field Coy. R.E. to march independently under orders of C.R.E.

The 1½ battalions now in VENDEGIES to march at 0900 hrs.

The 1½ battalions now forward will withdraw to VENDEGIES at an hour to be notified, where they will rest for a few hours in billets vacated by 1½ battalions who have marched, and will march during the afternoon."

ACKNOWLEDGE.

(Sd.) C.H. Dowden, Maj.
1.11.18.   for Lt.Col.,
           G.S. 61 Div.

SECRET.   *War Diary*   G.C.31/6.

1/5 D.C.L.I.
61 Division "Q"

Appendix

Reference Movement Table issued with D.O.231 dated 1.11.1918.

One Company 1/5 D.C.L.I. will remain to work under C.R.E. and will march on 3rd inst.

ACKNOWLEDGE.

1st November, 1918.

Lieut. Col.,
G.S., 61st Division.

SECRET

G.C. 31/1

182 Inf. Bde.
184 Inf. Bde.
"Q".

Appendix VI

Reference Movement Table issued with D.O. 231 dated 1.11.18.

184 Inf. Bde. will remain at BERMERAIN on completion of relief on night 2nd/3rd, and will march at 1100 hrs. on 3rd inst.

182 Inf. Bde. on relief may halt and rest about VENDEGIES for a few hours, but must march by 0800 hrs. on 3rd inst.

2.11.18.

for Lieut.-Col.,
G.S., 61st Divn.

War Diary   Appendix VII

SECRET.   G.C. 79.
                          61st DIVISION.
               Locations of Units at 0600, 2.11.18.
                                                          Probable moves
                                                          during next
      61st DIV.H.Q. "G"   VENDEGIES, (Q.14.d.1.7).   24 hours.
         do.   "Q"   do............... ST. AUBERT.

      C. R. A.   do.
      C. R. E.   do.

      182 Inf.Bde. (SUPPORT BDE.) Q.4.c.6.7.)
         2/6 Warwicks,   Q.4.c.5.7.   )   AVESNES-LEZ-
         2/7 Warwicks,   K.35.a.3.8.   )   AUBERT
         2/8 Worcesters,   K.35.a.2.1.   )   (on relief,
                                                          night 2/3).

      183 Inf.Bde. (RESERVE BDE.) BERMERAIN.)
         9th North. Fus.   LA FOLIE (Q.23.a)   AVESNES-LEZ-
         11th Suffolks,   SOMMAING.   )   AUBERT.
         1st E. Lancs.   Q.4.c.6.5.   )

      184 Inf.Bde. (LINE) K.35.a.1.1.   )
         2/5 Glosters,   K.30.b.8.2.   )
         2/4 Oxfords,   do.   )   BERMERAIN
         2/4 R. Berks.   Q.6.b.6.2.   )   (on relief
                                                          night 2/3).

      61 Bn. M.G.C.   VENDEGIES (Q.14.a.8.1).

      476 Field Coy. R.E. Q.14.a.8.5.
      478   do.   Q.22.d.0.3.   AVESNES-LEZ-AUBERT
      479   do.   Q.21.b.8.0.   do.

      1/5 D.C.L.I.(P).   Q.27.b.6.5.   ST. AUBERT.

      2/1 Field Amb.   Q.20.a.1.7.   AVESNES-LEZ-AUBERT
      2/2   do.   P.30.b.   do.

      P.O.W. Cage,   VENDEGIES (Q.14.b.1.4).

                                                    A.O. Stephenson Capt.
                                                        G.S., 61st Divn.
      1.11.18.

WAR DIARY. Appendix VIII

S E C R E T. G.C.79.

61st DIVISION.
Location of Units at 0600, 3.11.18.

			Probable moves during next 24 hours.
61st Div.H.Q.	"G"	VENDEGIES	ST.AUBERT
do.	"Q"	ST.AUBERT	
C.R.A.		VENDEGIES	ST.AUBERT
C.R.E.		VENDEGIES	ST.AUBERT
182 Inf. Bde. H.Q.		ST.AUBERT	
2/6 Warwicks		do.	
2/7 Warwicks		do.	
2/8 Worcesters		do.	
183 Inf. Bde. H.Q.		AVESNES-LEZ-AUBERT	
9th North Fus.		SOMMAING	AVESNES-LEZ-AUBERT
11th Suffolks		AVESNES-LEZ-AUBERT	
1st East Lancs.		AVESNES-LEZ-AUBERT	
184 Inf. Bde. H.Q.		AVESNES-LEZ-AUBERT	
2/5 Glosters		BERMERAIN	AVESNES-LEZ-AUBERT
2/4 Oxfords		do.	do.
2/4 R.Berks.		do.	do.
61 Bn. M.G.C.		VENDEGIES	AVESNES-LEZ-AUBERT
476 Field Coy.		ST.AUBERT	
478 do.		AVESNES-LEZ-AUBERT	
479 do.		do.	
1/5 D.C.L.I.(P).		ST.AUBERT	
2/1 Field Amb.		AVESNES-LEZ-AUBERT	
2/2 do.		do.	

2.11.18.

A.D. Stephenson
Captain,
G.S., 61 Division.

Appendix IX

SECRET.   Copy No. 29.

61st DIVISION ORDER No. 232.

3.11.18.

Reference Map 51^A, 1/40,000.

1. The enemy is now retiring along the front of the 1st and 3rd Armies.

2. Moves as shown on attached table will therefore take place tomorrow 4th inst.

3. In order to avoid congestion, Dismounted troops will march across country or on the side of the roads wherever this is possible.
    The usual distances will be maintained on the line of march.
    Accommodation for Infantry and all transport must be carefully arranged before either enters villages so that there is no delay in clearing roads through the villages.
    If necessary Infantry must halt, and transport park off the road clear of the villages until arrangements can be made to receive them.
    Transport will not halt in any village.

4. All further details of moves will be arranged direct by Commanders concerned.

5. Completion of moves will be reported to D.H.Q. by wire as early as possible.

6. Divisional H.Qrs. will remain at ST.AUBERT.

7. ACKNOWLEDGE.

C.H.Bowden Maj
for
Lieut.Col.,
G.S., 61 Division.

Issued at 1800 hours ~~6 p.m.~~

DISTRIBUTION.

No. 1 - A.D.C. for G.O.C.   16-17 - "Q"
    2 - 61 Div.Signal Coy.   18 - "G"
  3-4 - 61 Div.Arty.   19 - D.G.O.
    5 - C.R.E.   20 - Camp Commandant
    6 - 61 Bn.M.G.C.   21-22 - XVII Corps ADV.
    7 - 1/5 D.C.L.I.   23 - 20th Div.
    8 - 182 Inf. Bde.   24 - Div.Reception Camp
    9 - 183 Inf. Bde.   25 - S.A.A. Sect.D.A.C.
   10 - 184 Inf. Bde.   26 - M.V.S.
   11 - A.D.M.S.   27 - 19 Div.
   12 - 61 Div.Train   28 - 24 Div.
   13 - D.A.P.M.   29-30 - War Diary
   14 - D.A.D.O.S.
   15 - D.A.D.V.S.

P.T.O.

MOVEMENT TABLE ISSUED WITH 61 DIVISION ORDER No. 232 dated 3.11.18.

Serial No.	Date	Formation or unit.	From	To	Route	Remarks
1	4.11.18	182 Bde. Group 182 Inf. Bde. Coy. 61 Bn.M.G.C. 476 Fd.Coy.R.E. No.2 Co.Div.Train S.A.A.Sec.D.A.C. 2/2 Field Amb.	ST.AUBERT	HAUSSY	direct	To be clear of ST. AUBERT by 1000 hours.
2	do.	1/5 D.C.L.I.	ST.AUBERT	FERMERAIN	MONTRECOURT – CHAUSSEE-BRUNE HAUT	To march at 1015 hrs.
3	do.	184 Bde. Group 184 Inf. Bde. Coy.61 Bn.M.G.C. 479 Fd.Co.R.E. No. 4 Co.Div.Train 2/1 Field Amb.	AVESNES-LEZ-AUBERT	do.	do.	To march at 1100 hrs.
4	do.	183 Bde. Group 183 Inf. Bde. 61 Bn.M.G.C.(less 2 coys.) 478 Fd.Coy.R.E. No.3 Co.Div.Train Mob.Vet.Sec.	TO REMAIN AT AVESNES – LEZ – AUBERT			
5	do.	Div. H.Q. H.Q. Div. Arty. Div. Signals. H.Q. Div. Engrs. H.Q. Div. Train	TO REMAIN AT ST. AUBERT			

Postponed 24 hours (margin note by row 3)

War Diary.   *Appendix* X

SECRET.   G.C.79.

61st DIVISION.
Locations of Units at 0600, 4.11.18.

Probable moves
during next
24 hours

61 Div.H.Q.	ST.AUBERT, U.24.b.6.1.	
C.R.A.	do.	
C.R.E.	do.	
182 Inf. Bde. H.Q.	ST.AUBERT	HAUSSY
2/6 Warwicks	do.	do.
2/7 Warwicks	do.	do.
2/8 Worcesters	do.	do.
183 Inf. Bde. H.Q.	AVESNES-LEZ-AUBERT, U.28.a.5.5.	
9th North. Fus.	do.	
11th Suffolks	do. U.27.b.30.05.	
1st E. Lancs.	do. U.28.a.8.0.	
184 Inf. Bde. H.Q.	AVESNES-LEZ-AUBERT	BERMERAIN
2/5 Glosters	do.	do.
2/4 Oxfords	do.	do.
2/4 R.Berks.	do.	do.
61 Bn. M.G.C. (less 2 Coys.)	AVESNES-LEZ-AUBERT, U.27.d.9.8.	
476 Field Coy.R.E.	ST.AUBERT	HAUSSY
478 do.	AVESNES-LEZ-AUBERT, U.22.c.0.2.	
479 do.	do.	BERMERAIN
1/5 D.C.L.I.(P).	ST.AUBERT, U.18.d.4.1.	BERMERAIN
2/2 Field Amb.	AVESNES-LEZ-AUBERT	BERMERAIN
2/1 do.	do.	HAUSSY

A.D.Stephenson
Captain,
G.S., 61 Division.

3.11.18.

War Diary.   Appendix XI

SECRET.   G.C.79.

61st DIVISION.
Locations of Units at 0600, 5.11.18.

Probable moves during next 24 hours.

61 Div. H.Q.	ST.AUBERT, U.24.b.6.1.	
C.R.A.	do.	
C.R.E.	do.	
182 Inf. Bde. H.Q.	HAUSSY, V.12.c.4.8.	
2/6 Warwicks	do. V.11.d.6.6.	
2/7 Warwicks	do. V.12.c.00.55.	
2/8 Worcesters	do. V.12.a.5.2.	
183 Inf. Bde. H.Q.	AVESNES-LEZ-AUBERT, U.28.a.5.5.	
9th North Fus.	do.	
11th Suffolks	do. U.27.b.30.05.	
1st E. Lancs.	do. U.28.a.8.0.	
184 Inf. Bde. H.Q.	AVESNES-LEZ-AUBERT	BERMERAIN
2/5 Glosters	do.	do.
2/4 Oxfords	do.	do.
2/4 R. Berks.	do.	do.
61 Bn. M.G.C. (less 2 Coys.)	AVESNES-LEZ-AUBERT, U.27.d.9.8.	
476 Field Coy. R.E.	HAUSSY, V.12.c.3.7.	
478 do.	AVESNES-LEZ-AUBERT, U.22.c.0.2.	
479 do.	do.	BERMERAIN
1/5 D.C.L.I.(P).	ST.MARTIN, Q.27.b.6.5.	
2/1 Field Amb.	HAUSSY, V.11.d.8.8.	
2/2 do.	AVESNES-LEZ-AUBERT	BERMERAIN
S.A.A.Section, D.A.C.	HAUSSY, V.18.a.2.8.	

A.D.Stephenson
Captain,
G.S., 61 Division.

4.11.18.

War Diary. Appendix XII

SECRET.   G.C.79.

                       61st DIVISION.
              Locations of Units at 0600, 7.11.18.

                                                  Probable moves
                                                  during next
                                                  24 hours.

61 Div. H.Q.   ST.AUBERT, U.24.b.6.1.

C.R.A.   do.

C.R.E.   do.

182 Inf. Bde. H.Q. HAUSSY, V.12.c.4.8.
   2/6 Warwicks   do.   V.11.d.6.6.
   2/7 Warwicks   do.   V.12.c.00.55.
   2/8 Worcesters   do.   V.12.a.5.2.

183 Inf. Bde. H.Q. AVESNES-LEZ-AUBERT, U.28.a.5.5.
   9th North Fus.   do.
   11th Suffolks   do.   U.27.b.90.05.
   1st E. Lancs.   do.   U.28.a.8.0.

184 Inf. Bde. H.Q. BERMERAIN, Q.22.c.1.7.
   2/5 Glosters   do.   Q.22.a.2.0.
   2/4 Oxfords   do.   Q.22.c.0.9.
   2/4 R.Berks.   do.   Q.22.c.1.6.

61 Bn. M.G.C.   AVESNES-LEZ-AUBERT, U.27.d.9.8.
   (Less 2 Coys.)

476 Field Coy.R.E. HAUSSY, V.12.c.3.7.
478   do.   AVESNES-LEZ-AUBERT, U.22.c.0.2.
479   do.   BERMERAIN, Q.21.d.6.9.

1/5 D.C.L.I.(P).   ST.MARTIN, Q.27.b.6.5.

2/1 Field Amb.   HAUSSY, V.11.d.8.8.
2/2   do.   BERMERAIN, Q.22.a.2.2.

S.A.A.Sect.,D.A.C. HAUSSY, V.18.a.2.8.

                                              D. Stephenson.
                                                 Captain,
                                              G.S., 61 Division.
6.11.18.

APPENDIX XIII

SECRET.   Copy No. 29

61st DIVISION ORDER No. 233.

Reference Map 51^A. 1/40,000

1. The Division will march forward tomorrow the 8th inst. in accordance with movement table attached.

2. In order to avoid congestion on roads, all dismounted troops will move across country or by the side of and off the roads where possible.
   The usual distances will be maintained on the line of march.

3. Completion of moves and location of H.Qrs. will be wired to Div. H.Q. as early as possible.

4. All further details will be arranged direct by commanders concerned.

5. Advanced Div. H.Q. will close at ST.AUBERT and open at VENDEGIES at 1130 hours on 8th inst.
   Rear Div. H.Q will close at ST.AUBERT and open at VENDEGIES on the 9th inst. at an hour to be notified later.

6. ACKNOWLEDGE.

                                            C.H. Dowden Major
                                            for Lieut.Col.,
Issued at 1800 hours.   G.S., 61 Division.
Nov 7th 1918
                    DISTRIBUTION :-

No. 1 - A.D.C. for G.O.C.   15 - D.A.D.V.S.
    2 - 61 Signal Coy.   16-17 - "Q"
  3-4 - 61 Div. Arty.   18 - "G"
    5 - C.R.E.   19 - D.G.O.
    6 - 61 Bn. M.G.C.   20 - Camp Comdt.
    7 - 1/5 O.C.L.I.   21-22 - XVII Corps ADV.
    8 - 182 Inf. Bde.   23 - 20 Div.
    9 - 183 Inf. Bde.   24 - Div. Reception Camp
   10 - 184 Inf. Bde.   25 - S.A.A.Sect. D.A.C.
   11 - A.D.M.S.   26 - M.V.S.
   12 - 61 Div. Train   27 - 19 Div.
   13 - D.A.P.M.   28 - 24 Div.
   14 - L.A.D.O.S.   29-30 - War Diary

                                                        P.T.O.

MOVEMENT TABLE ISSUED WITH 61 DIVISION ORDER No. 233 dated 7.11.18.

Serial No.	Date	Formation or Unit.	From	To	Route	Remarks.
1	8.11.18	184 Bde. Group 184 Inf. Bde. Coy.61 Bn.M.G.C 479 Fd.Coy.RE No.4 Coy.Train 2/2 (S.M.) Fd.Amb.	BERMERAIN area	SEPMERIES and MARESCHES	Cross rds. Q.16.a. - Rd. junction Q.11.d. - PARQUIAUX	To be clear of BERMERAIN by 0930 hours.
2	do.	1/5 R.G.L.I.	BERMERAIN	PARQUIAUX	do.	To march at 0930 hours.
3	do.	182 Bde. Group 182 Inf. Bde. Coy.61 Bn.M.G.C. 476 Fd. Coy. R.E. No. 2 Coy.Div.Train S.A.A.Sect.D.A.C. 2/1 (S.M.) Fd.Amb.	HAUSSY	VENDEGIES and SOMMAING	Cross Rds. W.1.d. - Cross Rds. P.19.b.9.9.	To march at 0900 hours and be clear of HAUSSY by 1000 hours.
4	do.	183 Bde. Group 183 Inf. Bde. 61 Bn. M.G.C.(less 2 Coys.) 478 Fd.Coy. R.E. No. 3 Coy.Div.Train Mob. Vet. Sect.	AVESNES-LEZ AUBERT	BERMERAIN and ST. MARTIN	ST.AUBERT - HAUSSY - Cross Rds. W.1.d. - Cross Rds. Q.31.b.9.9.	To be clear of ST.AUBERT by 1015 hours. Not to arrive at HAUSSY before 1000 hours.
5	do.	Adv. Div. H.Q. H.Q. Div. Arty. H.Q. Div. Engrs. H.Q. Div. Train	ST.AUBERT	VENDEGIES	MONTRECOURT - Cross Rds. P.33.b. - CHAUSSEE BRUNEHAUT	To march at 1030 hours in order shown. Rear Div. H.Q. will move to VENDEGIES on 9th inst.
6	do.	Div. Signals.	do.	do.	do.	To march at 1030 hours.

APPENDIX XIV

"A" Form
MESSAGES AND SIGNALS.

Army Form C. 2121 (In pads of 100.)

No. of Message............

Reference D.O. 233 aaa Groups march today as follows aaa Serial No. 1 march at 1200 hrs No. 2 at 1330 hrs No. 3 at 1130 hrs. Serial No. 4 at 1130 hrs No. 5 at 1100 hrs No. 6 at 1115 hrs aaa Troops and transport must move straight to billets on arrival aaa If halt is necessary both troops and transport must clear the road aaa Adv. D.H.Q. closes 1500 hrs. and opens VENDEGIES same hour aaa added all recipients D.O. 233

From
Place: 61 Div.

S E C R E T.   G.C.79.

61st DIVISION.
Locations of Units at 0600, 9th Nov.1918.

61 Div. H.Q. Adv.	VENDEGIES, Q.14.d.1.7.	
61 Div. H.Q. Rear	ST.AUBERT, U.24.b.6.1.	Moving to VENDEGIES
C.R.A.	VENDEGIES	
C.R.E.	VENDEGIES	

<u>182 Inf. Bde. H.Q.</u>   SOMMAING, Q.7.d.5.5.
  2/6 Warwicks   VENDEGIES, Q.8.d.4.3.
  2/7 Warwicks   SOMMAING, Q.7.d.3.2.
  2/8 Worcestors   VENDEGIES, Q.14.a.8.6.

<u>183 Inf. Bde. H.Q.</u>   BERMERAIN, Q.22.c.2.6.
  9th North.Fus.   do.   Q.22.c.4.7.
  11th Suffolks   do.   Q.22.c.0.9.
  1st East Lancs.   do.   Q.22.c.1.9.

<u>184 Inf. Bde. H.Q.</u>   PARQUIAUX, Q.6.b.4.7.
  2/5 Glosters   MARESCHES, L.25.b.3.4.
  2/4 Oxfords   do.   L.25.d.1.8.
  2/4 R.Berks.   SEPMERIES, K.36.d.8.4.

61 Bn. M.G.C.   ST.MARTIN, Q.21.d.6.4.
  (less 2 Coys.)

476 Field Coy. R.E.   SOMMAING, Q.7.d.9.1.
478   do.   BERMERAIN, Q.21.d.7.8.
479   do.   SEPMERIES, K.36.d.2.2.

1/5 D.C.L.I.(P).   do.   K.36.d.4.2.

2/1 Field Amb.   VENDEGIES, Q.20.a.1.7.
2/2   do.   SEPMERIES, K.36.c.7.2.

S.A.A. Sect.D.A.C.   VENDEGIES, Q.8.d.3.2.

8.11.18.

                                           Captain,
                                    G.S., 61 Division.

APPENDIX XVI

"A" Form
MESSAGES AND SIGNALS.

Army Form C. 2121 (In pads of 100.)

(Copy)

To	61 Div.		

Sender's Number.	Day of Month.	In reply to Number.	AAA
GB.575	11		

Hostilities will cease **1100** hours today Novr. 11th aaa Troops will stand fast on line reached at that hour which will be reported by wire to Corps H.Q. aaa Defensive precautions will be maintained aaa There will be no intercourse of any description with the enemy

From Adv. 17 Corps.
Place
Time 0655.

"A" Form
MESSAGES AND SIGNALS.

Army Form C. 2121 (in pads of 100.)

TO
All recipients Divl. Orders.

Sender's Number.	Day of Month.	In reply to Number.	AAA
G 415	11		

From 17 Corps begins aaa Hostilities will cease 1100 hours today Novr. 11th aaa Troops will stand fast on line reached at that hour which will be reported to Corps H.Q. aaa Defensive precautions will be maintained aaa There will be no intercourse of any description with the enemy aaa Ends

From: 61 Div.
Place:
Time: 0800

APPENDIX XVII

SECRET.   Copy No. 28

61st DIVISION ORDER No. 234.

13.11.18.

Ref. Map 51^A. 1/40,000.

1. The 61st Division (less Artillery) will move by march route tomorrow, 14th inst., in accordance with Movement Table attached.

2. All dismounted troops will move off the roads where necessary. The usual distances will be maintained on the line of march. Units will not halt in villages whilst on the march.

3. Completion of moves and locations of H.Q. will be wired to Div. H.Q. as early as possible.

4. All further details will be arranged by Commanders concerned.

5. Div. H.Q. will close at VENDEGIES and open at RIEUX at 1100 hrs., 14th inst.

6. ACKNOWLEDGE.

Issued at 2230 hours.

A.D. Stephenson Cap
for Lieut.-Col.,
G.S., 61st Division.

Distribution :-

Copy No. 1 - A.D.C. for G.O.C.	15 - D.A.D.V.S.
2 - 61 Signal Coy.	16-17 - "Q".
3-4 - 61 Div. Arty.	18 - "G".
5 - C.R.E.	19 - D.G.O.
6 - 61 Bn. M.G.C.	20 - Camp Comdt.
7 - 1/5 D.C.L.I.	21-22 - XVII Corps.
8 - 182 Inf.Bde.	23 - 19th Div.
9 - 183 Inf.Bde.	24 - 20th Div.
10 - 184 Inf.Bde.	25 - 61 Div. Reception Camp.
11 - A.D.M.S.	26 - S.A.A.Sec. D.A.C.
12 - 61 Div. Train.	27 - Mob.Vet.Sec.
13 - D.A.P.M.	28-29 - War Diary.
14 - D.A.D.O.S.	

(P.T.O.)

Movement Table to accompany 61 Div. Order No. 234, dated 13.11.18.

Serial No.	Date.	Formation or Unit	From	To	Route	Remarks
1	14.11.18.	182 Bde. Group. 182 Inf.Bde. 476 Fd.Coy.R.E. 2/1(SM)Fd.Amb. No.2 Coy.Div.Train.	VENDEGIES & SOMMAING	AVESNES-LEZ-AUBERT.	Cross-roads Q.19.b.9.9 - SAULZOIR - VILLIERS-CAUCHIES - AVESNES.	To march at 1000 hrs.
2	do.	Coy. 61 Bn.MGC.	do.	ST. AUBERT.	do.	To march under orders of G.O.C. 182 Inf.Bde. To rejoin 61 Bn.MGC. at ST.AUBERT.
3	do.	SAA.Sect. D.A.C.	do.	RIEUX.	do.	To march under orders of G.O.C. 182 Inf.Bde.
4	do.	183 Bde. Group. 183 Inf.Bde. 478 Fd.Coy.R.E. No.3 Coy.Div.Train. 61 Bn.M.G.C.(less 2 coys.).	BERMERAIN & ST. MARTIN.	ST. AUBERT.	Cross-roads Q.31.b.9.9.- cross-roads W.l.d.- HAUSSY - ST. AUBERT.	To march at 1000 hrs.
5	do.	61 Mot.Vet.Sec.	do.	RIEUX.	do.	To march under orders of G.O.C. 183 Inf.Bde.
6	do.	1/5 D.C.L.I.	SEPMERIES.	AVESNES-LEZ-AUBERT.	BERMERAIN - cross-roads Q.31.b.9.9.- cross-roads W.l.d.- HAUSSY - ST. AUBERT.	To march at 1030 hrs.
7	do.	184 Bde. Group. 184 Inf.Bde. 479 Fd.Coy.R.E. No.4 Coy.Div.Train	SEPMERIES & MARESCHES.	HAUSSY.	BERMERAIN - cross-roads Q.31.b.9.9 - cross-roads W.l.d. - HAUSSY.	To march at 1100 hrs.
8	do.	Coy. 61 Bn. M.G.C.	do.	ST. AUBERT.	do.	To march under orders of G.O.C. 184 Inf.Bde. & rejoin 61 Bn.M.G.C. at ST.AUBERT.
9	do.	2/2 (SM) Fd. Amb.	do.	do.	do.	To march under orders of G.O.C. 184 Inf.Bde. & join 183 Bde.Group on arrival at ST. AUBERT.
10	do.	Div. H.Q. H.Q. Div.Arty. H.Q. Div.Engrs. H.Q. Div.Train.	VENDEGIES	RIEUX	CHAUSSEE-BRUNE HAUT- SAULZOIR - VILLIERS CAUCHIES - RIEUX.	To march at 11.15 hrs.
11	do.	Div. Signals.	do.	do.	do.	To march at 11.45 hrs.

APPENDIX XVIII

SECRET.   Copy No. 26

61st DIVISION ORDER No. 235.

Reference Map 51ᴬ. 1/40,000.   14.11.18.
           51   1/40,000.

1. The Division (less Artillery) will march to CAMBRAI Main town on 15th and 16th inst. in accordance with attached movement table.

2. (a) Dismounted troops will march across country or clear of the roads. Routes will be carefully reconnoitred.
   (b) The usual distances will be maintained by units and transport on the line of march.

3. Completion of moves and location of H.Qrs. will be reported to Divisional H.Qrs. through Town Commandant as soon as possible.

4. Representatives of Billeting Parties will meet the D.A.A.G. at the Town Commandant's office at 0930 hours 15th inst. Guides will be stationed on the main SOLESMES road at railway crossing in A.11.b.0.3. to meet units.

5. All further details will be arranged direct by Commanders concerned.

6. Divisional H.Qrs. will close at RIEUX and open at CAMBRAI at 1100 hours on the 15th inst.

7. ACKNOWLEDGE.

                                              A.D.Stephenson Capt.
                                              Lieut. Col.,
Issued at 1800 hours.   G.S., 61 Division.

DISTRIBUTION:

No. 1 - A.D.C. for G.O.C.	15 - D.A.D.V.S.
2 - 61 Signal Coy.	16-17 - "Q"
3-4 - 61 Div. Arty.	18 - "G"
5 - C.R.E.	19 - Camp Comdt.
6 - 61 Bn. M.G.C.	20-21 - XVII Corps
7 - 1/5 D.C.L.I.	22 - 19 Div.
8 - 182 Inf. Bde.	23 - Div. Reception Camp
9 - 183 Inf. Bde.	24 - S.A.A. Sect. D.A.C.
10 - 184 Inf. Bde.	25 - Mob. Vet. Sect.
11 - A.D.M.S.	26-27 - War Diary.
12 - 61 Div. Train	
13 - D.A.P.M.	
14 - D.A.D.O.S.	

P.T.O.

MOVEMENT TABLE ISSUED WITH 61st DIV. ORDER No. 235, dated 14.11.18.

Serial No.	Date.	Formation or Unit.	From	To	Route	Remarks
1	15.11.18.	1/5 D.C.L.I.	AVESNES-LEZ-AUBERT	CAMBRAI "A" (N.W.) Area.	Cross-roads C.3.b.8.4 - SOLESMES - CAMBRAI Road.	To march at 0930 hrs.
2	do.	182 Bde. Group. 182 Inf.Bde. 476 Fd.Co.R.E. No.2 Coy.Div. Train. 2/1(SM)Fd.Amb.	do.	"C" CAMBRAI (S.W.) Area.	do.	To march at 1000 hrs.
3	do.	183 Bde. Group. 183 Inf.Bde. 478 Fd.Co.R.E. No.3 Coy. Div. Train. 2/2(SM)Fd.Amb.	ST. AUBERT	"B" CAMBRAI (N.E.) Area.	AVESNES - Cross-roads C.3.b.8.4 - SOLESMES - CAMBRAI Road.	To march at 1030 hrs.
4	do.	61st Bn.M.G.C.	ST. AUBERT	"B" CAMBRAI (N.E.) Area.	do.	To march at 1130 hrs.
5	do.	184 Bde. Group. 184 Inf.Bde. 479 Fd.Co.R.E. No.4 Coy.Div. Train.	HAUSSY	CAGNONCLES	ST. AUBERT - AVESNES - cross-roads C.3.b.8.4 - SOLESMES - CAMBRAI Road.	To march at 1100 hrs. To be clear by 1200 hrs.
6	do.	61 DIV.H.Q. H.Q. Div. Arty. H.Q. Div. R.E. H.Q. Div.Train. S.A.A.Sec.D.A.C. Mob.Vet.Sec.	RIEUX	CAMBRAI "A" (N.W.) Area.	Cross-roads U.13 - CHAUSSEE-BRUNEHAUT.	To march at 1000 hrs. Guides from billeting parties will meet Units where railway crosses road at A.11.a.2.4.
7	do.	61 Signal Coy.	do.	do.	do.	To march at 1020 hrs. } do
8	16.11.18.	184 Bde.Group. 184 Inf.Bde. 479 Fd.Co.R.E. No.4 Coy.Div. Train.	CAGNONCLES	CAMBRAI "D" (S.E.) Area.	No restrictions.	To march at 1000 hrs.

War Diary   *Appendix XIX*

SECRET.
                                                                                           G.C. 79

61st DIVISION.
Locations of Units at 1200 hrs., 16.11.18.

61st DIV. H.Q.	CAMBRAI, A.9.d.95.80.
C. R. A.	do. RUE NEUVE DES CAPUCINS.
C. R. E.	do. 18, RUE D'ARRAS.
182 Inf. Bde.	A.16.c.6.4.
2/6 Warwicks,	A.22.b.75.50.
2/7 Warwicks,	A.16.d.0.4.
2/8 Worcesters,	A.22.a.95.95.
183 Inf. Bde.	A.12.c.5.3.
9th North. Fus.	A.11.b.7.0.
11th Suffolks,	A.18.a.
1st E. Lancs.	A.12.c.
184 Inf. Bde.	A.10.c.6.2.
2/5 Glosters.	BARRACKS, A.10.a.
2/4 Oxfords,	A.10.d.2.9.
2/4 R. Berks	BARRACKS, A.10.a.
61 Bn. M.G.C.	A.11.a.6.7.
476 Field Co. R.E.	A.16.d.8.4.
478 do.	A.17.b.90.65.
479 do.	A.10.c.6.7.
1/5 D.C.L.I.(P).	The HOSPITAL, CAMBRAI, A.10.a.6.3.
2/1 Field Amb.	A.17.d.0.3.
2/2 do.	A.12.c.2.2.
2/3 do.	COLLEGE NOTRE DAME LE GRACE.
S.A.A. Sec. D.A.C.,	A.10.c.85.05.

                                                                       A. Stephenson.
16.11.18.   Captain,
                                                                   G.S., 61st Divn.

War Diary   Appendix XX

SECRET.   G.C. 79.

61st DIVISION.
Locations of Units at 0600 hrs. 20.11.18.

61st DIV. H.Q.	CAMBRAI, A.9.1.95.80.
C. R. A.	RUE NEUVE DES CAPUCINS, A.10.a.75.40.
306 Bde. R.F.A.	CAVALRY BARRACKS, A.10.a.
307 do.	RUE DE L'EPEE, A.10.c.80.05.
D.A.C.	do. A.10.c.70.10.
182 Inf.Bde.H.Q.	RUE DE ST. QUENTIN, A.16.c.6.3.
2/6 Warwicks,	A.22.b.75.50.
2/7 Warwicks,	A.16.d.0.4.
2/8 Worcesters,	A.22.a.95.95.
183 Inf.Bde.H.Q.	RUE LALLIER, A.12.c.5.3.
9th North. Fus.	A.11.b.7.0.
11th Suffolks,	A.18.a.
1st E. Lancs.	A.12.c.
184 Inf.Bde.H.Q.	RUE WATTEAU, A.17.c.3.8.
2/5 Glosters,	A.17.c.15.25.
2/4 Oxfords,	A.10.b.2.9.
2/4 R. Berks.	A.23.a.30.85.
1/5 D.C.L.I. (P).	HOSPITAL, CAMBRAI, A.10.a.6.3.
C. R. E.	CAMBRAI, 18, RUE D'ARRAS.
476 Field Co.R.E.	A.16.d.8.4.
478 do.	A.17.b.90.85.
479 do.	A.10.c.6.7.
61st Bn. M.G.C.	A.11.a.6.7.
2/1 Field Amb.	A.17.d.0.3.
2/2 do.	A.12.c.2.2.
2/3 do.	COLLEGE NOTRE DAME DE GRACE, CAMBRAI.
61 Div. Train, ASC.	A.10.a.70.05.

19.11.18.

                                                    Capt
                                                p. G.S., 61st Div.

Appendix XXI

S E C R E T.   Copy No. 24

61st DIVISION ORDER No. 236.   21.11.18.
WARNING ORDER.

1. The 61st Division will be prepared to move, by tactical trains and march route, to the BERNAVILLE area.

2. Transport, less portion proceeding by rail, will move by road on 23rd and 24th inst., in accordance with attached Table.

3. Brigade Groups will travel by tactical trains as follows :-

    24th :- 182 Bde. Group (including 2 coys. 1/5 D.C.L.I. & 1 coy. 61 Bn. M.G.C.).
            183 Bde. Group (including H.Q. & 1 coy. 1/5 D.C.L.I & H.Q. & 1 coy. 61 Bn.M.G.C.).

    25th :- 184 Bde. Group (including 2 coys. 61 Bn.M.G.C.).
            61 Div.H.Q.

4. 315 Army Bde. R.F.A. will move with 61st Div. Arty., probably on 24th inst.

5. Full details will be issued later.

6. ACKNOWLEDGE.

Issued at 1800 hrs.

A.D.Stephenson Capt
for Lieut.-Col.,
G.S., 61st Divn.

DISTRIBUTION :-

Copy No. 1 - A.D.C. for G.O.C.
       2 - 61 Signal Coy.
    3-4 - 61 Div. Arty.
       5 - C.R.E.
       6 - 61 Bn.M.G.C.
       7 - 1/5 D.C.L.I.
       8 - 182 Inf.Bde.
       9 - 183 Inf.Bde.
      10 - 184 Inf.Bde.
      11 - A.D.M.S.
      12 - 61 Div. Train.
      13 - D.A.P.M.
      14 - D.A.D.O.S.
      15 - D.A.D.V.S.
  16-17 - "Q".
      18 - "G".
      19 - Camp Comdt.
  20-21 - XVII Corps.
      22 - Div. Reception Camp.
      23 - Mob.Vet.Sec.
  24-25 - War Diary.

MARCH TABLE ISSUED WITH 61.DIV. ORDER NO. 236,
dated 21.11.18.

Serial No.	Date	Formation or Unit.	From	To	Route	Remarks
1	23.11.18	Transport of 182 Bde.Group. 182 Inf.Bde. 476 Fd.Coy.R.E. 2/1 Fd.Amb. 1/5 D.C.L.I. No.2 Coy.; Div.Train.	CAMBRAI	vicinity of BAPAUME.		By road to staging camp about BAPAUME to be notified later.
2	do.	Transport of 183 Bde.Group. 183 Inf.Bde. 478 Fd.Coy.R.E. 2/2 Fd.Amb. 61 Bn.M.G.C. No.3 Coy.; Div.Train.	do.	do.		do.
3	do.	61st Div. Arty. (less 1 Bde.). No. 1 Coy.; Div.Train.(less portion proceeding 24th inst.).	do.	do.		do.
4	24.11.18	Transport of 184 Bde.Group. 184 Inf.Bde. 479 Fd.Coy.R.E. No.4 Coy.; Div.Train.	do.	do.		do.
5	do.	1 Bde.R.F.A. Mob.Vet.Sec. Remainder of No.1 Coy.Div.Train.	do.	do.		do.
6	do.	61 Div. H.Q. 61 Div.Signals. H.Q., R.E. H.Q. Div.Train.	do.	do.		do.

APPENDIX XXII

SECRET.   Copy No. 24

                    61st DIVISION ORDER No. 237.
                                                               22.11.18.

Reference Maps: LENS 1/100,000.
                VALENCIENNES   do.

1.   The 61st Division (less 2/3 Field Amb.) will move from
    CAMBRAI to the BERNAVILLE Area, commencing 23.11.18 as follows:-

    (a) Divisional Artillery (less 315 Army Bde. R.F.A. attached) and
        transport of Division (less portion proceeding by rail) will
        move by march route in accordance with Movement Table attached.

    (b) Remainder of Division by tactical trains on 24th and 25th inst.

2.   The following distances will be maintained on the march :-

    (i) Between Batteries, Sections of D.A.C., Field Ambulances,
        transport of units   ...   .   100 yds.

    (ii) Between Artillery Brigades, transport of Brigades   500 yds.

    (iii) Between groups of 6 vehicles, whether mechanical or
        horse-drawn   ...   .   25 yds.

3.   182 Inf. Bde. will detail a Field Officer to be in charge of
    the Divisional transport (less Artillery).   He will be
    responsible for arranging halting places for watering and for
    alloting areas at each staging point.

4.   Administrative and train arrangements will be notified by "Q".

5.   All further details will be arranged by Commanders concerned.

6.   ACKNOWLEDGE.
                                              A.D.Stephenson Capt.
                                                 for Lieut.Col.,
Issued at 1800 hours.   G.S., 61 Division.

                            Distribution:

    Copy No. 1 - A.D.C. for G.O.C.   13 - D.A.P.M.
           2 - 61 Signal Coy.   14 - D.A.D.O.S.
         3-4 - 61 Div. Arty.   15 - D.A.D.V.S.
           5 - C.R.E.   16-17 - "Q"
           6 - 61 Bn.M.G.C.   18 - "G"
           7 - 1/5 D.C.L.I.   19 - Camp Comdt.
           8 - 182 Inf. Bde.   20-21 - XVII Corps
           9 - 183 Inf. Bde.   22 - Div. Reception Camp
          10 - 184 Inf. Bde.   23 - Mob. Vet. Sec.
          11 - A.D.M.S.   24-25 - War Diary.
          12 - 61 Div. Train

MARCH TABLE ISSUED WITH 61st DIV. ORDER No. 237, dated 22.11.18.

Serial No.	Date	Formation or Unit.	From	To	Route	Remarks
1	23.11.18	Div.Arty.Group. Div.Arty. D.A.C. Mob.Vet.Sec. No.1 Coy.Train	CAMBRAI	Staging Camp at BEUGNATRE and FAVREUIL.	CAMBRAI - BOURSIES - FREMICOURT.	Time of start to be given by C.R.A. 315 Army Bde. RFA. will also march under orders of C.R.A., 61 Div., 24 hours after 61 Div. Art.
2	do.	182 Bde.Group. 182 Inf.Bde. 476 Fd.Coy.RE. No.2 Coy.Train 2/1 Fd.Amb. 1/5 D.C.L.I.	do.	Staging Camp at BERTINCOURT and HAPLINCOURT.	Fbg.de Paris - N.end of MASNIERES - MARCOING - RIBECOURT - FIESQUIERES - HAVRINCOURT - HERMIES.	To be clear of road junction immediately S. of Fbg. de PARIS by 0830 hrs.
3	do.	183 Bde.Group. 183 Inf.Bde. 478 Fd.Coy.RE. 2/2 Fd.Amb. No.3 Coy.Train 61 Bn.M.G.C.	do.	do.	do.	Head of column not to pass starting point before 0825 hrs. and be clear by 0930 hrs.
4	do.	184 Bde.Group. 184 Inf.Bde. 479 Fd.Coy.RE. No.4 Coy.Train	do.	do.	do.	Head of column not to pass starting point before 0940 hrs. and to be clear by 1020 hrs.
5	do.	Div.H.Q.Group. 61 Div.Signals 61 Div.H.Q. H.Q. R.E. H.Q. Train.	do.	do.	do.	Head of column not to pass starting point before 1030 hrs.
6	24.11.18	Div.Art.Group.	BEUGNATRE - FAVREUIL area.	COIGNEUX	FAVREUIL - SAPIGNIES - BIHUCOURT - ACHIET - LE GRAND - ACHIET - LE PETIT - BUCQUOY - HEBUTERNE - SAILLY-AU-BOIS.	To march in order given.

(P.T.O.)

(2)

Serial No.	Date	Formation of Unit	From	To	Route	Remarks
7	24.11.18.	182 Bde. Group.	BERTINCOURT - HAPLINCOURT area	STATION, ALBERT.	HAPLINCOURT - BANCOURT - Fbg.de PERONNE (BAPAUME) - N.end of THILLOY - X roads 1 mile S.E. of GREVILLERS - ALBERT.	To be clear of X roads, HAPLINCOURT, by 0800 hrs.
8	do.	183 Bde. Group.	do.	do.	do.	Not to pass starting point before 0605 hrs., and to be clear by 0650 hrs.
9	do.	184 Bde. Group.	do.	do.	do.	Not to pass starting point before 0800 hrs., and to be clear by 0930 hrs.
10	do.	Div.H.Q. Group.	do.	do.	do.	Not to pass starting point before 0940 hrs.
11	25.11.18	Div.Art.Group.	SOIGNEUX	BERNAVILLE Div.area	Any	
12	do.	182 Bde.Group.	ALBERT	do.	HEDAUVILLE - VARENNES - BEAUQUESNE - BEAUVAL - CANLAS - FIENVILLERS.	To be clear of road junction ½ miles due S. of B in BUZIECOURT by 0600 hrs.
13	do.	183 Bde.Group.	do.	do.	do.	Not to pass starting point before 0605 hrs., and to be clear by 0650 hrs.
14	do.	184 Bde.Group.	do.	do.	do.	Not to pass starting point before 0700 hrs., and to be clear by 0730 hrs.
15	do.	Div.H.Q. Group.	do.	do.	do.	Not to pass starting point before 0740 hrs.

2nd Division.
4th Division.

G.C.31/1.

G.R.12/7

Herewith amended Map to accompany 61st Division Order No.230, dated 31.10.1918, shewing DISPOSITIONS ON RELIEF at 1800 hours, 2/3.11.1918.

2nd November, 1918.

Major General,
Commanding, 61st Division

Secret

APPENDIX XXII

S E C R E T.

G.O.31.

Amendment to
61 Div. Order No. 237, dated 22.11.18.

Reference March Table issued with above Order.

Serial No. 6 - Div. Art. Group.

Destination will be POMMIER, and not COIGNEUX as stated.

Route - FAVREUIL - SAPIGNIES - BIHUCOURT - ACHIET-LE-GRAND - ACHIET-LE-PETIT - BUCQUOY - ESSARTS - HANNESCAMPS - BIENVILLERS.

J.B. Stephenson Capt

Lieut.-Col.,
G.S., 61st Divn.

22.11.18.

Copies to - A.D.C. for G.O.C.
          61 Signal Coy.
          61 Div. Art.
          A.D.M.S.
          61 Div. Train.   "Q".
          D.A.P.M.   XVII Corps.
          D.A.D.O.S.   Mob.Vet.Sec.
          D.A.D.V.S.   War Diary.

APPENDIX - XXLII

"A" Form.
MESSAGES AND SIGNALS.

Army Form C.2121 (in pads of 100).

TO: War diary

Sender's Number.	Day of Month.	In reply to Number.	
* GS 761	23		A A A

Reference 61 Div. Order No. 237 aaa Div. H.Q. will close at CAMBRAI at 0900 hrs on 25th inst. and open at BERNAVILLE at 1500 hrs on the same date aaa Addsd all recipients of above Order.

(D.R.L.S.)

From 61 Div.

O Stephenson
Capt GS

War Diary.   Appendix XXIV

S E C R E T.   61st DIVISION.   G.C. 79.
              Locations of Units at 0600, 28.11.18.

        61st DIV.H.Q.   BERNAVILLE.

        C.R.A.   CHATEAU DE BEAUVOIR.
          306 Bde. R.F.A.   BEALCOURT.
          307   do.   WAVANS.
          D.A.C.   ACQUET.
          315 Army Bde.RFA.   MAIZICOURT.
          M.T.M.B.   MONTLOUIS FM.

        182 Inf.Bde.H.Q.   MAISON PONTHIEU.
          2/6 Warwicks,   YVRENCH.
          2/7 Warwicks,   MAISON PONTHIEU.
          2/8 Worcesters,   CRAMONT.
          182 L.T.M.B.   YVRENCH.

        183 Inf.Bde.H.Q.   DOMLEGER.
          9th North. Fus.   LONGVILLERS.
          11th Suffolks,   HEUZECOURT.
          1st E. Lancs.,   LE MAILLARD.
          183 L.T.M.B.   AGENVILLE.

        184 Inf.Bde.H.Q.   DOMART.
          2/5 Glosters,   DOMQUEUR.
          2/4 Oxfords,   DOMART.
          2/4 R.Berks.,   FRANSU.
          184 L.T.M.B.   DOMART.

        1/5 D.C.L.I.(P).   BEAUMETZ.

        C.R.L.   BERNAVILLE.
          476 Field Co.RE.   L'ABBAYE D'AMMONT Fm.
          478   do.   PROUVILLE.
          479   do.   ST. HILAIRE.

        61 Bn. M.G.C.   BERNEUIL.

        A.D.M.S.   BERNAVILLE.
          2/1 Field Amb.   HEIRMONT.
          2/2   do.   MESNIL DOMQUEUR.

        61 Div.Train H.Q.   BERNAVILLE.
          No. 1 Coy.   FROHEN-LE-GRAND.
          No. 2 Coy.   CRAMONT.
          No. 3 Coy.   PROUVILLE.
          No. 4 Coy.   DOMART.

                                           A.D. Stephenson.
                                                Captain,
                                           G.S., 61st Divn.
        27.11.18.

Confidential

61st Division
War Diary.
Vol. XXII
December 1918.

61st Division No A 36.

CONFIDENTIAL.

D. A. G.
    Base.

      Reference this office Number A.36 of 12th inst.
Herewith War Diaries of Headquarters 61st Division
"G" & Headquarters 61st Division "A" & "Q".

D. H. Q.
14-12-18.

                for Major-General,
            Commanding, 61st Division.

A.G's BRANCH.
G.H.Q., 3RD ECHELON.
RECEIVED.

CAPTAIN.
for D.A.G.

DATE

Army Form C. 2118.

WAR DIARY
of VOLUME XXXII.
~~INTELLIGENCE~~ SUMMARY.

(Erase heading not required.)

Instructions regarding War Diaries and Intelligence Summaries are contained in F. S. Regs., Part II. and the Staff Manual respectively. Title pages will be prepared in manuscript.

Place	Date	Hour	Summary of Events and Information	Remarks and references to Appendices
BERNAVILLE	1.12.18.		3 lectures on Demobilization delivered by Rev. Studdart Kennedy (Woodbine Willie) to 182 and 183 Bdes. and Div. Arty. Locations of units altered as per attached amendment.	Appendix I.
	3.12.18.		2 lectures on Bolshevik Russia delivered by Mr A.L.Williams to 182, 183 and 184 Brigades. 2/3rd Field Ambulance at PUCHVILLERS reverted to the command of G.O.C. 61st Division.	Appendix II.
	6.12.18.		Orders for move of certain units; the Divisional area having been extended Westwards. Meeting of representatives from Brigade Groups for deciding details as to Sports, Football, etc., held under Presidency of Major-General F.J.Duncan, C.M.G., D.S.O.	
	7.12.18.		183 Inf. Brigade, less 9th Northumberland Fusiliers, moved to AILLY area in accordance with orders.	
ST.RIQUIER	8.12.18. 1000		9th Northumberland Fusiliers moved to VAUCHELLES. 61st Div. H.Q. moved to ST. RIQUIER, opening at 10.00 hours.	
	9.12.18.		Locations at 06.00 hours as per attached list. 182 Inf. Brigade H.Q. moved to HIERMONT. Amendment to location list dated 9.12.18 issued. Professor A.D. CROMMELIN of Greenwich Observatory lectured on "Astronomy" to 61 Div. Arty. and 182 Brigade Group.	Appendix III. Appendix IV.
	10.12.18. 12.12.18. 16.12.18.		Mr TURTLE lectured on "Under Big Ben" to 61 Div. Arty. and 184 Inf. Brigade Group. Locations at 0600 hours as per attached list. Capt. BEWSHER, R.A.F. lectured on "Night Bombing Raids" to 183 and 184 Brigade Groups.	Appendix V.
	17.12.18.		Col. BOURNE lectured on "Land Settlement" and "Agriculture" to 61 Div. Arty. and 182 Brigade Group.	
	19.12.18.		Col. SWAYNE, R.E. lectured on "Exploration in Siberia" to 182 and 184 Brigades.	

Army Form C. 2118.

WAR DIARY
or
INTELLIGENCE SUMMARY.
(Erase heading not required.)

Place	Date	Hour	Summary of Events and Information	Remarks and references to Appendices
ST.RIQUIER	21.12.18.		Capt. TAYLOR lectured on "Agriculture" to 183 and 184 Brigades.	Appendix VI.
	25.12.18.		A fine frosty day. Special arrangements made for men's dinners etc.	
	27.12.18.		1st Bn. E.Lancs (183 Inf. Brigade) moved to ABBEVILLE, with H.Q. at CAOURS, for work under G.O.C. L.of C. - looking after German prisoners. This Battalion was still to be administered by this Division except for rations.	
	29.12.18.		H.Q. 1st E.Lancs moved to NEUILLY L'HOPITAL.	
			The weather throughout the month has been very poor, the only really bright day being Christmas Day.	
			Units have devoted a considerable amount of time to recreation during the month; though enough military training has taken place to keep up the discipline in the Division.	
			The Education Scheme has proved very popular, and in addition to well attended classes in various subjects, (under arrangements made by units), courses in various trades outside the Division have been attended with beneficial results.	

12.1.19.

[signature]
for Major-General,
Commanding 61st (S.M.) Division.

War Diary Appendix I

SECRET.

G.C. 79

Amendment to Locations dated 28.11.18.
----

    61 D.A.C.   LA NEUVILLE.

    No.1 Coy.,
       61 Div.Train.   LANNOY.

    No.2 Coy. do.   CONTEVILLE.

1.12.18.

                                            W.H. Dowden, Maj.
                                            Capt.
                                            G.S., 61 Div.

War Diary   S E C R E T   Appendix II
G.S.31

Reference 61 Div. Order No. 238, dated 6.12.18; Div.H.Q. will close at BERNAVILLE at 1000 hrs. and reopen at ST. RIQUIER at the same hour on the 8th inst.

6.12.18.

To all recipients of
61 Div. Order No.238.

John Hunter Capt.
G.S., 61st Divn.

Appendix II

SECRET.   Copy No. 24

                    61st DIVISION ORDER No. 238.   6.12.18.

Reference maps - LENS 1/100,000,
                 ABBEVILLE 1/100,000.

1. In accordance with a readjustment of Divisional areas, the
    following units will move to new areas as shown on the
    attached Movement Table.

2. The usual distances will be maintained between units on the
    line of march.

3. On completion of moves, Divisional, Brigade Group, and Unit
    areas will be as shown on the attached tracing.

4. Completion of moves and locations of Headquarters will be
    wired to Divisional Headquarters as soon as possible.

5. All further arrangements will be made by Commanders concerned.

6. ACKNOWLEDGE.

                                                M. Wetherly.
    Issued at 0900 hours.   Lieut.-Col.,
                                                G.S., 61st Division.

                        Distribution :-

Copy No. 1 - A.D.C. for G.O.C.   14 - D.A.D.O.S.
       2 - 61 Signal Coy.   15 - D.A.D.V.S.
     3-4 - 61 Div. Art.   16-17 - "Q".
       5 - C.R.E.   18 - "G".
       6 - 61 Bn. M.G.C.   19 - Camp Comdt.
       7 - 1/5 D.C.L.I.   20-21 - XVII Corps.
       8 - 182 Inf. Bde.   22 - 61 Reception Camp.
       9 - 183 Inf. Bde.   23 - Mob. Vet. Sec.
      10 - 184 Inf. Bde.   24-25 - War Diary.
      11 - A.D.M.S.   26 - 19th Div.
      12 - 61 Div. Train.   27 - 20th Div.
      13 - D.A.P.M.   28 - Area Comdt.,
                                          BERNAVILLE.

P.T.O.

Movement Table to accompany 61st Div. Order No. 238, dated 6.12.18.

Serial No.	Date	Formation or Unit.	From.	To	Route.	Remarks
1.	7.12.18	Battery R.F.A.	FROHEN-LE-GRAND FROHEN-LE-PETIT	LE MEILLARD	Direct	To be clear of villages by 1000 hrs.
2.	do.	183 Inf.Bde.Group. 183 Inf.Bde. 478 Fd.Co.R.E. No.3 Co.Train.	Present area	Area west of present Divisional area. B.H.Q. to AILLY-LE-HAUT-CLOCHER.	Any.	PROUVILLE to be cleared by 1000 hrs.
3.	do.	2/1 Field Amb.	HEIRMONT	BUIGNY-L'ABBE	Any.	To march under orders of G.O.C. 183 Inf.Bde. and to join 183 Inf.Bde.Group. To be clear of HEIRMONT by 1000 hrs.
4.	do.	1/5 D.C.L.I.	To concentrate in BEAUMETZ and PROUVILLE under orders of O.C. 1/5 D.C.L.I.			
5.	8.12.18	Div. H.Q.	BERNAVILLE	ST.RIQUIER	Direct	To march at 1000 hrs.
6.	do.	61 Div.Signals	BERNAVILLE	ST.RIQUIER	Direct	To march at 1015 hrs.
7.	do.	61 Bn. M.G.C.	BERNEUIL and GORGES	BERNAVILLE	Direct	To march at 1000 hrs.
8.	do.	Mob. Vet. Sec.	VACQUERIE	ONEUX	Any	To march at 1030 hrs.

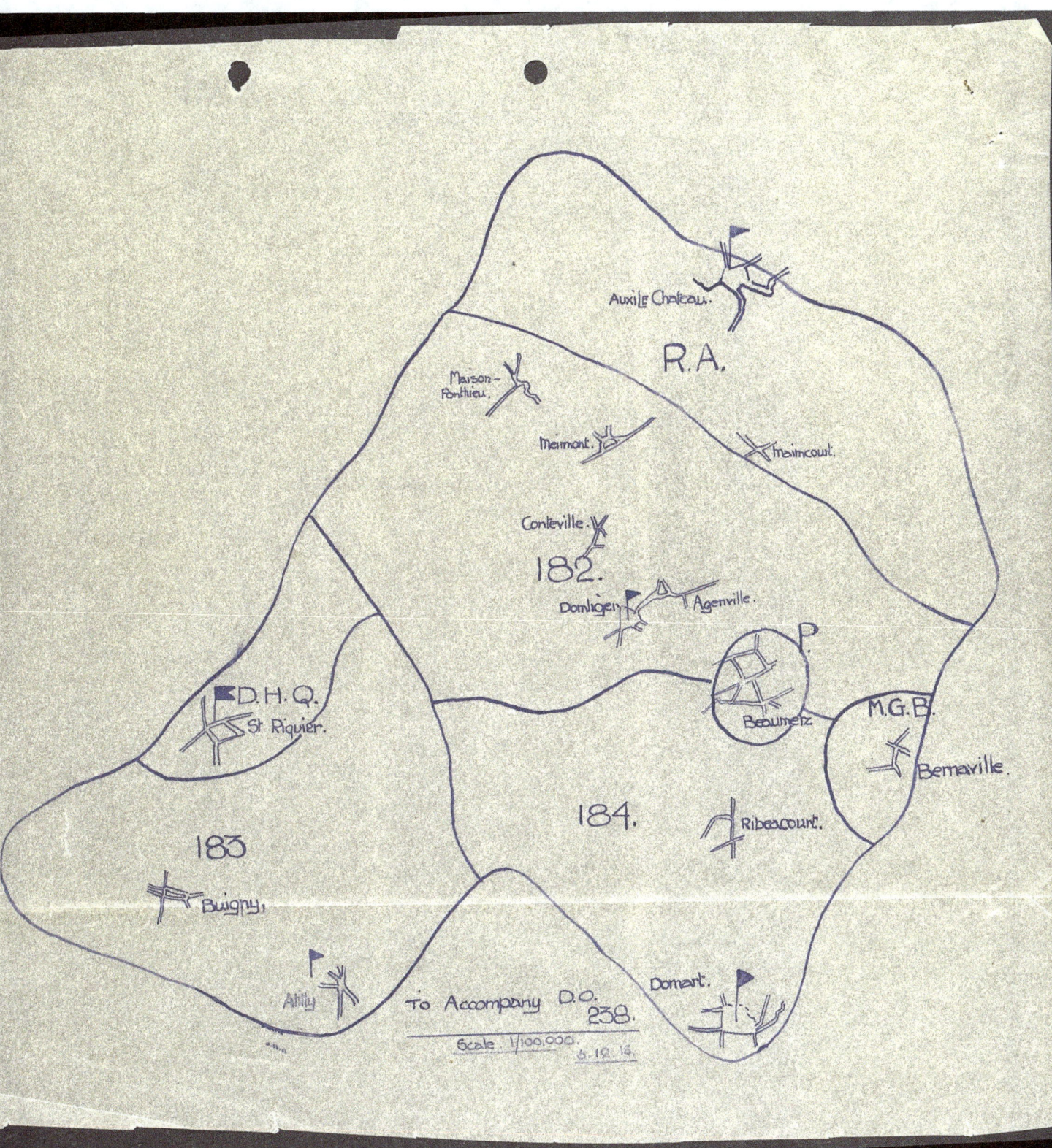

War Diary   *Appendix* III

SECRET.   G.C. 79.

61st DIVISION.
Locations of Units at 0600 hours, 9.12.18.

61st DIV.H.Q.	ST. RIQUIER.
C. R. A.	AUXI-LE-CHATEAU.
306 Bde. R.F.A.	CHATEAU DE BEAUVOIN.
307 do.	WAVANS.
D. A. C.	LA NEUVILLE.
315 Army Bde.RFA.	MAIZICOURT.
M.T.M.B.	MONTLOUIS FM.
182 Inf.Bde.H.Q.	MAISON PONTHIEU.
2/6 Warwicks,	YVRENCH.
2/7 Warwicks,	MAISON PONTHIEU.
2/8 Worcesters,	CRAMONT.
182 L.T.M.B.	YVRENCH.
183 Inf.Bde.H.Q.	AILLY-LE-HAUT-CLOCHER.
9th North. Fus.	VAUCHELLES.
11th Suffolks,	ALLIEL.
1st E. Lancs.	YAUCOURT.
183 L.T.M.B.	AILLY-LE-HAUT-CLOCHER.
184 Inf.Bde.H.Q.	DOMART.
2/5 Glosters.	DOMQUEUR.
2/4 Oxfords,	DOMART.
2/4 R. Berks.	FRANSU.
184 L.T.M.B.	DOMART.
1/5 D.C.L.I. (P).	BEAUMETZ.
C. R. E.	ST. RIQUIER.
476 Field Co. R.E.	L'ABBAYE D'AMMONT FM.
478 do.	FAMECHON.
479 do.	ST. HILAIRE.
61 Bn. M.G.C.	BERNAVILLE.
A. D. M. S.	ST. RIQUIER.
2/1 Field Amb.	BUIGNY-L'ABBE.
2/2 do.	AGENVILLE.
2/3 do.	MESNIL DOMQUEUR.
61 Div. Train H.Q.	ST. RIQUIER.
No. 1 Coy.	AUXI-LE-CHATEAU.
No. 2 Coy.	CONTEVILLE.
No. 3 Coy.	AILLY-LE-HAUT-CLOCHER.
No. 4 Coy.	DOMART.

John Hunter Capt-
for G.S., 61 Div.

8.12.18.

Appendix IV

SECRET.

G.C. 79.

61st Division.
Amendment to Location List dated 9.12.18.

182 Inf.Bde.H.Q.,	HIERMONT.
476 Field Co. R.E.,	DOMLEGER.
2/3 Field Amb.,	DOMART.

9.12.18.

John Hunter Capt.
/vr G.S., 61 Div.

SECRET.   G.C. 79.

61st DIVISION.
Locations of Units at 0600 hours, 12.12.18.

61st DIV. H.Q.	ST. RIQUIER.
C.R.A.	AUXI-LE-CHATEAU.
306 Bde. R.F.A.	CHATEAU DE BEAUVOIN.
307 do.	DRUCAS.
D.A.C.	LA NEUVILLE.
315 Army Bde. RFA.	MAIZICOURT.
M.T.M.B.	LANNOY.
182 Inf.Bde.H.Q.	HEIRMONT.
2/6 Warwicks,	YVRENCH.
2/7 Warwicks,	MAISON PONTHIEU.
2/8 Worcesters,	CRAMONT.
182 L.T.M.B.	YVRENCH.
183 Inf.Bde.H.Q.	AILLY-LE-HAUT-CLOCHER.
9th North. Fus.	VAUCHELLES.
11th Suffolks,	ALLIEL.
1st E. Lancs.,	YAUCOURT.
183 L.T.M.B.	AILLY-LE-HAUT-CLOCHER.
184 Inf.Bde.H.Q.	DOMART.
2/5 Glosters.,	DOMQUEUR.
2/4 Oxfords,	DOMART.
2/4 R.Berks.,	FRANSU.
184 L.T.M.B.	DOMART.
1/5 D.C.L.I.(P),	BEAUMETZ.
C.R.E.	ST. RIQUIER.
476 Field Co. R.E.	DOMLEGER.
478 do.	FAMECHON.
479 do.	ST. HILAIRE.
61 Bn. M.G.C.	BERNAVILLE.
A.D.M.S.	ST. RIQUIER.
2/1 Field Amb.	BUIGNY-L'ABBE.
2/2 do.	AGENVILLE.
2/3 do.	DOMART.
61 Div. Train,	ST. RIQUIER.
No. 1 Coy.,	AUXI-LE-CHATEAU.
No. 2 Coy.,	CONTEVILLE.
No. 3 Coy.,	AILLY-LE-HAUT-CLOCHER.
No. 4 Coy.,	DOMART.

11.12.18.

John Hunter Capt
G.S., 61st Divn.

"A" Form.
MESSAGES AND SIGNALS.

Army Form C. 2121.
(In pads of 100.)

APPENDIX VI (COPY)

TO — 183 Bde.
Commandant, ABBEVILLE area

| Sender's Number. | Day of Month. | In reply to Number. | AAA |
| G.553 | 24 | | |

Detail 1st Bn. East Lancs. Regt. to proceed by march route to ABBEVILLE on the 27th inst. for work under G.O.C. L. of C. aaa Send representative to report to Commandant, ABBEVILLE area on 26th inst. to arrange accommodation for battalion and to get details of work to be carried out aaa Report completion of move aaa Battalion will probably be away for about one month aaa acknowledge aaa addsd 183 Bde repeated Commandant ABBEVILLE area and Q

From 61 Div.
Place
Time

(Z) (sgd) C.H. DOWDEN, Maj.

98 33

G.S.

War Diary
61st Division
January 1919
Vol XXXIII

17

Confidential

61st Division - Volume XXXIII
WAR DIARY
or
INTELLIGENCE SUMMARY.
(Erase heading not required.)

Army Form C. 2118.

Instructions regarding War Diaries and Intelligence Summaries are contained in F.S. Regs., Part II and the Staff Manual respectively. Title pages will be prepared in manuscript.

Place	Date	Hour	Summary of Events and Information	Remarks and references to Appendices
ST. RIQUIER	1919 Jan. 1st to 31st		There have been few items of special interest to record during the month. The Division has remained located in the ST.RIQUIER - AUXI-LE-CHATEAU - DOMART area as it was during the previous month. The 1st East Lancs. Regt. has not yet rejoined. A considerable amount of good work has been put in under the Education Scheme, but this is now being very seriously hampered owing to demobilization, which is proceeding. The semi-finals and final of a Divisional Football Competition have been played during the month. This competition was won by a team from the S.A.A. Section of 61st D.A.C. with the Headquarters 184 Inf. Bde. second. Each formation and unit has had its football competition and cross country runs, and in addition various other items of sport and pastime. Demobilization has been proceeding at a progressive rate during the month and men are now leaving the Division at the rate of about 1,000 per week. On the 29th inst. orders were received to despatch 3 Battalions to Base Ports for duty : 2/4 Oxford & Bucks. Light Infantry to ETAPLES. 2/4 Royal Berks. Regt. to BOULOGNE. 2/6 Royal Warwickshire Regt. to HAVRE. The 2/4 Royal Berks. Regt. and 2/6 Royal Warwickshire Regt. were despatched on the 31st inst. A telephone message was received on the 31st inst. warning the Division to be prepared to	

Army Form C. 2118.

WAR DIARY
or
INTELLIGENCE-SUMMARY.

(Erase heading not required.)

Place	Date	Hour	Summary of Events and Information	Remarks and references to Appendices
ST. RIQUIER	1919 Jan.	(contd)	detach an additional Battalion for duty at Base Ports. The 2/5 Gloucester Regt. was selected for this duty.	
	31.1.19.			

Muirhead Lintot.
G.S.
for Major-General,
Commanding 61st Division.

Confidential

WR 34
68

- War Diary -
- 61st Div: -
- February 1919 -
- Vol. XXXIV -

Army Form C. 2118.

61 Division - Vol. XXXIV

WAR DIARY

~~INTELLIGENCE~~ SUMMARY

(Erase heading not required.)

Instructions regarding War Diaries and Intelligence Summaries are contained in F.S. Regs., Part II. and the Staff Manual respectively. Title pages will be prepared in manuscript.

Place	Date	Hour	Summary of Events and Information	Remarks and references to Appendices
ST. RIQUIER 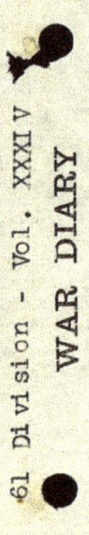	Feb. 1st		2/4 OXFORDS & BUCKS LIGHT INFANTRY entrained for ETAPLES for duty in connection with demobilization.	
	2nd		2/5 GLOUCESTER REGT. entrained for ROUEN for duty at that Base.	
	3rd		Orders received to hold in readiness the following for despatch to ETAPLES for duty :- H.Q. 184 Inf. Bde., 2/7 ROYAL WARWICKSHIRE REGT. and 1/5 D.C.L.I. (Pioneers).	
	4th		Orders received to hold in readiness 2/8 WORCESTER REGT. for duty at CHERBOURG.	
	5th		184 Inf. Bde. H.Q., 2/7 ROAYL WARWICKSHIRE REGT. and 1/5 D.C.L.I. proceeded to ETAPLES for temporary duty at Base Ports.	
	6th		Division notified by telephone from G.H.Q. that it had been placed at the disposal of G.O.C., L. of C.	
	7th		Orders received to despatch 11 SUFFOLK REGT. to CALAIS and 61st Bn. M.G.C. to ABBEVILLE for temporary duty.	
	8th		Division placed at disposal of L. of C.	
	9th		Orders received that 61st Division (less Artillery) will be transferred to L. of C. from 13th February inclusive.	
	10th		61st Bn. M.G.C. moved to ABBEVILLE by march route and came under orders of G.O.C., L. of C.	
	11th		11 SUFFOLK REGT. to AUDRUICQ by train for temporary duty. Orders received to despatch 182 Inf. Bde. H.Q. and 9th NORTHUMBERLAND FUSILIERS to DIEPPE for temporary duty. Information received that Division (less Artillery) was to be made up to strength and would be one of the Divisions temporarily retained for duty on the coast.	
	12th		80 men from 9 NORTHUMBERLAND FUSILIERS to ABBEVILLE for duty under Commandant.	

Army Form C. 2118.

WAR DIARY
or
INTELLIGENCE SUMMARY.
(Erase heading not required.)

Instructions regarding War Diaries and Intelligence Summaries are contained in F. S. Regs., Part II. and the Staff Manual respectively. Title pages will be prepared in manuscript.

Place	Date	Hour	Summary of Events and Information	Remarks and references to Appendices
ST. RIQUIER	Feb. 13th		Divisional area readjusted and troops disposed as in Division Order No. 239 attached as Appendix I. Division (less Artillery) came under orders of G.O.C., L. of C. Area.	Appendix I
	14th		H.Q. 182 Inf. Bde. with Signal Section, 182 L.T.M.B., and 9 NORTHUMBERLAND FUSILIERS entrained at ST.RIQUIER for DIEPPE for duty at that port. Appendix II giving present locations of units.	Appendix II
	15th		Orders received that the 1st EAST LANCS REGT. would be replaced by the 11 EAST LANCS REGT. from 31st Division. The 1st EAST LANCS. to be reduced to cadre for transfer to ENGLAND. Retainable men to be posted to 11 EAST LANCS.	
	16th to 27th		Nothing of interest.	
	28th		Information received that 2/6 ROYAL WARWICKSHIRE REGT. would be transferred from HAVRE to DIEPPE at an early date. It has been decided to complete all Infantry Battalions to 900 men and drafts of Officers and other ranks are under orders to join. There has been very little Educational or other training carried out during the month owing to demobilization and to all infantry battalions being employed at Base Ports. Demobilization of men who are not eligible to serve with the Army of Occupation has been carried out steadily throughout the month.	

28.2.19.

C.H.Dowden Major
Major-General,
Commanding 61st Division.

War Diary

APPENDIX I

Amendment No. 1 to 61st Division Order No. 239.

Para. 2. - Serial No. 5.

For "VAUCHELLES" read "NEUF MOULIN"

12.2.19.

Distribution.

G.S., 61st Division.

To all recipients of 61 Div. Order No. 239.

APPENDIX I

SECRET.   Copy No. 25

               61st DIVISION ORDER No. 233.   12.2.19.

Reference maps - LENS 1/100,000,
                 ABBEVILLE 1/100,000.

1. The Division (less Artillery) is transferred to L. of C. Area from 13.2.19.

2. All units remaining in the present Divisional area (less those under orders to move to Base Ports) will close up into the present 183rd. Inf. Bde. area, and the following moves will take place on the 13th inst.:-

No.	Unit.	From	To	Instructions.
1.	476 Fd. Coy. R.E.	DOMLEGER	AILLY-LE-HAUT-CLOCHER.	A. Transport arrangements as necessary will be made by Div. "Q".
2.	479 Fd. Coy. R.E.	DOMART	- do -	
3.	184 L.T.M.B.	-do-	- do -	B. Billets for No. 2 Coy. Train from O.C. Div. Train.
4.	478 Fd. Coy. R.E.) 183 Bde. H.Q.) No. 3 Co. Train.) 183 L.T.M.B.)	remain at	AILLY-LE-HAUT-CLOCHER	C. 476 Fd. Coy. R.E. will leave a guard of 1 N.C.O. & 4 men on the R.E. Dump at DOMLEGER.
5.	No. 4 Coy. Train	DOMART	NEUF MOULIN VAUCHELLES	This guard will be relieved and the Dump taken over by Corps if possible on 13th inst.
6.	2/1 Field Amb.	to remain at	BUIGNY L'ABBE	
7.	2/2 Field Amb.	AGENVILLE	YAUCOURT BUSSUS	
8.	2/3 Field Amb.	DOMART	BUSSUS BUSSUEL	
9.	Div. H.Q.) 61 Mob.Vet.Sec.) 61 Div.M.T.Coy.)	to remain at	ST. RIQUIER	
10.	No. 2 Coy. Train	CONTEVILLE	ST. RIQUIER	

3. Refilling point for all units will be at YAUCOURT on the 14th; Train wagons will deliver to Q.M.Stores.

4. All area stores will be collected into dumps - R.E. being kept apart from Ordnance Stores.
   A Guard with three days rations will be left behind in charge. It is anticipated that sufficient lorries will be available on 14th and 15th inst. to clear these dumps.
   The Guards should clearly understand that all R.E. Stores are to be sent to C.R.E's dump DOMLEGER; all Ordnance stores to the Corps Intermediate Collecting Station in the R.A.F. Hangars situated at the bottom of the C in CANDAS.

5. The 61st Divisional Reception Camp at BERNATRE will be broken up on the 13th inst. Personnel will be temporarily attached to

                                                              P.T.O.

- 2 -

Divisional Headquarters and despatched from there to rejoin their units.
In future casuals and returning leave personnel will report to Camp Commandant, Divisional Headquarters and will be despatched to rejoin their units.

Personnel Railhead will be at ABBEVILLE from 14th inst.

Issued at 1200 Hours.

[signature]
Lieut. Col.
G.S., 61st Division.

Distribution:-

Copy No. 1 A.D.C. for G.O.C.
2. 61 Signal Coy.
3. 61 Div. Art. (for information)
4. 61 Div. Eng.
5. 182 Inf. Bde.
6. 183 Inf. Bde.
7. A.D.M.S.
8. 61 Div. Train.
9. D.A.P.M.
10. D.A.D.O.S.
11. D.A.D.V.S.
12. "Q"
13. "G"
14. Camp Comdt.
15. H.Q., L. of C.
16. XVII Corps.
17. 61 Reception Camp.
18. 61 Div. M.T. Coy.
19. 184 L.T.M.B.
20. Mob. Vet. Sec.
21. Area Commandant ST. RIQUIER.
22. Commandant ABBEVILLE.
23. Town Major VAU HELLES (thro' 183 Inf. Bde)
24.) War Diary.
25.)

SECRET.   G.O.79

61st DIVISION.
Locations of Units at 1200 hours 15.2.19.

61st DIV. H.Q.	ST. RIQUIER.
C. R. A.	AUXI-LE-CHATEAU.
306 Bde. R.F.A.	CHATEAU DE BEAUVOIN.
307 do.	AUXI-LE-CHATEAU.
D.A.C.	LA NEUVILLE.
315 Army Bde. R.F.A.	MAIZICOURT.
182 Inf. Bde. H.Q.	DIEPPE.
2/6 Warwicks.	HAVRE.
2/7 Warwicks.	ETAPLES.
2/8 Worcesters.	CHERBOURG.
182 L.T.M.B.	DIEPPE.
183 Inf. Bde. H.Q.	AILLY-LE-HAUT-CLOCHER.
9th North. Fus.	DIEPPE.
11th Suffolks.	AUDRUICQ.
1st East Lancs.	ABBEVILLE.
183 L.T.M.B.	AILLY-LE-HAUT-CLOCHER.
184 Inf. Bde. H.Q.	ETAPLES.
2/5 Glosters.	ROUEN.
2/4 Oxfords.	ETAPLES.
2/4 R. Berks.	BOULOGNE.
184 L.T.M.B. (attached 183 Bde)	AILLY-LE-HAUT-CLOCHER.
1/5 D.C.L.I. (P).	ETAPLES.
C. R. E.	ST. RIQUIER.
476 Field Coy. R.E.	AILLY-LE-HAUT-CLOCHER.
478 do.	do.
479 do.	do.
61 Bn. M. G. C.	DRUCAT.
A. D. M. S.	ST. RIQUIER.
2/1 Field Amb.	BUIGNY L'ABBE.
2/2 do.	YAUCOURT BUSSUS.
2/3 do.	BUSSUS BUSSUEL.
61 Div. Train.	ST. RIQUIER.
No. 1 Coy.	AUXI-LE-CHATEAU.
No. 2 Coy.	ST. RIQUIER.
No. 3 Coy.	AILLY-LE-HAUT-CLOCHER.
No. 4 Coy.	NEUF MOULIN.
Mob. Vet. Sec.	ST. RIQUIER.

14.2.19.

C.H.Dowden
Major,
G.S., 61st Division.

Confidential

Vol 35

G S

War Diary
61st Division
March 1919
Vol: XXXV

Army Form C. 2118.

WAR DIARY
or
INTELLIGENCE SUMMARY.
(Erase heading not required.)

Instructions regarding War Diaries and Intelligence Summaries are contained in F. S. Regs., Part II. and the Staff Manual respectively. Title pages will be prepared in manuscript.

Place	Date	Hour	Summary of Events and Information	Remarks and references to Appendices
St.RIQUIER.	1/3/19.		No further change in Units, all of which, except administrative Units, are located at the various Base Ports for duty connected with demobilization, etc. Letter No. G.C. 31/1/1 issued on 3.3.19. attached as Appendix "A". There are no further incidents of facts of value to record.	App. "A".
	7/3/19.		2/6th Warwicks Regt., arrived at DIEPPE from HAVRE.	
	13/3/19.		Information received that 2/7th Bn. R.Warwick Regt., would be transferred from ETAPLES to DIEPPE forthwith.	App. "B" & C
	18/3/19.		Advance party proceed to arrange accommodation of D.H.Q. at LE TREPORT.	
	21/3/19.		G.C. 31/1. Letter on Policy issued.	App. "D".
24-	25/3/19.		D.H.Q. moved to LE TREPORT.	App. "E".
	31/3/19.		Units located as in appendix "F".	App. "F".
4.4.1919.				

Earl Bowden Major
for Major-General,
Commanding 61st. Division.

Appendix 'A'

G.C.31/1/1.

```
182 Inf. Bde.    Commandant, ABBEVILLE Area.
183 Inf. Bde.    Commandant, DIEPPE Base.
184 Inf. Bde.    Commandant, ABANCOURT Area.
1/5 D.C.L.I.     H.Q., L. of C. Area (for information)
                 "Q" (for information)
```

1. The 61st Division (less artillery) has been allotted to the L. of C. for duty in the Areas specified below :-

> ABBEVILLE.
> ABANCOURT.
> DIEPPE (with a detachment at CHERBOURG).

2. The areas so allotted are shewn on the attached tracing.
The eventual distribution proposed for formations and units of the Division will be as follows :-

```
ABBEVILLE Area          183 Inf. Bde.
                        183 L.T.M.Battery.
                        11th Bn. E.Lancs. Regt.
                        11th Bn. Suffolk Regt.
                        478 Field Coy. R.E.
                        2/1st Field Ambulance.
                        No. 3 Coy. Train.

DIEPPE Area             182 Inf. Bde.
                        182 L.T.M.Battery.
                        2/6 R.Warwick. Regt.
                        2/7 R.Warwick. Regt.
                        9th Bn. Northd. Fus.
                        61st Bn. M.G.Corps.
                        476 Field Coy. R.E.
                        2/2nd Field Ambulance.
                        No. 2 Coy. Train.

ABANCOURT Area          1/5th Bn. D.C.L.I.

Reserve Bde. Area       184 Inf. Bde.
  (LE TREPORT)          184 L.T.M.Battery.
                        2/5th Gloucester. Regt.
                        2/4th Ox. & Bucks. L.I.
                        2/4th R.Berks. Regt.
                        479 Field Coy. R.E.
                        2/3rd Field Ambulance.
                        No. 4 Coy Train.

LE TREPORT              Divl. H.Q.
                        H.Q. Div. R.E.
                        H.Q. Div. Train
                        61st Div. Signal Coy.
                        61st M.T.Coy.
                        61st Div. Mob. Vet. Sect.
```

In the meantime the Field Companies, Field Ambulances and 2 Train Companies will not be moved to join their Brigade Groups until such time as they have been brought up to sufficient strength to enable them to move and function as units.

- 2 -

3. The Divisional Commander will command all troops in the Divisional Area and delegates to Brigade Commanders command of all troops in their area as under :-

    DIEPPE Area   -   G.O.C., 182 Inf. Bde.
    ABBEVILLE Area   -   G.O.C., 183 Inf. Bde.
    Reserve Bde. Area -   G.O.C., 184 Inf. Bde.
    ABANCOURT Area   -   O.C., 1/5 D.C.L.I.

4. The Command of troops in the areas specified must not disorganise the smooth working of the Bases.
It is not intended that Brigadiers shall administer Bases and Areas as well as command and administer their own troops. New machinery and new staffs are therefore not required and will not be formed for the running of these new commands.

5. The system of Base and Area Commandants working direct with H.Q., L. of C. Area will continue, and as far as possible the system will not be interfered with.

6. Brigade Commanders will be responsible for :-

(a) Studying the system of administration within their areas.

(b) Visiting and inspecting the Bases, Depots, etc., and all troops in their areas from time to time.

(c) Reporting to the Divisional Commander any matters which, in their opinion, might be improved upon, or might call for change or action.

(d) Supervising and assisting the existing system of administration in their areas.

(e) Providing Base and Area Commandants with the personnel they require for the working of their Base or Area. In doing this, they will allot such numbers as to allow that elasticity which it is essential for a Base or Area Commandant to have, owing to the impossibility of his being able to foretell exactly what duties he may be called upon to perform at short notice.

(f) Allotting certain definite duties to certain units, when convenient to do so and when it can be done without involving other responsibilities. In making all such rearrangement of work, the entire responsibility for the proper carrying out of the work must be definitely fixed so that there be no divided responsibility.

(g) Carefully considering the interests of Base and Area Commandants before collecting units together for training or any other purpose.

(h) Carefully watching and feeling the pulse of units known to be in a state of unrest and prescribing remedies where necessary.
In this connection it is most important that Brigade Commanders shall investigate any causes for discontent which they may elicit in the course of their inspections. It will then be possible to rectify matters before troubles arise

7.	It must be realised that both Base Commandants and Brigade Commanders have usually held their commands for a long time and seniority will sometimes come into the question. There will therefore be need for tact on both sides.

Base and Area Commandants will therefore give every facility to Brigade Commanders to study their system of administration and to visit and inspect the various organisations and troops in their areas. Brigade Commanders will give every help and advice to Base and Area Commandants to ensure the smooth and efficient working of the Bases in their Areas.

[signature]

Lieut.Col.,
G.S., 61st Division.

3.3.19.

APPENDIX B

G.C.31/1.

C.R.E.	"A" Mess.
61 Div. Train	"B" Mess.
A.D.M.S.	"C" Mess.
Div. Employ. Coy.	Capt. MORTIMORE
Div. Sig. Coy.	Lieut. HAWKEN
D.A.P.M.	Lieut. GIBSON
Camp Comdt.	Q.
D.A.D.O.S.	61 M.T.Coy.

Reference G.C.31/1 of 14.3.19.

1. No. 4 Company Divisional Train will march to LE TREPORT on Tuesday 18th inst., staging for the night at FRESSENVILLE.
   This company will be located in the Camp at LE TREPORT and will be at disposal of O.C. Advance Party until the arrival of the Division.

2. O.C., 61st Div. M.T.Coy. will detail 4 lorries to proceed with the Advance Party. These lorries will remain with the Advance Party for duty.
   Lorries will be at the Church at ST.RIQUIER at 0900 hours on the 18th inst. to convey Advance Party to LE TREPORT.

3. Advance Party will report to Capt. MORTIMORE at the Church at 0900 hours on Tuesday 18th inst.

15.3.19.

CH Dowden Maj
for Lieut.Col.,
G.S., 61 Division.

APPENDIX L

G.C.31/1.

C.R.E.   "A" Mess.
61 Div. Train   "B" Mess
A.D.M.S.   "C" Mess.
Div. Employ. Co. Capt. Mortimore
Div. Sig. Coy.   Lieut. Hawken.
D.A.P.M.   Lieut. Gibson.
Camp Comdt.   Q.
D.A.D.O.S.   61 M.T. Coy.

1. The undermentioned will proceed to LE TREPORT on Tuesday 18th inst. as advance party to Divisional Headquarters, which will proceed as soon as party have prepared the necessary accommodation :-

Officers

Capt. Mortimore,
Lieut. Hawken,
Lieut. Gibson.

Other Ranks.

Div. Employment Coy. & Baths.
    1 Sergt. & 10 men (to include 1 cook)

Div. Signal Coy.
    1 Sergt., 1 Corpl. and 8 men

D.A.P.M.
    Traffic Control - 6 men

C.R.E. H.Q.
    2 men

Train H.Q.
    1 N.C.O. & 6 men

A.D.M.S.
    1 man

"A" Mess
    2 men (old servants to G.O.C. and A.D.C.)

"B" Mess
    1 man

"C" Mess
    1 man

Ordnance
    1 Conductor and 2 men

"G" Office
    1 orderly

"Q" Office
    1 orderly

E.F.C.
    1 W.O.

	Officers	W.Os.	N.C.Os.	Men	Total
Total	3	2	4	41	50

P.T.O.

- 2 -

2. Rations for the 19th inst. will be taken by individuals. Camp Commandant and Div. Train will arrange to ration at LE TREPORT from 20th inst. until arrival of the Division.

3. Time of departure, etc. will be notified later; party will not return to ST. RIQUIER.

4. 61st M.T.Coy. will be prepared to send number of lorries required which will be notified.

                C H Dowden Major

14.3.19.   a/- Lieut.Col.,
                  G.S., 61st Division.

Appendix D

G.C.31/1.

182 Inf. Bde.
183 Inf. Bde.
184 Inf. Bde.
Commandant ABBEVILLE.
Commandant DIEPPE.
Commandant ABANCOURT.
Q.

---

1. In order to clear up any misunderstanding that may exist with regard to responsibility for the command and administration of units and detachments of the Division in the various Base Areas, the Divisional Commander wishes the following principles to be adhered to.

2. Officers Commanding Divisional Units and detachments from those units are responsible to their immediate superiors in the formation or unit to which they belong, for command, discipline and administration of the troops under their command.

3. In cases, however, where units and detachments are so situated that the command, discipline and administration of their troops cannot be efficiently carried out by Brigade and Unit Commander, they will be definitely placed by order of the Brigade Commander under the Base or Area Commandant or such subordinate commanders of L. of C. troops to whom they may be attached, for local discipline and local administration.

4. It must, however, be clearly understood that Brigade and Regimental authorities will still be held responsible for the frequent visiting and general supervision of their troops, so as to ensure the efficiency, discipline and well-being of such detached troops.

(Sgd) W.S.WHETHERLY,
Lt. Col.
G.S., 61st Division.

21.3.19.

Appendix E

Copy No. 28

61st DIVISION ORDER No. 240.

21.3.1919.

Ref. Map ABBEVILLE 1/100,000.

1. The 61st Division Headquarters will move from ST.RIQUIER to LE TREPORT on 24th and 25th March.

2. The following units will be included in Divisional Headquarters for this move:-

   61st Div. Signal Coy.   )
   H.Q., 61st Div. Train   )   To move 24th inst.
   61st M.T.Coy.   )

   2/1 Field Ambulance   )
   2/3   do.   )   To move 25th inst.

3. (a) Horse transport will proceed by march route, and will stage in each case at FRESSENVILLE for the night.   O.C. 61 Div. Signal Coy. will detail an officer to take command of all horse transport moving on 24th inst.

   (b) Two days' rations and forage will be carried by those proceeding by march route.

   (c) Application for billets at FRESSENVILLE will be made to a representative of 61 Div. H.Q. at the Mairie.

4. (a) The undermentioned units will, on the move of Div. H.Q., come under orders of G.O.C., 183 Inf. Bde. :-

   H.Q., Div. R.E.
   476 Field Coy.
   478   do.
   479   do.
   2/2 Field Amb.
   No. 2 Coy. Train
   No. 3   do.
   61 Mob. Vet. Sect.

   (b) O.C. 61 M.T.Coy. will detach two lorries and the Foden Thresh Disinfector to remain with H.Q. 183 Inf. Bde.

5. Div. H.Q. will close at ST.RIQUIER at 1000 hours and re-open at LE TREPORT at 1200 hours on the 24th.

E. M. Birch Co
G.S., 61 Division.

Issued at 1830 hours.

Distribution.

Copy No.					
1	A.D.C. for G.O.C.	11	2/8 Worcesters	21	H.Q. L. of C.
2	61 Div. Art.	12	2/4 R.Berks.	22	61 M.T.Coy.
3	61 Div. Eng.	13	A.D.M.S.	23	Mob.Vet.Sec.
4	61 Signal Coy.	14	61 Div.Train	24	Cdt. ABBEVILLE
5	182 Inf.Bde.	15	D.A.P.M.	25	Cdt. DIEPPE
6	183 Inf.Bde.	16	D.A.D.O.S.	26	Cdt. ABANCOURT
7	184 Inf.Bde.	17	D.A.D.V.S.	27	Area Cdt.ST.RIQUIER
8	1/5 D.C.L.I.	18	Q	28-29	War Diary.
9	11 Suffolks	19	G	30	Capt. MORTIMORE.
10	2/5 Glosters	20	Camp Comdt.		

Appendix "F"

61st DIVISION.

Locations of Units at 1200 hours 31.3.1919.

61st Division.	Le TREPORT.
<u>182 Inf. Bde. H.Q.</u>	DIEPPE.
2/6th R.Warwicks Regt.	DIEPPE.
2/7th R.Warwicks Regt) & 182 L.T.B.M.)	DIEPPE.
2/8th Worcesters.	CHERBOURG.
<u>183 Inf. Bde. H.Q.</u>	St. RIQUIER.
9th North'd. Fus.	DIEPPE.
11th Suffolks.	AUDRUICQ.
1st East Lancs.,) & 183 L.T.M.B.)	ABBEVILLE.
<u>184 Inf. Bde. H.Q.</u>	Le TREPORT.
2/4th Glosters.) & 184 L.T.M.B.)	VAUCHELLES.
2/4th Ox. & Bucks L.I.	Le TREPORT.
2/4th R. Berks.	Le TREPORT.
1/5th D.C.L.I. (P)	ABANCOURT.
<u>C.R.E.</u>	AILLY-LE-HAUT-CLOCHERS.
476 Field Coy.	do.
478 do.	do.
479 do.	do.
61st Bn. M.G.C.	DRUCAT.
<u>A.D.M.S.</u>	Le TREPORT.
2/1st Field Ambulance.	do.
2/2nd do.	YAUCOURT-BUSSUS.
2/3rd do.	Le TREPORT.
<u>61st Div. Train.</u>	Le TREPORT.
No.2 Coy.	St. RIQUIER.
No.3 Coy.	AILLY-LE-HAUT-CLOCHER.
No.4 Coy.	Le TREPORT.
<u>Mob. Vet. Sec.</u>	ONEUX.

D.H.Q.
31.3.1919.

Confidential

GS
WO 336

War Diary.
61st Division
April 1919
Vol: XXXVI

Army Form C. 2118.

WAR DIARY
of
INTELLIGENCE SUMMARY.
(Erase heading not required.)

Instructions regarding War Diaries and Intelligence Summaries are contained in F. S. Regs., Part II. and the Staff Manual respectively. Title pages will be prepared in manuscript.

Place	Date	Hour	Summary of Events and Information	Remarks and references to Appendices
			Instructions issued regarding the duties of the Division.	App. 1.
LE TREPORT	April 4th.	6th.	Major W. CARDEN ROE assumed the duties of G.S.O. 2, 61st Division.	
			During the month few events of importance took place. About the 20th April instructions were received from the L. of C. ordering the 2/4th R.Berks. Regt., and 2/4th Oxford & Bucks L.I. and 2/8th Worcester Regt., to be prepared to proceed to Egypt at short notice. Steps had then to be taken to bring these Battalions up to strength with retainable personnel.	
			Military Training and Educational Training was carried on wherever possible. In many instances, notable in the case of the 183 Infantry Brigade around ABBEVILLE little could be done on account of the number of guards and working parties which had to be found.	
	30.4.1919.			

L Carden Roe
Major-General,
Commanding 61st Division.

APPENDIX I

G.C.31/1.

```
182 Inf. Bde.        61 Signal Coy.
183 Inf. Bde.        A.D.M.S.
184 Inf. Bde.        61 Div. Train
61 Bn. M.G.C.        D.A.P.M.
1/5 D.C.L.I.         Camp Comdt.
C.R.E.               Q.
```

---

1.   The present role of the Division involves guard and demobilization duties and the movement of formations and units to quell any disturbances which may arise in any portion of the Divisional Area.

2. (a) The LE TREPORT Infantry Brigade will be prepared to move, in whole or in part, at short notice, to any portion of the DIEPPE, ABANCOURT or ABBEVILLE Areas to assist the Commanders of troops in these areas in the event of disturbances.
   "Q" Branch will arrange for the storage at LE TREPORT, and issue in emergency, of two days reserve supplies and forage, for the whole of the LE TREPORT Brigade.
   Movement of the LE TREPORT Infantry Brigade will be by march route, train, or lorry according to the special circumstances.   Detailed transport arrangements cannot be prearranged.   Units of the LE TREPORT Brigade will, if ordered to move proceed with Greatcoats and 120 rounds S.A.A. per man.   Blankets will not be taken.   24 drums per Lewis gun and 15 rounds per Stokes mortar will be carried. If the Brigade moves as a whole 4 Stokes mortars will be taken: If single units 1 Stokes mortar per unit.

   (b) The Commanders of troops in the DIEPPE, ABANCOURT and ABBEVILLE Areas will, in consultation with Area Commandants, draw up plans for the rapid movements of troops in their areas to deal with disturbances in any portion of their respective areas, and will notify Division Headquarters by the quickest means, (priority wire or telephone) the place and nature of any disturbance which may occur, and whether the assistance of the whole or part of LE TREPORT Infantry Brigade is required to deal with the situation.
   Copies of plans will be forwarded to D.H.Q.

3.   In order to be able to carry out their possible role of dealing with disturbances the discipline and training of the troops must be maintained at a high standard.   The idea that the war is over and that therefore any slackness will be permitted is to be energetically combated; in fact this is just the moment when everything should be done to discourage this idea. The Divisional Commander looks to all Commanders to ensure these essentials.

4.   The Divisional Commander does not, however, wish training overdone, but adapted to suit the special cases of :-

   (a) Demobilisable men,

   (b) Men subject to retention in the Army of Occupation, whose training should be directed to fit them to take their places in the Army of the Rhine, if ordered there.

P.T.O.

- 2 -

5. Training will be :-

      (a) Military,
      (b) Educational,
      (c) Recreational.

In the case of demobilisable men who possess already a reasonable standard of military training, effort should be concentrated largely on educational and recreational training. In the case of retainable men military, educational and recreational training should be combined equally.

6. The Divisional Commander fully appreciates that facilities for training vary according to the duties and situation of troops, but trusts that Commanders will do their utmost to meet existing circumstances.

He wishes the importance of keeping troops busy each day impressed on all Commanders in order to :-

(a) Keep up the spirit of all ranks and obviate all tendency to discontent.

(b) Fit them for such tasks as may devolve upon them.

(c) Assist them in their normal peace occupations after their return to civil life.

He also wishes the importance of Officers being present with their men insisted upon, and everything done to ensure the maximum comfort of all ranks.

7. Commanders will arrange to acquire the necessary ground for recreation and training through the local authority on the spot. If requirements cannot be met reference will be made to Divisional Headquarters.

8. The Divisional Commander directs especial attention to the following points during military training :-

(a) Musketry - rapid loading - snap shooting - judging distance - fire control - fire discipline.

(b) Training of Lewis gunners and signallers.

(c) Duties should as far as possible be found by one Company of a Unit at a time and the remainder freed for training.

9. Training programmes of units and detachments, (military, educational and recreational) will be made out weekly in advance and forwarded so as to reach Divisional Headquarters each week on Saturday, commencing April 12th.

E. M. Birch
Colonel,
G.S., 61st Division.

4.4.19.

Duplicate

Confidential

War Diary

61st Division

May   1919

Vol: XXXVII

Army Form C. 2118.

WAR DIARY

or

~~INTELLIGENCE SUMMARY~~

(Erase heading not required.)

Instructions regarding War Diaries and Intelligence Summaries are contained in F.S. Regs., Part II. and the Staff Manual respectively. Title pages will be prepared in manuscript.

Place	Date	Hour	Summary of Events and Information	Remarks and references to Appendices
LE TREFORT			On the 9th & 10th Majors R.D.JOHNSTON and N.D.H.CAMPBELL joined the 61st Division as D.A.Q.M.G., and D.A.A.G., respectively.	
			About this time the whole of the personnel of the 2/4th Oxford & Bucks L.I., 2/4th R. Berks Regt., and 2/8th Worcester Regt., proceeded on 14 days leave to U.K., prior to the departure of their Battalions to Egypt. The actual entrainment for MARSEILLES took place as follows:-	

			2/4th Oxford & Bucks L.I. 23.5.1919.
			     2/4th R.Berks Regt., 24.5.1919.
			     2/8th Worcester Regt 25.5.1919.	

			At this time a reorganisation of the whole of the L. of C. Area commenced, the 61st Division Area being extended to include HAVRE & ROUEN, whilst the ABBEVILLE Area was taken over by the 30th Division. Moves took place as follows:-	

			2/5th Gloucester Regt from ABBEVILLE to HAVRE. 24.5.1919.
			   11th East Lancashire Regt from " " " 27.5.1919.
			   183 Inf.Bde H.Q. " " " 27.5.1919.
			   ~~11th Suffolk Regt.,~~ " ~~ABBEVILLE to ROUEN.~~ ~~29.5.1919.~~	

			On the 18th May trouble arose at ABANCOURT between the Chinese Labour Coys., and the B.W.I. Regt. Several casualties were inflicted on the Chinese and the 1/5th D.C.L.I. had to be called out to quell the trouble.	
			During the month considerable progress was made on Educational Training particularly in the 182 Inf. Bde. Shakespearean Recitals were given to all Battalions by Capt., HAWKEN and very much appreciated.	
	31.5.1919.			

[signature] for Major,
Cimmanding 61st Division.

Confidential

WO 95 61D
VN 38

War Diary

61st Division

June 1919

Vol.: XXXVIII

Army Form C. 2118.

WAR DIARY
or
INTELLIGENCE SUMMARY.
(Erase heading not required.)

Instructions regarding War Diaries and Intelligence Summaries are contained in F. S. Regs., Part II. and the Staff Manual respectively. Title pages will be prepared in manuscript.

Place	Date	Hour	Summary of Events and Information	Remarks and references to Appendices
LE TREPORT.	2/6/19.		Orders received as to the re-distribution of the Division and Areas under this Division.	
	2/6/19.) 3/6/19.)		61st Bn. Machine Gun Corps moved from ABBEVILLE to ROUEN.	
	6/6/19.		D.R.I. Service ceased.	
	9/6/19.		"B" and "D" Companies of 11th Bn. Suffolk Regt. and part Transport left AUDRUICQ for ROUEN.	
	14/6/19.		Bt.Lieut-Colonel S.G. SCOBELL, D.S.O., G.S.O. 1, 33rd Division, appointed G.S.O. 1. 61st Division.	
	16/6/19.		The Tug of War Team of 9th Bn. Northumberland Fusiliers won the Divisional Competition, and was ordered to proceed to ENGLAND to pull in the Olympia Military Tournament.	
	17/6/19.		"A" and "C" Companies and remainder of Transport of 11th Bn. Suffolk Regt. arrived at ROUEN.	
	18/6/19.		Lieut-Colonel WILKINSON, D.S.O. (Gloucester Regiment) appointed to command Units under 61st Division at ROUEN, namely, 11th Bn. Suffolk Regiment, 33rd Bn. Machine Gun Corps, 61st Bn. Machine Gun Corps.	
	21/6/19.		Orders received for reduction to Equipment Guard of 194th Infantry Brigade Headquarters prior to proceeding to ENGLAND.	
	26/6/19.		Orders received that various Units of 33rd Division notably 100th Infantry Brigade are to be administered by 61st Division on the breaking up of 33rd Division Headquarters.	

Army Form C. 2118.

WAR DIARY
or
INTELLIGENCE SUMMARY.
(Erase heading not required.)

Instructions regarding War Diaries and Intelligence Summaries are contained in F. S. Regs., Part II. and the Staff Manual respectively. Title pages will be prepared in manuscript.

Place	Date	Hour	Summary of Events and Information	Remarks and references to Appendices
	27/6/19.		Orders received that this Division need no longer be held in a state of mobility.	
	10.7.1919.		The following Units of the Division were down to Equipment Guard at the end of the month and awaiting orders to entrain for Base Ports:- 61st Division R.E., 2/1st, 2/2nd, 2/3rd (S.M.) Field Ambulances, 61st Divisional Signal Company R.E., 184th Infantry Brigade Headquarters.	

L. Carden Roe Maj.
Major-General,
Commanding 61st Division.

Confidential:

War Diary
61st Division
July 1919
Vol. XXXIX

Army Form C. 2118.

WAR DIARY
or
INTELLIGENCE SUMMARY.
(Erase heading not required.)

Instructions regarding War Diaries and Intelligence Summaries are contained in F.S. Regs., Part II. and the Staff Manual respectively. Title pages will be prepared in manuscript.

Place	Date	Hour	Summary of Events and Information	Remarks and references to Appendices
Le Treport.	July 1st.		Nothing of interest.	
	2nd.		Nothing of interest.	
	3rd.		Wire received from G.H.Q. that Peace had been signed at 16.00 hours on 28/6/1919.	
	4th.		Orders received from Headquarters, L. of C. Area that following Battalions of 61st Division had been nominated to go home as Cadres when no longer required for their present duties.	
			100th. Infantry Brigade. 182nd. Infantry Brigade.	
			17th. Bn. The Worcestershire Regiment. 2/6th. Bn. Royal Warwickshire Regiment.	
			1/9th. Bn. Highland Light Infantry. 2/7th. Bn. Royal Warwickshire Regiment.	
			16th. Bn. King's Royal Rifle Corps. 9th. Bn. Northumberland Fusiliers.	
			183rd. Infantry Brigade. 61st. Divisional Units.	
			2/5th. Bn. Gloucestershire Regiment. 11th. Bn. Suffolk Regiment.	
			11th. Bn. East Lancashire Regiment.	
	5th.		Nothing of interest.	
	6th.		Notification received from Headquarters, L. of C. Area that French Peace Celebrations would take place on 14th. July and that British celebrations would be held on 19th. July.	
	7th.) 8th.) 9th.) 10th.)		Nothing of interest.	
	11th.) 12th.) 13th.)		Notification received that Officers still serving might invest their gratuities in Victory Loan.	
			Nothing of interest.	
	14th.		Orders received from the Army Council that it had been decided to despatch 33rd. Bn. Machine Gun Corps to EGYPT in the near future.	
	15th.) 16th.) 17th.		Nothing of interest.	
			Orders received that the Headquarters, 184th. Infantry Brigade not to go home as a Cadre, but would be broken up in this Country.	
	18th.		Nothing of interest.	

Army Form C. 2118.

WAR DIARY
or
INTELLIGENCE SUMMARY.
(Erase heading not required.)

Instructions regarding War Diaries and Intelligence Summaries are contained in F.S. Regs., Part II. and the Staff Manual respectively. Title pages will be prepared in manuscript.

Place	Date	Hour	Summary of Events and Information	Remarks and references to Appendices
Contd.	19th.		Orders received that the following Units would supply drafts for EGYPT and the Black Sea:- 17th. Bn. Worcestershire Regiment, 11th. Bn. Suffolk Regiment, 2/5th. Bn. Gloucestershire Regt., 11th. Bn. East Lancashire Regiment, 2/6th. & 2/7th. Bns. Royal Warwickshire Regiments.	
	20th.) 21st.) 22nd.)		Nothing of interest.	
	23rd.		Approval received for the wearing of the ribbband of British War Medal 1914-1919.	
	24th.) 25th.) 26th.)		Nothing of interest.	
	27th.		Authority received for Headquarters Divisions to fly the Union Jack.	
	28th.) 29th.)		Nothing of interest.	
	30th.		Orders received for the closing of Headquarters, 61st Divisional Units, ROUEN. Orders received that drafts selected for EGYPT and Black Sea were to proceed home on Draft Leave. Orders received that Base Commandant, DIEPPE would assume command of ROUEN Base. Orders received that 61st. Divisional M.T. Company would move to DIEPPE and thus enable 43rd Aux. (Petrol) Company to be broken up.	
D.H.Q. 13.8.19.				

[signature]
Major-General,
Commanding 61st Division.

www.ingramcontent.com/pod-product-compliance
Lightning Source LLC
Chambersburg PA
CBHW080831010526
44112CB00015B/2493